Effective Group Discussion

Effective Group Discussion

eighth edition

John K. Brilhart

University of Nebraska, Omaha (Emeritus)

Gloria J. Galanes

Southwest Missouri State University

WCB Brown & Benchmark
PUBLISHERS

Madison, Wisconsin • Dubuque, Iowa

Book Team

Editor *Stan Stoga*
Developmental Editor *Kassi Radomski*
Production Editor *Peggy Selle*
Designer *Anna Manhart*
Art Editor *Jodi Wagner*
Photo Editor *Carol Judge*
Visuals/Design Developmental Consultant *Marilyn A. Phelps*
Visuals/Design Freelance Specialist *Mary L. Christianson*
Marketing Manager *Pamela S. Cooper*
Advertising Coordinator *Susan J. Butler*

WCB Brown & Benchmark

A Division of Wm. C. Brown Communications, Inc.

Executive Vice President/General Manager *Thomas E. Doran*
Vice President/Editor in Chief *Edgar J. Laube*
Vice President of Marketing and Sales Systems *Eric Ziegler*
Director of Production *Vickie Putman Caughron*
Director of Custom and Electronic Publishing *Chris Rogers*

WX212

Wm. C. Brown Communications, Inc.

President and Chief Executive Officer *G. Franklin Lewis*
Corporate Senior Vice President and Chief Financial Officer *Robert Chesterman*
Corporate Senior Vice President and President of Manufacturing *Roger Meyer*

Cover image by Inga Spence/Tom Stack & Associates

Copyedited by Marilyn Frey

Part Opener Credits: Part 1: © Tom Pettyman/Photo Edit; Part 2: © Steve Niedorf/Image Bank; Part 3: © Larry Gale Gordon/Image Bank; Part 4: © Paul Conklin/Photo Edit; Part 5: © Jeff Hunter/Image Bank

A Times Mirror Company

Library of Congress Catalog Card Number: 93–74332

ISBN 0–697–20129–5

Printed in the United States of America by Wm. C. Brown Communications, Inc., 2460 Kerper Boulevard, Dubuque, IA 52001

10 9 8 7 6 5 4 3 2 1

CONTENTS

This eighth edition of *Effective Group Discussion* continues the dual emphases of the previous editions: a comprehensive survey and interpretation of the small group research literature accompanied by practical, prescriptive guidance to help the reader become a more productive member and leader of small groups. We believe that the quality of our lives and the joys we experience can be enhanced immeasurably by the interpersonal and small group relationships we experience. Humans have a need to participate, and small groups can serve as vehicles for this participation. People who understand how groups function and can adapt their communicative behavior appropriately are positioned to make the most of small group participation. Conversely, people who lack this understanding are in for frustrating times in small groups.

We advocate sharing responsibility, work, and the rewards of small group life. For both of us, small group work is too important to be left to chance or to "conventional wisdom." We have seen too many mistakes made by groups of otherwise well-meaning members, and we know from recent experience that group work in the United States will increase as corporations and governments expand their reliance on teams. We simply *must* learn how to work together cooperatively, productively, and ethically if we want to remain viable as a nation in which people desire citizenship. That is our mission—to help people understand small group communication so they can be more effective group members and leaders in groups that work for the common good.

Effective Group Discussion is about secondary groups of all kinds: work groups, committees, task forces, self-directed work teams, and other small groups whose objectives include finding solutions to problems, producing goods, and creating policies. Although we have written this text primarily for the academically prepared beginning student of small group communication, it should also serve well as a reference source for advanced communication students, consultants, or people appointed to leadership positions in groups or organizations—in short, for anyone active in small groups. Instructors in academic fields such as communication, social psychology, business communication, a variety of health-related fields, and education will find it an appropriate and teachable textbook for their small group-oriented courses.

New Features

With every new edition of *Effective Group Discussion,* the problem of what to include becomes both more exciting and challenging. Much recent research by scholars in communication and allied disciplines reflects the burgeoning societal and corporate interest in groups. We know more than ever before about what makes groups operate effectively. However, the resulting explosion of information about both small groups and interpersonal communication directly relevant to small groups has meant that we have had to make difficult choices about what to include and what to emphasize. In making changes, we have relied heavily on the advice of our reviewers, instructors who use the text, and our own experiences in teaching from the text. We have tried diligently to keep the text manageable and affordable for students.

In this edition, we have reorganized early chapters in response to requests of several instructors who asked that information about human communication processes be introduced before we discuss members and throughput processes. Therefore, chapters dealing with communication, verbal and nonverbal behavior, and intercultural communication establish a foundation for the subsequent chapters on group members, development, leadership, and so forth. However, as in previous editions, the chapters after 1 and 2 may be presented in any order without hurting comprehension.

We have tried to streamline the text by consolidating similar information previously found in several chapters into a single chapter. For example, the information about critical thinking, gathering information, and use of questions is now all in the chapter on decision making. In addition, information we thought sidetracked the development of a major theme (though important to many instructors) has been placed in appendices. Instructors who want to use the material about conducting research, engaging in learning discussions, and making public presentations of group findings will still have ready access to it.

We have strengthened the communicative focus throughout the text, particularly regarding leadership and conflict, by emphasizing the relationship between what people *say* and *do* and the various group processes and structures that result. In this regard, we embrace the trend in the communication discipline to define concepts using communication terminology. We welcome this direction for our discipline.

We have added information about ethics. Every day, the news media provide stories about unethical conduct by public officials, corporate leaders, educators, and so forth. It seems that all too often groups support and even encourage the unethical and immoral behavior of their members. We think it is important for students explicitly to consider the ethical and moral implications of their actions in groups, whether as members, leaders, or observers.

As in previous editions, we have incorporated the most recent research findings we believe are relevant to small group communication, such as information about structuration theory and Leader-Member Exchange theory. We have augmented the information about intercultural communication to include recent information assessing intercultural communication in groups. Whereas in the previous edition we presented intercultural information about interpersonal encounters and extrapolated it to small groups, we now have been able to include information specifically about the effects of culture on behavior in small groups. In addition, we have augmented information about gender and added information about race. We also have responded to requests from several instructors for additional information about increasing group creativity by adding information about creativity-enhancing techniques such as synectics.

Finally, we have revamped our *Instructor's Manual* to reflect new directions we are taking in our own classes. In particular, we suggest a variety of ways to use a number of videotapes and films to clarify several concepts. We also suggest activities that use "writing to learn" techniques.

This book continues to be written primarily for *students,* many of whom lack extensive experience with committees, task forces, work teams, quality circles, and other small groups. Numerous specific examples from both campus and industry are included for this reason. Visual illustrations were incorporated to teach rather than to entertain or capture attention. In that regard, this book is differentiated from our other small group text, *Communicating in Groups,* by the inclusion of more reports of current research, use of a more extensive vocabulary, and greater emphasis on theoretical principles and models. A freshman well prepared for college should find this text understandable; juniors and seniors will find their needs for research summaries and theoretical explanations well met.

Approach

We continue to use the general model of open systems to unify the book because we believe this is the most appropriate paradigm available for understanding groups in all their complexity. We have intentionally avoided much of the jargon of general systems theory.

As before, the book was written so that the chapters may be used selectively or in an order other than the one presented. Each chapter is self-contained in terms of content. Part 1 presents an overview of small group theory. Chapter 1 introduces the importance and types of small groups in our lives, and chapter 2 introduces the organizing framework—systems theory—that provides the underlying structure for the rest of the text. Part 2, "The Foundations of Communicating in Small Groups," presents a theoretical description of the communication process, thereby providing a foundation for understanding the centrality of communication in a group's throughput processes. Chapter 3 explains the communication process, chapter 4 concentrates on verbal and nonverbal signals, and chapter 5 describes the effects of culture and cultural differences on communication in small groups. Part 3 focuses on the development of the group as an entity. Chapter 6 discusses the members, and chapter 7 deals with how the members develop from a collection of individuals to a group. Chapter 8 presents theoretical perspectives about leadership, while chapter 9 offers guidelines for designated small group leaders. Part 4 links throughput processes with outputs as it presents information about effective problem solving. It begins with an overview of problem solving in chapter 10, moves to a discussion of decision making in chapter 11, and concludes in chapter 12 with information about how properly managed conflict can enhance these important small group processes. Part 5 contains specific techniques and tools for evaluating and improving small groups. Chapter 13 presents specific discussion techniques designed to maximize small group effectiveness. Techniques and tools for observing, analyzing, and evaluating small group communication are presented in chapter 14.

The chapters were designed to follow each other in a logical way, but instructors need not assign them in the sequence presented. Some teachers want to address leadership or problem solving early in the course. Others want their students to know how to observe and evaluate interaction in groups so that the theoretical explanations can be applied to specific real-life examples. In addition, some instructors may want or need to omit some chapters or sections. These and other changes in the order of chapters should not interfere with student understanding of the concepts.

We gratefully appreciate your use of *Effective Group Discussion.* We welcome your written reactions to its content and composition. You can send such comments to us via Brown & Benchmark Publishers or to the Department of Communications, Southwest Missouri State University, Springfield, MO.

May all your groups be enjoyable and satisfying!

Acknowledgments

We appreciate the contributions made to this book by numerous persons; we can name only a few. First, we acknowledge our debt to such instructors and writers as Freed Bales, Ernest Bormann, Elton S. Carter, B. Aubrey Fisher, Kenneth Hance, Randy Hirokawa, Alex Osborn, Sidney J. Parnes, J. Donald Phillips, Marvin Shaw, and Victor Wall. Many colleagues in the study of small group dynamics and communication have expanded our vision through their papers and research reports. We thank our department head, John I. Sisco, for both his moral and tangible support.

The reviewers provided through Brown & Benchmark Publishers were exceptionally helpful in supplying thoughtful, carefully considered suggestions: Carol Armbrecht, North Central College; Thomas Endres, University of St. Thomas; Judith Hoover, Western Kentucky University; Bruce Kinghorn, American River College; Edward Lamoureaux, Bradley University; and Doris Werkman, Portland Community College. We have chosen to incorporate many of their suggestions and thereby improved the book appreciably. Fellow members of many small groups provided numerous examples, many of which we have included in the book. Students in our classes continue to teach us, and their insights have been incorporated as well. Finally, our friends and families have supplied support in countless ways. To all these people, and many left unmentioned, our sincere thanks!

Introduction to the Study of Small Groups

The two chapters in part 1 provide introductory information to focus your study of small groups. Chapter 1 introduces important terms and concepts used throughout the text, and chapter 2 presents systems theory as a framework for studying and understanding small groups.

The Small Groups in Everyone's Life

Central Message

Any person who wants to succeed in modern corporate and social life must understand how to communicate effectively as a member of a group.

Study Objectives

As a result of studying chapter 1 you should be able to:

1. Explain why it is important for you to understand small group communication and be able to participate productively in small group discussions.

2. Use correctly the terms presented in this chapter, particularly *group, small group, discussion, small group discussion,* and *ethics.*

3. Classify any group on the basis of its major purpose.

4. Describe the three ethical principles most relevant to small group communication.

Key Terms

Activity group
Committee
   Ad hoc or special committee
   Standing committee
Conference group
Discussion (small group discussion)
Ethics

Group
Group dynamics
Grouphate
Interaction
Interdependent goal
Learning group (study group)
Personal growth group

Primary group
Problem-solving group
Quality control circle
Secondary group
Self-managed work group
Small group
Small group communication

In the city where we work (Springfield, Missouri), a recent controversy developed over the location of a materials recovery facility (MERF). Like many cities, Springfield has a problem with solid waste disposal. The landfills are nearly overflowing, and something must be done to handle the ever-growing accumulation of solid waste. The city council assembled a task force to investigate how the city might dispose of the waste. After the task force recommended construction of the MERF, it was charged with selecting the best location, which turned out to be near a relatively undeveloped area north of Springfield. As you might imagine, residents near the proposed site objected, formed a neighborhood task force to organize opposition to the MERF, distributed petitions, lobbied legislators, and conducted a public relations campaign to stop the MERF. The task force caused the MERF proposal to be placed on the ballot, where a majority of Springfieldians voted in its favor. At last word, members of the neighborhood task force vowed to continue their opposition.

What does this have to do with small groups? The MERF controversy involved a number of small groups, including the original task force that recommended the facility, the city council that accepted the recommendation, and the neighborhood task force that organized the opposition. Furthermore, this example is not unusual. Most of the work of corporations, government agencies, religious and educational institutions in present-day American society is conducted in groups. We spend a tremendous amount of our time in formal and informal groups. For example, Cole reported in 1989 that executives spent an average of half their time in business meetings,[1] and Lawren noted that there are an estimated 20 million meetings *each day* in the United States.[2] Add to these figures the amounts of time people spend in groups not connected with jobs, and you have an idea of how pervasive groups are in modern society. Moreover, the ability to work effectively as part of a team requires skills that must be practiced. In a recent national survey of 750 leading American companies, 71.4 percent of respondents mentioned "ability to work in teams" as an essential skill for MBA graduates—more important by far than knowledge of quantitative and statistical techniques.[3] If you plan to advance in your career—if you even just want to get anything *done*—you must learn how to participate as a member of a team.

To help you with that learning, four important ideas are introduced in this chapter. First, groups exist to meet important human needs, and humans are willing to exchange items of value—time, energy, money—to participate in groups. Schutz explained that groups meet needs for inclusion, affection, and control: a need to belong and be identified with others; a need for love and esteem from others; and a need to achieve and exert power over others and our environment.[4] These are needs that humans cannot meet by themselves—participation with others is mandatory. In addition, these needs are so important that humans willingly give of their own resources to participate in groups. Consider the amount of time members of the MERF neighborhood task force spent trying to convince voters to reject the MERF. They worked long and hard *as a group,* not only because the issue was so important to them but also because they knew they had a better chance of succeeding if they worked collectively rather than individually. Moreover, sharing the work both lightened the workload for each individual and reaffirmed the values and opinions the neighbors held. An important extension of this idea is that, although group membership certainly confers benefits on members, it also requires that members in return exchange a degree of autonomy, the license to do whatever they want whenever they want. Thus, participation in groups always requires trade-offs—you get something, but you give up something, too.

A second important point is that because the formation of groups is natural to humans, groups are everywhere. List all the small groups in which you participated during the past week, regardless of how briefly—and don't forget to list your family! Students in college classes average about eight to ten, and sometimes list as many as twenty-four groups. For example, one student listed the following: family, *Bible* study, sorority, executive committee of sorority, study group in small group class, project group in marketing class, intramural volleyball team, car pool, work group of clerks in clothing department. One of us lists family, church board, ministerial search committee, departmental personnel committee, planning committee for departmental annual banquet, search committee, curriculum committee, three graduate student thesis committees, three faculty senate committees, the American Association of University Professors, Phi Kappa Phi executive committee, and informal faculty support group (probably for being a member of all those groups!). This is not unusual; Goldhaber found that the average tenured faculty member served on six committees simultaneously and spent eleven hours per week in meetings.[5]

If this seems like a lot of groups, consider this: reliance on groups in our society is increasing and expected to increase further, perhaps dramatically. American managers are recognizing the value of participative decision making, with the small group as one important vehicle through which employee participation can be encouraged and by which corporate decision making can be improved. For example, American automobile executives are finally beginning to learn from their counterparts in Japan and Sweden about the value of group work in the design, manufacture, assembly, and marketing of their cars. The Ford Taurus and General Motors Saturn success stories are in large part the stories of successful group work. Saturn, for example, was praised by *Consumer Reports* for having a much better than average reliability record in its first year of production,[6] a far cry from the poor records of other General Motors cars throughout the 1980s. Years ago, Ouchi, developer of Theory Z management, warned American managers that their ability to counter Japanese competition depended on how well they learned to work in groups.[7] More recently, Waterman identified teamwork as a key element in companies that have kept their competitive edge.[8] It seems that Americans are getting the message; Donald Petersen, retired CEO of Ford Motor Company, led that company from deep losses in the early 1980s to the highest profit of any American auto company in the late 1980s, largely by developing teamwork. *Employee Involvement and Participative Management* was Petersen's slogan to emphasize this approach, which involved extensive use of Japanese-style small groups.[9]

Why has group work been successful? Groups are usually better problem solvers, in the long run, than solitary individuals because they have access to more information than does an individual, can spot flaws and biases in each other's thinking, and then think of things an individual may have failed to consider. Moreover, if people participate in planning the work of solving the problem, it is more likely that they will work harder and better at carrying out the plans. Thus, participation in problem solving and decision making helps guarantee continued commitment to those decisions and solutions.

The third key point is this: communicating in groups is so much a part of our lives that most of us take it for granted, failing to perceive and understand what is happening in these groups or how to make them more effective. We chuckle at the saying "A camel is a horse designed by a committee," but when we participate in ineffective committees, we don't know how to help the group improve unless we have a clear idea about *where* the group is getting off track and *what* we can do about it. We as teachers have experienced on many occasions the groans from students when we tell them that a major portion of their grade will be based on a group project. Sorensen coined the term **grouphate** to describe the antipathy many people feel about working in groups.[10] Interestingly, she found that lack of training in effective group communication skills is associated with grouphate. Knowledge of the process of group communication and education in effective discussion techniques is crucial. Petersen learned this during his rise at Ford. At first he envisioned his role as that of a solitary engineer designing cars, but later discovered that a successful company requires interaction and teamwork: "Communication skills are crucial. And I mean that in both directions—not only the ability to articulate . . . in a good fashion, but to listen."[11]

The fourth and final point is that groups provide the vehicle by which the individual can make a contribution to the organization and the society as a whole. Larkin postulated that humans have a motivation to *give:*

> The basic ingredient cementing social cohesion is not the satisfaction of basic needs, but rather the availability for contribution. What best binds individuals to groups may not be so much the pressure to obtain necessities as the opportunities to give of oneself to something beyond merely self-interested acquisition.[12]

The dignity of individuals, he states, comes not from basic needs but from people's contributions to something greater than themselves. People who *do* give, of their time, money, energy and other resources, live healthier, happier, and more fulfilled lives; and report that their lives are more meaningful than those who do not.[13] Groups facilitate giving because they enable people to participate directly in something greater than self. For example, legendary pitcher Nolan Ryan remembers as one of the high points of his distinguished twenty-seven-year career the 1969 pennant-winning season of the New York Mets because of the unity and team spirit he experienced.[14] We agree with these humanistic principles presented here, and believe that the success of work-related committees stems from this need to create and share one's creation with others. What better way to do this than through a group?

The focus of this book is the *communicative* behavior of group members— what people say and do in groups. Although we will draw upon findings from other fields, we will concentrate on the process of communication among members, especially on how you as a group member can influence this process. In psychology, you may have studied how groups modify the behavior of individuals or provide therapeutic benefits, and, in sociology, how groups help establish and maintain social organization. In communication, you will study what happens as members talk and work together, and what you can do to make your own communication as productive as possible.

Small group discussion, the talk among group members, cannot be reduced to a set of prescriptions; it is far too complex for simplistic rules. Each element of group discussion influences each other element in the group system, which we describe in depth in chapter 2. Because the only person you can directly control is yourself, this book is designed to promote your awareness of your own behavior in small groups and its implication for other members. We occasionally give guidelines and suggestions for you to consider, but we assume you will remember to take into account the group's entire situation before you blindly follow someone else's guidelines.

In the remainder of this chapter, we present definitions of key terms we will be using throughout the book to reduce the possibility of misunderstanding between you and your classmates. We also present information about the types of groups you will encounter, particularly those you are likely to find in organizations, and we conclude with a brief discussion of ethical behavior important to effective group functioning.

Important Concepts and Terms

Group is the first term we must consider. Although a variety of definitions exists, we believe none surpasses Marvin Shaw's: "persons who are interacting with one another in such a manner that each person influences and is influenced by each other."[15] Shaw's conception of a group emphasizes interaction and mutual influence. **Interaction** implies *communication,* the exchange of signals (words, gestures, and so forth) among people who belong to the group. It also implies that at least some of these signals are perceived and responded to in such a way that each member can potentially affect each other member's behaviors, beliefs, opinions, values, and so on. By this definition, a collection of people in one place would not necessarily constitute a group unless there were reciprocal awareness and influence. By this same logic, group members who are widely scattered geographically, but who interact and mutually influence each other by way of newsletters, telephone conversations, computer networks, closed circuit TV, or radio *do* constitute a group.

The study of groups may include large groupings (e.g., whole societies) or small ones; our focus is on *small* groups. The notion that "each person influences and is influenced by each other" implies that members are *aware* of each other, and from this mutual awareness we derive our definition of *small* as being based on *perceptual awareness.* A **small group,** therefore, is a group small enough that each member is aware of and able to recall each other group member. We admit that this is fuzzy, but attempts to define *small* on the basis of number of members have never worked. By this definition, a small group is one in which the members can perceive, at least peripherally, all other members at once, with some awareness of who is and who is not in the group, and the role each is taking. At the low end, we can certainly perceive all members in a group of three (we arbitrarily eliminate the dyad, or two-person unit, as a small group because dyads function differently from units of three or more). At the high end, most of us can take in up to eleven similar units and, with training, may learn to handle twelve to fourteen.[16] At the end of a semester, even a class as large as twenty-five may seem small to a teacher.

One key feature of a group is an **interdependent goal,** meaning that all members succeed or fail together in the accomplishment of the group's purpose. For example, one player on a softball team cannot win while the others on the same team lose. The players are interdependent. Their fates are linked—they all succeed or fail as a group. Without an interdependent goal, a collection of people is not a group as we use the term.

Discussion, another term essential to the concept of group, is the primarily verbal exchange among members through which the work of the group is accomplished. In this book, **small group discussion** refers to *a small group of persons talking with each other (usually face to face) in order to achieve some interdependent goal, such as increased understanding, coordination of activity, or a solution to a shared problem.* We will now "unpack" this definition, which suggests several characteristics of small group discussion:

1. A small enough number of people for each to be aware of and have some reaction to each other (typically three to seven, rarely more than fifteen).

2. A mutually interdependent purpose, making the success of one member contingent on the success of all.

3. Each person having a sense of belonging, of being part of the group.

4. Interaction involving verbal and nonverbal channels, with words conveying the content of the discussion (this definition includes as "verbal" manual languages such as American Sign Language used by the hearing impaired). Members continuously respond and adapt their actions to each other. Impromptu communication rather than prepared speeches is the essence, which involves give and take.

5. A sense of cooperation among members. Although there may be disagreement and conflict, all members perceive themselves as searching for a group outcome that will be as satisfactory as possible to all, so that no one is frustrated at losing to another group member.

The term **small group communication** refers in this book to the study of interaction among small group members as well as to the body of communication theory yielded by such study. Later, we will examine in detail this body of theory and principles.

The study of small group communication is part of the broader field of **group dynamics,** which comprises the study of "the nature of groups, the laws of their development, and their interrelations with individuals, other groups, and larger institutions."[17] The study of group dynamics is a relatively new phenomenon. As Cathcart and Samovar note, the field received its greatest impetus when Kurt Lewin established a center specifically for the investigation of group dynamics in the 1930s.[18] Early researchers, such as Muzafer Sherif, W. F. Whyte, and Robert Bales, were often social psychologists who were particularly interested in how groups influenced individual behavior and the development of norms in groups. One thread of group dynamics research contributed to the human potential movement of the

Figure 1.1   Types of groups on the continuum from primary to secondary.

Primary Groups (satisfy needs for love, belonging)						**Secondary Groups** (satisfy needs for control, power)
Families Live-together groups	Social groups Close friends	Activity groups (sports teams, card clubs, hunt clubs, etc.)	Learning groups Study groups Interest groups	Growth groups Therapy groups Self-help groups	Problem-solving groups Committees Task forces Conference groups Quality circles	Production teams Self-managed work teams Work crews

1960s and 1970s, which focused on how individuals could grow through group activities. As *communication* evolved from its initial focus on public speaking, some communication researchers began to examine the communication within groups and to link members' communicative behaviors to group outcomes such as the effectiveness of decisions and the degree of cohesiveness. Now, as the field of communication has matured, researchers have increasingly attended to the process of communication within the group, including how ideas are developed, how the communication creates and maintains group structure, and how leadership is enacted by what people say and do. These trends are expected to continue and are being encouraged as appropriate directions for small group communication scholars.[19] Communicative behavior, not the comprehensive field of group dynamics, is the focus of this book.

Types of Small Groups

We classify groups on the basis of the reason they were formed and the human needs they serve. The two major classifications created by sociobiologists are called *primary* and *secondary;* this book emphasizes the latter. The major categories and several subtypes are shown in figure 1.1. We emphasize again that our focus is on communication within the *small* group, so we do not include much information about large public discussion groups such as forums, panel discussions, and public interviews.*

Primary Groups

Primary groups exist chiefly to satisfy human needs for inclusion (affiliation, belonging) and affection (love, esteem), rather than to accomplish a task. Primary groups are usually long term. Examples include a nuclear family, roommates, several friends who meet daily around a table in the student center, co-workers who regularly share coffee breaks, and other groups principally designed for friendship. Although such groups may make decisions and tackle particular tasks, they exist mainly to provide personal attention and support for the members, who may chat about a variety of topics, let off steam, and generally enjoy each other. The tasks they perform are less important than their primary purpose of providing affection. Their talk can be productive even though it is often disorganized and informal because it is not so much the means to an end as *it is the end in itself.* More than

*If the final product of your group will be a public presentation of some kind, the information about forums, panel discussions, and public interviews in the Appendix will help you.

any other forces in our lives, primary groups socialize and mold us into the people we become; their importance is *tremendous*. However, primary groups are not the major emphasis of this book, though most of the information and advice regarding effective communication in groups applies to them. Readers who want more information about primary groups should direct their attention to courses and books labeled *interpersonal communication,* or to the disciplines of psychology and sociology.

Secondary Groups

Secondary groups are formed for the purpose of doing work, such as completing a task, solving a problem, or making a decision. Secondary groups meet primarily the human needs for control and achievement as they enable members to exert power over their environment and others. For example, the teams studied by Larson and LaFasto in their efforts to define effective teamwork are clearly secondary in nature because they have "a specific performance objective or recognizable goal to be attained; and coordination of activity among the members of the team is required for attainment of the team goal or objective."[20] All groups initiated to accomplish some task are more secondary than primary, although many task groups also help members achieve primary needs for socialization and affection.

As you may have discerned by this point, there are no *pure* primary or secondary groups. Although we classify groups according to the *main* reasons for their formation, it is probably clear to you that primary groups do engage in work, and secondary groups provide affection and belonging to their members. Thus, groups blend primary and secondary characteristics and meet many human needs in addition to the ones for which they are initially formed.

Many types of secondary groups exist, and the distinctions among the categories are not always (or even often) precise. We now present several main types of secondary groups. The first three possess many primary group qualities, and the fourth is more purely secondary in nature.

Activity Groups

Activity groups enable members to participate in an activity, both for the sake of doing the activity and for the affiliation provided by doing the activity with others. The following are examples: a gourmet club whose members meet regularly to eat together at different restaurants, bridge and poker clubs, road rally clubs, hunting and bird-watching groups, and numerous other interest groups. Members of such groups solve problems and make choices such as when and where to meet, how to pay for their activities, how group membership is determined, and all the other decisions necessary when several people's efforts must be coordinated. Of course, members enjoy the fellowship and camaraderie of others whose interests are similar. It is easy to see the blend of primary and secondary qualities in activity groups.

Personal Growth Groups

All therapy, encounter, and support groups are called collectively **personal growth groups.** They are composed of people who come together to develop personal insights, overcome personality problems, and grow as individuals from the feedback and support of others—to engage in personal learning and growth. Examples include local chapters of twelve-step programs such as Alcoholics Anonymous and Al Anon, mutual support groups like gay or women's rights groups, outpatient

Sharing information and ideas in a small group is usually more enjoyable and enlightening than being silent in a large group.

groups for clients with personal adjustment problems, support groups for parents whose babies died of SIDS, cancer survivors' support groups, and therapy groups for spouse abusers. Members of such groups typically do not choose each other; they join to help themselves with problems that are both highly personal and social. Because no purely *group* goal is sought, goal interdependence is low; rather, members meet their individual needs for personal learning, awareness, and help in the context of the group. Many such groups have a professional facilitator to guide the interaction. Most of these groups have a limited term of existence; in some, membership changes gradually while the group itself continues.

Learning Groups

Learning groups are similar to growth groups in that they are formed as a medium for learning and growth of the participants. Rather than seeking personality growth as the primary end, members of such groups meet to understand a subject more thoroughly by pooling their knowledge, perceptions, and beliefs. For example, your class may be organized into several learning groups, and local public libraries often organize issue-oriented learning discussions so citizens can become better informed regarding important or controversial issues. Members of such groups often learn much more than the specific subject matter they gather to study; participants also learn skills of effective speaking, listening, critical thinking, and effective interpersonal communication.

There is much value in learning groups. Look at the bulletin boards on your campus, and you are likely to see posters advertising *Bible* study groups, philosophy discussion groups, meditation groups, issue discussion groups, and many others. In addition, many churches, libraries, schools, hospitals, and volunteer organizations produce opportunities for such informal learning.

Problem-solving groups formed to address some condition or problem vary widely in their composition and functioning. For example, the teams studied by Larson and LaFasto functioned primarily in one of the following three ways: problem resolution, creation and innovation, or tactical execution of a well-defined task.[21] These researchers note that each type of group must have a *results-driven structure,* which means that the group's structure must match the group's purpose to help it achieve its goals. For example, a problem-resolution team, such as the health care task force led by Hillary Rodham Clinton or the Springfield MERF neighborhood task force, depends upon trust among team members, effective discussions, and assessment of information for its success. Creative teams, such as advertising agency creative groups or the team that developed the Apple Macintosh, need freedom and autonomy to be able to work without bureaucratic hassles. On the other hand, tactical teams, such as heart transplant and automobile assembly teams, require clearly defined tasks and dependable members.

Whatever the main function of a problem-solving group, such groups are so classified because they are created expressly to solve problems. There are many ways of describing subtypes of problem-solving groups. In this book, we deal with four major categories we believe are prevalent in modern organizational and social life: committees, conference groups, quality control circles, and self-managed work teams. The latter two are relatively new to the American scene but are rapidly gaining in both numbers and acceptance.

Committees.   **Committees** are groups that have been assigned a task by a parent organization or person with authority in an organization. Committees may be formed to investigate and report findings (such as the original MERF task force constituted by the Springfield city council), recommend a course of action for the parent group, formulate policies, or plan and carry out some action. All these tasks require discussion among members. Boards, councils, and staffs are special kinds of committees. For example, a *board of directors* is often called *an executive committee* and represents a larger organization. It may have extensive power to make and execute policy.

Committees are usually classified as either *ad hoc* or *standing.* The **ad hoc** or **special committee** is established to perform a specific task and normally ceases to exist when that task has been completed. A special committee is often referred to as a *task force,* with members appointed from various departments of an organization or political body. Examples of what special committees might be asked to do include evaluating credentials of job applicants, drafting bylaws, hearing grievances, planning social events, conducting investigations, devising plans to solve work-related problems, advising legislators on what to do about statewide problems, and evaluating programs and institutions. Once the task force has reported its action or recommendations, it disbands.

Standing committees are ongoing committees established through the constitution or bylaws of an organization to deal with recurring types of problems or to perform specific organizational functions. The most important standing committee of most organizations is given a name such as *executive committee, board,* or *steering committee.* Usually this group is charged with overall management of the organization and can function for the entire organization when general membership

A committee of health care specialists prepares a recommendation.

Photo by James Shaffer

meetings are not feasible. Other commonly encountered standing committees go under such names as *membership committee, personnel committee, parking and traffic committee, program committee,* and *bylaws committee.* These groups continue indefinitely, even though the membership may change. Frequently, some members of a standing committee are replaced annually so that the group includes both experienced members and those with a fresh perspective. Standing committees often meet regularly, typically resolving a number of problems at a single meeting.

Conference Groups.   By general usage, *conference* refers to almost any type of face-to-face communication, whether between two people or among many participants at large gatherings. However, we use **conference group** to refer to a meeting of representatives from two or more other groups. Since every large organization contains within it many functioning small groups, conferences are critical for coordination within and among organizations. Conferees communicate information from one group to another, often to coordinate their efforts. Intergroup conflicts and competition must be mediated to find a solution acceptable to all groups represented. For example, representatives from the community theatre, art museum, ballet, symphony orchestra, and jazz ensemble may meet to coordinate their scheduling, marketing, and publicity efforts so that individual events do not compete with each other. Conferences between delegates of the U.S. Senate and House of Representatives routinely meet to resolve differences in legislation on the same issue. In the workplace, representatives of business and labor meet to negotiate a contract. Often, conference committees do not have authority to resolve matters within committee meetings, but must submit their tentative decisions to their respective constituent groups for final approval.

Quality Control Circles.   American businesses have experimented with quality control circles for nearly two decades, but only fairly recently have many companies made a serious commitment to their success. A **quality control circle,** sometimes shortened to *quality circle,* consists of workers (usually five to seven) in a company who either volunteer or are selected to meet regularly on company time to recommend ways to improve the quality of finished products, efficiency, worker safety, and other work-related problems. Quality circles represent attempts to capitalize on the fact that groups usually make better and more readily accepted decisions about complex problems than individuals do, and that individuals actually performing the work are in the best position to recommend ways to improve it. Several conditions are essential for quality control circles to work. The people who lead the groups must be trained as problem-solving discussion leaders who remain open-minded toward all ideas suggested. Members must also be trained in discussion procedures and the responsibility of members. Upper management must be committed to the quality circle concept, must respond to all recommended solutions, and must either act on the recommendations or explain why they are being delayed or rejected. Workers must share in the benefits of any cost-saving ideas, and job security must be guaranteed when efficiency is increased.

Self-Managed Work Groups.   **Self-managed work groups,** also called *autonomous work groups* or *peer-led work teams,* are groups of workers given a defined area of freedom to manage their productive work within certain preset limits established by the organization. For example, an automobile assembly team may be responsible for assembling a car from start to finish. It may be given a deadline by which the car must be fully assembled, but within that limit the team members are free to elect their own leaders, plan their work procedures, and schedule individual assignments for the members. Members of self-managed work groups are often *cross-trained,* meaning that each member can perform several jobs competently. This permits human and other resources to be allocated efficiently and effectively, gives workers the chance to develop a variety of skills, and reduces boredom. As with quality circles, workers in self-managed work groups must be well trained,[22] but the benefits are that the immediate group can allocate resources more expediently than a somewhat distant manager, employees with some say in their work are more committed and productive than workers given less choice, and involvement in decision making meets psychological needs of employees without reducing the technical quality of their work. In the future, more employees will be involved in self-managed work teams and quality control circles, so sensitivity to group phenomena and skills in discussion leadership becomes increasingly important.

In the same way that no group is purely primary or secondary, most small groups you encounter will combine elements of all four major types—activity, personal growth, learning, and problem-solving—we have just described. Recall for a moment the several groups involved in the MERF controversy. Although the initial committee charged by the city council to investigate and recommend solutions to Springfield's solid waste problem was an *ad hoc* task force, members had to educate themselves about solid waste, various disposal options, and pros and cons of the options before they could make their recommendations to the city council. They also had to manage their own resources of time and information and be concerned with the comprehensive quality of life in the Springfield area. Thus, this group comprised elements of a learning group, problem-solving group, quality circle, and self-managed work team. The same was true for the city council and for the neighborhood task force that opposed the MERF. This is likely to be the case for many of the groups to which you will belong.

In this edition of *Effective Group Discussion,* we explicitly address the ethical behavior of group members, whether they serve as leaders, members, or observers. **Ethics** refers to the "rules or standards for right conduct or practice. . . ."[23] While appropriate standards of behavior from the general culture apply also to behavior within groups, the unique nature of small groups requires attention to special ethical concerns regarding the treatment of speech, of people, and of information.

Ethical Behavior of Group Members

First, the field of communication has evolved from what was originally the study of speech. Our field has a long and distinguished tradition, dating from Aristotle, that supports the value of free speech.[24] Many secondary groups are formed because several heads perform better than one, but that advantage will not be realized if group members are unwilling or afraid to speak freely in the group. Therefore, an important ethical principle for small group communication is that group members should, first, be willing to share their unique perspectives and, second, should refrain from saying or doing things that prevent others from speaking freely. Each member of a group must feel free to share his or her facts, beliefs, and opinions within the group, according to the appropriate discussion rules established in the group.

Second, group members must conduct themselves with honesty and integrity. In a small group, this takes various forms. An obvious implication of this principle is that group members should not intentionally deceive one another or manufacture information or evidence in an unethical attempt to persuade other members to their points of view. Integrity takes several forms. We mentioned earlier that participation in a group requires trade-offs. In order to receive the benefits of group participation (such as inclusion, affection, and control), members give up something in return (total autonomy, or the ability to do whatever they want whenever they want). Sometimes you may be asked to do something for a group that violates your personal values, beliefs, morals, or principles. For example, what if a group on which you serve decides to suppress information that is contrary to a decision the group wishes to make, and pressures you to go along. What will you do? Only *you* can answer that question. One option is to try your best to persuade the group to see things your way; another option is to leave the group. All we can do is urge you to think carefully about actions that profane your integrity, and make the best choice you can. If you choose to stay with the group, make sure you can support the group's actions and decisions wholeheartedly. To do otherwise is unfair both to the group and to yourself. Integrity also implies that you are willing to place the good of the group ahead of your own individual goals. We believe that if groups are to function effectively, members should make public their private agendas so they are not operating from motives unknown to the other members. We have known individuals who are not able to become part of a team. For whatever reasons, they are unable or unwilling to merge their personal agendas with that of the group. These individuals make lousy team members, and the group is better off without them. If you make a commitment to join a group, be the kind of team member who benefits, not harms, the group.

Third, the ethical principles for interpersonal interaction apply strongly to members of a group. Deetz stresses that ethical interpersonal behavior should strengthen one's personal identity and should have mutual understanding as its goal.[25] Our first goal, as we interact, should be to strive to understand others to their satisfaction. If this happens, we will confirm and support each other's self-concept and identity, even when we disagree. So, another ethical principle is that members should perform no actions intended to disconfirm, belittle, or ridicule other members, and, before agreeing or disagreeing with another, members should make sure that they have first understood that member.

Finally, it is essential that we mention the ethical treatment of information. Many consequential decisions are made in groups, from where to locate a MERF to whether or not it is safe to launch a space shuttle in cold weather. These decisions will be only as good as the information on which they are based and the reasoning members use to assess the information. It is absolutely crucial that group members consider all relevant information in an open-minded, unbiased way by employing the best critical thinking skills they can; to do otherwise can lead to tragedies such as the fatal decision to launch the Challenger. It follows from this that members must credit the sources of information they share with the group, and must not falsify data or information. The fourth ethical principle for effective group discussion, therefore, is that members must make a conscientious effort to find and present to the group all information and points of view relevant to the group's work, to set aside personal biases and prejudices when evaluating that information, and to refrain from doing anything that short-circuits this process. We will return to this subject of ethical behavior at various points throughout the book.

Summary

In this opening chapter, we have considered the vital and ubiquitous roles small groups play in our lives. They provide a source for our identity, a means for problem solving in a complex society, a vehicle to satisfy many basic needs, and we willingly give up time, energy, and total autonomy in order to belong to small groups. Yet grouphate is pervasive because many small groups are ineffectual and frustrating to their members. Even so, the use of groups in the workplace and in society will continue to increase. Learning to operate effectively in small groups is an essential skill that can be learned.

Key terms have been defined to facilitate communication, and a scheme for classifying groups according to their main purpose. Primary groups include the family and groups of close friends, while secondary groups are task-oriented and include activity groups, therapy and encounter groups, learning groups, and problem-solving groups such as committees, conference groups, quality control circles, and self-managed work groups. Three principles pertaining to ethical treatment by group members of speech, people, and information were presented.

With your understanding of these basic terms and concepts, we now turn to a more detailed consideration of communication in the small group.

1. This icebreaker exercise is designed to help you get acquainted with classmates **Exercises** and reduce the tension and formality that exist among strangers. The entire class should sit in a circle so members can see each other face to face. Use a name tag or card large enough to be read across the table.

    a. First, draw a picture (stick figures are fine) to illustrate each of the following statements about yourself. Each person responds to the first statement before proceeding to the next. Begin each set of answers with a different person and proceed around the circle until all have answered.

    I am taking this course because . . .
    Being in a small group makes me feel . . .
    The thing I like best about myself is . . .
    The thing I like least about myself is . . .
    It would surprise most people if they knew that I . . .
    No matter what anyone says, I will not change my mind about . . .
    I really dislike . . .
    My favorite activity is . . .
    Ten years from now I see myself as . . .
    The thing I am most proud of about myself is . . .

    b. Briefly discuss the following:

    Who is most like you?
    Did anybody's answers particularly surprise you? Why?
    Who impressed you most? Why?
    How do you feel now about your class?
    What have we learned from this exercise?

2. For the next week, keep a list of all the small groups in which you actively participate. Classify these groups according to the scheme presented in this chapter. Next, rate your personal satisfaction with each group, from 1 (very dissatisfied) to 7 (very satisfied). Compare your lists in class. What do you conclude? Do your classmates like and dislike the same things in a group that you do? Using these lists, can you develop a list of general principles for having an effective group?

Bibliography

Cathcart, Robert S. and Larry A. Samovar, eds. *Small Group Communication: A Reader.* 6th ed. Dubuque, IA: Wm. C. Brown Publishers, 1992, sections 1 and 2.

Larson, Carl E. and Frank M. J. LaFasto. *Teamwork: What Must Go Right/What Can Go Wrong.* Newbury Park, CA: Sage Publications, 1989.

Notes

1. Diane Cole, "Meetings That Make Sense," *Psychology Today* (May 1989): 14.

2. Bill Lawren, "Competitive Edge," *Psychology Today* (September 1989): 16.

3. Charles C. DuBois, "Portrait of the Ideal MBA," *The Penn Stater* (September/October 1992): 31.

4. William C. Schutz, *FIRO: A Three-Dimensional Theory of Interpersonal Behavior* (New York: Rinehart, 1958).

5. Gerald Goldhaber, "Communication and Student Unrest" (Unpublished report to the president of the University of New Mexico, undated).

6. "Road Test," *Consumer Reports* (April 1992): 266; (July 1992): 427.

7. Ouchi, William, *Theory Z: How American Business Can Meet The Japanese Challenge* (Reading, MA: Addison-Wesley, 1981).

8. Robert H. Waterman, Jr., *The Renewal Factor: How the Best Get and Keep the Competitive Edge* (New York: Bantam Books, Inc., 1987).

9. Lisa Stroud, "No CEO is an Island," *American Way* (November 15, 1988): 94–97, 140–41.

10. Susan Sorensen, "Grouphate" (Paper presented at the International Communication Association, Minneapolis, May, 1981).

11. Stroud, "No CEO is an Island," 97.

12. T. J. Larkin, "Humanistic Principles for Organization Management," *Central States Speech Journal* 37 (1986): 37.

13. Douglas M. Lawson, *Give to Live: How Giving Can Change Your Life* (LaJolla, CA: ALTI Publishing, 1991).

14. Nolan Ryan, Personal Interview, *Today Show* (May 25, 1993).

15. Marvin E. Shaw, *Group Dynamics: The Psychology of Small Group Behavior,* 3d ed. (New York: McGraw-Hill, 1980): 8.

16. Robert F. Bales, *Interaction Process Analysis* (Cambridge, MA: Addison-Wesley, 1950): viii, 35–39.

17. Dorwin Cartwright and Alvin Zander, *Group Dynamics: Research and Theory,* 3d ed. (New York: Harper & Row, 1968): 7.

18. Robert S. Cathcart and Larry A. Samovar, *Small Group Communication: A Reader,* 6th ed. (Dubuque, IA: Wm. C. Brown Publishers, 1992): 1–3.

19. Richard E. Sykes, "Imagining What We Might Study If We Really Studied Small Groups From a Speech Perspective," *Communication Studies* 41 (Fall 1990): 200–211.

20. Carl E. Larson and Frank M. J. LaFasto, *TeamWork: What Must Go Right/What Can Go Wrong* (Newbury Park, CA: Sage Publications, 1989): 19.

21. Larson and LaFasto, *TeamWork,* 66–69.

22. Charles C. Manz and Henry P. Sims, Jr., "The Potential for 'Groupthink' in Autonomous Work Groups," *Human Relations* 35 (1982): 773–84.

23. *The Random House Dictionary of the English Language,* 2d ed. unabridged (New York: Random House, 1987): 665.

24. Ronald C. Arnett, "The Practical Philosophy of Communication Ethics and Free Speech as the Foundation for Speech Communication," *Communication Quarterly* 38 (Summer 1990): 208–17.

25. Stanley Deetz, "Reclaiming the Subject Matter as a Guide to Mutual Understanding: Effectiveness and Ethics in Interpersonal Interaction," *Communication Quarterly* 38 (Summer 1990): 226–43.

The Small Group as a System

Central Message

All components of a small group operate interdependently with one another, just as the group itself is interdependent with its environment. To understand a group fully, we must examine the components in relationship to one another, not in isolation.

Study Objectives

As a result of studying chapter 2 you should be able to:

1. Consciously and intentionally adopt a participant-observer perspective during group discussions.

2. List and explain the major input, throughput, and output variables in a small group system and provide examples of their interdependence.

3. Define the main terms and types of variables pertaining to systems, listed below.

4. Describe the characteristics of an ideal discussion group.

Key Terms

Boundary spanners
Closed systems
Environment
Feedback
Individual-level variables
Input variables

Interdependence
Multiple causation
Nonsummativity
Open system
Output variables
Participant-observer

Social loafers
System
System-level variables
Throughput variables
Variables

We have already discussed how pervasive small groups are in our daily lives and why it is important to study them. What we present in this chapter is a framework, from general systems theory, to help you see how a small group operates; how the group's parts relate to each other; and how the input, throughput, and output variables function together. Once you understand these basic principles of systems theory, you can apply them to *any* group. You then can understand what is happening and why, and adjust your behavior to achieve desired outcomes for yourself and the group.

Participant-Observer Perspective

A major purpose of this book is to help you develop a participant-observer perspective. A **participant-observer** is a regular member of the group who engages actively in its discussions, but at the same time observes, evaluates, and adapts to the group's processes and needs. Participant-observers direct part of their attention to participating in the group and part to assessing how the group is functioning; they try always to be aware of what the group needs at the moment. For example, if the group seems confused, a participant-observer will try to clarify; if group members seem tired of the task, a participant-observer may suggest a break. Because such members simultaneously pay dual attention to the group's processes and the content of the discussion, they can supply essential information, ideas, procedural suggestions, and interpersonal communication skills *when needed.* But to be effective participant-observers, members need a mental model of how an ideal group would function.

Some members supply valuable information but have little understanding of group processes. As long as the group is operating well, these members contribute needed facts and ideas, but they are of no help in resolving conflicts, reducing misunderstandings, offering procedural suggestions, or helping solve other process problems.

Other people are members in name only; they are **social loafers** who watch and listen but contribute little and seem content to let the rest of the members carry the workload. Even if they detract little from the group's energy and resources, they add almost nothing to the group's inputs. We all have experienced groups with social loafers, such as the committee member who makes no suggestions or the classmate in a discussion group who has not read the assignment to be discussed. Although this behavior may result from a lack of understanding of group processes, it nevertheless is inappropriate and unhelpful.

In contrast to both these types of members, participant-observers with extensive knowledge about groups as well as communication competencies can contribute to the quality of both the process and the product of the group. They help lead by articulating relevant information and ideas, promoting harmonious relationships among members, and suggesting procedures helpful to the group. To be an all-around valuable member of the group, you need *both* a participant-observer focus *and* information and expertise essential to completing the group's task.

As a beginning student of small group discussion, you need an overall model of interaction to use as a standard against which to compare the groups to which you belong. We next present an actual example of an exceptionally productive and cohesive small group, then develop a model of a small group as a system, and finally establish a standard of excellence for each major small group variable.

Just like you, most of the groups in which we participate fall short of the ideal. However, one of us has participated for the past eighteen months in a small group that comes close to the ideal. The group began as a steering committee composed of a minister and three lay people working to establish a new church, whose congregation would be the second of its particular denomination in Springfield. The original congregation had split several years before, with people such as the steering committee members feeling uncomfortable about attending the original church. During one traumatic week, the minister died and the chair of the steering committee suffered a stroke. The remaining two members of the steering committee decided to continue their efforts, and recruited three more members to help. They operated at first without a chairperson, but when two more members were added, the committee decided to select a chair to provide more structure to the meetings. The committee faced many serious challenges, including how to handle Sunday services without a minister, how to pay for the lease they had recently signed on an older building, how to overcome opposition from the denomination's headquarters, and objections by the original church's minister to creation of a second congregation in Springfield. The original two members were Sunni, director of a university speech and hearing clinic, and Marina, a college professor. The new recruits were Bill (a lawyer), Norm (a massage therapist), and Sally (a widowed secretary whose husband had been a minister). Sally understood the denomination's rules well, and also knew many people at the association headquarters. The last members added were Don (a retired business owner) and Gary (a maintenance worker). As you can see, the committee included people with diverse experiences.

Commitment of all members to the group's purpose is essential for a productive team. During the first meeting after the death of Chuck (the minister), members affirm their commitment to the task and the group.

Sunni: I'm still in shock from the past week, but I really don't want to give up!

Norm: I feel the same way. We're just on the verge of creating something that fills a hole for lots of people, and I want to see us continue.

Bill: I feel that way, too, but are we all aware of everything that needs to be done? I don't want to give up, but I want us to be realistic about the amount of work it's going to take to form a new congregation.

[Bill affirms the commitment, but encourages members to examine their commitment realistically.]

Marina: It's really important to me to have a church where I feel comfortable, so I'm willing to give whatever time is necessary to pull this off! Are we all feeling the same way? Is this important enough for all of us to give it the time and energy it's going to take?

Group: Yes. Absolutely. Whatever it takes. You bet.

Marina: Then why don't we make a list of what exactly *does* have to be handled for the service on Sunday, and we can see where we are and what needs to be done.

An Example of an Effective Problem-Solving Group

The group planned the service for the following Sunday, then reaffirmed its commitment to the common task:

Sunni: This feels really good to me—that we're all 100 percent behind this, and also that we'll be working together.

Norm: Me, too. I have a feeling we'll be spending lots of time together in the next few months, and I can't think of a better group of individuals to spend time with!

[This reinforces the group's solidarity.]

Bill: Let's see if we can start to get a handle on the things that need to be done immediately. Let's make a list.

Sally: Okay, I'll take notes as we talk.

Having all expressed their commitment, group members were ready to work. The listing of jobs to do continued for about half an hour, with members jumping in to clarify and elaborate as needed. Often, the member who presented a job simultaneously volunteered to do it. Sally read the list and members added a few items. Members volunteered either to perform the "unclaimed" duties or to recruit congregation members. Then the group created an agenda for future meetings:

Marina: Even though we have Sunday services handled, we've got a lot of work to do to get square with the association. Not only that—we have to file for our tax-exempt status, both federal and state. We have to think about bylaws and finding a more permanent location, and lots of other things, too.

[Marina brings up long-range goals.]

Norm: You're right, but my brain is fried and I can't think well anymore. Can we do some of this at another meeting?

Bill: We've accomplished a lot so far, we should probably give it up for tonight.

Group: (Nods of agreement.)

Bill: I have a suggestion, though, for next week. Why doesn't everybody think of the important things that must be accomplished over the next, say, six months, and next week let's make a tentative schedule and organize how we're going to get everything done. Does that sound all right with you?

[All members are encouraged to take responsibility for the group's problem-solving agenda. Although Bill hasn't been named coordinator yet, you can see how he is providing task-oriented, procedural leadership in a completely democratic way.]

Group: That sounds like a great idea. Yes. Good idea.

Sunni: Bill, would you mind typing up the list and giving everybody a copy at the next meeting? That way we won't have to reinvent the wheel every time!

[Sunni emphasizes the importance of keeping written records, thereby sharing in the procedural leadership.]

Bill: Oh, absolutely! I'll have it for everybody at next week's meeting.

Sally: Speaking of meetings, can we talk about meeting times? I was willing to cancel my regular Tuesday meeting to come tonight because this was so important, but can we pick another day? I'd hate to have to miss either meeting.

[Good groups do what they can to accommodate needs of members.]

The group selected Wednesday evening as its meeting time. Members decided to meet weekly until they felt things were going smoothly enough to meet less often. At the next few meetings, the group monitored closely how well Sunday services were being handled and identified long-range tasks that needed to be accomplished. Often the group would address specific problems that concerned one or more members. For example:

Norm: It seems like we've gotten lazier and lazier about making sure the service starts on time. Last Sunday we started ten minutes late, and I noticed several older people leaving before it was over. Why can't we get started on time? Or am I the only one who's bothered by this?

[Norm points out a bad habit by sharing an observation, and then suggests the group make it a *group* issue by inviting the others to share their perceptions.]

Marina: No, it bugs me, too. Unless we do something about it, people will come later and later and the problem will get worse.

Sally: It doesn't bother me very much, but I can see where it would be annoying for somebody on a tight schedule. What could we do about starting on time?

[Sally acknowledges the legitimacy of Norm's concern, even though she doesn't share it to the same degree.]

Sunni: One problem, I think, is that guest speakers don't feel comfortable taking charge. And, starting on time hasn't been identified as someone's specific responsibility. Maybe we could designate a specific person to get the service started?

[Sunni diagnoses a possible cause of the problem, then *tentatively* suggests a solution.]

Bill: Yes, I think you're right—the speakers should be able to rely on *us* for time management and structure. What if we had a platform coordinator for Sundays, just to make sure that the microphone is on, the speaker has a water glass, and the people involved in the service are ready to start on time? For instance, we could make it a platform coordinator's job duty to have everyone in place five minutes before the service.

[Bill elaborates on Sunni's suggestion. He, too, *suggests* rather than saying "We should . . ."]

Norm: Yes, and not only that, we might ask the pianist to play something rousing that will remind people to come in and sit down.

          [Notice how the *group* is building a solution collectively.]

Group: Great idea. I think that will work. Sounds good.

Bill: Then we are agreed? We'll try assigning a platform coordinator and having the pianist start at five minutes 'til the hour.

          [Bill summarizes the decision he believes the group agreed to and tests for consensus.]

The group's norm has become decision making by consensus. While the group continued to address the myriad ordinary problems that cropped up every week, it also began to tackle the major long-range problems that were important to formation of a new congregation, in particular healing its relationship with the association and creating an acceptable set of bylaws.

At this point, Don and Gary were added to the steering committee. The members decided they could function more efficiently with a coordinator. Bill was unanimously acclaimed as group coordinator. He said that he would not "boss" the group, but would prepare an agenda and work to keep the discussions more organized than they had been. The next important task the group tackled was creation of the bylaws:

Bill: Now that we're approved, we need to think about hiring a minister. The association rep told us that we will be permitted to hire a minister when we have a set of bylaws approved by the association and when it looks like we can afford a minister's salary.

Don: Well, the finances seem to be taking care of themselves, but it's time to start working on bylaws. Any ideas?

          [Don supports and extends Bill's initiation of a new topic.]

Sally: Yes, actually. I have a sample of bylaws from the church where my late husband was pastor. Maybe those can give us a start.

Sunni: I do, too, from a church where I was a board member.

Gary: You know, we might have some problem with the congregation. Some people are still mad at our former church and want to make sure the bylaws give the minister absolutely no power whatsoever, including no voting rights!

          [Gary is alerting the group to opinions that must be considered.]

Bill: I've been thinking about that problem, and I have an idea. What if we constituted a bylaw committee that included members from the congregation, especially one or two people who are most angry at our old minister?

Marina: Bill, that's brilliant! We need to make sure their point of view is included. Will you be willing to be the representative from the steering committee to the bylaws subcommittee? With your background as a lawyer, I feel we could trust whatever you came up with.

[Marina supports and confirms Bill's idea.]

Norm: Yes, I trust your judgment too, Bill. And, I just thought of something else we could do. Do you remember Rev. Lacy, the minister of the Columbia church? She has said she'd help us out any way she can. I bet she'd be willing to look at the bylaws and give us some idea about how the association will react to them. That might save us some headaches, if we sent them up there and they hated them!

[Notice how the group willingly asks trusted outsiders for help.]

Gary: Yeah, both the association and the congregation need to be satisfied. I know someone from the congregation who has a real strong opinion about the bylaws and should be on this committee, Rich Jones. If he's part of creating them, I think he'll support them, but if we leave him out, he will be a lot harder to convince.

[Gary follows up on Bill's suggestion with a specific person who fulfills the necessary criteria.]

Group: Good idea! Sure. Yes, let's use all the resources we have.

After the bylaws subcommittee had been working for several months, Bill shared a first draft with the board:

Bill: Well, here's draft one of the bylaws! They aren't carved in stone; we still have lots of time to make changes. I suggest that everybody take them home, read them carefully, and come prepared with suggested changes next week.

[Democratic leadership.]

Norm: Hang on a second, Bill. We said we wanted Rev. Lacy to look at them and give us the association perspective. That will take longer than a week.

[Norm reminds Bill of something he forgot; everyone can share in leading the group.]

Don: Norm's right, we don't want to rush this. Norm, could you call her and tell her we're faxing them, and ask when we could have her comments and suggestions?

Norm: Sure, I'll call tomorrow.

Bill: I'm sorry, I forgot. You're absolutely right. Let's schedule our discussion of the bylaws after Norm gets Rev. Lacy's feedback. Is there anything else you all can think of that I forgot?

[Bill apologizes and reaffirms his expectation that members will share leadership.]

Two weeks later, Norm relayed Rev. Lacy's comments to the group. Her comments resulted in some important changes in the proposed bylaws, which were finally approved by all committee members. Now it was time to present them to the congregation for its consideration and vote:

Don: I'd like for us to plan a strategy session to talk about how we can present these bylaws to the congregation. I don't want all this work to go down the tubes!

Sally: That makes a lot of sense. We can anticipate objections and decide how to handle them.

The bylaws were approved overwhelmingly by the congregation. It was now eight months since the steering committee had initially formed. What had it accomplished? Bylaws had been approved. A board (which included five members of the steering committee) had been elected. The congregation had moved to a more cheerful building. Both financial resources and attendance had continued to grow. The association now supported the new congregation and was sending ministerial students to conduct the services. This was certainly a highly productive team!

Members of the board felt that they had developed such good working and friendship relationships that they "didn't want to break up the family." So, in a very unusual move, the board asked the remaining members of the steering committee (who were not eligible for board membership) to continue to meet with the board as nonvoting consultants. After about a year, the board decided it didn't need weekly meetings; it began to meet every other week. Near the anniversary of Chuck's death, the following meeting occurred. Group members acknowledged their accomplishments as a group, reminded themselves of how far they had come, and demonstrated their continued commitment to the group and each other:

Sunni: Can you believe it? It's been a year since we first got together to decide whether to continue or quit after Chuck died.

Don: As much as we sometimes complain about how much we have to do and how things will be better once we have a minister, take a look at our finances! We have half a year's salary in the minister's fund!

Bill: At times when I'm swamped and feel like giving up, I think about what we've created and I'm energized again.

Marina: I know. Sometimes I get discouraged about all the things we *haven't* done, and all the things that have fallen through the cracks, but when I come here on Sundays and see the attendance and the enthusiasm of the people, I'm overcome with amazement and gratitude.

Gary: Speaking of gratitude, I'm not sure I told you all how hesitant I was to be part of this committee at first, because I don't have the education most of you have, and I didn't feel like I could express myself as well as you all, but this has been one of the best experiences of my life, and I'm grateful to you all for your encouragement and support.

[Gary can admit this only because he trusts the other members.]

Sally: I'm glad you feel that way, but you also should know that we think you've more than pulled your own weight. We really need your expertise, and you express yourself just fine!

Group: Yes! You do! You express yourself well!

This is clearly a productive, cohesive group. As we write this, the board continues to meet bi-weekly. It now is in the process of searching for a minister who will be a full-fledged member with voting rights. The combination of high cohesiveness and high productivity is similar to the excellent teams studied by Larson and LaFasto.[1] As with those teams, a major factor contributing to cohesiveness and productivity was the commitment of all members to create something greater than themselves. This group met all three of Schutz's needs: inclusion, affection, and control. All decisions were made by consensus, and Bill, who eventually was elected board president, continues to serve as a democratic coordinator who always asks for members' input and never behaves in a bossy or dogmatic way. Each member contributed unique skills and talents: Don had extensive financial experience; Gary worked hard to maintain the physical plant; Sally's contacts with the association provided needed liaison; Sunni helped mediate several conflicts; Norm supplied enthusiasm and outside resources; Marina's organization skills made her an adept special events manager; and Bill's problem-solving and people skills made him an amiable and openminded chair. This group had both diversity of perspectives and commonality of values, important elements for group success. With the example of this group as a model of excellence, we are now ready to consider the meaning of the phrase "a small group as a system."

The Small Group as an Open System

You have probably noticed that when a new person joins a group, the group changes in some ways. For example, when a new baby is brought into a family, *all* family relationships will change, including between the parents, between the other children, and between the parents and the children. In addition, new relationships must be accommodated—between *everyone* else and the new baby. This illustrates the idea of a **system**—a set of relationships among interdependent, interacting components and forces. General systems theory is built upon an analysis of living entities—including groups and organizations—as they attempt to remain in dynamic balance with the environment by constant adjustments. Systems theory provides a useful framework to help you keep track of all the individual elements and components of a small group as they interact as a complex whole.

Several principles of systems theory are especially relevant to your study of small groups. One of the most important is the principle of **interdependence,** which states that the parts of a system do not operate in isolation but continuously affect each other, as well as the system as a whole. The new baby affects every other family member. Similarly, if the normally cheerful chair of a committee comes to a group meeting in a grouchy mood, the other members will feel uneasy and the group's normally effective decision-making processes may be impaired. In the church board we described, *every* decision was accomplished through open discussion that emphasized member interdependence. When Sally couldn't make the initial meeting time, the rest of the members adjusted the time so she could participate. No individual's views (including those of board president Bill) were treated as more important than another's. You probably noticed how the open-minded behaviors of Bill and Marina encouraged the others to be open-minded, too, which in turn increased the group's cohesiveness and satisfaction with both the process and the product. Notice, also, that the board recognized its interdependence with both the rest of the congregation and the association headquarters that would have to approve its status as a congregation. Members strove to create something that would be fully acceptable to both organizations to which they were responsible—congregation and association. They paid attention to the *environment* so they could adjust appropriately.

Another key principle is the system property of **nonsummativity** (nonadditivity), which states that the whole system is *not* the sum of its parts. It may be either greater or less than the sum of its parts, with either *positive synergy* or *negative synergy* operating. Imagine a collection of individuals when they first begin to interact and coordinate their efforts to form a competitive basketball team. The team (group) involves much more than the simple addition of the abilities of each player. The group will take on a life of its own and become an identifiable entity. Sports fans know they will lose money on a basketball or football game if they add up the statistics for each player, arrive at team totals, and bet on the team with the higher total. On any given day, a so-called poor team can play beyond its apparent potential (positive synergy), or a terrific team can have an off day (negative synergy). Why? Because each team or group is a living system in which everything is interdependent, and no one can predict precisely how the new system will function during any particular time.

In other arenas of endeavor, groups frequently design technologies beyond the collective capacities of the individual members. For example, most recent Nobel prizes in science have been given for breakthroughs that required teams of scientists. On the other hand, groups of intelligent, knowledgeable, and committed members sometimes make lousy decisions, such as the groups of scientists and managers who decided to launch the space shuttle Challenger on its ill-fated trip. Both examples, good and bad, illustrate nonsummativity.

The systems perspective helps keep us from oversimplifying our understanding of how a group functions and perhaps missing something important. For example, systems theory emphasizes **multiple causation,** the fact that whatever happens in a system is not the result of a single, simple cause, but is produced by complex interrelationships among multiple forces. For example, several factors contributed to the church board's successful efforts, including the board's shared leadership, Bill's democratic coordination, the commitment and expertise of the members, the fact that creation of a new congregation filled a need in the community, and probably some fortuitous factors, such as the availability of an affordable location. Similarly, the systems perspective leads us to look for multiple outcomes of any change in a group.

The **variables** of a system are its characteristics or dimensions. They may be classified as either *individual-level* or *system-level* features of a group.[2] **Individual-level variables** are properties of the individual members, such as their traits, skills, abilities, expertise, values, and attitudes. **System-level variables** are characteristics of the group as a whole, including preexisting societal and cultural norms, the degree of cohesiveness, and procedures the group uses. The individual-level and system-level variables are interdependent within themselves and with each other. For example, a new member may be well informed about a topic the group is discussing (an individual-level variable), but if the group has established a norm that new members should be seen and not heard until they have "paid their dues" (a system-level variable), the group will not benefit from that member's information. Thus, individual characteristics and group (system) characteristics mutually influence each other, as well as the group's final outputs.

Small group variables may be classified into three broad categories: *input, throughput,* and *output.* **Input variables** are components from which a small group is formed and that it uses to do its work, including: the members; the reasons for the group's formation; resources such as information, expertise, money, and tools; and environmental conditions and forces that influence the group. In the church committee, members with their diverse areas of expertise were inputs. For instance, both Sunni and Sally had examples of bylaws from other churches, and Bill knew what to do to incorporate and receive tax-exempt status. This information, possessed by individuals but shared with the group, served as resource input variables that ultimately affected both the group's deliberations and its success.

Throughput variables involve *how* the group transforms inputs into final products and are characteristics of how the system *functions,* what it actually *does.* Examples include: roles, rules, and norms; procedures the group follows; communication among members; and all the other things that are part of the process in which the group engages as it works toward completing its task. In our exemplary group, observe how certain rules and procedures evolved. First, the members complimented each other and affirmed their commitment to the group's task. This led to a pattern of expressing cohesiveness and mutual respect, which later made it easier for members to contribute freely and frankly. Bill established his role as a democratic chair who encouraged norms of equality and shared leadership ("Does that sound all right with you?" and "Is there anything else that you can think of that I forgot?"). Other members then felt comfortable jumping in with suggestions or comments.

Output variables are the results or products of the group's throughput processes, including the tangible work accomplished (such as written reports, items built, and policies developed), changes in the members (such as increases in commitment and increased self-confidence), the group's effect on its environment, and changes in the group's procedures. The church board's most obvious output to its environment was the formation of a church now serving many people in southwest Missouri. Internal outputs included the strong bond that occurred among members and the increased self-esteem Gary felt about being able to express himself in a group.

As you can see, input, throughput, and output variables are not separable; everything influences and is influenced by everything else. For example, attitudes affect interaction, which in turn affects the outcome. Moreover, both the interaction itself and group outcomes can produce changes in members' attitudes. In addition, changes in such variables can change roles; the output of increased cohesiveness after completion of one task can then become an input as members tackle a new task. These reciprocal relationships among a system's parts and processes illustrate the interdependence discussed earlier.

Figure 2.1 is a diagrammatic model of some of the many variables in each of the three major categories: input, throughput, and output. The hopper at the top of the figure represents inputs flowing into the throughput machinery of the system, where they are processed and changed. The exit channel at the bottom of the diagram represents the outputs of the system. The tube on the left side looping from output to input represents the **feedback** channel, through which a portion of the group's outputs are recycled as system inputs. For example, if the basketball team we mentioned earlier becomes successful, the output of repeated winning will produce more enthusiasm and commitment to the team by the players, who will continue to polish their performance together and to feel positive about each other and the coach. Their success may then produce greater attendance at the games and more funds to buy better equipment, which may in turn lead to greater success.

The model in figure 2.1 represents an **open system,** meaning that the group interacts freely with its **environment,** the setting in which the small group exists, rather than operating in isolation. In contrast, there are relatively **closed systems,** meaning that there is little interchange between the group and its environment. For example, a classroom discussion group may receive relevant information from the instructor, from other classmates, from friends outside the class, or from news media sources. The church board was influenced by information and opinions outside the group. On the other hand, a cloistered monastery, where monks interact with each other but have little contact with outsiders, illustrates a closed system. However, there can be no *completely* closed human system.

The relationship between a group's internal processes and its outputs is obvious, but how a group manages its relationship with its environment, while less obvious, is equally important. Ancona and Caldwell note that this aspect of group processes has been largely ignored by group researchers.[3] They suggest that groups need members who serve as **boundary spanners** by constantly monitoring the group's environment to bring in and take out information relevant to the group's success. The first of the three major functions that boundary spanners serve is initiating transactions to import or export needed resources, such as information or support. For instance, in our example of an effective group, Norm contacted his minister friend for advice about organizing the new congregation and help in gaining approval from the association. Another boundary spanning function consists of responding to initiatives of outsiders. Someone may ask a group member what the group discussed at a particular meeting; that member must then decide whether and what information to relate. The final function involves changes in the membership of the group—new people may be brought into the group either temporarily or permanently. For example, members decided to invite Gary's wife, Christy, to attend church board meetings in his place as a nonvoting member during the weeks he was unable to attend, so that he would be able to keep up with the information and maintain, through Christy, relationships that had formed. The management of the group's relationship with the environment is crucial and can spell success or failure for the group. If the church board had decided to be secretive and not share openly

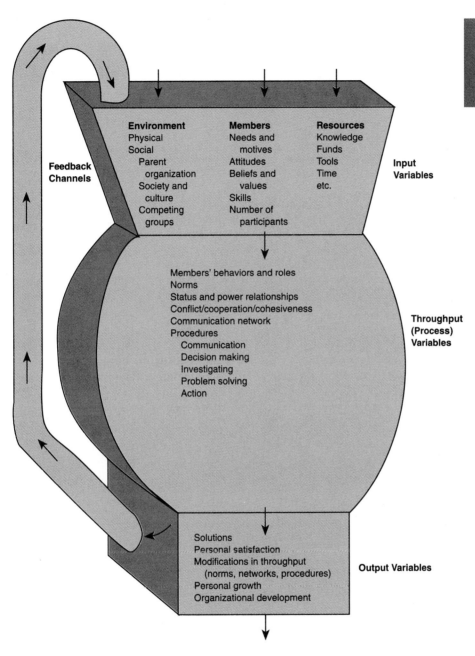

Figure 2.1
A model of the
small group as an
open system.

Environment
Physical
Social
 Parent
  organization
 Society and
  culture
 Competing
  groups

Members
Needs and
 motives
Attitudes
Beliefs and
 values
Skills
Number of
 participants

Resources
Knowledge
Funds
Tools
Time
etc.

**Input
Variables**

**Feedback
Channels**

Members' behaviors and roles
Norms
Status and power relationships
Conflict/cooperation/cohesiveness
Communication network
Procedures
 Communication
 Decision making
 Investigating
 Problem solving
 Action

**Throughput
(Process)
Variables**

Solutions
Personal satisfaction
Modifications in throughput
 (norms, networks, procedures)
Personal growth
Organizational development

Output Variables

with the congregation what was discussed and decided at board meetings, the congregation would likely have not approved the bylaws.

Now that you have seen an example of the interaction of an effective committee and have an understanding of the complexities of small group systems, we can proceed to identify standards against which you can evaluate the major input, throughput, and output variables of any small group to which you belong.

Figure 2.2
Characteristics of
an ideal discussion
group.

Input Variables
1. Members share values and beliefs toward the purpose of the group and each other.
2. The number of members is small enough for all to be active participants who are aware of each other, yet large enough to supply knowledge and competencies.
3. The group's purpose is understood and accepted by all members.
4. Resources needed to achieve group goals are available.
5. The group's relationships to other groups and organizations are clear.
6. The group has sufficient time to do its work.
7. The group has a meeting place that provides for members' needs and is free of distractions.

Throughput Variables
1. Members can predict each other's behaviors.
2. Roles are stable, mutually understood, and accepted.
3. Members have relatively equal status, so they can exert influence based on knowledge, ideas, and skills.
4. Norms and the values underlying them are understood and adhered to, or discussed openly and changed if counterproductive.
5. Communication flows in an all-channel network.
6. Members are skilled and considerate when expressing themselves.
7. All members understand and share procedures that are efficient and lead to goal achievement.

Output Variables
1. Members perceive that the group purpose has been achieved.
2. Members feel satisfaction with their roles, the group process, and their relationships with other members.
3. Cohesiveness is high.
4. There is consensus on the role and leadership structure.
5. The parent organization (if one exists) is strengthened by the group's work.

Characteristics of an Ideal Secondary Group

The worth of any secondary group can be determined only from its outputs, its effectiveness. The quality of a group's outputs is directly related to the quality of the group's inputs and throughputs. We do not mean to underestimate environmental factors or limits placed on the group by its parent organization, but our focus is on the discussion that occurs within the group. The following standards, summarized in figure 2.2, represent the ideal input, throughput, and output variables toward which discussion groups should strive, even though most will fall short.

Input Variables

1. **Members share basic values and beliefs about the purpose of the group and each other.**

   For instance, if one member of a project group believes deeply that the project is worthwhile and intends to commit substantial time to it but another member thinks the assignment is busywork and decides to "blow it off," the group is not likely to reach consensus or interact smoothly. Ideally, members' attitudes toward each other, the group, and the group's task are positive. Members should be able to count on each other to complete tasks, support the decisions of the group, and act in a trustworthy way toward the other members. In our story about the effective church board, members demonstrated their commitment to the group and to doing a good job with such statements as "It's really important to me to have a church where I feel comfortable," and "I'm willing to give whatever time is necessary to pull this off!"

2. **The number of members is small enough for all to be active participants and to be perceptually aware of each other as individuals, yet large enough to supply the variety of knowledge and competencies needed to achieve high-quality outputs.**

   A divergence of backgrounds and perspectives is needed, but similarity in goals and values will make it possible for all members to support group decisions. Ideal groups achieve a balance between diversity and similarity; this balance is more important than size. For example, five people with different perspectives but similar values might agree on a goal, yet supply different sets of information about the problem and possible solutions. Thus, they will perform more effectively than ten people whose perspectives are exactly the same or three people who can't agree on basic values and goals.

3. **The group's purpose is understood and accepted by all members.**

   All members perceive the goal alike and give it priority over personal goals or needs incompatible with group objectives. Members whose personal values or goals are at odds with a group goal interfere with efficiency. For example, if one or two members of a religious study group attempt to convert others, but the purpose of the group is to share and understand a variety of beliefs, the group will have problems.

4. **Resources needed to achieve the goals of the group are available.**

   Members have what they need in order to accomplish the task. This includes reliable information, physical resources, communication media, funds, and any other needed objects. For example, a group in which one of us served could not do its work until a highly detailed set of data on computer tapes was made available from a government agency and a member with computer programming skills was added to the group.

5. **The group's relationships to other groups and organizations in its environment are clear, and members know what resources are available from these groups and organizations.**

   Group members perform the appropriate boundary spanning activities and know how they relate to the organization that created the group, to competing groups, and to the environment. The area of freedom and limitations on the group are understood both by the group and by affected people in the environment. The group knows how to adapt to changing environmental circumstances.

6. **The group has sufficient time in which to do its work.**

   If research is needed to understand the problem, group members should have enough time to do it thoroughly. Groups need time to work through all the phases of the problem-solving procedure or to digest and process information and ideas. In short, members must have and commit enough time to do their work as a group thoroughly and well. For example, they should not try to find a solution to a city's congested traffic in a forty-minute meeting. Recall that the church board met for six months before it received the association's approval to organize as a congregation.

7. **The group has a place to meet that provides for members' needs and allows discussions without distractions.**

A committee that has no adequate room in which to meet regularly will expend much energy just finding and changing meeting places and trying to get members to those places. A quality circle cannot discuss well in a noisy assembly room, nor can a personnel committee evaluate job candidates in a room where privacy is compromised by strangers wandering in and out.

Throughput Variables

1. **Members are dependable and reliable.**

A member who undertakes an assignment can be counted on to carry it out, whether that involves gathering information, typing and distributing a report, or scheduling a Sunday speaker for the service. Members can be counted on to attend scheduled meetings, notify the group if this is not possible, and perhaps send a knowledgeable substitute in their place if appropriate.

2. **Roles of members are relatively stable, mutually understood, and accepted by all members.**

There is both sufficient role definition to permit members to predict each other's behavior (for example, on the church board Marina was consistently task oriented and organized and Bill was consistently democratic), as well as sufficient flexibility to permit anyone to make needed contributions to task or group maintenance (other members were task oriented and organized, and Marina also contributed to the positive feelings: "I'm overcome with amazement and gratitude!"). There is an equitable division of labor. The leadership position has been settled satisfactorily, *but leadership functions are shared by all members.* In our example of an effective group, all members made suggestions and volunteered for assignments.

3. **Members have relatively equal status, so all can exert influence based on their own knowledge, skill, and ideas rather than status differences internal or external to the group.**

On the church board, Bill's external status as a lawyer was relatively high, but that didn't stop Norm, the massage therapist, from saying "Hang on a second, Bill . . . that will take longer than a week" when he reminded Bill of something. That was possible because *inside* the group, the status of members was relatively equal, partly because the designated leader served as a coordinator, not a supervisor. Equal status promotes teamwork in the sharing of rewards, mutual support, and decision making by consensus. Members spend their energies achieving the goals of the group, not competing against each other for power and position. When all members feel equal, they freely contribute ideas, opinions, and suggestions; they don't hold back. This gives the group more information to work with.

4. **Norms (rules) and the values underlying them are understood and adhered to, or are discussed openly and changed when found to be unproductive.**

   A consistently productive problem-solving group has a culture of beliefs, values, and standards that encourages thorough searching for and testing of facts and ideas. For example, diversity of opinion was important to the church board; when Bill suggested putting one or two people on the bylaws committee who felt strongest about limiting the power of the minister, Marina said, "Bill, that's brilliant! We need to make sure their point of view is included." Earlier, when Norm expressed concern about the service consistently starting late, he checked his concern with the others: ". . . am I the only one who is bothered by this?" This allowed the others to express their views, to address the unproductive habit that had developed, and to participate in finding a solution.

5. **The flow of communication reveals an all-channel network.**

   A high proportion of remarks is directed to the group as a whole, not to individual members. There are no sidebar conversations during the group meeting, yet members are free to approach any and all other members when a meeting is not in progress. Members build on each other's ideas. For example, when Norm brought up the problem of the service starting late, Sunni suggested giving the responsibility to a specific person, Bill expanded that to suggest creating a position of "platform coordinator," and Norm followed up with a suggestion to have the pianist start to play as a signal to the congregation to sit down.

6. **Members are skilled in expressing themselves interpersonally and are considerate of other members.**

   In the church board, Gary felt insecure about his ability to express ideas, but he was willing to share his opinion, did so clearly, and was encouraged by the other members. Group members should express their ideas with sensitivity so as not to evoke defensiveness in the others. In our example, before Norm mentioned that he wanted a minister friend to evaluate the bylaws Bill has been working on, he affirmed his faith in Bill: "Yes, I trust your judgment, Bill." Then he stated his suggestion *provisionally,* not dogmatically: "I just thought of something else we *could* do. . . . I bet she'd be willing to look at the bylaws and give us some feedback. . . . That might save us some headaches, if . . . they hated them!" Norm *didn't* say, "You've wasted a lot of time on bylaws without taking into account how the association will react, and you'd better get that feedback before we go any further!" Instead, he first demonstrated his basic agreement with and respect for Bill, then made his suggestion.

7. **All members understand and share procedures that are efficient, prevent overlooking important issues and facts, and lead to goal achievement.**

   In a problem-solving group, this means all members understand and follow a procedure that is based on systematic methods of problem solving, and they share in exercising control over this procedure. The *group* decides to change its procedures. In addition, it is helpful for group members to share specific discussion techniques appropriate to the purpose of the group, and to participate in establishing the agenda. For example, after the church board tried biweekly meetings for a while, Norm concluded they weren't working for him. He brought it up to the group, gave the members reasons why they might reconsider ("Things really pile up in two weeks, and sometimes there's a big delay in our response. . . .") and asked the others what they thought.

Output Variables

1. **Members of the group perceive that its purpose has been achieved.**
   Decisions and solutions to problems are supported by members as the best ones possible. In the example, all members stated openly that they thought the bylaws they had created were excellent, and should be adopted by the congregation. Solutions decided upon will be accepted by most or all of the people affected.

2. **Members experience personal satisfaction with their respective roles in the group, the discussion and group-work process, and their relationships with the members.**
   For example, Bill says, "I can honestly say it's been worth the work," and Gary says, "I'm grateful to you all for your encouragement and support." The fact that at one point the board decided to meet *more* frequently, not less, indicates a high degree of satisfaction with the activity.

3. **Cohesiveness is high.**
   Members have a strong sense of identification with the group and give it high priority among competing demands for their time and attention. Cohesiveness among board members was evident ("I'm swamped with things to do, but this is my priority" and "I think about what we've created, and I'm energized again."). A high degree of trust exists among members.

4. **There is consensus on the leadership and role structure of the group.**
   If asked independently, each member would name the same person(s) as designated leader of the group and as choice for leader in the future. For example, Bill emerged as the group's designated leader because he organized well, was democratic, and put in considerable work. He was *drafted* to coordinate the steering committee, and was later *elected* board president. The rest of the members' roles developed as a result of their interests and expertise in relation to the needs of the group. Thus, members shared in leading the group.

5. **The parent organization (if one exists) is strengthened as a result of the small group's work.**
   The organization is better off as a result of the group's work. In the church board's case, this requirement clearly was met. The board helped create a viable church that is growing, has received its denomination's approval, and will soon have its own minister.

Probably few groups you experience will measure up to these standards as well as the church board did. However, you now have a model of an effective small group as a basis for comparison and should be able to spot at least some of the sources of difficulty in any group that is not producing satisfactory outputs.

Summary

This chapter began with a discussion of the value to groups of participant-observers, members who attend both to the content and process of the group's discussion. Variables with which small group observers must be concerned may be either individual- or system-level features of the group. To help you become an astute participant-observer, the small group was described as an open system with input, throughput (process), and output variables, and was characterized as having properties of interdependence and nonsummativity. Input variables include such items as members' skills, knowledge, and other resources. The group, as a system, processes these resources through communication among members, thereby transforming them into outputs such as physical products, solutions to problems, recommendations, and changes in cohesiveness, perceptions, and the group members. A model of an ideal group was presented as a standard by which to evaluate the effectiveness of any secondary small group, and to provide perspective for further study. In the next section, we will discuss the basic communication principles that provide the foundation for effective group throughput processes.

Exercises

1. Discuss the following issues with a small group of classmates or with the entire class sitting in a circle.
   a. How important is it to develop a participant-observer focus?
   b. How could you tell whether a group member had such a focus?
   c. How can we develop such a focus while working in this class?

2. Compare a small group system to other living systems: an individual plant cell, the human body, an organization (for example, General Motors or the Mafia). Discuss the following terms in relation to these other systems.
   a. Open versus closed systems
   b. Interdependence of the parts of the system
   c. Nonsummativity
   d. Boundary-spanning activity

3. In this chapter, several input, throughput, and output variables of small secondary groups were identified. What others do you think should be included? Why? Your answer should include a modification of figure 2.1.

4. Think of the best and the worst small secondary groups in which you have participated. Why were they the best and worst? What characteristics of the inputs and the throughputs seem to have made the most difference? As a class, generate your own criteria for effective inputs and throughputs.

5. Study carefully the excerpts from the discussion of the church board presented in this chapter. What are the characteristics of the variables that made this a highly productive and cohesive group? Compare your answers with those of classmates.

Bibliography

Katz, Daniel and Robert L. Kahn. *The Social Psychology of Organizations.* 2d ed. New York: John Wiley, 1978. See chapter 2.

Von Bertalanffy, Ludwig. *General System Theory.* New York: George Braziller, 1969.

Wood, Julia T., Gerald M. Phillips, and Douglas J. Pedersen. "Understanding the Group as a System." In *Small Group Communication: A Reader.* 3d ed., eds. Robert S. Cathcart and Larry A. Samovar. Dubuque, IA: Wm. C. Brown Publishers, 1992, 5–17.

Notes

1. Carl E. Larson and Frank M. J. LaFasto, *TeamWork: What Must Go Right/What Can Go Wrong* (Newbury Park, CA: Sage Publications, 1989).

2. Randy Y. Hirokawa and Dierdre D. Johnston, "Toward a General Theory of Group Decision-making: Development of an Integrated Model," *Small Group Behavior* 20 (November 1989): 500–523.

3. Deborah G. Ancona and David F. Caldwell, "Beyond Task and Maintenance: Defining External Functions in Groups," *Group & Organization Studies* 13 (December 1988): 468–94.

The Foundations of Communicating in Groups

The three chapters in part 2 provide theoretical information about communication that is particularly relevant to communicating in small groups. They are intended to serve as a foundation on which to build your understanding of throughput processes in a small group. This foundation includes information about how humans use language, how nonverbal and verbal behaviors function together, and how individuals from different cultures communicate differently in small group settings. Specific guidance based on communication theory is provided for improving your personal competencies as a group member, especially in speaking, listening, and interpreting during group meetings.

Human Communication Processes in Small Groups

Central Message

Communication is a complex, symbolic process that must be both understood and attended to by group members in order to coordinate their efforts to achieve the group goal.

Study Objectives   As a result of studying chapter 3 you should be able to:

1. Explain communication as a symbolic, personal, transactional process that is not always intentional.

2. Differentiate among the content, relationship, and affective levels of interpersonal communication.

3. Explain the fallacy in each of five communication myths.

4. Describe how signals are encoded, transmitted, received, interpreted, and responded to in a communication transaction.

5. Give an example of a complete communication transaction and explain why such transactions are important.

6. Identify and describe each of seven pitfalls to effective listening.

7. Demonstrate both active and focused listening.

Key Terms

Active listening	Interpersonal communication	Paraphrase
Communication	Intrapersonal communication	Pseudolistening
Complete communication transaction	Listening	Sidetracking
Defensive listening	Message	Signs
Feedback	Mind raping	Signals
Focused listening	Noise	Symbols

Communication is the very heart of a small group; it is the verbal and nonverbal process by which individuals forge themselves into a group, maintain the group, share information, reach agreements, and coordinate their efforts. No communication, no group. This chapter provides a foundation for understanding the term *communication,* which is *the* fundamental throughput process of all groups.

If you have previously studied communication, much of the next two chapters may be a review for you. Nevertheless, because communication scholars sometimes use key terms in different ways, we recommend that you at least survey them to understand how we are using them.

What is Communication?

Many definitions of the term *communication* exist. We define it as the process by which people create and send signals that are received, interpreted, and responded to by other people. The purpose of this process, for the small group, is to develop meaning that is shared sufficiently for the members to accomplish the group task. We acknowledge that not all scholars agree that "shared meaning" is the purpose because there are limitations to this definition.[1] For one thing, meaning between two people, let alone among the four or five who typically constitute a small group, will never be completely shared. However, limitations aside, common sense tells us that if group members are to achieve their interdependent goal, they must strive for mutual understanding; at least *some* shared meaning must occur.

Principles of Communication

This straightforward definition contains several implications that must be addressed for you to understand fully how the process works in small groups. In this section, we first present several principles that govern the communication process before we elaborate on that process in greater detail and discuss several myths associated with communication. We note, again, that different authors subscribe to different communication principles. The following are the ones that make the most sense to us; if you understand these principles, you will appreciate why communication is at best an *inexact* activity. Several of these principles are considered in greater detail in chapter 4.

1. **Human communication is symbolic.**

   This, perhaps, is the most important principle of communication. *Meaning* is not transferred from one person to another; rather, people send *messages that must be interpreted* to each other. In the movie *Brainstorm,* the main character invented a headphone device that could transfer experiences directly from the brain of one person to another without first having to *encode* the experiences into words. Of course, we can't do this—yet! We must use verbal and nonverbal signals to send our thoughts to another person. In this encoding process, we convert our thoughts, feelings, beliefs, and experiences into the words, sounds, and gestures that we hope others will interpret as we mean them. The receiver then uses the reverse process of *decoding,* attending to what was sent and interpreting it, to try to determine what was meant.

   The **signals** that humans exchange may be either *signs* or *symbols.* **Signs,** nonverbal elements such as tone of voice, face and body characteristics, have an inherent, natural connection with what they represent. For example, if you scowl because you hear something you dislike, there is a natural connection between your feeling of dislike and your scowl. Similarly, your blush of embarrassment is a sign directly connected with your feeling of embarrassment. In contrast, **symbols** are arbitrary signals created by people to represent experiences, objects, or concepts. For example, there is no automatic reason why we call something we write with a *pen.* We could just as easily have agreed to call it a *dog, tree,* or *la plume.* Similarly, the *okay* gesture, the circle we make with thumb and forefinger, is an arbitrary symbol; it means something different in other cultures, such as in South America, where it means something obscene. This reliance on symbols is an important characteristic of human communication and is a major reason why *meaning* is never shared exactly.

2. **Communication is personal.**

   Meaning itself is not conveyed. A person sends signals that evoke meaning in a receiver; the signals will have different associations for the receiver than they do for the sender. Because much human communication is symbolic, the same word can have different meanings to different people. Thus, as is sometimes stated, "meanings are in people, not in words." This principle is even more important when we consider that many of the concepts we necessarily use in everyday conversation are abstract: *fairness, excellence, effective.* For instance, *excellence* to you may mean striving for an A grade on a project, with no typographical errors and all information thorough and complete; for a fellow group member, *excellence* may mean getting the project completed on time, even if there are mistakes and missing information. Both of you are using the same word, but you aren't meaning the same thing at all! Your backgrounds, experiences, the culture from which you came—all of these things affect the meanings you give to the words you and others use. We discuss in detail the effects of culture on the communication process in chapter 5.

3. **Communication is a transactional process.**

   This principle follows from the previous two. *Transactional* implies that participants in a communication encounter must cooperate and work together to achieve mutual meaning and understanding. To extend the previous example, if we know that the symbol (i.e., word) *excellent* has different connotations to different people, and we want to make sure we understand each other about *our* project, then we must work together, communicatively, to determine what we jointly mean by *excellent.* In addition, *transactional* implies that the sender-receiver roles in a communication transaction occur simultaneously. While I am describing what an excellent project means to me, I am simultaneously seeing your frown, and guessing that you don't agree with my description. Thus, communication is *both* a sender *and* receiver phenomenon simultaneously for each person involved in the process. Finally, the concept of *process* implies that communication is an ongoing event with no clear beginning or end. If we argue about how excellent our project will be, then the next time we meet we will carry the memory of that argument with us. Thus, communication is ever-changing, not static, but constantly in flux.

4. **Communication is not always intentional.**

   This principle is sometimes stated as "You cannot NOT communicate," and not all communication scholars agree with this position. For example, Infante et al.[2] believe that for an event to "count" as communication, the sender must have intended to communicate with the receiver. However, we believe that when two or more humans are in each other's perceptual awareness they cannot stop sending nonverbal signals to each other, which the receivers pick up, interpret, and respond to. True, the way signals are interpreted may not be the way they were intended. Moreover, people do not always *know* what they intend, and may have multiple intentions for their words.[3] Nevertheless, in a group, you do not have the option of *not* communicating, because even silence will be interpreted by your fellow group members.

5. **Communication involves content, relationship, and affective levels.**

   A **message,** the set of signals from one person to others, contains all three levels. The *content* or denotative level of the message is the subject or topic of the message. The *relationship* level of the message refers to what the message reveals about how the speaker views his or her relationship to the other participants, and the *affective* level of the message reveals how the speaker feels about what he or she is saying. These latter two levels provide the connotative, or implied, level of the message. The following example, excerpted from a meeting of students, will illustrate. Chris, the designated leader, Lori, Deidre, and Tony are waiting for Kevin, who is always late:[4]

   Deidre: Man, what time is it already? Kevin—he's ten minutes late! If he would have gotten here on time we'd have been done by now. I'm tired of this.

   Chris: I'm tired of waiting on the jerk, okay?

   Lori: I don't have time for this.

   Chris: I'm kind of tired of it, too. Let's just go ahead and get started and try to get the ball rolling. Tony, did you find out how much money we've got to spend?

   At the content level, Deidre's first remark presents a fact—that Kevin is ten minutes late—and an opinion—that the group could have finished its meeting if members had been able to start on time. However, the level of communication most striking here, and in Chris' and Lori's subsequent remarks, is the affective level. Clearly, these students feel angry and frustrated that Kevin has failed them again. Chris' calling Kevin "a jerk" indicates that Kevin's behavior pattern is straining the good will of the others. Now notice Chris' final remark: "Let's just go ahead and get started. . . . Tony, did you. . . ?" This comment clearly illustrates the relationship level of communication, which concerns how the speaker views his or her relationship to the other members. Chris takes charge here by suggesting the group begin without Kevin, then asks Tony for a report. At the content level, Chris seems to be making a procedural suggestion ("Let's get started") and asking Tony for information. At the relationship level, however, Chris is saying, "I have enough authority in this group to suggest how to proceed, and I'm taking charge now." The rest of the members comply with Chris' request, and the meeting gets under way. Why? Chris is the designated leader of the group, and he is behaving appropriately for his position. The members *expect* him to coordinate and structure the group's discussion. In this instance, Chris does not overstep his relational bounds.

The relationship level, which is often conveyed nonverbally through tone of voice and movement, can show that the speaker considers him- or herself to be dominant, subservient, or equal to the other members. Attitudes of arrogance, dominance, submissiveness, distrust, superiority, neutrality, or concern are not often stated; rather, listeners interpret them from nonverbal cues. In our experience, this level causes many of the misunderstandings we observe in small groups. To illustrate, what if Lori had turned to Deidre and said, in a commanding tone of voice, "Deidre, you take notes for the meeting." Deidre would probably have wanted to say, "Who died and made you queen?" Group members often react strongly to a peer who seems to command and direct because the manner suggests superiority to the other members. Unless the group members have agreed to give someone extra authority (such as by electing that person the group's leader), they will usually reject a bid to take over.

Misunderstandings about communication are perpetuated by a number of communication myths. Here are five of the most pervasive ones:

Myths about Communication

1. **I understand communication. I've been communicating all my life!**
   What if your 90-year-old Aunt Tilly said, "I know how to drive—I've been driving all my life!" Just because we do something often doesn't mean we do it well. Most people do not *think reflectively* about their communication behavior so they can improve it.

2. **All human problems are communication problems.**
   This statement trivializes the very real value differences that divide humans. Environmentalists who want to save old growth forests in the Pacific Northwest may understand perfectly well the concern of loggers who fear for their jobs and livelihoods—but they disagree over values and appropriate courses of action. Communicating *more* and *better* may do nothing to resolve their disagreements. This does not imply, though, that most of us communicate clearly and well most of the time; we don't. Ineffective communication is the rule, not the exception.

3. **If communicators use good communication techniques, they will automatically have good communication.**
   It *is* true that becoming a good communicator requires practicing techniques of effective encoding and decoding. However, communication involves much more than that. The most important "skill" for improving communication involves having an *attitude* of wanting to be a good communicator more than it involves techniques. You can make mistakes with the techniques you use, but if people sense your basic good intentions they will often forgive your communicative lapses and you can be quite effective in coordinating

meanings with them. Only if you *want* to be a good communicator can
the skills and suggestions in most communication books help you.

What *does* promote good communication? Almost always, good
communication is enhanced by the communicator's understanding of the
communication process and his or her attitudes toward both the process and
other people. In addition, although this myth implies that communicators
should work to improve their sending skills, improvements in the *listening*
aspects of communication are the most beneficial.

4. **I didn't misunderstand him, he misunderstood me.**
   Both sender and receiver must cooperate to create clear, mutually understood
   messages. If a message is misunderstood, the effective communicator will
   accept a share of the responsibility (*not* blame!) and work to improve future
   transactions.

5. **Good communication achieves perfect understanding among participants.**
   Perfect understanding is impossible. Moreover, some messages are *intended* to
   mislead rather than enlighten. Have you ever answered vaguely to the question,
   "How do you like my new hair style?" In this case, the lack of clear,
   unambiguous communication purposefully avoids hurting someone's feelings.
   In addition, we discussed earlier the fact that communication is both symbolic
   and personal; the best we can do is come close enough to understanding that
   we can complete the work of the group.

A Description of a Communication Transaction

Now that we have looked at main principles and widespread myths about communication in general, let's go back to our definition of communication (*the process
by which people create and send signals that are received, interpreted, and responded to by other people*) and use it to analyze a communication transaction,
which is modeled in figure 3.1. **Noise,** or interference with the participants' ability
to achieve mutual understanding, can happen at any point in the communication
process. Noise is always present to some extent; that doesn't mean that communication has broken down, but that the limitations of human communicating always
make perfect understanding an impossibility.

To start the process, something occurs to a group member that he or she
wants to share. That member then encodes the thought, feeling, or idea by putting it
into words and gestures. This process, of course, happens without a lot of conscious
thought. You typically don't stop to think how to arrange your face into a scowl
when you are expressing your displeasure—you just *do* it. However, you probably
have had the experience of intending to say something, but the words came out
wrong, or the thought was not expressed as precisely as you would have liked. This
glitch in encoding is a type of noise, the first place where fully shared meaning is
compromised.

In small group communication, we assume the communicators are face
to face. After the speaker has encoded the thought and sent it (i.e., spoken the
words with accompanying nonverbal signals), another person must then receive
the communication. This may sound simple, but the receiving process, which we
call *listening,* is tricky, an additional source of noise. First, the receiver must *hear*
what the speaker has said. Listeners often mishear, or hear only part, of what a

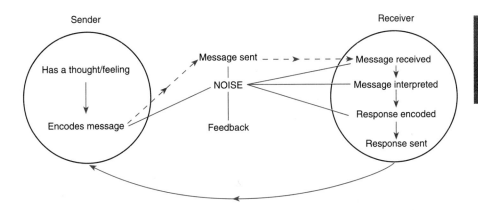

Figure 3.1
An interpersonal communication transaction.

speaker said. One of us attended a group meeting where a member said, "I don't have time to do that," but another member failed to hear the *don't,* and assumed the first member would handle a particular task. Fortunately, the problem was quickly straightened out by a third member, who suspected the misunderstanding and clarified it.

Once the receiver has physically heard the message sent, he or she must then *interpret* the message, another stage where noise interference often occurs. Major misunderstandings can occur during this step because of the very nature of communication—it is symbolic and personal. We may use the same words or gestures but mean very different things by them. For example, Darren comes to the first meeting of his group early. He greets everyone in a friendly way when they arrive, sits at the head of the rectangular table, and makes numerous suggestions. One member thinks, "Wow, I like his self-confidence. He'll really be an asset to the group." Another member thinks, "What an arrogant jerk. What makes him think he's in charge?" Same actions, different interpretations on the part of the receivers. Later, as the members get to know each other better, they will likely modify their interpretations. The second member may conclude, "Well, he comes on a little strong to begin with, but actually he's really friendly and hard working." Our experiences, including our past experiences with the particular individual who is the sender of the message, color our interpretation of the message. A vital determinant of how we interpret messages comes from the culture in which we were raised. Our culture gives us the rules for what is appropriate communication behavior. These various cultural rules are another important source of noise, or interference, in a small group. The effects of culture on the interpretation process are extremely significant and are covered in detail in chapter 5.

The final step in the communication transaction is **feedback,** the process by which the receiver responds to the listener. Feedback provides a number of important functions in the communication process. First, it helps reduce the harmful consequences of noise that interferes with mutual understanding. For instance, a member who isn't sure she heard a speaker correctly can say, "I didn't catch that, could you run it by again?" Or, a member who heard the speaker but isn't sure how to interpret the statement can say, "Does that mean that you can help me with that assignment, or not?"

In addition, giving feedback to members implies, "You are a valued member of this group." Lack of feedback is demoralizing; it disconfirms the speaker's existence. Confirming actions reinforce an individual's sense of self-worth, while disconfirming actions cheapen it.[5] In addition to ignoring a speaker, specific disconfirming behaviors include interrupting the speaker, making a response that is irrelevant to what preceded it, and responding tangentially by acknowledging minimally what the speaker said but taking the conversation in another direction. Confirming responses, on the other hand, include direct acknowledgement of the speaker and expressing positive feelings toward the speaker. Many of the groups Sieburg studied exhibited impervious and tangential remarks, but members of effective groups had fewer impervious, tangential, and ambiguous remarks and responded more to the content of remarks. Clearly, confirming feedback behaviors improve understanding while disconfirming behaviors lessen it. Chopra observed, for instance, that when group members did not respond to and reinforce one another, retaliation, withdrawal, and defensive behaviors increased.[6]

Feedback of the type we have been discussing helps complete the communication transaction. A **complete communication transaction** occurs only when a receiver verifies a sender's meaning during discussion. A receiver must respond to the initial message, and the sender must in turn acknowledge that response. Then both parties can judge whether they have communicated as desired. For example:

Sarah: What happened in the student center that everyone is talking about? (initiation)

John: A big fight broke out between members of two fraternities. (response)

Sarah: Oh, I see. (acknowledgment)

Each speaker addressing a small group needs this kind of overt, perceivable response—feedback—and in turn needs to acknowledge those responses. The speaker may find it necessary to revise or correct the original message if the responses indicate some lack of understanding. For instance, if puzzled looks follow a statement, the speaker (sensing confusion) may rephrase the remark. If members make no observable response, the speaker has three choices: give up, restate in a different way, or ask for an overt response.

In the groups to which you belong, notice whether there is a difference in how much members typically respond to each other. Are you, like most of us, more comfortable in groups where members react openly and clearly (even to disagree), or ones where reaction is minimal? Do you agree with Jablin, who found that subordinates would rather have a boss disagree openly than ignore, which is perceived as highly insulting?[7] We suggest you monitor your own response behavior and change it if you routinely fail to respond to speakers. Don't break the communication circuit. Many student journals have contained observations of disconfirming behavior: "Even though Jean didn't say much, I was able to tell where she stood. You could tell from her face and movements that she was involved. Ed was another story. It was hard to tell how he felt, and I never could trust him."

Communication transactions can involve from one to many communicators. **Intrapersonal communication,** often called *self-talk,* occurs within the mind of one person. For example, Deidre is angry at Kevin because he has let the group down by failing to complete assignments and attend meetings as expected.[8] She probably says to herself something like this: "I could kill him, he's such a jerk! I'd really like to tell him off, but he and Tony are friends, and if I say what I'm thinking, I might make Tony mad. Should I say something or not? How can I tell him I don't like his behavior without making the situation worse for everybody?" This process occurs in Deidre without any of the others being aware of it; nevertheless, it is a very real and meaningful transaction to Deidre, and is directly relevant to her behavior in the group.

Interpersonal communication involves a minimum of two people responding to each other's signals simultaneously. We emphasize again that it is not *meaning* that is transmitted; instead, a sender encodes the meaning into signals that are then decoded by a receiver. Such transactions are the building blocks of small group communication. For example, at the conclusion of the meeting Deidre chooses to act on her internal conversation by saying, "Kevin—we need a commitment from you. Man, you've missed the last two meetings out of four, and you were late for the other two that you *did* show up for, and you didn't do what you said you'd do for this meeting. We all feel pretty much let down by you. What's up?"[9] She has chosen to encode her anger, frustrations, and observations directly to Kevin. Her self-talk has now been encoded and has become interpersonal.*

The interpersonal communication that occurs in small groups is not just communication that occurs between two people, but more; it is more complicated than that. For instance, Deidre has chosen to address her remarks directly to Kevin, but all the other group members are hearing her and interpreting her remarks from their own unique perspectives. In a way, Deidre has initiated four conversations at once, and is receiving four sets of messages at once. When you think about it, the human capacity to keep track of all this is quite remarkable—yet we do this all the time in small groups!

Beyond the small group context are public and mass communication contexts. In both contexts, the focus shifts increasingly to the speaker rather than to the individual receivers, who generally are *not* perceived as unique individuals and are collectively called an *audience.* In addition, communication contexts with large numbers of listeners are usually less *immediate,* or first-hand and personal. *Public communication* involves a primary source (e.g., a public speaker) communicating to many others; it becomes *mass communication* when the messages are carried by some medium available to an indeterminately large number of people—television, radio, newspapers, magazines, books, films, and so forth. In mass communication, there is usually no face-to-face transacting.

We realize that courses in interpersonal communication involve many more components in the process of communication. We have touched only briefly on this process.

Listening and Responding during Discussions

The level of understanding among group members depends more on how they listen and respond than on how they speak. Earlier, we explained that communication involves encoding, sending, hearing, interpreting, and responding to messages. **Listening** comprises the steps of hearing and interpreting. *Hearing* is a physiological process that involves the reception of sound waves by the ear. It is only the first element of listening, which also includes the *interpretation* of those sound waves (and other signals) to determine what the sender meant. A person with acute hearing may be a poor listener who does not interpret others' statements accurately or respond appropriately. In contrast, someone with considerable (or even total) hearing loss may be a good listener who is motivated to understand others the way they want to be understood. Such group members attend closely to the interaction, ask others to speak up, and check the accuracy of their interpretations.

Roach and Wyatt suggest four important things to remember if you want to be a good listener.[10] First, good listeners pay attention to the context of what is said. Have you ever been quoted "out of context"? If so, you know that context can change the entire meaning of what is said. Suppose Mary says she's not sure the president of your organization will read your group's entire report right away because she's in the middle of performance reviews with all the committee heads. Saying "Mary said the president won't bother to read our report" seriously distorts what Mary said and ignores the context of the president being too busy *at the moment* to give the report full attention.

Second, good listeners pay attention to the feelings of the speaker. Remember the affective component of a message? When Tom says, "Yes, that idea is fine" in a resigned, flat tone of voice, he's probably expressing a negative feeling about the idea, without actually saying so. A good listener will verify that interpretation: "Tom, you said you like it but you don't sound too enthused. Would you share your concerns with us?"

Third, when the organizational pattern a speaker uses is confusing, good listeners help speakers make themselves clear by asking questions to clarify. For example, Shanda is a statistics whiz who completed all the computer analyses for your group's project. She knows her stats so well that she skips steps in explaining them to the rest of you, who are lost. You can help her communicate more clearly by asking her questions that encourage her to fill in the gaps.

Finally, it is important to interpret silence carefully. Silence can mean that people don't understand what was said, that they don't agree, that they are apathetic, or that they are hoarding information as a power play. Group leaders often mistake silence for agreement when it is something else. Again, a well-timed question will help interpret silence correctly.

Poor listening is easier to detect in a dyad than in a small group, where one person can "hide" for long periods of time. Because people can fake listening, only when someone speaks do other participants have a basis for judging that person's listening behavior. Making irrelevant comments and asking questions about something that has already been explained are evidence of poor listening.

Most of us think we are good listeners, but evidence suggests otherwise. At times, group members are not even aware of the current topic of discussion. Berg found, for instance, that topics were switched about one time per minute in discussions he observed. Members were hardly listening or responding to what previous speakers had said.[11] This finding was confirmed by other investigators in a variety of cultures and situations.[12] We've both been frustrated, repeatedly, by this phenomenon. Nichols and Stevens reported that students listening to lectures on which they knew they would be tested retained only about half of the new information presented.[13] We have found that when members of small groups (whether college students or corporate personnel in training groups) are required to paraphrase what a previous discussant said to that person's satisfaction, they can do so only about half the time. This is true even when participants know that they will be assessed for accuracy in listening. How much, then, must group members misunderstand when they are *not* on guard?

The cost of poor listening is high. In the work scene, many jobs are done incorrectly, shipments go awry, time and material are wasted, and people are hurt or killed because they did not understand what was intended. In groups, much time is lost repeating ideas for people who were listening poorly or not at all.

Our listening is impaired when we are tired, preoccupied, or overloaded with information and noise. But even when we are not bothered by such concerns, we still may listen poorly as a result of bad habits we are not aware of. We either do not pay attention carefully to the speaker, or we pay too close attention—to the wrong things! The following are behaviors that interfere with good listening:

Pitfalls to Listening Effectively

1. **Pseudolistening.**
   Pseudolistening refers to faking the real thing. Pseudolisteners nod, smile, murmur polite responses, look the speaker in the eye, and may even give verbal support like "right" or "good idea." But behind the mask, the pseudolistener has "zoned off" on a daydream, a personal problem, sizing up the speaker, or mentally preparing a response. When such behavior is challenged, most pseudolisteners blame the speaker ("That stuff he was saying was boring") when they really hadn't given the speaker a chance.

2. **Sidetracking.**
   Related to pseudolistening is **sidetracking,** where you allow something another member said to send you off into your own private reverie. Meanwhile, you have missed several points in the discussion when you finally return.

3. **Focusing on irrelevancies and distractions.**
   Sometimes distractions such as background noises, furnishings, and the temperature make it difficult for us to concentrate on the speaker. At other times, undue attention to speaker characteristics such as dialect, appearance, or personal mannerisms interfere, causing us to miss important points. As one woman from Georgia said to her group: "Damn it, listen to what I have to say, not to how I speak. It makes me really mad when someone says, 'Oh, how you talk is so cute I just can't pay attention to what you are saying.' "

4. **Silent arguing.**
   Many people listen selectively for information that confirms views they already hold. When they hear information that contradicts their chosen positions, silent arguers carry on an intrapersonal argument that opposes what they think the speaker has said.

You cannot listen both to yourself and a fellow group member. You cannot mentally rehearse a reply at the same time you are striving to understand another. If you listen primarily to find flaws and argue them in your mind, you are unlikely to understand the speaker, the context of the remarks, and the meaning the speaker intends. We are not saying, "Don't argue." We are suggesting that you make sure you understand others first, well enough to be able to paraphrase their remarks *to their satisfaction,* before you argue.

5. **Premature replying.**
Similar to silent arguing, premature replying need not involve disagreement. Most commonly, a person prepares mentally to make a remark before fully understanding the speaker's comment or question. It is also common for group members who know each other well to think they know what others are going to say before they say it—but they aren't always right! Jumping to a conclusion before the other has finished speaking results in a disjointed discussion where the subject keeps switching.

6. **Listening defensively.**
When we feel psychologically threatened, we don't listen well. Feeling vulnerable, we generally quit listening in order to invent ways to defend ourselves and attack the perceived threat. This is called **defensive listening.** For example, later in the meeting of the student group we discussed earlier, Lori verbally attacks Kevin several times. Kevin defends himself by attacking Lori back: "What's your problem? You've been riding my case all day!" Unfortunately, this usually doesn't help solve the group's problem. It is often the very time when we most need to understand the perceptions and values of the other person. Still later, after Deidre politely but directly confronts Kevin's behavior, his honest, nondefensive response to her indicates that he is not feeling attacked.

The flip side to defensive listening is aggressive speaking, which attacks others' self-concepts. It is especially important to watch for emotive or trigger words that may offend others. Keep in mind that what sounds like an innocent remark to you may trigger an emotional response in someone else because people have their own individual "hot buttons." Be sensitive to how others might hear your words. You may not be able to avoid offending someone inadvertently, but you certainly can, and should, avoid offending someone deliberately.

7. **Mind raping.**
This term was coined by psychiatrist George Bach to refer to a listener insisting that what the speaker meant by a particular statement is what the listener *says* the speaker meant: "I heard what you said, and I know exactly what you mean by that!"[14] Underlying such obnoxious behavior is the faulty assumption that words have only one meaning—the one the mind raper holds. Mind rapers are unwilling to admit the symbolic and personal nature of communication transactions. They tend to be rigid, dogmatic people.

You may have noticed that evaluation or judgment is part of all these nonlistening behaviors. Poor listeners are so busy judging the speaker and the speaker's ideas that they do not take the time to respond empathically and supportively. The sequence is entirely reversed from what it should be. Only *after* we understand each other's ideas are we able to judge appropriately. As Kelley put it, we need to be empathic listeners who try to understand what the other means *from his or her point of view,* with the motivation to receive information being greater than the motive to evaluate and criticize.[15]

We assume now that you *want* to improve your listening behavior in groups. With your attitude in the right frame of mind, we present tested techniques to help you take responsibility for your listening habits.

Small group members must work at understanding each other while they keep the group discussion structured and organized. Two types of listening are especially helpful for accomplishing this: active and focused.

Effective Listening in the Small Group

Effective listening is an *active* process requiring as much effort as speaking. The person trying hard to understand and recall shows signs of physical activity, including an accelerated heartbeat and postural shifts. In contrast, heart rates of poor listeners frequently slow to the level of sleep! Listening takes an act of will, a decision to listen.

Active Listening

A good test of how well you have been listening is a technique called **active listening.** This technique virtually forces the listener to understand a speaker before replying or adding to a discussion. The main rule is that you must state *in your own words,* or **paraphrase,** what you understood the previous speaker to mean, then ask for a confirmation or correction of your paraphrase. Active listeners paraphrase, not repeat word for word. After all, a parrot can repeat, but that doesn't mean that the parrot has understood! A paraphrase in the listener's own words forces the listener to process the information cognitively, allowing the speaker to determine whether the message was understood as intended or not. The original speaker can then reply to the paraphrase (i.e., give feedback) by accepting it or revising and asking the listener to try again. Only when the original speaker is fully satisfied that the listener has understood what was intended does an active listener proceed with agreement, disagreement, elaboration, change of topic, or whatever. The following dialogue illustrates the technique:

Ed: Requiring landowners to farm in such a way that topsoil is not lost is absolutely necessary if we really want to protect the earth for our children. (opinion)

Gail: If I understand you, you think we should require that farming practices prevent possible erosion of the topsoil because erosion destroys the earth for living things? (paraphrase of Ed's opinion)

Ed: Right, Gail. (confirmation and acceptance of the paraphrase; also a complete communication transaction)

Another example:

Consuelo: If every college graduate were required to demonstrate some competence in using a computer, that might help right at graduation. But computers are changing so rapidly that grads would be no better off in a few years than if they had no such training, unless they kept up to date or had to use a computer all along. (opinion)

Taylor: Do I understand you right? Are you saying that a computer science course should *not* be required to get a degree? (attempted paraphrase of Consuelo's opinion)

Consuelo: No, just that it should be more than just how to use a computer. You ought to understand computers, and what they do and don't do. (rejects the paraphrase and attempts to clarify)

Taylor: So you think there should be a requirement for a graduate to be able to explain what computers can and can't do, as well as be comfortable with a computer. (second attempt at paraphrasing Consuelo's opinion)

Consuelo: Yes, more than a course as such. (confirms Taylor's paraphrase)

Taylor: I agree with that idea, and think we should also have a requirement for ability to investigate, organize, and write a term paper. (His paraphrase confirmed, Taylor is now free to add his opinion, on a new topic, to the discussion.)

Every idea proposed in a discussion should be evaluated, but only when you are sure you understand it to the satisfaction of the speaker. Active listeners confirm their understanding *before* they express their positive or negative evaluation. Only at that point is critical listening in order, where the listener may comment on whether the statement is relevant, defensible, likely to be effective, carefully thought through, and so forth.

Sometimes active listeners cannot hear adequately or are not confident of their understandings. If so, they will say so quickly, asking the speaker to repeat or clarify. Only then will they disagree, add more information, or express whatever is their honest reaction.

Active listening slows the pace of interaction. If you are not used to listening actively, you may at first find yourself with nothing to say for a moment after the other finishes speaking. Keep practicing; soon you will find yourself making spontaneous responses instead of preplanned or irrelevant remarks. Note the comparability between the communicative model represented in figure 3.1 and the concept of active listening. Only overt feedback can provide the speaker with the responses needed, and confirming feedback response is the best response of all. Positive feedback indicating that a message has been received doesn't have to be a big deal; *uh-huh, gotcha, yeah,* or nonverbal responses such as a head nod, frown, or smile will work. More expansive nonverbal cues usually indicate agreement, so loosen up when you listen and allow yourself to be spontaneous. Above all, don't pseudolisten, which often damages trust and cooperation more than argumentative listening.

Becoming an active listener in a small group takes practice, but the supportive climate you help create when you listen actively increases cohesiveness and cooperation in your group. You also will learn when this technique is needed, and when it will unnecessarily slow the group's progress.

Group members often have problems recalling what was discussed. During the excitement of exploring a new idea, it is easy to forget vital information, even though that is the responsibility of each member. **Focused listening** helps members recall important information, ideas, and issues discussed during a meeting.

Focused Listening

Human memory is limited. We have a terrible time memorizing unrelated lists of items, but we can more easily recall information grouped into sets of related items. Try to remember the following list of numbers: 4178365218. Now try again: (417) 836–5218. Grouping a string of digits into area code, exchange, and number helps you remember it better. This is the key to focused listening.

Group members can maintain their perspective on the discussion as a whole by focusing their listening on the *main points* of the discussion. They organize the details—specific facts and opinions—by issue. Ironically, focusing on the main points helps them remember details better. If you want to be a productive group member, keep a notepad to record important information, listen for and record the main issues by using key words rather than complete sentences, and keep track of essential facts by issue. This type of focused listening helps you keep on track so you can reorient the group when someone switches topics before closure has been reached. Focused listeners can serve as process observers who readily keep track of the discussion. They often provide an internal summary, or brief review of what has transpired up to that point in the discussion, thus keeping the discussion orderly and easy for other members to follow. The group benefits greatly from focused listeners, who help keep it on target.

Summary

Human communication is a complex transactional process that involves the generation, transmission, receipt, and interpretation of signals that may be verbal or nonverbal in nature. In small group communication, the purpose of this activity is to share meaning so that group members can coordinate their efforts to complete the task of the group. Human communication is necessarily an inexact process because it is a complex symbolic, personal, transactional, and often unintentional process. Messages include content, relationship, and affective levels. Several myths help perpetuate misunderstandings about what communication is. During a communication transaction, a sender encodes a message by putting it into words and nonverbal signals; a receiver then decodes the message by hearing it, interpreting it, and responding to it. Noise, or interference with understanding meaning, can occur at any juncture during this process. Understanding is facilitated, however, through feedback. A complete communication transaction includes feedback as an important step to help the speaker determine whether the message sent was received accurately, or whether the speaker should try again.

Communication transactions can involve from one to many people, with varying degrees of immediacy. Transactions can occur intrapersonally, interpersonally, or in small group, public, or mass communication contexts. As the listeners increase in number, the focus shifts increasingly to the skills of the speaker. Listening is itself a complex process that involves both hearing and interpretation. Many factors, including one's culture, can affect the interpretation process. Several specific pitfalls to listening include focusing on irrelevancies, pseudolistening, sidetracking, silent arguing, premature replying, defensive listening, and mind raping. Mutual understanding is helped by active listening, during which a listener paraphrases what the speaker has said in order to try to understand the speaker as he or she wants to be understood. Focusing on main issues and decisions helps members keep discussions structured and organized.

Exercises

1. Discuss in small groups, then share your ideas with the class as a whole: "How and where in the small group system can noise interfere with the process of communication?"

2. Select a topic (preferably a controversial one), and then discuss it in small groups while you practice active listening. A discussant may not have the floor or add anything new to the conversation until he or she has paraphrased what the previous speaker meant (*both* ideas and feelings) to the speaker's complete satisfaction. If the paraphrase is not accepted, the discussant may try again until the speaker accepts the paraphrase. One member of the group should not participate but should keep count of how many times paraphrases are accepted or rejected. Be sure to count *every* attempt to rephrase. Afterward, discuss the implications of active listening, how to improve communication, and how you felt during this discussion.

3. Think of the most recent time you felt that someone listened to you and understood you. Try to recall exactly what was said and done. *How* did you know you were understood? What are the implications for a small group?

4. Prepare a chart for recording observations of listening behaviors and responses of members of a discussion group. This chart should have four columns headed as follows: *active listening, premature replying, sidetracking,* and *mind raping.* With several classmates, observe either a live or recorded discussion. As you observe, note each instance of these behaviors.

   Now compare your observations with those of your fellow observers. What do you conclude about the listening-responding behavior of discussants? What was the effect of the members' listening behaviors on the group outcomes?

Bibliography

Mader, Thomas F., and Diane C. Mader. *Understanding One Another: Communicating Interpersonally.* Dubuque, IA: Wm. C. Brown, 1990.

Roach, Carol A., and Nancy J. Wyatt, "Successful Listening," in *Small Group Communication: A*

Reader, 6th ed., eds. Robert S. Cathcart and Larry A. Samovar. Dubuque, IA: Wm. C. Brown Publishers, 1992, 301–25.

Stewart, John. *Bridges Not Walls.* New York: McGraw-Hill, 1990.

Notes

1. Tom D. Daniels and Barry K. Spiker, *Perspectives on Organizational Communication,* 2d ed. (Dubuque, IA: Wm. C. Brown Publishers, 1991): 29–46.

2. Dominic A. Infante, Andrew S. Rancer, and Deanna F. Womack, *Building Communication Theory* (Prospect Heights, IL: Waveland Press, 1990): 8–10.

3. Glen H. Stamp and Mark L. Knapp, "The Construct of Intent in Interpersonal Communication," *Quarterly Journal of Speech* 76 (1990): 282–99.

4. This excerpt comes from the videotape *Communicating Effectively in Small Groups,* part of the ancillary package for this text. The excerpt comes from the second segment of the video, *Conflict.*

5. Evelyn R. Sieburg, "Dysfunctional Communication and Interpersonal Responsiveness in Small Groups" (Unpublished doctoral dissertation, University of Denver, 1969).

6. Amarjit Chopra, "Motivation in Task-Oriented Groups," *Journal of Nursing Administration* (1973): 55–60.

7. Fred Jablin, "Message-Response and 'Openness' in Superior-Subordinate Communication," *Communication Yearbook ii,* ed. Brent Ruben (New Brunswick, NJ: Transaction-International Communication Association, 1978): 293–309.

8. From ancillary videotape *Communicating Effectively in Small Groups,* segment 2, *Conflict.*

9. From ancillary videotape, *Communicating Effectively in Small Groups,* segment 2, *Conflict.*

10. Carol A. Roach and Nancy J. Wyatt, "Successful Listening," in *Small Group Communication: A Reader,* 6th ed., eds. Robert S. Cathcart and Larry A. Samovar (Dubuque, IA: Wm. C. Brown Publishers, 1992): 301–25.

11. David M. Berg, "A Descriptive Analysis of the Distribution and Duration of Themes Discussed by Task-Oriented Small Groups," *Speech Monographs* 34 (1967): 172–75.

12. Ernest G. and Nancy C. Bormann, *Effective Small Group Communication,* 4th ed. (Minneapolis: Burgess, 1988): 120.

13. Ralph G. Nichols and Leonard Stevens, "Listening to People," *Harvard Business Review* 35 (1957): 85–92.

14. George Bach and Peter Wyden, *The Intimate Enemy* (New York: Avon Press, 1968).

15. Charles M. Kelley, "Empathic Listening," in *Small Group Communication: A Reader,* 4th ed., eds. Robert S. Cathcart and Larry A. Samovar (Dubuque, IA: Wm. C. Brown Publishers, 1984): 296–303.

Verbal and Nonverbal Signals in Small Group Communication

Central Message

Since verbal and nonverbal signals create and maintain groups, members who want to be effective send and interpret verbal signals in harmony with nonverbal signals and realize that all their actions are potential messages to other members.

Study Objectives   As a result of studying chapter 4 you should be able to:

1. Describe the structuration process whereby members' verbal and nonverbal signals create and maintain the group.

2. Describe the nature and function of each of the three major components of language.

3. Describe the nature of bypassing, abstract language, and emotive words, including their disruptive effects on discussions and how to prevent or correct such disruptions.

4. Express your ideas during a discussion so that your statements are organized, clear, and relevant to the preceding remarks.

5. Explain three major principles of nonverbal communication.

6. Explain six major communicative functions performed by nonverbal signals.

7. Name and give examples of eight types of nonverbal signals, and explain how each contributes to communication among small group members.

Key Terms

Ambiguity	High-level abstractions	Regulators
Bypass	Kinesics	Sociofugal
Cliches	Nonverbal signals	Sociopetal
Code	Paralanguage	Structuration
Concrete	Proxemics	Syntactic rules
Emotive words	Referent	

Group communication begins before any member says a word. We begin to form opinions about each other on the basis of what we see. One member slinks into the room without looking at anyone and takes a seat in a corner: "Better not count on much from that one," you think. The next person, dressed in a dark business suit, strides confidently to the head of the table and deposits a briefcase: "Arrogant, will try to boss us around," you think. Members' clothing, looks, manners, where they sit, how much space they claim—all these and other nonverbal signals affect how relationships among members develop.

In a small group, the primary medium for exchange of information and ideas are the words members use. Although *discussion* is the heart of group interaction, the verbal and nonverbal signals operate together to create meaning; in practice they operate indivisibly. Although it is artificial to separate verbal from nonverbal signals, we do so here to help you assess the contribution each makes to *meaning* during discussions. At different times and for various reasons we may attend more to the words, or more to the nonverbal signals, but almost no human communicating is entirely verbal or nonverbal.

A group does not exist apart from its verbal and nonverbal communication. In this chapter, we first discuss how communication creates and maintains the group. We then present an overview of the nature of language, some things that often go wrong when we speak to each other, and how informed word choices and arrangements can facilitate group process. The latter part of the chapter summarizes research and theory about the characteristics of nonverbal communication, including the types and functions of nonverbal signals affecting small group communication.

Communication and the Structuring of Small Groups

We noted earlier that a small group is created and maintained by communication among the members. This concept is known as **structuration,** which refers to *how* individuals form a small group by exchanging verbal and nonverbal signals that establish the norms and rules shaping members' behaviors. The theory of structuration, developed by Poole, Siebold, and McPhee, embraces three important assumptions.[1] First, the behavior of group members is constrained by such things as the general rules of the society in which they live, the structures of the particular group in which they find themselves, and the behavior of the other members. For example, the rules of corporate America frown on executives settling their differences with a fist fight. Members of a group that has developed a formal, polite atmosphere would be embarrassed by a member who slaps another on the back and says, "Hey, babe, how's your sex life?" The other members would probably ignore the offending member, and if the behavior continued, might try to remove that person from the group. The second important assumption is that people have free will— they can choose to follow the rules of the group or not. Although there may be unpleasant consequences for a member who doesn't follow a group's rules, there is no *law* that says he or she *must* conform, like the law of gravity that says objects dropped from a high place must fall to the ground. The third important assumption is that group creation is a process; the group not only creates itself initially but continuously *re-creates* itself, changing in incremental ways, always in a state of *becoming,* with communication as the instrument for this creation and re-creation.

The theory of structuration is quite complex. However, the main point is this: the *communication among members* is what creates group rules in the first place, and once rules and structures are in place, communication is what keeps them there, or changes them, as the case may be. Let's examine how this process might occur. Suppose a company appoints a group of several managers to develop long-range strategy. Two members, Anita and Bob, have worked together before and naturally call each other by first names. Anita introduces Bob to Carol, an acquaintance of hers, by his first name, and pretty soon the rest of the group members are calling each other by first name instead of Mr., Ms., or Dr. As they wait for the meeting to begin, members talk about mutual interests such as sports and jazz music, and several find common outside interests with other members. Norms of informality and friendliness have begun to develop among these members, and these norms will begin to affect other aspects of the communication among members, such as how they deal with disagreement. For instance, assume that at a later group meeting, Bob says, in a formal and accusing tone of voice, "I respectfully disagree with the proposal offered by my esteemed colleague Ms. Hernandez," and continues to make a formal speech relating his objections. The rest of the members will probably say something like: "When did we get so formal, Bob? What's the big deal here? Why are you sounding like a prosecutor?" What they are saying, in another way, is: "We've developed norms of informality and friendliness, which you are violating. Your behavior seems inappropriate to us." Of course, Bob has free choice about his behavior. He can choose to continue in his formal, prosecutorial way, but if he *does,* that may either change the informality and friendliness norms to something more formal and adversarial, or it may cause the other members to ignore Bob and ostracize him from the group.

Notice, through this example, that it was communication through verbal and nonverbal signals that established the norms initially and, once established, served to maintain them. The members' friendly talk at the initial meeting set the stage for expectations of informal and friendly behavior later. Bob's words ("my esteemed colleague Ms. Hernandez") and his harsh tone of voice violated the norm, and members called this violation to Bob's attention with words ("Why are you sounding like a prosecutor?") and perhaps nonverbal actions such as not looking Bob in the eye or glaring at him out of anger.

A variety of internal and external factors influences the types of structures groups create, including member characteristics and preferences, the nature of the group's task, and such structural dynamics as the interplay between important (but perhaps conflicting) values. For instance, one group that Poole observed valued democratic principles, but the pressure to get the job done led members to encourage controlling leadership.[2] This contradiction caused tension within the group and an eventual split.

We agree with Poole that structuration offers advantages over other social scientific theories. Structuration captures the complexity of human behavior by recognizing that, although human beings are free agents, certain limitations and constraints keep their behaviors in small group systems within certain boundaries. We especially like the communicative focus of structuration theory, for it reminds us to look at the *communicative behavior* of members to learn about a group. We now turn to a discussion of language and its role in the small group process.

Symbolically, he is a *chien, hund, cane, perro, hunt,* and *dog;* or Butch to his best human pal.

The Nature of Language

Any language—Spanish, Vietnamese, English—consists of a code of symbols, rules about how and when to use words, and some assumptions about the nature of the world. Each of these components affects the quality of a discussion.

The **code,** a set of signals used in language, is the basic building material of language. In spoken language the codes are the sounds (phonemes, such as "ay" or "sss") and words, along with the patterns in which they are spoken. In the written version of the spoken language, we have the alphabet code and the code of all written words (vocabulary) in the language. Each community of users of a language (i.e., subculture) develops its own unique subcode. Cultures, subcultures, corporations, families, clubs, and other groups often have their own special codes, and membership in a continuing group is contingent upon using its special language. For example, theatre students call the *waiting room* the *green room.* One of us had some young women in a speech class who referred to all men they didn't like as *Ernies.* This special use of that name came about because they once encountered at a party a particularly obnoxious man named Ernie.

In addition to the codes themselves, languages have both formal and informal rules governing the use of these codes, many of which vary depending on the situation. We all have learned to adapt our codes for a variety of situations. For instance, none of us would write a love letter in the same style we'd use for a job application. We use a different code when we meet someone in a church or synagogue from the one we use during a tailgate party at a football stadium. Physicians use a different code to explain a medical procedure to a patient from the one they use to discuss the procedure among themselves. We must use the code shared by group members if we want to be understood. If we don't use the code appropriate to the context and group, others may be annoyed and distracted from the purpose of the discussion.

The formal rules governing language use include syntactic and grammatical rules. **Syntactic rules** govern the arrangement of code units. In English, we do not say "The lights out I put," but that word arrangement does conform to the rules of Latin. We have extensive rules governing where to place verbs in sentences, uses of connectives, placement of modifiers, and so on. Violations of these rules impair the speaker's credibility and status.

Every language reflects in its code and structure some assumptions about the nature of the world and human perception that are shared by most users of the language. For example, in English we routinely say things such as "The American Civil War began in 1861." However, in some Native American languages, we would be required to use a verb form that told the reader we were not actually there: "The American Civil War is said to have started in 1861, although I was not there to see it and I am merely relating something I have been told." While this is cumbersome to English speakers, in some Native American languages verb forms can distinguish among whether you are relating something you actually saw, whether you heard about it from someone who actually saw it, whether you heard about it from someone who read about it, whether you read about it yourself, and so forth. In other words, these languages are quite particular about what constitutes evidence and truth.

Of all the characteristics of language, the most important to keep in mind is that *all language is symbolic.* As we said in chapter 3, words have no inherent meanings but are used in conventional ways by a community of users to represent specific things and classes of experience. As symbols, *words have no meaning or reality apart from the person using them and responding to them.* Different languages use different words to refer to the same objects, further demonstrating that the meanings are not in the words themselves, but in the users. For example, the object or experience to which a symbol refers is called the **referent.** The referent Americans call a *dog* is symbolized in other languages by the words *chien, hund, cane, perro,* and *hunt.* Same referent, different symbols. The main point is this: human communication is symbolic, and only if speakers and listeners have approximately the same referent for a word will they have perceptual similarity. *This cannot be taken for granted!*

Speakers in a discussion must use the same or similar codes in order to be understood. However, even if discussants speak the same language, they may use the same word to refer to different things. Consider a word less concrete than *dog,* such

Figure 4.1
One statement,
different referents.

as *food*. As illustrated in figure 4.1, when Joe says "Let's go get some food," his referent is a cupcake and soft drink from the nearest vending machine. Mary envisions alfalfa sprouts on whole wheat bread, and Herbie pictures a five-course meal at a fine restaurant. Obviously, Joe's words have different meanings to these three people. If this were a group recommending a break for lunch, clarification would be necessary!

Clearly, we communicate effectively with symbols only when we have similar referents for them. Imagine that the designated leader of your group asks you to keep a "detailed" list of what the group discussed. The leader means "word for word account of the entire discussion," and you assume that "a broad description of major decisions" will suffice. Your group will have problems, even though neither of you was wrong! Each of you used the same symbol (*detailed*) to refer to something different, which emphasizes the personal nature of communication—meanings are in people, not in words.

You have seen how easy it is even for people who speak the same language to misunderstand each other, and you already know that an important ethical principle for group members is to make a sincere effort to comprehend one another. Fortunately, your understanding that symbols (including all words) have no absolute or certain referents can help you prevent a variety of misunderstandings and problems common in discussions. Three of the most troublesome problems include bypassing, using ambiguous or unnecessarily abstract language, and using emotive words.

Two discussants **bypass** each other when they have different referents for the same word or phrase but think they have the same meanings, or when they think they disagree but really do not, because they use different words to indicate the same referent. Each hears the same words, but interprets them differently; they end up talking past each other, as in the *food* and *detailed* examples provided earlier. For example, one of us observed a group arguing about whether *feminism* was good or bad. One young woman, believing *feminism* meant that men and women should have the same rights, particularly in the workplace, could not understand how another group member could be opposed to it. On the other hand, the man who disagreed with her believed *feminism* meant that women should be preferred over men and should receive higher salaries than men because of past discrimination and underpayment. This group wrangled for fifteen minutes before someone, listening carefully, said, "I think you two actually agree" and asked each to explain what *feminism* meant. When they realized they had been using the word to refer to different phenomena, they were then free to discover that they actually *agreed* with each other that men and women performing the same work should receive the same pay. In another example, a boss asked a new secretary to "burn this memo." Although she thought his request was strange, she set fire to the memo. Later, when the boss asked for the copy, she realized that, in this company, *burn it* means *make a photocopy of it.* We have both watched members of many groups chatter on as if they understood each other when any careful observer could tell that members had very different meanings for some key term. Unfortunately, by the time the misunderstanding is discovered, serious problems have occurred.

Bypassing results from two myths about language: that words have meanings (*right* meanings) in and of themselves and that a message coded in words can have only one meaning. Even though we know these aren't true, *we often act as if they were true.* We sometimes behave as if we thought anyone who doesn't understand what we mean when we utter words is somehow foolish, stubborn, or wrongheaded. In the earlier example of *detailed,* if both you and the designated leader act as if the other's use of the word *detailed* is wrong, then feelings will be hurt, as will the group's productivity. Instead, remember that it is normal for people to use words differently and that effective communication occurs only if discussants use the same code and definitions; they must be in agreement on the referents for their words at any given time. Just as in poker we agree on the value of the various chip colors, in small group communication we must have a shared understanding of the referents for the words we use. Whenever a symbol is used that could be misunderstood, we are smart to ask for clarification: "What do you mean by *detailed? How much detail do you want me to go into?"* Taking a bit of extra time initially saves time in the long run.

Problems
Resulting from
Language Choices

Bypassing

Lack of Clarity

Two factors contribute to lack of clarity in discussions, abstractness and ambiguity. In discussions of ideas, many statements are necessarily **high-level abstractions,** lacking specific referents. Think of such terms as *justice, fairness, democratic, high quality, civil rights,* and so on. As we move away from terms referring to specific and unique items, the degree of abstractness and ambiguity increases, as does the potential for misunderstanding. Consider the following set of terms, each of which is higher in level of abstraction and thus more vague than the ones preceding it:

> The 1993–94 Curriculum Committee of the Department of Communication
> Departmental committees
> Committees
> Problem-solving groups
> Small groups
> Groups
> Living systems

When the first term is used between members of the Department of Communication, the picture in the listener's mind is almost certain to be similar to the picture in the speaker's mind. However, when we talk of *departmental committees* or just *committees,* any one of many committees could come to mind. Only terms that name unique objects are likely to be clear. For example, one member of a group discussing classroom procedures and policies said, "Lecturing is a poor method of teaching." Another responded, "Oh, no it isn't." An argument ensued until a third member asked for **concrete** examples (lower-level abstractions). The speakers were then able to agree on specific instances of effective and ineffective lecturing, and particular contexts in which lecturing was both a good and a poor choice of teaching strategy. The vagueness reduced, the group agreed on a less abstract statement: "Lecturing, if well organized, filled with concrete examples, and done by a skilled speaker, can be an effective means of presenting factual information and theoretical concepts. It is usually less effective than discussion for changing attitudes or developing critical thinking skills."

Leathers found that highly abstract statements consistently disrupted subsequent discussion, with the degree of disruption increasing as the statements became more abstract. His groups contained "plant" discussants who were trained to say abstract statements like, "Don't you think this is a matter of historical dialecticism?" After such a statement, most of the other discussants became confused and tense; some withdrew from further participation.[3]

Several factors can cause **ambiguity,** which results from phrases that could reasonably be interpreted in more than one way. For example, one of our colleagues once wrote in a letter of recommendation: "You will indeed be fortunate if you can get him to work for you." The writer meant that the person being "recommended" was a lazy employee and "you'll be lucky if you can get him to do any work." However, the recipient of the letter likely took it to mean that the future employer of this job candidate would be fortunate indeed to have such a promising employee.

Ambiguity can also result from a mixed message, one in which the words seem to imply one meaning but the vocal cues indicate something different. For example, the group leader might say, "Take as long as you like to consider this item," while at the same time looking at the clock and stuffing things into a brief-case. Such ambiguous messages are difficult to interpret and disrupt effective communication in the group.

These two forms of ambiguity and abstractness can be prevented or at least mitigated if other group members ask for clarification. When you realize that a speaker's words could be interpreted in a number of ways, ask for specific examples or illustrations. Use active listening. Paraphrase and ask the speaker to confirm or correct your understanding: "Tom, you said we could take as long as we liked, but you seem rushed. Would you prefer we table this discussion to a later meeting?" When you are the speaker, use terms you think the others will understand, and give plenty of examples for abstract concepts: "I think we can produce an excellent paper, one that covers the topic thoroughly, with up-to-date evidence, no grammatical or typographical mistakes, and professionally bound." Whenever possible, use specific descriptions rather than comparative terms: "six feet, four inches" instead of "tall."

Lack of clarity also results when opinions are uttered in sentence fragments or in an evasive manner. It is quite common for spontaneous participants to utter sentence fragments; they mention a subject, but never finish making a point about it, at least not in words. Sometimes, a nonverbal signal—a shrug, a face, a gesture—completes the sentence, but anyone not watching will miss the point, and those watching may misunderstand. Fragments like the following can confuse listeners:

Uh, I'm thinking that we might—well, what is going on here anyway?

Maybe we should divide . . . there seem to be a lot of issues . . . a lot of confusing bits and pieces . . . will make a lousy solution.

You know what members of that sorority are like (followed by a roll of the eyes and a smirk).

All these statements could have easily been uttered directly and clearly, leaving little doubt in listeners' minds about what was intended:

I think we might improve our understanding of what made it possible for the mechanic to steal so many auto parts if we ask the head of the motor pool how inventories are kept and revised.

Maybe we should divide our investigation of how student-athletes are treated academically by dividing the issue into component topics, such as recruitment, advising during orientation, advising after enrollment, and monitoring compliance with NCAA rules. Otherwise, we may get all these mixed up, overlook some problems, and produce an incomplete or shoddy report.

I think members of Lumba Dumba Sorority are vain and snobbish. They rarely speak to the women in Gamma Raya Sorority, who may not come from such wealthy homes, but seem friendlier to me and have the highest grade point average on campus.

Lack of clarity also results when members express opinions as loaded or rhetorical questions. Although the *form* of the utterance is a question, the *function* is to express a judgment. For instance, "You don't plan to support Clara's proposal, do you?" strongly suggests that the speaker would prefer the hearer *not* support Clara's plan. The classic example of this type of question is "When did you stop beating your wife?" This leaves the responder in a double bind where any plausible reply can be attacked. Even the innocuous "Isn't this a nice day?" is an indirect way of saying "I think it's a nice day." Rhetorical questions are not questions in intent; they are leading questions that suggest a particular answer, such as, "Wouldn't it be a good idea to brainstorm this issue?" or, "Don't you think prostitution should be legalized?" If you feel backed into a corner with a question, you may have been the target of a loaded or rhetorical question. When you hear such a question, you can eliminate confusion by encouraging the speaker to take responsibility and state his or her opinion directly: "You seem to think that we should brainstorm. I agree," or, "You seem to favor legalizing prostitution. What are your reasons?"

People use vague language for several reasons. Occasionally, a group member will try to enhance personal status by using technical jargon the others don't use. Sometimes, this is done to conceal ignorance of the issue. At other times, the speaker may be trying to cover up or evade answering the question directly, such as a politician saying: "Revenue enhancement is very important, and we will have to explore every available avenue for overcoming the economic paralysis caused by the deficit. No one likes new taxes, and I can promise you we'll investigate all options." (We think that means taxes are going up!) When you encounter this, don't be snowed by a show of technical expertise or jargon. Ask the speaker to explain in terms you know and insist that all group members understand.

Sometimes cliches are used to stop objective evaluation of an issue. All cliches are highly abstract because they can be made to fit a number of situations—or none at all. Although they may be true in a general way, they obscure the dimensions of a specific situation because each situation is unique, not general. For instance, a speaker trying to stop a proposal to spend money for a cost accounting program to control waste and inefficiency might say, "Let's not throw more money at the problem. After all, a penny saved is a penny earned." This brands the people who support the cost accounting program as spendthrifts, but they may counter with, "A stitch in time saves nine." Neither cliche is helpful because neither addresses the *specific* merits, or lack of them, of the particular proposal under review. Here are a few more "idea killers":

No one does it that way anymore.

He won't change. You can't teach an old dog new tricks.

A watched pot never boils.

It can't be done. There's no way to get there from here.

That's the tail wagging the dog. We're too small for that idea.

What can you do when someone uses the trite high-level abstractions we call **cliches?** First, be on guard for easy answers like this. When you spot one, point it out and suggest that group members examine the specifics of the situation to determine where the cliche fits, and where it does not. Sometimes you can counter the negative impact by giving a contradictory cliche: "You can't teach an old dog new tricks" can be offset with, "But you're never too old to learn. Now, let's really evaluate. . . ."

Group members can and should try to prevent the confusion produced by lack of clarity. Remember that an important ethical principle for group members is to strive for mutual understanding; this means members have an obligation both to be clear and to help others make themselves clear. This means that as a speaker, you should use the appropriate code for the particular group situation, use specific examples for the necessary high-level abstractions you use, make your actions and words congruent, persuade the group to conduct an honest evaluation of questions facing the group rather than relying on the easy answers cliches provide, and encourage others to give you feedback to determine whether you have been understood as intended. As a listener, when you perceive lack of clarity from any of the sources we have just discussed, ask the speaker to clarify. Paraphrase what you think the speaker said to make sure you have understood, and work *transactionally* with the speaker to create mutually understood meaning.

Emotive words are words that evoke strong feelings in others; these connotative words have been associated with highly pleasant or unpleasant images and experiences in our culture. The denotative impact on listeners is minimal compared to their blockbuster connotative impact. These are the *fighting* or *trigger* words that produce strong reactions—unthinking, instantaneous responses where the person reacts to the word as if it were the actual thing. For instance, the man with the strong negative feelings about the word *feminist,* mentioned earlier, had an image of feminists as man-hating, bra-burning, controlling females with no sense of humor. Powerful physiological reactions to words with highly negative connotations are normal, but they involve nonthinking responses. Recall that group members are ethically obliged to strengthen, not weaken, one another's identity and self-concept; therefore, intentionally using emotive words to hurt someone or to see if you can get a rise out of someone is not only inappropriate, it is unethical.

Emotive Words

When a discussant, or something he or she values, is called one of these negative terms, the response is usually defensive or hostile. Constructive, open-minded discussion ends. The group problem-solving process is disrupted as counterattacks are exchanged. But this doesn't need to happen. Some of the more common trigger words, including racial and ethnic slurs, sexist terms, and other epithets, have alternative denotative terms that are neutral or positive. You can state your opinion, even if it is controversial and others are likely to disagree, in a way that does not deliberately push somebody's "hot button." For example:

Negative Connotation	Neutral or Positive Connotation
Egghead	Intellectual
Broad	Woman
Manipulative	Persuasive
Jock	Athlete

Discussants must be sensitive to current usage and to the feelings of other group members. For example, a white group member with no prejudicial intention may say *colored* and a black member may respond defensively. Our black students have told us they now prefer the term *African-American* to *black,* which was the preferred term for many years. One discussant might say, "Nebraska has socialistic electric power distribution," meaning that such facilities are owned by the public and managed by a voter-elected board. Although *socialistic* is used appropriately to define a company owned by the social body (the citizens of Nebraska), some Nebraskans wouldn't take kindly to that adjective. *Publicly owned* would have been a better choice; it is equally descriptive, but doesn't carry the negative connotations of *socialistic.* Why should we pay attention to such things? Groups can get sidetracked from their goals by these types of problems that create hurt feelings and lost harmony. In addition, good members want their ideas and opinions to have a fair shake in the group's discussions, but someone you have offended with an emotive word will be unable to consider fairly and objectively the merits of what you propose. So, using such language hurts the group's ultimate outcome.

The use of sexist terms is a major problem for many groups. Terms that once were used interchangeably to refer to all people, as well as males specifically, are now rejected as biased against women. For instance, the word *man* has been used in the past when the person referred to could be either male or female (patrolman, chairman, businessman, postman). Language is dynamic; it changes to fit changing circumstances. What was once acceptable is now inappropriate. Any word that implies a sex criterion for filling a role or performing a task may disrupt many discussions. You will be a more valued and valuable group member if you consciously eliminate all sexually stereotyped terms from your speaking vocabulary.

The worst form of stigmatizing is name-calling. Adrenalin rises as we prepare to fight physiologically and psychologically when called by such names as *pig, chauvinist, feminazi,* or *nigger.* Such behavior deflects attention from the issues before a group, reduces trust, elicits defensive reactions, and does *nothing* to promote effective group discussion. It also is unethical.

What can you do to prevent or reduce the effects of stigmatizing? First, recognize that people have feelings about everything and these feelings are not to be rejected. When people or their beliefs are challenged, their concepts of self are also challenged and must be defended. Next, monitor your own behavior; be aware that your feelings and evaluations are just that—YOUR feelings and opinions, not *truths.* While some labeling and stigmatizing occurs normally when people express how they feel about things, we can reduce it in ourselves by taking responsibility for our opinions and expressing these opinions provisionally: "It seems to *me* that . . . ," or "I don't like . . . ," for example.

Finally, when you hear someone else express a trigger term, you can reduce the danger of wasteful conflict or defensiveness by restating the emotive statement in unloaded form and inviting contrasting feelings or points of view. For example: "Joe has called the ACTION program phony and fascistic. That's one point of view. What are some others?" A statement like "Doctors are money-grubbing pigs at the American feed trough. We can't get health care reform because of their greed!" might be rephrased as follows: "Helen believes that health care reform will be difficult because physicians have strong concerns about losing their current incomes. What do the rest of you think?" Replacing the emotive term with a denotative one and soliciting a variety of opinions and feelings allow the group to examine the idea objectively, in a mood of skeptical inquiry, so the conclusion will be based on more complete information.

As we noted, stigmatizing and name-calling are unethical behaviors because they attempt to undermine other members' self-concepts. They sidetrack the group into an argument that deflects it from its goal and cause the group to reject what may be valuable information because it was poorly stated. As a speaker, you should be sensitive to other group members so as not to stigmatize them, their values, or their beliefs. As a listener, rephrase stigmatizing statements so that they are neutral. That way, if members disagree, it will be on the merits of the idea, not because of the trigger words. If a member persists in stigmatizing others, make it clear—politely, but directly and firmly—that such behavior is not acceptable.

The ability to speak in a fluent and polished style is not essential to being a valuable group member but, as we have discussed, clarity is. Organizing your remarks clearly makes it easier for others to interpret them as you intend. The following are guidelines for organizing remarks:

Improving Communication by Organizing Remarks

1. **Relate your statements to preceding remarks.**
   It should be clear to your fellow group members how your remark contributes to the discussion. Your statement should not appear to come out of the blue, but should connect to the topic under discussion and, most of the time, to the immediately previous remark. Furthermore, you should state your idea, support it with evidence, and make the connection to the topic clear. For example, in a group investigating the loss of widely used library reference materials, Helen has just said, "A major problem for the library is replacing magazines with articles that have been cut out." You say, "Yes, that is a major reason why reference materials aren't available, and I *also* found out that every encyclopedia had articles removed. The librarian told me it costs $2,000 per year to replace them." Your remark will make sense to other group members because it relates directly to Helen's statement, it is relevant at this particular time in the discussion, and the point is clear.

2. **Use conventional and clear syntax (word arrangement).**
   For example, "Year last of all automobiles percent seventeen recalled from the past five years were" makes no sense because the syntax is illogical. This makes sense: "Last year, 17 percent of all autos made in the past five years were recalled." While you have more latitude with written English, spoken English requires conventional sentences to facilitate mutual understandings.

3. **Speak concisely.**
   When your listeners eyes glaze over, shut up; you've talked too long. State your ideas simply, briefly, and clearly—once! We all know participants who restate every point several times or use two hundred words for what could be said in twenty. This causes listeners to tune out and hogs "air time." For example, "Although I have no doubt about the possible efficacy of the operations of this proposal, there remain unresolved complications about it that might eventuate at some indeterminate point if untoward circumstances

tending toward time slippages were to arise and signal-exchange operations were conducted." Restated, it becomes clear: "This plan would fail if someone received a late signal or was not prepared to act when he got the signal." If you find others restating your ideas more succinctly, strive for a more concise style.

4. **State one point at a time.**

   This is not an inviolable rule, but usually you should not contribute more than one idea in a single speech because a group can discuss effectively only one idea at a time. If you attempt to give all the data on an issue or present a series of points, the group won't be able to follow you and respond to each one meaningfully. For instance, if you say, "Many people are injured when bumpers fail. Furthermore, I think cars should be required to have antilock brakes, and there's also a problem of the steering wheel that locks when the ignition shuts off." One person might reply about the bumpers, another about the brakes, and a third about the steering. A confused discussion will result. An exception to this guideline might be if you are submitting a multipoint report to the group, in which case it will be helpful for members to have a handout that lists or outlines the main points.

In this section we have described the nature of spoken language and several of the pitfalls to avoid during small group discussion. We now turn to an equally important component of communication, nonverbal signals.

Nonverbal Signals in Small Group Communication

Nonverbal signals include all signals *except* the actual words themselves. They are vital to small group communication. For instance, Birdwhistell, an early pioneer in the study of body-movement signals, believed that only about 35 percent of meaning is communicated verbally when people are face to face; the other 65 percent is evoked by nonverbal signals.[4] Mehrabian, a psychologist concentrating on interpersonal communication, agreed that the percentage of meaning derived from nonverbal signals is much higher than that derived from language alone.[5]

Nonverbal signals supplement our words and give listeners clues about how to interpret the words. However, nonverbal codes are culture bound. Most of what follows is about mainstream American culture and *is not necessarily valid* for people from other countries or from certain subcultures of the United States. We address the effects of culture in chapter 5; here, we first consider general principles about nonverbal communication, then the specific functions performed by nonverbal signals.

Principles of Nonverbal Communication

There are three major principles necessary for understanding how to interpret nonverbal signals among group members. These principles concern the flow of nonverbal signals, their lack of specificity, and what happens when nonverbal and verbal signals contradict one another.

1. **You cannot stop sending nonverbal signals to other members of a small group.**

   This is often stated as "you cannot *not* communicate" and means that, in the presence of another person, you cannot help sending signals that others can potentially receive and interpret (although the interpretation may be completely incorrect). We emit nonverbal signals continuously; we cannot stop them. Signals such as body shape, posture, movements, eyes, clothing and accessories, and skin color are among the signals we send, whether we intend to or not. One of us taught a small group seminar where one member, afraid that others would get to know her too well, decided she would not communicate. She refused to look at the other members, made few verbal contributions, and even turned her chair slightly aside so others could not see her face. Of course she communicated—that she did not care about other members and was "too good" for the rest of the group. Although this was not the message she intended, this was the meaning attributed to her by the others. You may not be an active verbal participant, but you cannot be physically present without affecting the mood, climate, cohesiveness, and interpersonal relationships of the group. The question is not "Will I communicate?" but "*What* will I communicate?"

2. **Nonverbal signals are highly ambiguous.**

   Consider what a smile can mean: feelings of friendship, agreement with a proposal, amusement, acknowledgement of another, gloating over someone's misfortune, feelings of superiority, or simple liking. Looking at your watch might be interpreted as boredom, but it could also mean the person has to take medication on a fixed schedule or has another meeting in a few minutes. To prevent misunderstandings, verbal clarification is needed.

3. **When nonverbal and verbal signals seem to contradict each other, people will usually trust the nonverbal signals.**

   A fellow group member, fists clenched and brows drawn tight, shouts, "NO, I'M NOT MAD!" Do you believe him? Marriage counselors are taught to look for these discrepancies, such as the wife who says, "I love my husband," while she shakes her head to indicate "no." There is good reason for the tendency to believe nonverbal elements when there is an inconsistency: nonverbal signals are less subject to a person's conscious control. Many nonverbal signals such as muscular contractions, blushing, and pupil dilation are controlled not by the higher, thinking centers of the brain's cortex but by primitive structures we share with virtually all other mammals. These structures—hypothalamus, brain stem, pineal body, limbic system—control bodily processes, hormone output, and feelings. Few of us are able consciously to control sweating, blood pressure, tension levels of internal organs, and so forth. Most of the time in group meetings we are not fully aware of what our feet, hands, faces, and bodies are doing. Some of us have been taught to control our speech rate, vocal tone, or pitch, and most of us exercise considerable control over the words we utter. Thus, nonverbal communication is relatively spontaneous and easier to trust than the more easily manipulated stream of words.

Just as nonverbal signals can be inconsistent with verbal ones, nonverbal signals are sometimes inconsistent with each other. For example, consider the group member who leans forward, nods at what you say, and seems to be paying rapt attention, but stifles a yawn while sneaking a peek at the clock. What are you to make of that? The pattern of overall nonverbal behavior is more important than any individual

"Are you *sure?*" Nonverbal signals supplement the verbal ones.
Photo by Billy Barnes/Photo Edit

signal. If we catch an incongruity, we become guarded in interpreting nonverbal signals, especially since mixed signals sometimes result from deliberate attempts to deceive or conceal. (Haven't you ever pretended to be keenly interested in someone while you thought about the exam you have to take tomorrow?) Having *sincerity, honesty, and integrity as a group member is the best way to prevent sending mixed messages that produce confusion.* Otherwise, our nonverbal behaviors betray us.

Nonverbal signals may also result from the sender's internal confusion or uncertainty. For example, a group member may both like and dislike different elements of someone's proposal; this genuine confusion may appear as mixed signals in the form of a positive head nod with a frowning face. Once again, ethical behavior requires honesty and clarity. If you as a speaker are confused, help other members interpret your remarks by honestly revealing your confusion. If you are confused or puzzled by the mixed messages of another, it pays to *say* so, thereby helping the other person clarify his or her intent and increasing your own and the group's understanding.

Functions of Nonverbal Communication

Awareness of the functions of nonverbal communication will enable you to respond appropriately to others and make your own signals more clear to them. Nonverbal signals serve six major functions during group interaction:

1. **Supplementing the verbal.**
   Nonverbal signals may repeat and reinforce the verbal message. For example, a person points to item three on a chart and simultaneously says, "Now look at the third item on our list of ideas." Sometimes, nonverbal signals complement

or elaborate what is said. For instance, a discussant may shake her head from side to side while saying, "I cannot accept that suggestion," or another may say, "It will be about *this* high when it is finished" and holds his hand three feet from the ground. Other nonverbal signals emphasize or accent the verbal message. A nod of the head, increased force on a particular word, and a shake of the finger can all indicate "this is an especially important idea I am now uttering." Thus, by repeating, complementing, and emphasizing, nonverbal signals supplement the verbal.

2. **Substituting for words.**

   Many gestures are substitutes for spoken words. Thumb and forefinger forming an *O* with the other three fingers held out stands for *okay* in the United States, as does the *thumbs up* signal. If a committee chair asks, "Are we ready to vote?" and members shake their heads from side to side, the group will not vote. Crooking your forefinger and moving it toward you indicates that you want someone to lean toward you. In an orderly group discussion, one member speaks at a time, but the rest are communicating nonverbally. Ignoring these nonverbal signals will cause you to miss potentially important information. For example, one of us observed a normally reticent group member fold his arms in a closed gesture in response to a question being addressed to the whole group. The chair, recognizing that the gesture could be interpreted in a number of different ways, asked the individual to share his opinion directly with the group. In fact, the member disagreed with an emerging group consensus for several excellent reasons the rest of the group had not considered; thus, his input improved the final proposal. This input would have been missed had the chair not been alert to nonverbal substitutions.

3. **Contradicting verbal messages.**

   As we discussed earlier, sometimes nonverbal signals contradict what a person says. For instance, a member might say, "Yes, I'll go along with that," but in such a way that you expect him or her to give no real support to the idea. In such a case, it will pay you to point out the contradiction and ask for clarification: "You said you'd go along with the proposal, but something about the way you said it sounded as if you really don't like it very much. What do you feel?"

4. **Expressing emotions.**

   As the previous example illustrates, our feelings are communicated more often by nonverbal signals than by what we say. Try to say, "I agree with you," in a variety of ways, and notice how each seems to indicate a very different feeling. Sitting near someone can show more positive feelings than any words will convey. A smile or nod can signal, "I like your proposal." Negative feelings are communicated nonverbally as well. For instance, some vocal aspects of anxiety are immediately detectable.[6] Particular voice characteristics are associated with both passive and active feelings.[7] Vocal qualities, posture, and facial expressions can all communicate feelings.

5. **Regulating interaction.**

   Certain nonverbal messages direct the flow of interaction among group members. For example, turn-taking is communicated nonverbally by such things as leaning forward, taking an audible breath, or relaxing. Turn-taking

Nonverbal signals regulate interaction.

Photo by James Shaffer

happens almost automatically, without much conscious thought, but discussion leaders also consciously employ head nods, eye contact, and hand movements to indicate who should speak next. Favorable nods indicate "keep talking," but lack of response or looking away may signal "shut up." Students raise their hands in classes to show they want to be recognized. Many of these regulatory cues are visual. A group that one of us observed had a blind member who could not see visual regulatory cues. He frequently talked out of turn or cut the other members' speaking turns short. The others were upset at what they perceived to be arrogant and self-centered behavior, but a discussion about regulatory cues helped the group discover the extent to which we depend on visual regulatory cues to regulate interaction. The discussion increased members' sensitivity to the communicative problems some handicapped people experience, which enabled the group to achieve its goal with greater harmony.

6. **Indicating status relationships.**
   Sitting at the end of the table indicates leadership or a desire for high influence in the group. A member who stakes out more than an average amount of territory at a table (briefcase, books, coffee cup, etc.) shows dominance or

superiority, as does suddenly getting very close to another, a penetrating stare, loud voice, or a patronizing pat or other touch.[8] High-status members tend to have more relaxed postures than lower-status members. On the other hand, uncrossing arms and legs, unbuttoning a coat, and a general relaxation of the body often signals openness and a feeling of equality.[9] Emergence as a perceived leader has been related to shoulder, head, and arm gestures.[10] Body orientation, the angle at which a participant's shoulders and legs are turned in relation to the group as a whole or another person, indicate how much one feels a part of the group and often that one is more committed to a subgroup than to the group as a whole.[11]

Interpreting nonverbal signals appropriately requires that we look at the pattern of simultaneous signals rather than at just a single cue. However, we need to be aware of the various types of nonverbal signals to avoid overlooking some. Those listed are especially relevant to communication among group members.

Types of Nonverbal Signals

Physical Appearance

Members of a new group react to each other's appearance long before they begin to judge each other's expertise, reasoning, and verbal competencies. The judgments may or may not be correct, but they are formed initially from nonverbal signals that cannot be concealed, such as race, sex, physique, and mode of dress. We attribute factors such as financial condition, status in the community, and educational background on the basis of what we initially observe. Of course, we may change our judgments later, but they are formed initially from nonverbal signals such as these.

Cultural factors influence our responses to physical appearance. For instance, Americans have a clear picture of the ideal body type. We tend to be prejudiced against endomorphs (heavy bodies), whom we often perceive as lazy, sloppy, stupid, and undependable, but also as jolly and easy to get along with. Ectomorphs (tall and skinny) are perceived as frail, studious, and intelligent. Mesomorphs (muscular types) are more likely than others to be perceived as leaders. Height is particularly important. The taller a person is, the more likely she or he is to be looked up to, literally, as a leader; short people have to try harder to be seen as potential group leaders.[12] We often are not aware we have these prejudices, so it is especially important that we teach ourselves to react to what a person *does* rather than to physical appearance.

Dress also influences initial judgments of others, as do hair style and items of adornment. John Malloy has made a systematic study of the influence of dress and has reported these findings in his daily newspaper column, "Dress for Success," and in his books. Jeans, T-shirt, and a pierced nose would reduce one's credibility in a group of bank managers, but the corporate "uniform" would be equally inconceivable in a group of *avant garde* artists. A group one of us belong to included a woman with a punk hairstyle that was long on one side, nearly shaved on the other, with an orange streak down the middle. "Bimbo," we concluded; we were wrong. The woman turned out to be one of the most perceptive, hard-working, and reliable members of the group. Looks can deceive; hold your initial judgments lightly, for you may need to change them.

Space and Seating

There have been many studies of how we use **proxemics,** or personal space and territory, to communicate. We signal our need to be included by how we orient our bodies to the group. A person who sits close to other members, directly in the circle in a flexible seating space, close to a circular table, or at a central point at a square or rectangular table signals a need to belong or a sense of belonging; a member who sits outside the circumference, pushed back from a table, or at a corner may be signalling a desire to withdraw. Sitting within range of touch indicates that we feel intimately or personally involved, whereas sitting from just outside touch distance to several feet away signals a more formal, businesslike relationship.[13] Patterson found that group members making collective (group) decisions sit closer together and in more of a circle than when making individual judgments.[14] Stacks and Burgoon discovered that closer distances (eighteen inches) make group members more persuasive and credible than distances of thirty-six or fifty-four inches.[15] What is a comfortable distance varies from one individual or one culture to another. Females tend to sit closer than males and tolerate crowding better. People of the same age and the same social status sit closer together than people of different ages and statuses. The better acquainted people are, the closer they tend to sit. Thus, members of a long-standing group characterized by high interpersonal trust would be comfortable sitting close together in a small room, but people just beginning to form into a group would need more space. Even so, humans are highly adaptable, so when a room or other constraint violates our preferred distances, we adjust, at least for a short time. If crowded for too long, though, people sweat, grow tense, fidget, and act defensively. Group leaders should watch for signs of discomfort from either too much or too little space and make adjustments by rearranging the room, taking a short break, or finding more comfortable accommodations for the group.

Once a group has formed, members appear to internalize what seems to be the most comfortable amount of space between them and to develop this as a space norm. Burgoon et al. found, for instance, that if low-status group members violated the group's norm regarding space, they suffered from reduced persuasiveness, sociability, and attractiveness in the eyes of the other members. In contrast, high-status members enhanced their status by moving closer than the group norm specified, and even more if they moved farther away.[16] Thus, it is generally advisable for you to follow group space norms rather than violate them, but if you are a high-status group member, you may increase your status even more by sitting slightly apart from other members.

Leadership emergence in a group is related to space. Dominant people and designated leaders usually choose central positions in the group, such as at the head of a rectangular table or across from as many others as possible. Other members frequently avoid sitting next to a designated leader, so the circle ends up looking like the diagram in figure 4.2.[17] This reinforces the leader's position and allows the leader a comprehensive view of the group, which facilitates coordination and control by the leader.

People sitting across from each other speak more often to each other than people sitting side by side.[18] However, when a group has a dominating leader, "sidebar" conversations tend to break out between people sitting next to each other. Thus, we can conclude that conversation normally flows across the circle, and leaders should sit where they can maintain eye contact with as many group members as possible.

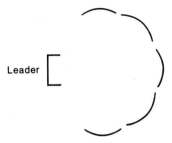

Figure 4.2
Typical spacing between designated leader and other members of a small task group.

Seating and spatial features of the group's environment, such as fixed-space permanent features like walls and doors, and semifixed, movable features like furniture, influence the group's interactions.[19] For example, in a large room, group members may choose to sit closer together than normal. If a group is meeting in a space normally used for another activity, the normal use of that space may change the group's interaction; for example, meeting in a member's living room may encourage informality. Meeting around a formal conference table encourages somewhat formal interaction, whereas meeting in a lounge with comfortable sofas does not. **Sociopetal** furniture arrangements encourage group interaction (for example, comfortable chairs moved into a circle), but **sociofugal** arrangements (for example, classrooms with seats facing front and bolted to the floor) discourage group interaction. Sometimes, simply rearranging a group's meeting place can turn a chaotic group into a productive one. For example, one of us advised a student committee whose meetings were characterized by general disorganization, repetition, and sidebar conversations. The room used by the group was normally set up for large assemblies, with a head table on a raised platform at the front, which the members used for their discussions. The president sat at the center of the long table, with the rest of the members sitting on either side of her along one side of the table. Only the members directly next to the president could both see and hear her without great difficulty. The group was advised to stop using the table and instead to rearrange the chairs in a circle. After just one meeting, members reported substantial improvement, and the president said she felt much more organized and in control. The group made eye contact and hearing easier by adapting its semifixed space to meet its needs.

Eye Signals

Eye movements can signal disgust, dislike, superiority, or inferiority, as well as liking; the rules for eye contact are highly culture dependent. For most middle-class white Americans, establishing eye contact is the first step to conversing. Americans use eye contact when they seek feedback, when they want to be spoken to, and when they want to participate more actively.[20] Burgoon reported that students given free choice of seating arrangements in small classes chose to sit in a circular or U-shaped pattern for their meetings so they could maintain eye contact with as many other members as possible.[21] Although a stare may indicate competitiveness, in a cooperative group it shows friendship and cohesiveness.[22] For many middle-class Americans, lack of eye contact is perceived as dishonesty, rudeness, apathy, or nervousness.[23] Eye contact is important, but must be interpreted carefully in context with other verbal and nonverbal signals.

Facial Expressions

Facial expressions indicate feelings and moods. Without a word being spoken, you can perceive anger, support, disagreement, and other sentiments. Eckman, Ellsworth, and Friesen found that at least six types of emotion could be detected accurately from facial expressions.[24] Some people change facial expression very little; they are said to have *poker faces.* They tend to be trusted less than people whose expressive faces signal their feelings more openly. But even poker-faced people leak their feelings by physiological changes they can't readily control, such as sweating or blushing.[25] If group members show few facial expressions, watch for other revealing physiological signs.

Movements

The study of how we communicate by movement is called **kinesics.** We reveal our feelings with bodily movements and gestures. We show tension by shifting around in a chair, drumming fingers, swinging a foot, or twitching an eye. Such behavior may signal frustration, impatience with the group's progress, or annoyance. Alert group members will attempt to track down the source of tension by pointing out the kinesic signs and asking what may be producing them.

According to Scheflen, how open to and accepting of others a group member feels is indicated by body orientation.[26] Members turn directly to those they like and away from those they do not like. Leaning toward others indicates a sense of belonging, whereas leaning away signals a sense of rejection. Members who sit at angles tangential to the rest of the group may not feel included or want to belong.

When members are tuned in to each other, they tend to imitate each other's posture and movements. This behavior is called *body synchrony.* Scheflen observed many instances of parallel arm positions, self-touching behavior, and leg positions indicating congruity.[27] Several studies found that group members are more likely to imitate the movements and gestures of members with high status and power than those with low status.[28] We can infer who has power and status in a group by observing which members are mimicked by others.

Nonverbal signals that control the flow of discussion are called **regulators;** in discussion groups, body movements and eye contact often perform this function. For example, speakers often signal that they are finished speaking by relaxing and stopping hand gestures.[29] Scheflen reported that a speaker who is concluding a point makes a noticeable postural shift.[30] A listener can bid for the floor by leaning forward, waving a hand, and simultaneously opening the mouth.

Vocal Cues

Vocal cues, or **paralanguage,** are any characteristics of voice and utterance other than the words themselves. Included are variables such as pitch, rate, fluency, pronunciation variations, force, tonal quality, and pauses. Extensive research since the 1930s indicates that listeners tend to agree on the characteristics they attribute to speakers based on these vocal cues,[31] including such things as attitudes, interests, personality traits, adjustment, ethnic group, education, and anxiety level and other emotional states.[32] Tone of voice is an excellent indicator of a person's self-concept and mood. For instance, frightened people tend to speak in tense, metallic tones; anxious people have nonfluencies such as interjections, repetitions, hesitations, sentence correction, and even stuttering in their speech.

How we react to statements such as "I agree" or "Okay" depends much more on the pitch patterns and tone of voice than on the words themselves. For example, sarcasm and irony are indicated primarily by a tone of voice that suggests the words should be taken *opposite* to what they seem to mean. Children generally do not understand sarcasm, and even one-third of high school seniors take sarcastic statements literally.[33] The possibility for misunderstanding sarcasm in a group is high; sensitive discussants listen actively for evidence of sarcasm, as well as for such signals of strong feeling as loudness, high pitch, a metallic tone, and a rapid speech rate.

In both movement and voice, animation tends to increase status within the group. People who speak quietly in a low key have little persuasive impact. They seem to lack much personal involvement with what they say. However, members whose vocal qualities change too extensively may be seen as irrational, not to be trusted as leaders or credible sources. Taylor found, however, that excessive vocal stress was judged more credible than a monotonous vocal pattern.[34] You are advised to vary your vocal tone and use vocal cues to emphasize the verbal content of your remarks.

Time Cues

Few of us think of time as a nonverbal dimension of communication. Perceptions of time are highly culture dependent, which we discuss in detail in chapter 5; here, we introduce you the concept of time as a component of nonverbal communication. Americans think of time as a commodity to be spent or saved. People in Western cultures tend to regulate their activities by the clock, but people in many other cultures act according to inner biological needs or natural events. For example, Native Americans on reservations structure their group events according to natural phenomena (e.g., sunrise, sunset, the full moon). In some places, work stops when it rains or when the sun is at a certain position in the sky. In rural America, the pace of life is slower than in large urban centers. The difficulty comes when people with different perceptions of time must coordinate their efforts to finish a group task.

In the fast-paced culture of the American business world, being considerate of group members' time is important; Americans usually will allow only about a five-minute leeway before they expect an apology.[35] People who come late to meetings (unless due to absolutely unavoidable circumstances) are judged to be inconsiderate, undisciplined, and selfish. Likewise, it is considered improper to leave a meeting before the announced ending time, unless some prior arrangement or explanation has been made. Forcing others to keep to your time schedule is the prerogative of high-status individuals.[36] It implies that your time is more important than that of the other members. Unless other group members have accorded you this prerogative (which is unlikely in the case of groups of peers), coming late to meetings will mark you as inconsiderate and arrogant.

Time also is a commodity in the group's interaction (i.e., air time). People can abuse this commodity by talking too much or too little. Harper, Weins, and Matarazzo found that persons who talked somewhat more than average were viewed favorably on leadership characteristics. Those who talked an average amount were the most liked. Extremely talkative members were regarded as rude and selfish, members the group could do without.[37] Derber refers to excessive talking as *conversational narcissism.*[38]

A valuable clock-watching service is pacing a meeting so that all agenda items receive some attention and decisions are made when required. The leader who is sensitive to time helps curb the narcissistic tendencies of members who shift the topic so they can exploit it for personal attention. A reminder that there are a certain number of minutes left for the meeting and two more items that must be settled will often curb unnecessary chatter and endless repetition of ideas, while encouraging members to be relevant and achieve closure on an issue.

Touch

Touch is an important nonverbal dimension in interpersonal communication. It is vital to group maintenance in most primary groups and athletic teams, but may be nonexistent in many American work groups and committees. The kind of touching people expect and enjoy depends on their acculturation and the type of relationship they share with others. For instance, touch between strangers, other than a handshake, tends to threaten most Americans.

Touch among group members can strengthen unity and teamwork. Families join hands to say grace before a meal; football players pile on hands in a huddle; actors hug each other after a successful performance. The type of touch, as well as the setting, determines the reaction. Pats are usually perceived as signs of affection and inclusion. Strokes are generally perceived as sensual, inappropriate in a small group meeting. A firm grip on an arm or about the shoulders is usually a control gesture, interpreted as a one-up maneuver; among a group of equals, this may be resented. A gentle touch may be a means of getting someone to hold back and not overstate an issue. Many a group member has been restrained from saying something hostile by a gentle touch on the arm during a heated argument.

As with other nonverbal cues, people vary widely in the extent to which they accept and give touches. It is crucial that you touch others in a group only when you sense they accept both you and the touch. Andersen and Leibowitz found that people range from those who enjoy touch to those who react negatively to being touched.[39] Have you placed what you thought was a friendly hand on a fellow group member's shoulder at a meeting and been surprised to feel the member flinch? Although touching can strengthen team bonds, you must respect the rights of those who prefer not to be touched, and never touch unless it is comfortable for you. A forced touch is detectable and seems phony or manipulative.

On the other hand, it is appropriate to give a gentle pat as a sign of solidarity to those who like being touched, even in work-related committee and task force meetings. However, jabbing, squeezing, or restraining another is rarely appropriate. You should go easy on touching in secondary groups, but you need less diligence in primary groups, many of which have norms of showing warmth and affection physically.

Summary

In chapter 4 we examined the structuration process, which describes how the verbal and nonverbal interaction among members serves to create and maintain a group. We then examined the functions of verbal and nonverbal signals, which constitute the heart of small group communication.

Effective discussion requires appropriate use of language. Languages are constituted by codes of symbols, rules for arranging these codes, and assumptions about the world. Symbols have no inherent meanings, so if coordination is to be achieved, people must use the same codes of words, and use them to refer to the same referents. The way language is employed can help group members understand one another or it can result in misunderstandings and problems for the group. Common language problems include bypassing, lack of clarity, use of cliches, and emotive words that stigmatize others. A group's progress is facilitated if members make concise and unambiguous remarks, relating them to prior remarks and stating them clearly.

Language is a major medium of effective discussion, but it does not function alone. Nonverbal signals communicate emotion and establish relationships among members, supplement and clarify verbal expressions, substitute for words, and regulate the flow of talk. One cannot stop sending nonverbal signals, so one cannot *not* communicate in the presence of other group members. When verbal and nonverbal signals contradict each other, most perceivers trust their interpretations of the nonverbal rather than the verbal signals.

Many types of nonverbal signals can be perceived and interpreted by group members, although interpretation is highly culture dependent. Body type, appearance, height, and dress contribute substantially to our initial impressions of personality traits, social status, and relative power. Spatial relations and body angles also indicate relative power, as well as how much a person feels included in or committed to a group. Seating arrangements influence who talks to whom. Distances among members reflect norms, position in the group, and personal liking. Eye contact signals both inclusion and control. Facial expressions reveal feelings toward specific members and the group as a whole. Body movements, including gestures, are used extensively, along with eye contact, to control turn-taking and to supplement statements. Personality characteristics and moods are interpreted from vocal cues, as is a speaker's seriousness or sarcasm. Vocal cues often clarify otherwise ambiguous words.

Americans often regulate their lives by the clock, the time dimension of nonverbal behavior. How we time our behavior in relation to other group members indicates our relative regard for them. Touch, though infrequent among members of most work groups, can be a means of enhancing solidarity if used appropriately, but caution is suggested because acceptance of touch is highly individual.

In the previous two chapters we have examined the process of communication in small groups and the kinds of signals involved in communication. In chapter 5 we address some of the special problems that are likely to occur when members of a group come from different cultures or subcultures.

Exercises

1. Listen to a recorded discussion or to a discussion among several classmates. Each time someone utters a cliche you recognize, write it down. Record your impression of any effect the cliche had on subsequent discussion. What did you discover? Share your findings with fellow observers.

2. Describe an instance of misunderstanding resulting from each of the following types of verbalization. You may do this from memory, direct observation, or recorded discussion. Describe specifically what was said and what happened in response.
   a. High level abstraction or ambiguity
   b. Sexist language
   c. Ethnic or racial epithet

3. In a practice group discussion session, all members should refrain from giving any bodily or vocal responses to the comments of others (i.e., no head nods, leaning forward, hand gestures, "uh huh" comments, facial expressions, etc.) for about ten minutes. Each person should make at least one major comment. Then, for the next ten minutes, everyone should react nonverbally (physically and vocally) as fully and completely as possible. Finally, talk about what *you* felt during each nonverbal response pattern and *what this shows* about group communication.

4. Watch a videotape of a small group meeting, but turn off the sound so the words cannot be heard. What do you think the members are talking about? What does each member's individual behavior seem to indicate? Watch the group again, this time with the sound, and see how accurate you were. Discuss what specific nonverbal behaviors contributed to your judgments.

5. Secure a play script. Choose a scene at random, and practice changing the meaning of the scene by varying the vocal qualities: pitch, rate, expression, tonal quality, and so forth. Next, practice reading the scene several times, this time keeping the vocal qualities constant but changing the gestures, distances between characters, facial expressions, and so forth. What did you discover?

6. During a fishbowl discussion, any observer may call "freeze" at any time, at which point each discussant should remain motionless, even regarding eye direction. The observer who called "freeze" then asks each other observer to comment on what each discussant's posture, position in the group, eye direction, and other nonverbal behavior indicate. Then, both observers and participants should discuss the implications of the observer's interpretations of nonverbal signals.

Bibliography

Andersen, Peter A. "Nonverbal Communication in the Small Group." In *Small Group Communication: A Reader.* 6th ed., eds. Robert S. Cathcart and Larry A. Samovar. Dubuque, IA: Wm. C. Brown Publishers, 1992, 272–86.

Burgoon, Judee K. "Spatial Relationships in Small Groups." In *Small Group Communication: A Reader.* 6th ed., eds. Robert S. Cathcart and Larry A. Samovar. Dubuque, IA: Wm. C. Brown Publishers, 1992, 287–300.

Condon, John C. *Semantics and Communication.* 3d ed. New York: Macmillan Company, 1985.

Leathers, Dale G. *Successful Nonverbal Communication: Principles and Applications.* 2d ed. New York: Macmillan Company, 1992.

Poole, Marshall Scott. "Group Communication and the Structuring Process." In *Small Group Communication: A Reader.* 6th ed., eds. Robert S. Cathcart and Larry A. Samovar. Dubuque, IA: Wm. C. Brown Publishers, 1992, 147–57.

Notes

1. Marshall S. Poole, David R. Siebold, and Robert D. McPhee, "Group Decision-Making as a Structurational Process," *Quarterly Journal of Speech* 71 (1985): 74–102; Marshall S. Poole, David R. Siebold, and Robert D. McPhee, "A Structurational Approach to Theory-Building in Decision-Making Research," in Randy Y. Hirokawa and Marshall S. Poole, eds. *Communication and Group Decision-Making* (Beverly Hills, CA: Sage Publications, 1986): 237–64; and Marshall S. Poole, "Group Communication and the Structuring Process," in *Small Group Communication: A Reader,* 6th ed., eds. Robert S. Cathcart and Larry A. Samovar (Dubuque, IA: Wm. C. Brown Publishers, 1992): 147–57.

2. Marshall S. Poole, "Group Communication and the Structuring Process."

3. Dale G. Leathers, "Process Disruption and Measurement in Small Group Communication," *Quarterly Journal of Speech* 55 (1969): 288–98.

4. Ray L. Birdwhistell, lecture at Nebraska Psychiatric Institute, Omaha, NE: May 11, 1972.

5. Albert Mehrabian, *Nonverbal Communication* (Chicago: Aldine-Atherton, 1972): 101–8.

6. J. Starkweather, "Vocal Communication of Personality and Human Feeling," *Journal of Communication* 11 (1961): 63–72.

7. Joel R. Davitz and Lois J. Davitz, "Nonverbal Vocal Communication of Feeling," *Journal of Communication* 11 (1961): 81–86.

8. Erving Goffman, *Relations in Public* (New York: Harper & Row, Publishers, 1971): 32–48.

9. Gerald E. Nierenberg and H. H. Calero, *How to Read a Person Like a Book* (New York: Pocket Books, 1973): 46.

10. Edward A. Mabry, "Developmental Aspects of Nonverbal Behavior in Small Group Settings," *Small Group Behavior* 20 (1989): 192–203.

11. Stewart L. Tubbs, *A Systems Approach to Small Group Interaction* (Reading, MA: Addison-Wesley, 1978): 185.

12. J. B. Cortes and F. M. Gatti, "Physique and Propensity," in *With Words Unspoken,* eds. L. B. Rosenfeld and J. M. Civikly (New York: Holt, Rinehart and Winston, 1976): 50–56.

13. Edward T. Hall, *The Silent Language* (Garden City, NY: Doubleday, 1959).

14. M. L. Patterson, "The Role of Space in Social Interaction," in *Nonverbal Behavior and Communication,* eds. A. W. Siegman and S. Feldstein (Hillsdale, NJ: Lawrence Erlbaum Associates, 1978): 277.

15. D. W. Stacks and J. K. Burgoon, "The Persuasive Effects of Violating Spacial Distance Expectations in Small Groups." Paper presented at the Southern Speech Communication Association Convention, Biloxi, MI (April 1979).

16. J. K. Burgoon, D. W. Stacks, and S. A. Burch, "The Role of Interpersonal Rewards and Violations of Distancing Expectations in Achieving Influence in Small Groups," *Communication* 11 (1982): 114–28.

17. R. F. Bales and A. P. Hare, "Seating Patterns and Small Group Interaction," *Sociometry* 26 (1963): 480–86; G. Hearn, "Leadership and the Spacial Factor in Small Groups," *Journal of Abnormal and Social Psychology* 54 (1957): 269–72.

18. B. Steinzor, "The Spatial Factor in Face to Face Discussion Groups," *Journal of Abnormal and Social Psychology* 45 (1950): 552–55.

19. Judee K. Burgoon, "Spatial Relationships in Small Groups," in *Small Group Communication: A Reader,* 6th ed., eds. R. S. Cathcart and L. A. Samovar (Dubuque, IA: Wm. C. Brown Publishers, 1992): 289–90.

20. J. McCroskey, C. Larson, and M. Knapp, *An Introduction to Interpersonal Communication* (Englewood Cliffs, NJ: Prentice-Hall, 1971): 110–14.

21. J. K. Burgoon, "Spacial Relationships in Small Groups," 295.

22. R. V. Exline, "Exploration in the Process of Person Perception: Visual Interaction in Relation to Competition, Sex and the Need for Affiliation," *Journal of Personality* 31 (1963): 1–20.

23. P. A. Andersen, "Nonverbal Communication in the Small Group," in *Small Group Communication: A Reader,* 6th ed., eds. R. S. Cathcart and L. A. Samovar (Dubuque, IA: Wm. C. Brown Publishers, 1992): 274.

24. P. Eckman, P. Ellsworth, and W. V. Friesen, *Emotion in the Human Face: Guidelines for Research and an Integration of Findings* (New York: Pergamon Press, 1971).

25. R. W. Buck, R. E. Miller, and W. F. Caul, "Sex, Personality, and Physiological Variables in the Communication of Affect via Facial Expression," *Journal of Personality and Social Psychology* 30 (1974): 587–96.

26. A. E. Scheflen, "Quasi-Courtship Behavior in Psychotherapy," *Psychiatry* 28 (1965): 245–56.

27. A. E. Scheflen, *Body Language and the Social Order: Communication as Behavioral Control* (Englewood Cliffs, NJ: Prentice-Hall, 1972): 54–73.

28. J. K. Burgoon and T. Saine, *The Unknown Dialogue: An Introduction to Nonverbal Communication* (Boston: Houghton Mifflin Company, 1978).

29. S. Duncan, Jr., "Some Signals and Rules for Taking Speaking Turns in Conversations," *Journal of Personality and Social Psychology* 23 (1972): 283–92.

30. A. E. Scheflen, *Body Language and the Social Order.*

31. N. D. Addington, "The Relationship of Selected Vocal Characteristics to Personality and Perception," *Speech Monographs* 35 (1968): 492; Ernest Kramer, "Judgment of Personal Characteristics and Emotions from Nonverbal Properties of Speech," *Psychological Bulletin* 60 (1963): 408–20.

32. Joel D. Davitz and Lois Davitz, "Nonverbal Vocal Communication of Feelings."

33. P. A. Andersen, J. F. Andersen, N. J. Wendt, and M. A. Murphy, "The Development of Nonverbal Communication Behavior in School Children Grades K–12" (Paper presented at the International Communication Association Annual Convention, Minneapolis, May, 1981).

34. K. D. Taylor, "Ratings of Source Credibility in Relation to Level of Vocal Variety, Sex of the Source and Sex of the Receiver," (M. A. thesis, University of Nebraska at Omaha, 1984).

35. E. T. Hall, *The Silent Language.*

36. Martin Remland, "Developing Leadership Skills in Nonverbal Communication: A Situational Perspective," *Journal of Business Communication* 3 (1981): 17–29.

37. R. G. Harper, A. N. Weins, and J. D. Matarazzo, *Nonverbal Communication: The State of the Art* (New York: John Wiley and Sons, 1978).

38. C. Derber, *The Pursuit of Attention* (New York: Oxford University Press, 1979).

39. P. A. Andersen and K. Leibowitz, "The Development and Nature of the Construct 'Touch Avoidance,' " *Environmental Psychology and Nonverbal Behavior* 3 (1978): 89–106.

The Effects of Culture on Small Group Communication

Central Message

The United States is becoming increasingly multicultural and business transnational, which means that members of small groups in the future will need to recognize, accept, and adjust to cultural differences in communication.

Study Objectives   As a result of studying chapter 5 you should be able to:

1. Define *culture* and explain why knowledge of cultural differences in communication is important for effective group discussion.

2. Describe five major dimensions on which cultures differ.

3. Describe the kinds of crosscultural differences that occur in language use and nonverbal behavior.

4. Explain why gender differences may be viewed as cultural differences, and describe differences that have been observed between male and female behavior in Western culture.

Key Terms

Activity orientation
Backchannel
Collectivist cultures
Crosscultural communication
Cultural identity
Culture
Dialect

Ethnocentric
Gender
High-context communication
Individualistic cultures
Intercultural communication
International communication
Intracultural communication

Low-context communication
Power distance
Sex
Subculture
Uncertainty avoidance
Worldview

In the next century, which is almost here, Americans of Asian, Hispanic, African, middle Eastern, and eastern European ancestry will outnumber Caucasians of western European ancestry. Called the "browning of America" by *Time* magazine,[1] this phenomenon will have a profound effect on *all* forms of communication. Transactions between people of different ethnic and racial groups require a great deal of patience and attention to the communication process. You don't have to visit another country or travel extensively for this phenomenon to affect you. The change, already well underway, will come to you; we can say with confidence that you will participate in groups with people whose backgrounds are markedly different from your own.

The culture in which a person is raised profoundly affects every aspect of that person's communication behavior, starting with the interpretation process we discussed in chapter 3. Communication among people of diverse backgrounds (and hence with diverse communication patterns) is challenging; it can result in an enriching experience or a disaster. Unfortunately, most people are **ethnocentric** in their responses to others: they believe in the superiority of their personal native culture and interpret the behavior of all people by the norms of that culture. But as Kim and Ruben have cautioned, successful communication among culturally diverse individuals requires them to give up their ethnocentricity.[2] For example, one of us observed a group of five students; four were white, middle-class Americans, and Qing-yu was Taiwanese. The American students, used to lively discussion and debate, expected all group members to speak up in support of or opposition to suggestions being proposed. However, Qing-yu kept quiet. Her eyes downcast, she contributed little to the group's interaction, even though her English was adequate for such discussions. The Americans interpreted her silence as lack of interest or stupidity, and they began to exclude her from other group activities. They were behaving *ethnocentrically,* assuming that because *American* students indicate lack of interest by not participating, Qing-yu's behavior meant the same thing. What they did not know is that in Taiwan and many other Oriental cultures, open disagreement is frowned upon. Instead, decisions are made by consensus gained through what seems to Westerners like endless discussion, with only subtle and indirect expressions of disagreement. For her part, Qing-yu believed the Americans were incredibly rude and inconsiderate to be so boisterous and direct. Qing-yu was behaving appropriately for her culture, and so were the Americans; everyone was behaving ethnocentrically. Neither was *inherently* right; all needed to develop a recognition and understanding of the differences so their meetings could be more productive.

As group membership becomes more heterogeneous, the need for intercultural understanding by members of teams and other small groups will increase greatly in the next decades. In this chapter we try to sensitize you to ways in which other cultures and subcultures differ from the "dominant culture" of the United States, thereby improving your communication in groups. Instead of presenting a laundry list of cultures and the characteristics associated with each (a lengthy catalog!), we focus primarily on several broad dimensions on which cultures differ. We offer three caveats as we present this information. First, the study of intercultural communication is a vast and growing field, from which we present only information we believe to be most relevant to small group communication. If the topic of intercultural communication intrigues you, we recommend that you take a course or read books devoted to the subject. Second, we recognize that in many instances we are overgeneralizing. For example, when we say that "white, middle-class Americans prefer direct eye contact," we know there is a lot of variation in the preferences of white, middle-class Americans. We urge you to remember that sometimes there will be as much within-group as between-group variation, especially for pluralistic cultures like the United States. Third, there has been relatively little research on intercultural communication *within small groups.* While much is known about how Mexicans and Arabs behave within their own cultures, almost nothing is known about how Mexicans and Arabs behave when they work *together* in the same small group. In many instances, we are making logical, best guesses about what happens when individuals of different cultures must interact within the same setting. Furthermore, much of what we know about small group behavior comes from research conducted on white, middle-class American college students. But as we noted earlier, the world is becoming more of a global village, and we can expect to see information about intercultural small group communication increase in the future. For now, we rely heavily on findings from studies of *interpersonal* intercultural communication, applying them to small group settings. We turn now to a definition of terms important to your understanding of the effects of culture on small group communication.

What is *Culture?*

Thus far we have used several terms in common usage, but now we define them according to our usage in this book. These terms are *culture, cultural identity, subculture, crosscultural, intercultural,* and *international communication.*

Culture refers to the pattern of values, beliefs, symbols (including language), norms, and behaviors that have been transmitted to and are shared by an identifiable group of individuals. During enculturation (becoming part of a culture), you are "programmed" or taught how to perceive the world, to think, to communicate, and to behave. The teaching is done both formally and informally as you learn the lifestyle of the family and community. This process happens so gradually and automatically that, unless something happens to make us question our behavior, we rarely are aware of the effects of culture on our behavior; we accept our own ways of behaving so thoroughly that the effect of culture is invisible, unless we make a point of looking for it. **Cultural identity** is the "identification with and perceived acceptance into a group that has shared systems of symbols and meanings as well as norms/rules for conduct."[3] In other words, cultural identity refers to the degree to which a person learns, accepts, and identifies with the symbols, meanings, and standards of behavior common to a particular group. Individuals are *taught* such things as language, how and when to speak, how to perceive the world, what is and is not appropriate behavior, and so forth. Each of us belongs to a culture, but, for the most part, we do not examine the cultural values and norms we accept. As in the example of the Taiwanese and American students misinterpreting each other's behavior, we often are oblivious to the behavior guidelines our culture has imparted to us, and we forget that group members from different cultures have been taught to act differently.

Our definition of *culture* is intentionally broad. *Culture* as we define it refers to *any* group of people with a shared identity. For example, a *cultural grouping* can refer to ethnicity (black, white, Hispanic, Greek), a professional grouping (college students, communication professors, nurses, accountants), an interest grouping (hunters, duplicate bridge players), or even gender. In short, any symbol system that is "bounded and salient" to individuals may be termed a culture.[4] Sometimes a grouping that sees itself as distinct, but is part of a larger culture, is termed a **sub-culture.** For example, your coauthors consider themselves to be part of the middle-class American culture, and also part of the subculture *professional educators.* We share certain values and beliefs with other professional educators that are very important to us: a belief in the value of education, both for its own sake and as the way to solve many societal problems; similar ideas about what does and does not constitute a good education; a desire to place education high on a list of funding priorities; and so forth. When we interact with professional educators (at our university, at professional conferences, during chance encounters on airplanes, etc.) we take these beliefs for granted—we accept them as "givens." Other examples of subcultural groupings include rural and urban; white collar and blue collar; eastern, southern, western, and midwestern United States; Roman Catholic and Jewish; and many more.

Each of us belongs to several different subcultures simultaneously. For example, Gloria is both white, middle class, AND Greek-American; Jack is both white, middle class, AND a shepherd. Whether a particular subcultural identification is important in a given circumstance depends on the specific features of that circumstance. For example, Gloria's identification as a Greek-American is more salient when she attends festivals where there is Greek food and dancing than when she attends professional conferences. Jack thinks of himself as a shepherd when he talks with other farmers, at sheep sales, or at workshops for shepherds.

It is important to understand and think about your culture because it affects *everything* you do, particularly your communication behavior.[5] The behaviors and attitudes we adopt from our culture are learned, not innate, but they are lasting. Cultures do change, but slowly. Later, we will examine several specific dimensions that vary by culture; for now, recognize that one's culture is an important determinant of communication behavior. During **intracultural communication** (among individuals from the same culture or subculture), much of the communication behavior can be taken for granted. However, during **intercultural communication** (among individuals from different cultures or subcultures), participants must be alert to the added potential for misunderstanding. An American manager talking to an Arabic counterpart is an instance of intercultural communication, as is a native of Springfield, Missouri, talking to someone from New York City. In a sense, *every* act of communication has intercultural elements because each individual is a *unique* blend of learned behaviors.[6] Kim describes a continuum of intercultural communication, with *intercultural communication* at one end and *intracultural* at the other.[7] As is shown in figure 5.1, all encounters are more or less intercultural, but none are *purely* one or the other. Thus, communication among members of an Eskimo family living in a remote area of Alaska will be almost purely *intra*cultural,

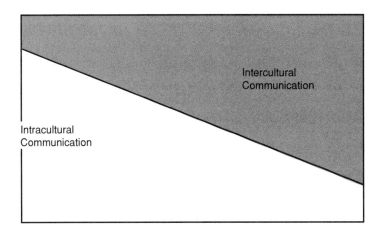

Figure 5.1
Degrees of
intercultural
communication.

Intercultural
Communication

Intracultural
Communication

whereas a conference of Japanese and American legislators who do not speak each other's languages would be extremely *inter*cultural. As you can imagine, the more intercultural communication becomes, the greater the potential for communication malfunctions.

Several other terms must be clarified. **Crosscultural communication** refers to the study of one particular phenomenon in two or more cultures. For example, a researcher may want to observe how personal space is used in the Native American, African-American, and midwestern white American cultures. *Intercultural communication,* on the other hand, focuses on how a mixed group of Native, African-, and midwestern white Americans negotiates personal space during meetings. More research has been conducted on crosscultural phenomena than on intercultural ones; crosscultural findings can help us understand intercultural interactions. **International communication** refers to interaction between individuals from two different countries, but it may be more *intra*cultural (e.g., between a white American and an English-speaking Canadian) than *inter*cultural (e.g., between an American and a Korean).

Now that we have introduced you to these important terms, we turn to a discussion of five broad characteristics that differ from culture to culture and that significantly influence group members' communication behaviors.

It is clear that cultures differ, and it is interesting to consider *why.* Factors such as a culture's history, ecology, biology, and availability of technology, contribute to creating the differences we all observe.[8] For example, life in cold climates is necessarily different from life in hot climates; therefore, communication patterns will evolve differently. Whatever the particular combination of factors that shaped a culture's communication behavior, a number of researchers have investigated particular characteristics that differ across cultures.[9] Although several characteristics have emerged, we focus on five that are especially relevant for communication in small groups. These are *worldview, individualism* versus *collectivism, power distance, uncertainty avoidance,* and *high-* versus *low-context communication.*

**Cultural
Characteristics
that Affect
Communication**

Worldview

Worldview encompasses how we perceive the nature of the world around us and our relationship to it, and the purpose of life. Every culture has a worldview that serves to explain why things are the way they are and where humans fit into the grand scheme of life; this cultural characteristic is highly resistant to change. For example, people from cultures that believe fate controls all human events are more likely to "go with the flow" because they believe their destinies are predetermined. They are not likely suddenly to become "movers and shakers" of events. In contrast, people from cultures emphasizing that change and progress depend solely on the efforts of people will respond quite differently. Eastern and Oriental cultures are much more likely to conceive of life as a river that flows, making it more appropriate for individuals to flow with the river than to try to navigate against it. North Americans and some western Europeans have the opposite conception. They say things like, "If at first you don't succeed, try and try again," indicating a worldview that hard work, with or against the river, is valued. In terms of communication behavior, developing *patience* and allowing discussion to proceed at its own pace without forcing it to a conclusion may be more natural in a go-with-the-flow culture, but difficult for many Americans who want to get to the point in a hurry so they can get things done. Try to imagine what might happen in a small group when individuals with vastly different worldviews attempt to create a solution to the world's global warming problem. Worldview affects one's activity orientation, values, customs and beliefs.

Activity Orientation

Worldview affects one's **activity orientation,** or whether a culture emphasizes *being* or *doing*.[10] Some cultures (e.g., the Hopi) emphasize spontaneity, being "in the moment" and in harmony with nature. In contrast, the majority culture of the United States represents a *doing* orientation, where activities that produce tangible accomplishments are highly valued. For instance, Americans usually ask, "What do you do for a living?" when they first meet someone. We tend to define people more by what they *do* or what they have achieved than by what they *are. Doing* cultures, such as the United States and many other Western countries, believe that the Earth, including nature, can be subjugated in service to humans; *being* cultures, such as the Chinese and many Native American cultures, believe that humans should try to mesh harmoniously with other animal and plant life. When divergent activity orientations such as these encounter one another, communication may be difficult and consensus decision making may be impossible.

Values

Worldview also affects values. The following story, highlighting differences between American and Arab values, exemplifies the types of value differences that can create communication challenges in a small group. Imagine that a man is in a small boat with his mother, wife, and child when it capsizes. Only he can swim, and he can save only one of the other three people. Whom should he save? Rubenstein found that *all* the Arabs he asked would save the mother because a man can always get another wife and child, but he has only one mother. Of one hundred American college freshmen, sixty said they would save the wife and forty the child. They laughed at the idea of saving the mother.[11] Such differences in worldview and values may be impossible to resolve. Imagine how difficult it must be for the Security Council of the United Nations, with such widely diverse cultures represented, to achieve consensus!

The customs, habits, and beliefs of a culture are also affected by that culture's worldview and values. Thus, in a culture where one's purpose in life is associated with bringing honor and good fortune to one's family, communication is likely to center on one's family. For example, a Nigerian student told us how unfriendly he thought Americans were when he first came to the United States. His friends on campus said "Hello" to him and kept walking. In Nigeria, the friends would have stopped, inquired about his mother, father, brothers and sisters, aunts and uncles, and so forth. They would have had a long conversation about their respective families. In another example, a colleague of ours who taught in Malaysia for two years was at first frustrated by the Malaysian students' unwillingness to speak up in class, challenge the professor, and engage in stimulating debate. Instead, the students, saying nothing, sat with downcast eyes. Eventually, he realized that Malaysian students are taught to respect authority and behave deferentially toward their professors, whereas American students are taught to question authority and challenge their professors. He had to change his habitual teaching style in order to communicate effectively with the Malaysian students.

Customs and Beliefs

Some cultures place higher value on individual goals, but others value group goals more. Gudykunst and Ting-Toomey note that in **individualistic cultures** the development of the individual is foremost, even when this is at the expense of the group, whereas in **collectivist cultures** the needs of the group are more important, with individuals expected to conform to the group.[12] As is suggested by the terms, conformity is valued in collectivist cultures, but diversity and dissent are more esteemed in individualistic cultures. People in the United States learn to be individualistic. We admire the person who "marches to a different drummer." The identity of *I* takes precedence over *we,* which leads us to give high priority to *self*-development, *self*-actualization, and *individual* initiative and achievement. We say things such as, "If you don't stand up for yourself, no one else will," and "It's important to stand out from the crowd." We go so far as to encourage group members to *leave* a group if they feel their individual values, beliefs, and preferences are being compromised. In contrast to this are most Oriental and African cultures. For example, a Chinese proverb states, "The nail that sticks up is pounded down." This means that if a member is standing out from the group, the group has the right—even the obligation—to force the individual to conform. In collectivist cultures, the goals, wishes, and opinions of the in-group (the dominant group) always prevail; such cultures value cooperation within the group and slow consensus building rather than direct confrontation in which individual opinions are debated. This was part of Qing-yu's problem described earlier in the chapter. She had been taught that what the Americans were doing was absolutely inappropriate behavior; she was caught in a very difficult bind because the culture surrounding her demanded that she abandon the values and habits of a lifetime.

Individualism versus Collectivism

This explanation about collectivist versus individualistic cultures is important in mixed-culture small groups, primarily because of the effect on communication behaviors. Perhaps some examples will clarify. A colleague of ours worked as a telecommunications consultant, living many months in China and Japan. Initially, he made direct requests and expected others to respond directly.[13] However, in those countries the preferred decision-making style, called *nemawashi* in Japanese,[14] is to talk to each group member individually about the decision without expressing a direct request, but allowing consensus to build gradually throughout the various discussions. Only when each person has moved incrementally to the same point of view can a group discussion be held that allows the decision (which really has been made behind the scenes) to be confirmed. The amount of time such a procedure takes frustrated our colleague. Because he is an American, the Chinese allowed him more leeway to violate their expectations than they would have permitted another Chinese, and once or twice he was able to speed a decision along by being direct. However, he pointed out to us that the leeway was given him only because he was providing a function the Chinese considered valuable—his violations of Chinese norms would not have been tolerated indefinitely.

Brislin et al. provide another example of the collectivist versus individualistic crosscultural theme.[15] A Caucasian teacher in a Hawaiian elementary school will find that native Hawaiian children do not perform well when rewarded for individual performance. Instead, Hawaiian children are socialized to support the group. They are taught not to stand out individually and may feel embarrassed or guilty if the teacher calls attention to them. On the other hand, Hawaiian children perform well when the teacher provides *group* reinforcement; *individual* reinforcement is something they are taught not to value.

Power Distance

Cultures differ with respect to their preferred **power distance,** which is the degree to which power or status differences are minimized or maximized.[16] In low power-distance cultures, such as Austria, Israel, and New Zealand, people believe that power should be distributed equally. For example, in the United States, which is a relatively low power-distance culture, we prize equality under the law; our Declaration of Independence asserts that "all men are created equal." We regard it as deeply unfair for some to receive privileges accorded to them only by accident of birth instead of being earned by hard work or merit. In contrast to this are high power-distance cultures, such as the Philippines, Mexico, and India, where there is a rigid, hierarchical status system and large power distances are preferred. In high power-distance cultures, people believe that each person has his or her rightful place, that leaders or others who have power should have privileges not given to others, and that the authority of those with power should not be questioned. People of some cultures (such as conservative Islam) believe that *God* grants all power to govern, so control of group action flows from a divine source. For example, the will of Saddam Hussein *is* the will of God (Allah), and only Satan (former President George Bush) will oppose him.[17]

Hofstede observed that high power-distance cultures typically have wealth that is distributed extremely unevenly, and access to the educational and political systems of the culture is equally uneven. He also noted that larger cultures usually develop higher power distances. Larger groups need more formalized leadership and communication structures to maintain themselves than smaller groups do. Power tends to be concentrated in the hands of a few people, and members of the culture accept the fairly rigid hierarchy as normal and desirable. (Compare, for example, the "old" General Motors with G.M.'s new Saturn Division.)

Lustig and Cassotta have summarized research that examines how power distance might affect small group communication.[18] They found that power distance is related to leadership styles and preferences, conformity, and discussion procedures. High power-distance cultures value authoritarian, directive leadership, whereas low power-distance cultures value participative, democratic leadership. An American group leader trying to use a participative leadership style in a group of Mexicans or Filipinos is likely to be seen as inept or incompetent. Related to this are the discussion procedures members prefer. Participation in group discussions and decisions is preferred by persons who believe their individual opinions should be valued regardless of status (i.e., low power-distance cultures), but decision making by the leader, with minimal participation from the group, is the norm in high power-distance cultures. People from high power-distance cultures believe it is appropriate for low-status group members to conform to the desires of high-status members; however, in low power-distance cultures, members will be less likely to conform. We Americans tend to assume, ethnocentrically, that everyone wants a chance to participate in decisions that affect them. That reflects our deeply held cultural values stemming from our relatively low power-distance culture. However, we should not assume that persons from other cultures share our preferences; many do not.

Uncertainty avoidance refers to how well people in a particular culture tolerate ambiguity and uncertainty.[19] Does unpredictability make us anxious or eager? Low uncertainty avoidance cultures have a high tolerance for ambiguity, are more willing to take risks, have less rigid rules, and accept a certain amount of deviance and dissent. These include countries such as Great Britain, Sweden, and Hong Kong. At the other end of the continuum are countries such as Greece, Japan, and Belgium, where people prefer to avoid ambiguous situations. These cultures use rules to help establish security and clear-cut norms of behavior; all members of the culture are expected to behave in accordance with the standards of behavior, and dissent is not appreciated. People from such cultures often have a strong internalized work ethic. The United States is a fairly low uncertainty avoidance culture.

Uncertainty Avoidance

Lustig and Koester note that when low and high uncertainty avoidance individuals come together, they may threaten or frighten each other.[20] Low avoidance people, such as most Americans, are perceived as too unconventional by their high avoidance counterparts. On the other hand, high avoidance people are seen as too structured or uncompromising by the low avoiders.

Uncertainty avoidance helps determine what people perceive as appropriate communication from supervisors. For example, Earley and Stubblebine investigated how American and British workers reacted to performance feedback from supervisors.[21] The performance of the Americans, who are higher in uncertainty avoidance than Britons, was more directly affected by the feedback they received. Americans want and expect their supervisors to suggest ways their performance can be improved. British workers have less of a need to reduce uncertainty; they also perceive feedback as interference rather than help.

Uncertainty avoidance also affects preferences for leadership styles, conformity, and discussion processes.[22] Cultures high in avoidance rely on clear rules, consistently enforced, with the leader expected to structure the work of the group and behave autocratically. Low avoidance cultures prefer democratic leadership approaches. High avoidance cultures value predictability and security; nonconformist behavior threatens this predictability. Conformity to the leader and group opinion is the norm for high avoidance cultures, whereas dissent and disagreement are tolerated, even encouraged, in low avoidance cultures. The need for structure and clear procedures is characteristic of high avoidance cultures. Lustig and Cassotta postulate that this should produce groups that are more task-oriented in high avoidance cultures and more relationship-oriented in low avoidance cultures.

Low- versus High-Context Communication

The final cultural characteristic we will consider is what Hall termed low-versus high-context communication.[23] A culture with **low-context communication** is one where the primary meaning of a message is carried by the verbal, or explicit, part of the message, whereas in **high-context communication** the primary meaning is conveyed by certain features of the situation. In other words, in a high-context culture, what is *not* said may be more important in determining meaning than what *is* said. In low-context cultures, such as those of Germany, Switzerland, the Scandinavian countries, and the United States, direct, clear, and unambiguous statements are valued. The suggestions we provided in chapter 4 for conducting organized and effective group discussions are appropriate for low-context cultures such as ours. We expect people to state precisely what they mean so there can be little room for doubt, no matter what the situation (i.e., context) happens to be. The same verbal message given in different contexts means about the same thing. For example, "No, I don't agree with that idea," said in a straightforward way means much the same thing whether you are in a meeting of co-workers, at the family dinner table, or meeting with your church board. In contrast, high-context cultures such as China, Japan, and South Korea prefer ambiguity, with several shades of meaning possible because this helps preserve harmony and allows people to save face. In China, instead of "No, I don't agree with that idea," you are more likely to hear, "Perhaps we could explore that option." You would have to be well versed in Chinese communication patterns to know whether that statement means "No, we don't like it" or "We like it very much, but we must build consensus slowly" or "We don't know whether we like it or not until we explore it more fully." Moreover, you would also have to be astute at reading clues in the situation—for instance, is this in reaction to the boss's suggestion, or to a younger co-worker's? Complicated, isn't it? To us, unfamiliar with the Chinese pattern, it seems as though the Chinese are beating around the bush.[24]

Gudykunst and Ting-Toomey note that low-context cultures also tend to be individualistic, and high-context cultures tend to be collectivist.[25] Collectivist cultures operate by consensus of the group; individuals try not to risk offending another member of the group as this might upset a delicate balance of agreement and harmony. Apparently, ambiguity allows individuals to express opinions tentatively rather than directly without the risk of affronting others and upsetting the balance. Okabe notes also that because low-context cultures such as the United States

In the future, effective group discussion will increasingly require sensitivity to cultural differences.

Photo by Blair Seitz/Photo Researchers

display cultural diversity where little can be taken for granted, verbal skills are probably more necessary, and thus more valued.[26] In a high-context culture such as Japan, the high degree of cultural homogeneity means that more can be taken for granted (and thus remain unspoken) during the communication process. In fact, most Japanese value silence more than we do and are suspicious of displays of verbal skills.[27]

You can imagine how difficult group communication can be when members from a high-context culture try to interact with members from a low-context culture. Again, this was part of the problem faced by Qing-yu and the Americans. The harder the Americans tried to force her to take a stand, get to the point, and be direct, the more she retreated into her familiar orientation of ambiguity and indirectness. The misunderstanding was severe.

The five characteristics we have just discussed determine what is considered appropriate verbal and nonverbal communicative behavior in a particular culture. We now present information about how communication differs from culture to culture.

Crosscultural Communication Differences

Differences in language and language use are probably the most obvious sources of misunderstanding. Our most important symbol system is our language, including both vocabulary and rules of usage. However, it is not just the fact that we use different symbol codes that makes communication difficult. Some researchers believed that language in fact *determines* how we experience our world; although

Language

deterministic views have been softened, it is clear that our language code helps shape what we perceive in several fundamental and profound ways.[28] For example, several languages, including German and Spanish, have more than one form of the pronoun *you*. A formal or polite version is used to address people the speaker doesn't know very well; another informal or familiar form is used to address family members and friends. What does this say about the relative formality, display of respect, and egalitarianism in such cultures? The Eskimo language has many words for *snow*, depending on the type of snow, whether it has already fallen or continues to fall, and so forth. It is important for a people who must survive in snow to recognize differences in snow patterns; it is also important that this recognition skill be passed along to new members of the culture (i.e., children) so they can learn to perceive survival-related features of their world. We discussed in chapter 4 how some Native American languages have different verb forms depending on whether the speaker actually observed the event being discussed or learned of it in some other way. Other Native American languages, such as that of the Hopi, have no past, present, or future tense. These cultures are spontaneous and experience *time* as what happens in the present moment. You can imagine the difficulty a Hopi and a white, middle-class American might have trying to coordinate efforts in a small group. Thus, language barriers are not limited to different code usages; rather, they include a number of *perceptual* differences that can be equally troublesome.

Not only are symbol systems and usages different, but preferred organizational patterns differ as well.[29] For example, consider what many of you have been taught by your English teachers, who suggest starting an essay with a main thesis, developing the thesis and supporting it with evidence, and presenting a clear conclusion that summarizes the main points. That linear presentation is the preferred organizational pattern for U.S. English. However, other cultures prefer different patterns. Many Eastern cultures, for instance, prefer an indirect approach to the topic and use a more inductive than deductive pattern. Sometimes students who complain about experiencing difficulty in courses taught by foreign teaching assistants or professors are reacting more negatively to the organizational pattern than to the mispronunciation of some words.

Inability to use the same language code (i.e., to speak the same language) presents significant obstacles to understanding. Gloria and her friend Noah, who speak no Czech, recently visited the Czech Republic, where they were entirely dependent on friends who spoke no English; they communicated using a common second language, Esperanto, which none of them spoke fluently. Although they had many wonderful encounters, the experience of trying to communicate in a language in which they were not fluent was stressful; much interesting and rich information was lost in translation. That is the experience of many foreign students in colleges and universities throughout the United States who must expend considerable energy listening and trying to decipher the content of messages; little energy is available for the nuances and subtleties of the interaction. For example, the word *yes* spoken by a Korean may mean something different than if it is spoken by an American. Park and Kim note that Koreans sometimes use *yes* when an American might say *no*. "Didn't you go to school yesterday?" elicits the following Korean response: "Yes, I didn't."[30] Although *yes* sometimes means agreement, it can also acknowledge that the Korean listener has heard a question, or that the Korean fully understands what the speaker is saying and is encouraging him or her to continue. Koreans use *yes* to maintain harmony and the appearance of harmony by avoiding appearing negative.

Communication difficulties can occur even between native speakers of the same language. For example, have you ever asked for *tonic* in the Midwest and received a puzzled look in return? *Tonic* in New England and *pop* or *soda* in the Midwest mean the same thing. Does *dinner* or *supper* mean *the evening meal* to you? One of our colleagues, a native-born Canadian, circulated a memo asking us to provide our yearly activity reports for merit in "point form." Faculty members were confused until someone noted that *point form* to a Canadian means *outline form* to someone from the United States. These misunderstandings are minor and easily overcome; not so with other misunderstandings.

We noted in chapter 3 that symbols do not have inherent meanings, only arbitrary ones. This makes it particularly difficult to translate from one language to another. For example, consider the word *family*. In English, *family* usually means one's nuclear family (parents and siblings, or spouse and children). The Turkish word *aile* translates as *family,* but the meaning includes a group of relatives that goes back to the oldest known living male relative, with all that man's male offspring, their wives, sons, and unmarried daughters.[31] An Englishman and a Turk talking about their families may think they are conversing about the same thing, but are bypassing each other to a large extent. In another example of translation difficulty, one of us heard a radio interview with a woman who develops sales presentations for American companies that want to conduct business in Japan. She nearly lost one client when, intending to say "I hope we have a long and productive relationship," she used a word that translates as *productive* in English but means something slightly different in Japanese. What the Japanese actually perceived her to say was "I hope we have many children together."

One final example illustrates pitfalls that can occur with the verbal aspects of intercultural communication. In graduate school, Gloria worked on a committee to analyze data by computer. Two Arab students were members of this committee. Responsible for writing the instructions for the computer analysis, Gloria named the file "BEGIN" to indicate "here's where to start." The Arab students, believing she had named the file *BEGIN* after Menachem Begin, prime minister of Israel, felt they had been deliberately insulted and protested vehemently to the course professor. They were focusing on cues most salient to them. It took a long time to unravel the source of the friction, but even though the mistake was innocent, trust among the group members was permanently impaired.

As important as language is to intercultural communication, nonverbal signals are often more important, as well as more difficult to interpret. In the next section, we highlight several of the best-documented cultural differences in nonverbal signal use.

As we explained in the previous chapter, nonverbal signals include every perceivable signal except the words themselves. There is considerable crosscultural variation in the types of nonverbal behavior exhibited by people.

Nonverbal Signals

Paralanguage

Intertwined with language is paralinguistic behavior, or the *way* a person speaks—speed, pitch, force, pronunciation, and so forth. Often what people react negatively to in another's speech is not the *content* of what is said so much as the *manner* in which it is spoken. For example, Tubbs and Moss explain that in Arab countries men are expected to show their strength and sincerity by speaking loudly; however, the volume acceptable to Arabs is perceived by Americans as aggressive and obnoxious.[32] A Saudi Arab may lower his voice to indicate respect to a superior, but in a conversation with an American this may create confusion. In the United States, when someone wants another to speak louder, the first person will raise his/her voice; when the American speaks louder, the Arab assumes he is being told his behavior is not respectful enough, so he lowers his voice even more, causing the American to raise his even more. This escalating cycle frustrates and angers both people.

Pierce relates the story of a woman from New York City who offended many guests by her bossiness at a party.[33] She appeared to be ordering everyone around, but Pierce, taking careful note of her behavior, observed that her *words* seemed perfectly polite and appropriate for the situation. It was her *intonation pattern* that was offensive. Her particular pattern, appropriate and customary for New York City dwellers, was perceived as domineering by persons from other areas. Similarly, one of us has a friend who grew up in New Jersey and has the same aggressive speech pattern as many New Yorkers. When she moved to the Midwest, she had to learn to soften the staccato quality of her speech and slow her rate so as not to create problems with her co-workers.

Cultural differences have been observed in the use of the **backchannel,** which refers to vocalizations such as *mm-hmmm, uh-huh,* and *yeah-yeah-yeah* that are uttered while another is speaking to indicate interest and active listening. Anderson claims that white Americans do not give such backchannel responses as frequently as African-Americans, Hispanics, and people of southern European origins.[34] This can lead to friction if members who use the backchannel frequently think those who do not are not really attuned and listening well, while the less active backchannel responders perceive their fellow members as being rude for interrupting so often.

Dialect may also cause misunderstandings. **Dialect** entails regional and social variations in pronunciation, vocabulary, and grammar of a language. Most countries, including the United States, Canada, Great Britain, and Japan, have regional and social class deviations to the "standard" dialect. We tend to stereotype individuals with nonstandard dialects. Klopf alerts us to the ways in which someone's dialect affects our perceptions of that person. For example, people who use *dees* and *does* instead of *these* and *those* are identified as lower-status speakers and accorded lower credibility ratings. Speakers of the general American dialect are rated higher than Appalachians and Bostonians on socio-intellectual status, dynamism, and being pleasant to listen to. Those who speak a French-Canadian dialect are rated as poor and ignorant in comparison with those who speak an English-Canadian dialect. Teachers tend to rate students who use dialects other than general American as less confident and more ignorant. Because dialect influences perceptions of a speaker's intelligence and competence, it can seriously affect employability and performance,[35] as well as credibility. It is important to be aware of judgment errors that result from such perceptions. Tubbs and Moss note, however, that as intercultural communication becomes more widespread, cultures become increasingly similar.[36] Although some of the richness and diversity is being lost, there is less misunderstanding as a world culture emerges from intercultural exchanges fostered by such forces as Cable News Network (CNN).

Kinesic behavior varies considerably from culture to culture.[37] Even facial expressions such as smiling cannot be assumed to mean the same in all cultures. For example, a smile in Japan may be a spontaneous expression of pleasure, but it may also represent the desire not to cause pain for someone else.[38] A smiling Japanese may say to you, "I just came from my mother's funeral." According to Japanese rules of etiquette, it is extremely bad form to inflict unpleasantness on someone else; thus, no matter how bad someone feels inside, a cheerful face must be presented to the world. *Kinesics*

Americans prefer direct eye contact with their conversational partners, but in some cultures (e.g., most Native American cultures) this is perceived as rude, while in still others (e.g., Arabic cultures) intense staring is the norm.[39] Hispanic children are taught to lower their gaze to indicate respect, but this can backfire in cases where Hispanic children interact with members of the dominant American culture.[40] For example, white American teachers and police officers sometimes misinterpret a lowered gaze as sullenness. Many African-Americans, too, tend to avoid eye contact, especially with someone of higher status.[41]

The handshake, a standard American greeting, is by no means universal. The willingness to touch hands suggests a belief in the equality of people.[42] This typically Western notion contrasts with the Hindu belief in a hierarchical society. Hindus greet each other by bringing their own palms together at the chest. Muslims, who according to the *Koran* are all brothers, hug each other shoulder to shoulder. The Japanese bow in greeting, but prefer to avoid physical contact. You can see how a culture's power distance (such as a belief in equality versus a belief in hierarchy) influences such things as the appropriate nonverbal form for a greeting, and also how easy it is for misunderstandings to occur in small groups with members of different cultures.

The use of space differs widely among cultures. In the high-contact cultures of South America, southern and eastern Europe, and Arab countries, people prefer to stand close, whereas in low-contact cultures such as northern Europe, North America, and Japan, people prefer more space.[43] In fact, members of Arabic cultures feel reassured when they stand close enough to be able to smell their conversational partners. Westerners, however, are usually uncomfortable with such close contact and tend to back away, causing Arabs to mistrust their intentions. *Space*

In small groups, individuals usually try to place themselves at a comfortable conversational distance according to the norms of their own cultures. Naturally, this can cause problems if the participants are members of cultures with divergent norms about appropriate distance; they may interpret unexpected behavior of others as rudeness or aggressiveness. For example, we know a New England native who has a somewhat greater than usual need to maintain physical distance between herself and others. In lines or other public places where people are crowded together, she becomes extremely uncomfortable and perceives as pushy those who try to close the space. On the other hand, one of us once had a friend from Alabama whose relatively small sense of personal space caused her to move in closer to her co-workers in Ohio, who kept backing away. Finally, they began to joke about her "invasion of their personal space," and both she and her co-workers learned something about their own subcultural rules.

Seating preferences have been found to vary across cultures. Summarizing research in this area, Ramsey explains that Americans show liking with close interpersonal seating, a forward lean, direct orientation toward the other, and eye contact. Leaders seem to gravitate to head positions, with high-status individuals sitting nearby. Similar behaviors occur in Japan, where the leader sits at one end of a rectangular table, and, the lower the rank, the farther away the seat. In some cultures, teachers and others need to be careful in assigning seats for fear of inadvertently violating cultural taboos about who may sit next to whom. In a few cultures, people sit opposite each other when they have differences to settle, but sit side-by-side in rows when eating or enjoying one another's company.[44] Ramsey cautioned that most of what we know about seating patterns comes from research on Westerners; it may not hold true for people of other cultures.

Time

In the previous chapter we explained that concepts of time are not consistent from one culture to another. Hall describes the Spanish culture of New Mexico as *polychronic,* while the Anglo culture is *monochronic.*[45] The Spanish do several things at a time, while the Anglos tend to do one thing at a time. The Spanish are casual about clocks and schedules; they are frequently late for appointments and meetings. Anglos are offended by such behavior. The collectivist cultures of Latin America, the Middle East, Japan, and France are polychronic, whereas the individualistic cultures of northern Europe, North America, and Germany are monochronic.[46] In individualistic cultures, time is treated as a tangible *thing* that can be spent, killed, and wasted; time is perceived as more relational in collectivist cultures, which integrate task and social needs and hold more fluid attitudes about time. People from individualistic cultures believe time can be controlled, but those from collectivist cultures tend to see time and space as renewing themselves without the imposition of people.

Differences in time and space patterns can cause irritation and resentment during intercultural encounters. For example, a colleague of ours, the author of a Spanish textbook, described her frustration with making appointments with colleagues in South America. She sometimes had to wait hours before she would be seen. As Hall says,

> One of the matters that keeps holding up progress is reluctance on the part of the human family to recognize the cultural and identity needs of their neighbors and fellow passengers on the "Spaceship Earth." We keep looking at each other in hierarchical, evaluative ways—as though some are less worthy or have less to contribute than others. But talent is everywhere, and I feel it can be not only shortsighted but sinful to fail to use talent wherever it is.[47]

Often the unconscious nonverbal signals we have discussed determine how much we like or trust someone. We all have a tendency to like people we perceive as similar to us, but we are unaware that our feelings are often based on *nonverbal* similarity.[48] It is important for us to recognize this normal tendency and consciously suspend judgments of others in intercultural settings where the same nonverbal behaviors have different meanings.

Earlier we described *culture* as something that is learned, a set of expectations and behaviors that we absorb. We view *gender* and *race* behavior, too, as largely culturally transmitted. With little conscious effort we learn to become *a female* or *a male,* or an *African-American* or *a Euro-American,* in the same way we learn to become *a salesclerk* or *a Protestant.*[49]

Gender and Race as Culture

We refer to learned characteristics and psychological attributes of masculinity and femininity as **gender,** and the inherent biological characteristics with which we are born as **sex.** We caution you that while there appear to be differences in the way men and women communicate, researchers do not know precisely which differences have biological origins (i.e., sex differences) and which have cultural origins (i.e., gender differences); however, research suggests that most differences are learned, not inborn. Moreover, research findings are often inconsistent. Female and male gender roles have been changing rapidly in the past thirty years, so differences observed many years ago do not necessarily hold true today. In addition, current research findings will almost certainly be out of date years from now because our roles as men and women continue to change.

Gender

An extensive review of findings about gender differences has been provided by Stewart et al.[50] In spoken communication gender differences have been observed in verbosity, interrupting, and initiating behaviors. Men talk more and interrupt more, but that may be changing, as recent research with college students did not find these differences. Women initiate more topics but, in part because men provide more minimal responses ("uh huh," or "yeah") without elaboration, more topics introduced by women are dropped in conversation than those introduced by men. Women often ask questions to maintain conversations; however, men usually ask questions to acquire information. Women speak more deferentially and tentatively. In the past, women were reported to ask more *tag* questions ("It's a good idea, *isn't it?*"), but recent research does not confirm those early findings.

Most researchers propose cultural rather than biological or psychological explanations for the differences that have been observed. For instance, Maltz and Borker concluded that men and women seem to have different rules about what constitutes friendly conversation, about how to conduct such conversation, and what certain behaviors mean.[51] For women, backchannel responses seem to mean, "I'm paying attention to you, keep talking," but for men they seem to mean, "I agree with you" or "I follow you so far." A male speaker receiving "mm-hmms" from a woman is likely to believe she agrees with him, but a woman speaker receiving only occasional "mm-hmms" from a man is likely to believe he is not listening. Men often complain that women *say* they agree with them but it's impossible to tell what women *really* think; women often complain that men don't listen. Both complaints may stem from misunderstandings caused by two conflicting sets of cultural rules for conducting conversation.

The view that male-female differences in communication are primarily culture based is further supported by Mulac et al.'s review of recent gender comparison studies.[52] These writers characterize men's talk as direct, succinct, personal (heavy use of "I"), and instrumental (task-oriented). Women's talk is characterized as indirect, elaborate, contextual, and affective. Note that these differences are tendencies, not inviolable rules. Mulac and associates attribute the differences between men's and women's communication to cultural learning rather than biology.

McCroskey et al. report that women display more facial and other signs of emotion than men.[53] In situations where males tend to sit or stand upright with their legs apart and hands on hips, women often clasp their hands together and fold their arms across their bodies. Women sit and stand closer to others, especially other females, than men do. Men sit closer to women than to other men, but require more personal space than females. Stewart et al. suggest that men's normal behavior signifies power and status, whereas women's conveys subordination.[54] Women display more signs of interpersonal liking (immediacy), men more signs of power (potency). Both sexes display responsiveness, although the nature of the responsiveness differs.

In the small group field, sex differences have been investigated more than other intercultural phenomena. In an early summary of such research, Baird reported that women were more expressive (paying attention to the relationships among group members, expressing concern for others, displaying emotions) and men were more instrumental (oriented to the task, factual, analytical).[55] More recent research indicates that male-female behaviors have changed, but some differences still appear. For example, Smith-Lovin and Brody found that men interrupt women more often than other men, but women interrupt men and women equally.[56] Men give more supportive interruption attempts in all-male groups, and the more women in the group, the less likely the men are to interrupt supportively. Men are less likely to yield to negative interruption attempts, women much more likely to yield to them. They concluded that men seem to consider sex to be a status variable, whereas women do not, but the findings are more complex than previously thought. Women do not simply give in to higher status individuals; instead, an interplay of sex, status, group composition, and gender salience affects the specific interaction. Verdi and Wheelan suggest that differences are exaggerated.[57] They found that all-male and all-female groups behaved the same, but mixed-sex groups behaved differently; group size seemed to be a more important factor than sex. Although early findings showed that men talked more than women, recent studies have produced mixed results. Mabry even found that women dominated group interaction and seemed to prefer interaction with other women more than with men, and that men showed subtle forms of resistance to a dominant presence of women.[58]

Some researchers have found that male leaders of small groups are more effective, but recent findings show that both men and women can behave in similar ways in groups, and neither sex is more effective than the other. Jurma and Wright

observed that the leader's sex made no differences in members' perceptions of
leaders who lost reward power during group discussions.[59] They concluded that
men and women are equally capable of leading task-oriented groups. This conclusion is supported by Andrews, who noted that it is more important to consider the
unique character of a group and the skills of the person serving as leader than sex.[60]
She suggested that a complex interplay of factors (including how much power the
leader has) influences effectiveness. Power was also a factor in Duerst-Lahti's
study of successful, high-status business women and men.[61] She observed that, contrary to the findings of others, women were not frozen out of conversations. The
women talked more often but for shorter periods, gave more indications of verbal
support, and freely challenged the men. They had power in the group, and their
ideas and proposals were included in the final product. They seemed to have mas-
tered the use of power just as effectively as the men.

Several studies suggest that, despite *actual* behavior, men and women are
perceived differently. For instance, Carli found that men and women behaved similarly, but that women spoke more tentatively in mixed-sex dyads. However, they
were more influential with men, but less so with other women, when they spoke
tentatively.[62] Burrell et al. compared trained and untrained mediators of both
sexes.[63] No male-female differences were observed in the behavior of trained mediators, but untrained female mediators were more controlling. However, the men,
whether trained or not, were *perceived* as more controlling. Other studies indicate
that perceptions of effectiveness depend on factors other than gender. Canary and
Spitzberg examined how men and women handled conflict episodes.[64] They concluded that the *approach* (i.e., using win-win strategies), not the sex, determined effectiveness, with each sex perceived as being equally effective.

About the only things we can conclude from this brief review are that gender
expectations and behaviors are in a state of rapid flux, and that differences are
largely a result of culture rather than sex. Remember, whatever is learned can be
changed.

Race

If multicultural societies like the United States are to succeed, it is absolutely
imperative that we learn to interact with people who are different from us. As we
noted earlier, intercultural groups of diverse Americans will become the norm in
the next century. In this section we discuss several of the communication differences between black and white Americans. We do not intend to imply that relationships between Hispanics and whites, or Asians and blacks, are not equally important. However, we elected to discuss black-white communication because
misunderstandings here appear to be among the most serious and volatile at
this time.

Foeman and Pressley have summarized research that describes "typical" (although we caution you again that there is no such thing as "typical") black communication, particularly in organizational settings.[65] Black culture in the United States
is an oral culture, so verbal inventiveness and virtuosity of expression are highly
valued. What many whites perceive as boastfulness Foeman and Pressley call assertiveness, which takes both verbal and nonverbal forms (trying to top someone
else's boast, strutting across the street). Black managers are perceived as forthright

or overly reactive. In a conflict, for instance, a black is more likely to confront an individual directly, whereas a white manager is more likely to approach the problem indirectly. Consequently, some blacks perceive whites as underreactive, but some whites see blacks as overreactive. Degree of responsiveness (expressiveness) differs; blacks are more likely to respond both verbally and physically (e.g., gesturing often with their hands), whereas whites tend to focus on verbal responses. Blacks make less direct eye contact, but they compensate by standing closer to their conversational partner than most whites. These differences in cultural communication patterns can create serious misunderstandings. For instance, a white expecting more eye contact may be likely to repeat or rephrase statements in order to get the expected signs of understanding (such as eye contact), while the black feels the white is being condescending.

The black culture is more collective than the more dominant white culture of the United States. According to Foeman and Pressley, this may lead to such strong black identification with blacks *as a group* that a black person may be unwilling or unable to work with people of different ethnic groups. However, the communal structure of the black culture helps offset the discrimination and prejudice many blacks still receive in this culture.

Blacks and whites express themselves verbally in different ways. Blacks are more playful than most whites in their use of language and relish playing verbal games. Foeman and Pressley explain that blacks *signify* (or hint) at questions rather than asking them directly because they perceive disclosure of personal information to be voluntary; thus, questions are implied so that the person being asked will not feel vulnerable or obliged to answer. In addition, blacks use the backchannel (also referred to as *call-response*) to indicate interest and involvement in the discussion. For example, in black churches the services resemble a dialogue, with congregation members freely calling *Amen, Go ahead, Preach* to the minister; such responses would be less frequent in most white churches. Differences in black-white uses of the backchannel, as we discussed earlier, can create misunderstandings and cause hurt feelings.

This discussion of race and gender has not even begun to scratch the surface, and is not intended to be exhaustive. It is intended to encourage you to think about your own behavior with an eye toward sensitizing you to ethnocentric behavior that may cause problems in a group. Two recent studies by Kirchmeyer indicate that minority members of groups are often the lowest contributors.[66] Two plausible explanations for this are that minorities may lack a sense of belonging to the group and that, while they may be skilled in communication within their own culture, they may lack the skills to communicate effectively in groups composed primarily of whites. Kirchmeyer found that the *gender* characteristics of low masculinity, high femininity, and minority status affected contribution levels, and she cautions that multicultural groups may not be encompassing the multiple perspectives of all their members in the final products. This represents a significant loss to all of us. Whether we are black, white, female, male, urban, rural, or whatever, we must begin to recognize that differences are just that—differences! They do not imply that someone from another culture is wrong, stupid, or uneducated. To be ethical group members, we must learn as much as we can about other cultures to help prevent serious misunderstandings and to ensure that all views are represented.

In intercultural small group communication,

Remember that every discussion is intercultural to some extent. Because each of us has a unique background, do not assume that we use verbal and nonverbal signals to mean exactly the same things.

Recognize and accept differences; abandon ethnocentricity. Instead of judging others wrong for behaving in ways different from yours, recognize that each of us is the product of our culture. Resolve to learn from each other, not try to change each other.

Resist making attributions of stupidity or ill intent; ask whether the other member's behavior could have a cultural origin. When another member's behavior seems rude, inconsiderate, or unusual, ask yourself whether you could be observing a cultural difference in what is considered appropriate behavior before you decide the other member is worthless to the group.

Initiate discussion of differences you observe. When you observe differences that seem to have cultural origins, you have the opportunity to enrich everyone's understanding by pointing out the cultural differences and initiating a discussion about how the cultures vary.

Be willing to adapt to differences. Instead of insisting that others follow the prescriptions of your culture, be willing to adapt your behavior to different cultural practices when appropriate.

Figure 5.2
Guidelines for intercultural small group communication.

Becoming Interculturally Competent

Becoming interculturally competent requires us to examine what we believe about ethical behavior. You know by now that various cultures and subcultures have different rules about what is appropriate communicative behavior. What is considered rhetorically sensitive and appropriate communication depends on the culture.[67] If cultures differ, are there any principles for communicating competently and ethically in intercultural groups? Kale has proposed two broad principles that should govern intercultural interactions: we should protect the worth and dignity of all human beings, and we should act in such a way as to promote peace among all people.[68] We believe two of the ethical principles described in chapter 1 extend logically from Kale's global principles: that we work to understand others as they want to be understood and that we act to support the identity and self-concept of others. Lustig and Koester suggest that this behavior can be promoted by acting with respect and empathy, encouraging others to explain themselves and their perceptions, and learning to tolerate some ambiguity.

Chen describes four communicative competencies that foster effective interpersonal intercultural communication that we think apply well to members of small groups.[69] First, *personal attributes* include high self-knowledge and awareness, the ability to self-disclose, and the ability to relax socially. Usually, persons who have these attributes also have high self-esteem, thinking well of themselves and others. Second, effective intercultural communicators need a variety of *communication skills,* including being flexible in interaction, empathic, and able to take turns during interaction. Third, *psychological adjustment* is needed so the member of a multicultural group can appropriately handle feelings of stress and frustration. Finally, *cultural awareness* is needed so members understand how differences in culture affect people's communicative behaviors. These principles are embodied in the guidelines suggested in figure 5.2.

Summary

The need for effective intercultural communicators in small groups increases as we move toward the twenty-first century. People are needed who will abandon their ethnocentricity and learn to appreciate, rather than denigrate, different communication assumptions and behaviors. A variety of important terms were defined, including *culture, subculture,* and *intracultural, intercultural, international,* and *crosscultural communication.* Among the most important characteristics that vary crossculturally are worldview, the levels of individualism and collectivism, power distance, uncertainty avoidance, and high- and low-context communication. *Worldview,* the encompassing set of beliefs about the nature and purpose of life, helps determine our values, activity orientation, customs, beliefs, and behaviors. In individualistic cultures, the needs of the individual take precedence over the group; in collectivist cultures, the needs of the group predominate. In high-power distance cultures, members prefer a rigid hierarchical structure with high-status individuals accorded more privileges. In high uncertainty avoidance cultures, people work hard to reduce uncertainty levels and prefer clarity and predictability of communication patterns and behaviors. People in low-context cultures convey their primary meaning with the words they speak, but people in high-context cultures value ambiguity and rely on contextual features to determine meaning. These broad aspects of culture influence both verbal and nonverbal communication patterns. The most obvious difference is in language, but nonverbal behaviors such as paralanguage, movements, use of space, and conceptions of time differ as well.

Gender and race differences appear to be primarily culturally determined and are undergoing rapid change. Verbally and nonverbally, men tend to display more signs of power and women more signs of liking. Men and women seem to have different rules about how conversations should be conducted and assign different meanings to such behaviors as asking questions and providing backchannel responses. However, since gender roles are changing rapidly, behaviors associated with males and females are also changing. Black and white differences in communication also are culturally based. Black culture, which is more oral and collective than traditional white culture, values verbal inventiveness and playfulness. Blacks learn to expect listeners to carry on a continuing dialogue with speakers in the form of an active backchannel. Being aware of such differences can help groups of black and white members avoid misunderstanding and unnecessary conflict.

Finally, suggestions for becoming an effective intercultural communicator were presented that spring from two overarching ethical principles that should guide intercultural encounters: the worth and dignity of humans should be protected, and peace among all people should be promoted.

Exercises

1. List all the cultures and subcultures with which you feel a strong identification. Form groups of five or six; share and discuss your lists. What do you think are the most salient characteristics of each item on your list? How do the members of each subculture expect you to behave? Do the features of any of the cultures contradict each other? If so, how? How do you handle it when you experience conflict between the expectations of two subcultures to which you belong?

2. One important subcultural grouping is your family. Form groups of five or six and have each person discuss what the communication norms are in his/her family. (You may want to narrow this to focus on only one kind of situation, such as having dinner with your family.) Are there norms that might surprise family members? Are there norms your family follows that differ from the norms of your classmates' families? Are there norms governing what you should *not* talk about?

3. As a class, look at movies that depict intercultural encounters of various kinds, including male-female encounters. For example, *Witness, Moscow on the Hudson, The Four Seasons, When Harry Met Sally, Guess Who's Coming to Dinner, Gandhi*, and *A Stranger Among Us* depict international or intercultural encounters. As a class, address the following questions:

   How did the two cultures differ? (Be sure to discuss the characteristics of worldview, collectivism versus individualism, low- versus high-power distance, low- versus high-uncertainty avoidance, and low- versus high-context.)

   What communication problems did this create?

   Were the communication difficulties resolved? If so, how?

   How were the people from the two cultures changed by the encounters?

   How realistic were the portrayals of the two cultures?

4. Ask several international students to visit your class and describe communication customs and behaviors in their home countries. Ask them what they found most different or hardest to adjust to in conversations in the United States. How do they think their communicative behaviors have changed as a result of encounters with Americans?

5. Ask native-born American students who have either traveled extensively or lived for long periods of time in other places to talk about their experiences adjusting to other cultures. What did they find most different or hardest to adjust to about the communication behavior of the people in the other cultures? How has their behavior changed as a result of their travels?

6. Use one or more of the intercultural "critical incidents" described in *Intercultural Interactions: A Practical Guide* (listed in the bibliography) to create a role-play or skit for the class. Discuss what each individual in the role-play or skit might do to repair the interpersonal damage that may have occurred and to prevent such "mistakes" in the future.

7. Go to a public place (e.g., airport, restaurant, or museum) and observe the differences between how men and women behave. Take note of such things as how they sit and stand, how they seem to use personal space, their facial expressions and gestures, and so forth. What generalizations are you comfortable making from your observations? Share your findings with the class.

Bibliography

Brislin, Richard W., Kenneth Cushner, Craig Cherrie, and Mahealani Yong. *Intercultural Interactions: A Practical Guide.* Beverly Hills, CA: Sage Publications, 1986. Provides 100 realistic intercultural case studies and asks the reader to speculate upon the sources of misunderstanding.

Kim, Young Yun, and William B. Gudykunst, eds., *Theories in Intercultural Communication, International and Intercultural Communication Annual,* Vol. 12. Newbury Park, CA: Sage Publications, 1988.

Lustig, Myron W. and Laura L. Cassotta, "Comparing Group Communication Across Cultures: Leadership, Conformity, and Discussion Processes," in *Small Group Communication: A Reader,* 6th ed., eds. Robert S. Cathcart and Larry A. Samovar. Dubuque, IA: Wm. C. Brown Publishers, 1992, 393–404.

Lustig, Myron W. and Jolene Koester. *Intercultural Competence: Interpersonal Communication Across Cultures.* New York: HarperCollins College Publishers, 1993.

Porter, Richard E. and Larry A. Samovar. "Communication in the Multicultural Group," in *Small Group Communication: A Reader,* 6th ed., eds. Robert S. Cathcart and Larry A. Samovar. Dubuque, IA: Wm. C. Brown Publishers, 1992, 382–92.

Stewart, Lea P., Alan D. Stewart, Sheryl A. Friedley, and Pamela J. Cooper, *Communication between the Sexes: Sex Differences and Sex-Role Stereotypes,* 2d ed. Scottsdale, AZ: Gorsuch Scarisbrick, Publishers, 1990, especially chapters 2, 3, and 4.

Notes

1. William A. Henry, "Beyond the Melting Pot," *Time* (April 9, 1990): 29–35.

2. Young Yun Kim and Brent D. Ruben, "Intercultural Transformation: A Systems Theory," in *Theories in Intercultural Communication: International and Intercultural Communication Annual,* Vol. 12, eds. Young Yun Kim and William B. Gudykunst (Newbury Park, CA: Sage Publications, 1988): 299–321.

3. Mary Jane Collier and Milt Thomas, "Cultural Identity: An Interpretive Perspective," in *Theories in Intercultural Communication: International and Intercultural Communication Annual,* Vol. 12, eds. Young Yun Kim and William B. Gudykunst (Newbury Park, CA: Sage Publications, 1988): 113.

4. Collier and Thomas, "Cultural Identity," 103.

5. Donald W. Klopf, *Intercultural Encounters: The Fundamentals of Intercultural Communication* (Englewood, CO: Morton Publishing Company, 1987): 27–30.

6. Larry E. Sarbaugh, "A Taxonomic Approach to Intercultural Communication," in *Theories in Intercultural Communication: International and Intercultural Communication Annual,* Vol. 12, eds. Young Yun Kim and William B. Gudykunst (Newbury Park, CA: Sage Publications, 1988): 22–38.

7. Young Yun Kim, "On Theorizing Intercultural Communication," in *Theories in Intercultural Communication: International and Intercultural Communication Annual,* Vol. 12, eds. Young Yun Kim and William B. Gudykunst (Newbury Park, CA: Sage Publications, 1988): 12–13.

8. Myron W. Lustig and Jolene Koester, *Intercultural Competence: Interpersonal Communication Across Cultures* (New York: HarperCollins College Publishers, 1993): 77–96.

9. Edward T. Hall, *Beyond Culture* (New York: Anchor Press, 1977); Geert Hofstede, *Culture's Consequences: International Differences in Work-Related Values* (Beverly Hills, CA: Sage Publications, 1980); F. Kluckhohn and F. Strodtbeck, *Variations in Value Orientations* (New York: Row, Peterson, 1961); Charles H. Kraft, "Worldview in Intercultural Communication," in *Intercultural and International Communication,* ed. Fred L. Casmir (Washington, D.C.: University Press of America, 1978): 407–28; Larry E. Sarbaugh, "A Taxonomic Approach to Intercultural Communication."

10. F. Kluckhohn and F. Strodtbeck, *Variations in Value Orientations.*

11. Moshe F. Rubenstein, *Patterns of Problem Solving* (Englewood Cliffs, NJ: Prentice-Hall, 1975): 1–2.

12. William B. Gudykunst and Stella Ting-Toomey, *Culture and Interpersonal Communication* (Newbury Park, CA: Sage Publications, 1988): 40–43.

13. Branch Lotspiech, international telecommunications consultant who lived in China for nine months, personal conversation, June, 1990.

14. Roichi Okabe, "Cultural Assumptions of East and West: Japan and the United States," in *Intercultural Communication Theory: International and Intercultural Communication Annual,* Vol. 7, ed. William B. Gudykunst (Beverly Hills, CA: Sage Publications, 1983): 33.

15. Richard W. Brislin, Kenneth Cushner, Craig Cherrie, and Mahealani Yong, *Intercultural Interactions: A Practical Guide* (Beverly Hills, CA: Sage Publications, 1986): 207–8, 219.

16. Geert Hofstede, *Culture's Consequences.*

17. Bernard Lewis, "Islam and Liberal Democracy," *The Atlantic Monthly* 271 (February 1993): 89–97.

18. Myron W. Lustig and Laura L. Cassotta, "Comparing Group Communication Across Culture: Leadership, Conformity, and Discussion Procedures," in *Small Group Communication: A Reader,* 6th ed., eds. Robert S. Cathcart and Larry A. Samovar (Dubuque, IA: Wm. C. Brown Publishers, 1992): 393–404.

19. Geert Hofstede, *Culture's Consequences.*

20. Myron W. Lustig and Jolene Koester, *Interpersonal Competence.*

21. R. Christopher Earley and Patrick Stubblebine, "Intercultural Assessment of Performance Feedback," *Group & Organization Studies,* 14 (June 1989): 161–81.

22. Myron W. Lustig and Laura L. Cassotta, "Comparing Group Communication Across Cultures."

23. Edward T. Hall, *Beyond Culture.*

24. Linda Wai Ling Young, "Inscrutability Revisited," in *Language and Social Identity,* ed. John J. Gumperz (Cambridge: Cambridge University Press, 1982): 79.

25. William B. Gudykunst and Stella Ting-Toomey, *Culture and Interpersonal Communication,* 45.

26. Roichi Okabe, "Cultural Assumptions of East and West," 21–44.

27. Donald W. Klopf, "Japanese Communication Practices: Recent Comparative Research," *Communication Quarterly* 39 (Spring 1991): 130–43.

28. Myron W. Lustig and Jolene Koester, *Intercultural Competence.*

29. Myron W. Lustig and Jolene Koester, *Intercultural Competence.*

30. Myung-seok Park and Moon-soo Kim, "Communication Practices in Korea," *Communication Quarterly,* 40 (Fall 1992): 398–404.

31. Joe E. Pierce, "Life Histories of Individuals and Their Impact on International Communication," in *Intercultural and International Communication,* ed. Fred L. Casmir (Washington, D.C.: University Press of America, 1978): 525.

32. Stewart L. Tubbs and Sylvia Moss, *Human Communication,* 5th ed. (New York: Random House, 1987): 402–3.

33. Joe E. Pierce, "Life Histories of Individuals."

34. Peter A. Anderson, "Nonverbal Communication in the Small Group," in *Small Group Communication: A Reader,* 6th ed., eds. Robert S. Cathcart and Larry A. Samovar (Dubuque, IA: Wm. C. Brown Publishers, 1992): 278.

35. Donald W. Klopf, *Intercultural Encounters,* 178.

36. Stewart L. Tubbs and Sylvia Moss, *Human Communication,* 5th ed., 414.

37. Donald W. Klopf, *Intercultural Encounters,* 177.

38. Branch Lotspiech, personal conversation, June, 1990.

39. Donald W. Klopf, *Intercultural Encounters,* 177.

40. Stewart L. Tubbs and Sylvia Moss, *Human Communication,* 5th ed., 414.

41. Dorothy L. Pennington, "Black-White Communication: An Assessment of Research," in *Handbook of Intercultural Communication,* eds. Molefi K. Asante, Eileen Newmark, and Cecil A. Blake (Beverly Hills, CA: Sage Publications, 1979): 387.

42. Donald W. Klopf, *Intercultural Encounters,* 178.

43. William B. Gudykunst and Stella Ting-Toomey, *Culture and Interpersonal Communication,* 124–28.

44. Sheila J. Ramsey, "Nonverbal Behavior: An Intercultural Perspective," in *Handbook of Intercultural Communication,* eds. Molefi K. Asante, Eileen Newmark, and Cecil A. Blake (Beverly Hills, CA: Sage Publications, 1979): 129–31.

45. Edward T. Hall, "The Hidden Dimensions of Time and Space in Today's World," in *Cross-Cultural Perspectives in Nonverbal Communication,* ed. Fernando Poyatos (Toronto: C. J. Hogrefe, 1988): 145–52.

46. Edward T. Hall, *The Dance of Life,* summarized in William B. Gudykunst and Stella Ting-Toomey, *Culture and Interpersonal Communication* (Newbury Park, CA: Sage Publications, 1988): 128–30.

47. Edward T. Hall, "The Hidden Dimensions of Time and Space in Today's World," 151.

48. Walburga von Raffler-Engle, "The Impact of Covert Factors in Cross-Cultural Communication," in *Cross-Cultural Perspectives in Nonverbal Communication,* ed. Fernando Poyatos (Toronto: C. H. Hogrefe, 1988): 96.

49. Brent D. Ruben, *Communication and Human Behavior,* 2d ed. (New York: Macmillan Publishing Company, 1988): 402.

50. Lea P. Stewart, Alan D. Stewart, Sheryl A. Friedley, and Pamela J. Cooper, *Communication Between the Sexes: Sex Differences and Sex Role Stereotypes,* 2d ed. (Scottsdale, AZ: Gorsuch Scarisbrick, Publishers, 1990): 43–114.

51. Daniel N. Maltz and Ruth A. Borker, "A Cultural Approach to Male-Female Miscommunication," in *Language and Social Identity,* ed. John J. Gumperz (Cambridge: Cambridge University Press, 1982): 195–216.

52. Anthony Mulac, Pamela Gibbons, and Stuart Fujiyama, "Male/Female Language Differences Viewed from an Inter-Cultural Perspective: Gender as Culture," paper presented at the *Speech Communication Association Annual Convention* (November 1990), Chicago.

53. James C. McCroskey, Virginia P. Richmond, and Robert A. Stewart, *One on One: The Foundations of Interpersonal Communication* (Englewood Cliffs, NJ: Prentice-Hall, 1986): 244–47.

54. Lea P. Stewart, Alan D. Stewart, Sheryl A. Friedley, and Pamela J. Cooper, *Communication Between the Sexes,* 2d ed., 92–106.

55. John E. Baird, "Sex Differences in Group Communication: A Review of Relevant Research," *Quarterly Journal of Speech,* 62 (1976): 179–92.

56. Lynn Smith-Lovin and Charles Brody, "Interruptions in Group Discussions: The Effects of Gender and Group Composition," *American Sociological Review* 54 (June 1989): 424–35.

57. Anthony F. Verdi and Susan A. Wheelan, "Developmental Patterns in Same-Sex and Mixed-Sex Groups," *Small Group Research* 23 (August 1992): 356–78.

58. Edward A. Mabry, "Some Theoretical Implications of Female and Male Interaction in Unstructured Small Groups," *Small Group Behavior* 20 (1989): 536–50.

59. William E. Jurma and Beverly C. Wright, "Follower Reactions to Male and Female Leaders Who Maintain or Lose Reward Power," *Small Group Research* 21 (1990): 97–112.

60. Patricia H. Andrews, "Sex and Gender Differences in Group Communication: Impact on the Facilitation Process," *Small Group Research* 23 (February 1992): 74–92.

61. Georgia Duerst-Lahti, "But Women Play the Game Too: Communication Control and Influence in Administrative Decision Making," *Administration and Society* 22 (August 1990): 182–205.

62. Linda L. Carli, "Gender, Language, and Influence," *Journal of Personality and Social Psychology* 59 (1990): 941–51.

63. Nancy A. Burrell, William A. Donahue, and Mike Allen, "Gender-based Perceptual Biases in Mediating," *Communication Research* 15 (1988): 447–69.

64. Daniel J. Canary and Brian H. Spitzberg, "Appropriateness and Effectiveness Perceptions of Conflict Strategies," *Human Communication Research* 14 (1987): 93–118.

65. Anita K. Foeman and Gary Pressley, "Ethnic Culture and Corporate Culture: Using Black Styles in Organizations," *Communication Quarterly* 35 (Fall 1987): 293–307.

66. C. Kirchmeyer and A. Cohen, "Multicultural Groups: Their Performance and Reactions with Constructive Conflict," *Group & Organization Management* 17 (1992): 153–70; C. Kirchmeyer, "Multicultural Task Groups: An Account of the Low Contribution Level of Minorities," *Small Group Research* 24 (February 1993): 127–48.

67. Stella Ting-Toomey, "Rhetorical Sensitivity Style in Three Cultures: France, Japan, and the United States," *Central States Speech Journal* 39 (Spring 1991): 28–36; Mary Jane Collier, "A Comparison of Conversations Among and Between Domestic Culture Groups: How Intra- and Intercultural Competencies Vary," *Communication Quarterly* 36 (Spring 1988): 122–44.

68. David W. Kale, "Ethics in Intercultural Communication," in *Intercultural Communication: A Reader,* 6th ed., eds. Larry A. Samovar and Richard E. Porter (Belmont, CA: Wadsworth, 1991).

69. Guo-Ming Chen, "Relationships of the Dimensions of Intercultural Communication Competence," *Communication Quarterly* 37 (Spring 1989): 118–33.

PART 3

Developing the Small Group

For a collection of individuals to coalesce into a small group, members must develop such group variables as roles, norms, communication patterns, a status hierarchy, procedures, and a stable leadership structure. This section examines key characteristics of the individuals who compose a group and explains how members develop these important throughput processes. In addition to theoretical perspectives, practical information to help you function as a group leader is also provided.

The Members

Central Message

The number of members and their personal traits and attitudes are input variables that seriously affect group communication and productivity.

Study Objectives
As a result of studying chapter 6 you should be able to:

1. Describe the most important cognitive and communicative competencies of productive group members.

2. Explain how to decide how many members should compose a specific small group.

3. Describe behaviors that indicate an attitude of responsibility for the success of a small group, and the ethical standards supportive of such an attitude.

4. Explain how a high level of apprehension about communicating in a small group affects both a member's behavior and how other members are likely to perceive the apprehensive member.

5. Describe the traits called *Preference for Procedural Order* and *Cognitive Complexity,* and explain what each has to do with problem solving discussions.

6. Explain how assertive persons behave differently from passive and aggressive persons during discussions, and why assertive speakers are preferable as group members.

7. Describe authoritarian and egalitarian attitudes, name behaviors indicative of each type, and explain why authoritarian attitudes impair decision making in small groups.

8. Describe the trait of self-monitoring and its relationship to rhetorical sensitivity, and how each contributes to the communicative competence of group members.

9. Describe and give examples of the kinds of behaviors typical of open-minded critical thinkers.

Key Terms

Aggressiveness
Assertiveness
Attitude
Authoritarianism
Cognitive complexity

Communication apprehension
Dogmatism
Egalitarianism
Least-sized groups
Passiveness

Preference for procedural order
Prejudice
Rhetorical sensitivity
Self-monitoring
Trait

Folk sayings reflect the generalization that nothing of value can be made from inferior materials: "You can't make a silk purse from a sow's ear." Both the individual characteristics of members and their mix affect how a small group will function and how productive it will be. Larson and LaFasto, in a study of what it took to make outstanding teams of all sorts, found that two types of member competencies were crucial: technical competencies essential for the task, and personal competencies necessary for working well with other members.[1] Productive group members are, or become, skilled and knowledgeable regarding the group's task, really want the group to succeed, are sound thinkers, and are communicatively competent collaborators. You've probably experienced the anguish of trying to be productive in a group of incompetent, uncommitted, or self-centered members. Yet the right people can make group work rewarding, even joyous. Chapter 6 describes how the number of members and their individual characteristics contribute to the characteristics (syntality) of the group. Or, what kinds of human components does it take to make a winning team?

Group Size

Theoretically, each member brings some different knowledge, perspectives, and skills relevant to the group's purpose. As Jackson notes, for complex, nonroutine problems, groups of individuals with diverse skills, information, and perspectives are more effective than homogeneous groups.[2] But that does not mean the more, the better. At some point the increasing cost and difficulty of coordinating the work of more and more people outweighs the gain. Following Thelen's principle of **least-sized groups,** we should strive for "the smallest groups in which it is possible to have represented at a functional level all the social and achievement skills required for the particular required activity."[3] Ideally, a group is as small as possible while having all the expertise and diverse points of view necessary to complete the task well.

As group size increases, the complexity of interpersonal relationships increases geometrically. In a three-person group, only three two-person relationships can exist, but in a group of ten members there can be forty-five. With two members, only one relationship is formed; with seven members, the number of possible relationships reaches 966![4] Furthermore, as their numbers increase, the discrepancy in the amount of talking done by different members increases drastically, with a tendency for one person to do relatively more talking.[5] Leadership tends to become more centralized and formal, with increasing demands on designated leaders to regulate and keep order. Other effects of more members are lower member satisfaction and cohesiveness, higher competitiveness, increased aggressiveness, increased withdrawal, and fragmentation of work.[6] On the other hand, Slater reported that groups of fewer than four members are often felt to be tension producing and constraining.[7]

Other factors being equal, a size of five to seven members is optimal for producing maximum participant satisfaction. For many years students in classes taught by one of the authors have consistently reported that they preferred working in classroom groups of five or six over groups of more than fifteen or fewer than four. A group of about five is small enough to permit informality, allow everyone a chance to speak up, keep down social loafing (nonparticipation), and facilitate consensus decisions, yet provide the diverse information and points of view needed for quality decisions.

Groups as large as this are more difficult to coordinate than smaller groups, have unequal participation rates, and usually produce less satisfaction.

A small group's most important resource is its members. A group cannot be productive if members are lazy, uncooperative, or incompetent. Your personal traits, attitudes, and competencies certainly affect every group in which you are a component. Fortunately, many of these can be improved. As you read this chapter, you can use it as a tool for self-evaluation and goal setting.

A **trait** is a consistent pattern of behavior or other observable characteristic. Traits are influenced by both genetics and environment, and our behavior is also determined by our attitudes. An **attitude** is a cluster of values and beliefs held by a person toward an object, person or type of persons, or concept. You can see that an attitude can also be a trait or personal characteristic. We infer attitudes from observed behaviors—what people say and do. Recent research has confirmed that some personal traits and attitudes produce behaviors that are better for groups than others.[8] For instance, we previously described the differences between an individualistic attitude and a collectivist attitude learned in different cultures, and how these differences affect groups formed from persons who hold them.

Among the personal traits relevant to what kind of group member someone can be, some of the most important are thinking patterns (cognitive complexity, reasoning, problem-solving strategies, etc.), self-monitoring, and preference for procedural order.

How members will act in discussions of complex problems, especially when there are wide differences among members' perspectives and preexisting beliefs, is seriously affected by a trait psychologists call *cognitive complexity*. Related to but different from general intelligence (which has frequently been correlated with positional or emergent leadership), **cognitive complexity** refers to the degree of development of an individual's construct system for interpreting signals: how

Personal Behavior: Characteristics, Attitudes, and Competencies

Personal Traits

Cognitive Complexity

differentiated, abstract, and organized. In common terms, this is a measure of complex-to-simplistic thinking, based on beliefs and assumptions about the nature of the world. Persons high in cognitive complexity employ more differentiated arguments in speaking, are better able to integrate their goals with those of listeners in these arguments, and can accept and build on others' feelings and beliefs during discussions.[9] Kline, Hennen-Floyd, and Farrell found that cognitively complex discussants asked more questions and provided more objective information during discussions of class policies than did their less-developed classmates; complex people did not assume to know the other's viewpoint. Less developed discussants used their own frames of reference as if these were also the viewpoints of others. During group decision making, high complexity persons may be able to arrive at consensus much better than less complex persons, who speak as if they already know the experience and viewpoints of fellow group members.[10] We suggest you seek and listen closely to feedback about your own speaking. If you seem to be low in cognitive complexity, you can begin to assume less, ask more questions, check out what you think others want, feel and think, and perhaps learn to evaluate reasoning to become a more analytical, critical thinker.

Self-Monitoring

A second cognitive variable important to how we discuss and work with others in problem solving is called self-monitoring. Investigated extensively in recent years, **self-monitoring** refers to the degree to which a person monitors and controls self-presentation in social situations: "*High self-monitors* attend closely to cues from other participants regarding situationally appropriate behavior and use these cues to guide their social actions. *Low self-monitors* . . . rely on their own attitudes in determining what social behavior to exhibit. . . ."[11] High self-monitors, then, are keenly aware of responses from others that indicate unstated norms for behavior and how the others feel about what the monitoring person is doing. They can adjust their behavior to achieve desired responses better than low self-monitors by displaying behaviors and role functions appropriate to the group. Ellis and Cronshaw suggest that modifying behavior instead of following initial inclinations ". . . is the primary mechanism by which high self-monitors emerge as leaders."[12] In other words, sensitivity to cues from others is not sufficient; flexibility and skill in *adjusting one's behavior* as a small group member is also necessary. We discuss how self-monitoring is related to leadership emergence in chapter 8.

Overlapping the trait of self-monitoring is the characteristic called **rhetorical sensitivity.** As conceptualized by Hart, Carlson and Eadie, rhetorically sensitive persons monitor what they say, adapting their statements to how they think other members of the group may react. You might have doubts about the ethical standards of self-monitors who are rhetorically sensitive, but we do not. The rhetorically sensitive person is not a *reflector* who says what she thinks others want her to say, or a *noble self* who says whatever comes to mind. Rather, before speaking out, the rhetorically sensitive person searches consciously for the most effective way to express a point in order to evoke a desired response from other group members.[13]

A third cognitive trait desirable in members of problem-solving groups is the ability to think critically and systematically. Gouran reported a tendency for most discussion participants to accept inferences without challenging them, even when patently flawed reasoning was involved.[14] For thorough evaluation of proposed solutions, both individuals skilled in all aspects of critical thinking and group procedures that encourage thorough critical evaluation of all solutions are needed. Critical thinking and systematic thinking may be linked in a personality trait referred to as **preference for procedural order** (PPO), which is characterized by a need or desire to follow a clear, linear structure during problem solving. Putnam described the rationale for such a personality measure, development of a questionnaire for measuring it, and its importance to how groups function as problem solvers.[15] Later research by Hirokawa and associates led to evidence that high PPO persons do much better in choosing among alternatives when a highly structured problem-solving procedure (such as presented in chapter 10) is followed by the group. However, groups of low PPO persons who are comfortable with less structured discussion did equally well whether following a procedure of high or low structure. No mixed-PPO groups were considered, but this research suggests that systematic procedures would improve (or at least not reduce) the output quality of most decision-making groups.[16] High PPO persons do not seem to think as well as possible during loosely structured discussions.

Preference for Procedural Order

Most groups are likely to be composed of members with varying preferences for order and structure. Pavitt found that half of the students he surveyed preferred a loose "reach testing" decision-making process and the other half preferred a more linear structure, perhaps combined with reach testing.[17] Pavitt suggests that groups whose members' preferences are similar will have an easier time conducting a discussion.

Attitudes about personal responsibility and communicating, involving self-perception, other people, and ways of expressing thoughts, are vital to how much a member contributes to group goal achievement. We think that you should examine especially carefully your attitudes about self in relation to your group and fellow members, your willingness to communicate, and how you communicate.

Communicative Attitudes

Perhaps the most important attitude of ideal small group members is summarized by the phrase *a sense of responsibility for the success of the group*. Constructive members feel a personal responsibility to do whatever they can to see that the group achieves its goals. In a word, they are *dependable*. Responsible members show that they put accomplishment of group goals ahead of selfish wants. They guide their conduct as group members by a number of ethical standards, such as:

A Sense of Responsibility for a Group's Success

1. No member has a right to act in a way that would be disastrous if done by all members.

2. No one has a right to expect more effort from other members than he or she makes for the group.

3. Every member should be faithful in carrying out assignments for the group, and if prevented from doing so, should immediately notify the group and explain what went wrong.

4. A member should share any relevant information and ideas for the group to use in solving problems.

The kinds of pronouns used by such members to refer to the group reveal a sense of commitment: *we, us,* and *our* rather than *you* and *your.* These members volunteer to do a fair share of the work, and can be counted on to get it done. Failure to do a fair share of the work is the biggest source of friction among members of student project groups in our classes. In sum, the valuable group member behaves in a way that colleagues perceive as fully responsible and trustworthy. If you will not act that way, other members are better off without you; maybe they can replace you with a useful member.

*Egalitarianism-
Authoritarianism*

Contrasting ways of seeing human relationships are referred to as *egalitarianism* and *authoritarianism.* **Egalitarianism** is the belief in the equal importance of all persons; this is a tenet of the U.S. Declaration of Independence. Egalitarian people encourage full participation by all group members; they tend to be free of bigotry and stereotypes. They abhor bossiness and dictatorial behavior in self and others. At the other extreme are members high in **authoritarianism,** who prefer a controlling leader and who dominate a group when placed in a position of leadership. High authoritarians accept uncritically information and ideas expressed by or attributed to "experts." They ask opinions of others less often, act less friendly, and make more directive comments ("Do this!") than egalitarians.[18]

*Willingness to
Communicate*

To be a productive member, you must have a greater *willingness to communicate* than to protect yourself from disagreement or embarrassment. People who have relevant information or see flaws in proposals but do not speak up fail to help the group and actually harm it by taking up a member slot that a more outspoken person with needed resources might have occupied. They could be called *excess baggage* or *useless appendages* of the group. These people manifest the trait of **communication apprehension** (CA, sometimes called *shyness* or *reticence*), which manifests itself with varying degrees of self-concern, self-doubt, fear, anxiety about speaking, and defensiveness toward others. In this book we are concerned only about communication apprehension experienced by participants in a group's discussion, not in public speaking, family relations, etc. McCroskey and Richmond say that high CA group members speak much less than members low in CA, choose seats where leaders can overlook them, make more irrelevant comments, and are likely to express strong agreement when inwardly they disagree. High CAs are perceived as making little contribution to the group and as less desirable members than low CAs.[19]

If you discover that you are relatively high in CA as a group member, what can you do? Your college or university may have a center where you can learn such helpful techniques as *systematic desensitization* or *cognitive restructuring.* McCroskey and Richmond say that an in-depth understanding of the communication

Aggressive	Assertive	Nonassertive (passive)

Figure 6.1
Assertiveness
lies between
aggressiveness and
nonassertiveness.

process and of specific skills can help. To that end, we next consider the attitudes and skills of communicating assertively as opposed to communicating either aggressively or passively.

Assertiveness refers to communicative behavior reflecting respect both for oneself and for other group members. Assertive people communicate openly as equals to other members. Assertiveness lies on a continuum, illustrated in figure 6.1, between **passiveness** (nonassertiveness) and **aggressiveness** in communicating. Aggressive people are highly dominant and often authoritarian; they try to force ideas and practices on others. They call names, demand, insult, threaten, command, shout, pound the table, and frequently drown out others who are speaking. Rather than challenging information or reasoning as such, they attack other people. Emotional bullies, their motto might be, "Do it my way or fight!" Aggressive behavior may stem from psychopathology, from cultural practices, inability to handle frustration, or just a lack of verbal skills for dealing constructively with conflict.[20] No matter what the cause, this behavior is destructive to productive discussion, cohesiveness, and teamwork. If you find it in your behavior, you will want to eliminate it. Ethically, you can do no less!

Passive discussants, like high CAs, go along with a majority rather than argue, even when they disagree. In going along despite doubts, they are unethical, untrue to themselves, and therefore untrue to the group. Passive members tend to make little eye contact, speak so softly they are hard to hear, and won't resist aggressors. The stereotyped "yessers" shown in figure 6.2 epitomize passive behavior. Their motto might be, "We'll do it your way; nothing is worth fighting over." The most harmful type of passive member engages in behavior referred to as *passive-aggressive,* highly destructive to teamwork. Passive-aggressives attempt to get their way subtly; they sabotage rather than confront as an assertive person does. Instead of saying, "I don't like that policy" or "I disagree," they may be late with an assigned report, "forget" to carry out an assignment, fail to show for a meeting, or neglect to do their share of the group work.

In contrast to both aggressors and passives, assertive members disagree openly and explain why. They explain what they think as clearly as possible and state what they want. Even more important, they try hard to understand the information, ideas, perspectives, and wants of other members, and to **co**-orient so a mutually satisfactory decision may be found.

The preceding description of cognitive traits and attitudes toward other persons and communicating have implied the attitude of productive team members toward new information and ideas—*open-minded,* or curious and low in prejudices. Open-minded members are low in the trait called **dogmatism.** The more dogmatic

Attitude toward New Information and Ideas

Figure 6.2
Passive "yessers" do
not express genuine
agreement.

"All those in favor say 'Aye.' "

"Aye."   "Aye."   "Aye."

"Aye."   "Aye."

people are, the less willing they are to try to understand new ideas, to listen to or accept evidence that contradicts their present beliefs, and to base conclusions on the total pool of information available to the group.[21] Arguments based on evidence and sound reasoning can change the positions of open-minded persons, but will not influence dogmatic persons, whose decisions are based on prior beliefs, internal needs, and emotions more than a desire to know the truth and be logically consistent.

Dogmatic people see things in either-or, black-or-white terms. One of us, while discussing the relative merits of collective bargaining with several highly educated individuals, was dismayed to hear such dogmatic utterances as, "I'm just against unions in principle. They're wrong. I wouldn't even consider joining one." Others said, "Unionism is good. Management just doesn't care about us who do the real work." Neither statement demonstrates open-minded use of evidence or reasoning, and makes no allowance for exceptions. You can see how people who talk like this, without qualification, question, or evidence, can block group consensus. As one famous cartoon character said, "It ain't what people don't know hurts 'em so much as what they know that ain't so." Lee called this attitude the "mood of allness," in which a person indicates "he wishes to go no farther, to talk no more about something which to him is impossible, unthinkable, wrong, unnecessary or just plain out of the question. He has spoken, and there is little use in trying to make him see otherwise."[22]

A special kind of closed-mindedness is called **prejudice,** which indicates a judgment or opinion formed without full and sufficient inquiry regarding a specific individual or thing. Actually, we can never know everything about anything, so we need to be open to new ideas and evidence. As Allport said, "Attitudes become prejudices only if they are not reversible when exposed to new knowledge."[23] Your mind is closed to the degree that you consistently reject ideas you disbelieve, cannot distinguish nuances among beliefs and practices different from your own, and see no similarities between your own beliefs and disbeliefs.[24]

Ideally, group members would all be open-minded and free of prejudices. We are sure you do not want to behave dogmatically and so create roadblocks to group co-orientation and unity. A little self-monitoring can help a lot. *Ask* for points of view that differ from yours, and be sure you listen actively to them. If you observe dogmatism to be a problem in a continuing group, it may help to tackle the problem head-on by describing it. It may help to keep reminding the group that mutual respect is essential for group cooperation.

Summary

In this chapter we have explored those inputs we call *members* of a group and those individual-level variables we call traits and attitudes underlying all behavior. To function well, a group needs enough competent members to supply the knowledge and skills necessary to accomplish its goal, but only members who are responsible, communicative, cooperative, co-oriented, and thoughtful participants. Secondary groups should be *least-sized,* meaning that the number of members is kept as low as possible while supplying all the resources of information, perspectives, and skills necessary to do the job for which the group was created instead of having some individual do it. Apart from other considerations, an optimal number of members for such groups as small task forces and committees seems to be about five.

A group of people unprepared to do the group task and function well in a team cannot produce excellent results. Teamwork is no accident. Individual-level variables such as traits, attitudes, and competencies of members are ignored at the expense of group productivity. In chapter 6 we have asked you to examine systematically your personal traits and attitudes as a potential group member and to change when indicated.

Ideally, a member of a group facing a typical discussion task should be high in *cognitive complexity* to deal with a complex multifaceted problem, reason critically, and listen to new information and ideas with an open mind that is free of *dogmatism* or *prejudices.* Such an ideal member is high on the trait of *self-monitoring,* thus being aware of responses of other members as subtle clues to norms, and *able* to modify personal behaviors in ways likely to be influential. High self-monitors are likely to be *rhetorically sensitive,* meaning they consider alternative ways of expressing a point before speaking, and choose the one most likely to achieve the desired response. Such persons are not *reflectors* who say what they think others want to hear, but are communicatively competent in presenting self in ways that help the entire group apply tests of critical thinking to information and proposals. Most groups will include members who are high in *preference for procedural order,* suggesting that problem-solving and decision-making procedures that are relatively systematic and structured will likely produce better outcomes than more unorganized discussions. Members with pro-social ethical standards for determining their own behavior and evaluating that of other members tend to be highly responsible and dependable in working for a group. They care deeply about the effects of their behaviors on the group and its outputs, and work conscientiously to be as valuable as is feasible. Toward other members they are highly *egalitarian* rather than *authoritarian,* assertive in communicating without being aggressive or passive/withdrawn. Most likely, they are low in apprehension about communicating openly as group members, and expressing pertinent information, interpretations, and judgments when relevant. We will look further at such members in chapter 7 with the tool called SYMLOG.

Exercises

1. Discuss the following questions with your classmates, first in small groups, then as an entire class: How much can we trust each other to be truthful and carry a fair share of work in the small groups we form in this class?

2. For one week keep a journal in which you write daily reports and evaluations of your efforts to be highly self-monitoring and rhetorically sensitive in discussions. At the end of the week, sum up any and all progress you have made, and goals yet to be accomplished as a high self-monitoring and sensitive individual.

3. First, identify three small secondary groups of which you are currently a member. Then ask all other members to rate anonymously the degree to which they perceive you as a *responsible* member on a scale of from 7 (highly responsible and dependable) to 1 (usually irresponsible, can't be counted on). Personally and privately, decide what behaviors of yours have led to these assessments by fellow group members. What are the implications of the ratings for your future behavior as a group member?

4. Issues for discussion: Are there any kinds of groups in which an authoritarian personality might be beneficial to goal achievement? Under what conditions are such persons likely to be detrimental to the group's purposes? Can you give any examples of cultures in which authoritarianism is considered a virtue?

5. In a small group of fellow students discuss each of the following questions. One person should report your conclusions to the class.
   a. What kinds of behaviors would lead us to think that a discussant was open-minded? Dogmatic?
   b. What effects have dogmatic persons had in groups to which you have belonged?
   c. Are there any differences in how you feel when a fellow group member is speaking dogmatically from when a member speaks with an open-minded, non-allness attitude?

6. Plan and present a skit of a part of a problem-solving discussion in which a member disagrees with another, first in an aggressive way, then in a passive way, and finally in an assertive way.

7. After a topical discussion of some issue on which class members are widely divided in opinions (such as abortion, gun control, smokers' rights, or responsible sex), have each participant rate each other on the degree to which his or her behavior manifested open-mindedness versus dogmatism.

8. List two or three prejudices you once held, but have now abandoned. Then describe how you changed each. With fellow classmates discuss what you can learn from this review of your collective pasts.

9. For discussion: How can we become more cognitively complex, or is this an unchangeable trait?

Bibliography

Larson, Carl E. and Frank M. J. LaFasto. *Teamwork: What Must Go Right/What Can Go Wrong.* Newbury Park, CA: Sage Publications, 1989, 59–72.

McCroskey, James C. and Virginia P. Richmond. "Communication Apprehension in the Small Group." In *Small Group Communication: A Reader,* 5th ed., eds., Robert S. Cathcart and Larry A. Samovar,

Dubuque, IA: Wm. C. Brown Publishers, 1988, 405–19.

Rokeach, Milton. *The Open and Closed Mind.* New York: Basic Books, 1960.

Shaw, Marvin E. *Group Dynamics: The Psychology of Small Group Behavior.* 3d ed. New York: McGraw-Hill, 1981, chapter 6.

Notes

1. Carl E. Larson and Frank M. J. LaFasto, *Teamwork: What Must Go Right/What Can Go Wrong* (Newbury Park, CA: Sage Publications, 1989): 59–72.

2. Susan E. Jackson, "Team Composition in Organizational Settings: Issues in Managing a Diverse Work Force," in *Group Process and Productivity,* eds. Stephen Worchel, Wendy Wood, and Jeffry A. Simpson (Newbury Park, CA: Sage Publications, 1992): 138–73.

3. Herbert A. Thelen, *Dynamics of Groups at Work* (Chicago: University of Chicago Press, 1954): 187.

4. Robert K. Napier and M. K. Gershenfeld, *Groups: Theory and Experience,* 5th ed. (Boston: Houghton Mifflin, 1985).

5. Robert F. Bales et al., "Channels of Communication in Small Groups," *American Sociological Review* 16 (1952): 461–68.

6. J. A. Schellenberg, "Group Size as a Factor in Success of Academic Discussion Groups," *Journal of Educational Psychology* 33 (1959): 73–79; E. B. Smith, "Some Psychological Aspects of Committee Work," *Journal of Abnormal and Social Psychology* 11 (1927): 73–79; Richard B. Powers and William Boyle, "Common Dilemma Choices in Small vs. Large Groups," (Paper presented at American Psychological Association, Anaheim, CA, August 1983).

7. Phillip E. Slater, "Contrasting Correlates of Group Size," *Sociometry* 21 (1958): 129–39.

8. Brian H. Spitzberg, "Interpersonal Competence in Groups," in *Small Group Communication: A Reader,* 6th ed., eds., Robert S. Cathcart and Larry A. Samovar (Dubuque, IA: Wm. C. Brown Publishers, 1992): 431.

9. Susan L. Kline, Cathy L. Hennen-Floyd, and Kathleen M. Farrell, "Cognitive Complexity and Verbal Response Mode Use in Discussion," *Communication Quarterly,* 38 (1990): 350.

10. Kline, Hennen-Floyd, and Farrell, 357–58.

11. Robert J. Ellis and Steven F. Cronshaw, "Self-Monitoring and Leader Emergence: A Test of Moderator Effects," *Small Group Research* 23 (1992): 114–15; see also Robert J. Ellis, Raymond S. Adamson, Gene Deszca, and Thomas F. Cawsey, "Self- Monitoring and Leadership Emergence," *Small Group Behavior* 19 (1988): 312–24.

12. Ellis and Cronshaw, 123.

13. Roderick P. Hart, Robert E. Carlson, and William F. Eadie, "Attitudes toward Communication and the Assessment of Rhetorical Sensitivity," *Communication Monographs* 47 (1980): 2–22.

14. Dennis S. Gouran, "Inferential Errors, Interaction, and Group Decision-Making," in *Communication and Group Decision-Making,* eds. Randy Y. Hirokawa and Marshall Scott Poole (Beverly Hills, CA: Sage Publications, 1986): 93–111.

15. Linda L. Putnam, "Preference for Procedural Order in Task-Oriented Small Groups," *Communication Monographs* 46 (1979): 193–218.

16. Randy Y. Hirokawa, Richard Ice, and Jeanmarie Cook, "Preference for Procedural Order, Discussion Structure, and Group Decision Performance," *Communication Quarterly* 36 (1988): 217–26.

17. Charles Pavitt, "Describing Know-How About Group Discussion Procedure: Must the Representation be Recursive?" *Communication Studies* 43 (Fall 1992): 150–70.

18. William A. Haythorn, Arthur Couch, D. Haefner, P. Langham, and L. F. Carter, "The Behavior of Authoritarian and Equalitative Personalities in Groups," *Human Relations* 3 (1956): 54–74; Stanley Milgram, "Some Conditions of Obedience and Disobedience to Authority," *Human Relations* 9 (1965): 57–76.

19. James C. McCroskey and Virginia P. Richmond, "Communication Apprehension and Small Group Communication," in *Small Group Communication: A Reader,* 5th ed., eds. Robert S. Cathcart and Larry A. Samovar (Dubuque, IA: Wm. C. Brown Publishers, 1988): 405–19.

20. Dominic A. Infante and Charles J. Wigley III, "Verbal Aggressiveness: An Interpersonal Model and Measure," *Communication Monographs* 53 (1986): 61–67.

21. Milton Rokeach, *The Open and Closed Mind* (New York: Basic Books, 1960).

22. Irving J. Lee, *How to Talk with People* (New York: Harper & Row, Publishers, 1952): 46.

23. Gordon Allport, *The Nature of Prejudice* (Garden City, NY: Doubleday, 1958): 9.

24. Dale G. Leathers, "Belief-Disbelief Systems: The Communicative Vacuum of the Radical Right," in *Explorations in Rhetorical Criticism,* eds. C. J. Stewart, D. J. Ochs, and G. P. Mohrman (University Park, PA: The Pennsylvania State University Press, 1973): 127–31.

From Individuals to Group

Central Message

When individuals with an interdependent goal begin to interact, their communication shapes them into a group with its own unique culture that comprises norms, an assortment of roles and a status hierarchy, communication patterns, levels of cohesiveness, and a shared understanding of reality.

Study Objectives   As a result of studying chapter 7 you should be able to:

1. Explain the sources, characteristics, and remedies for both primary and secondary interpersonal tensions among group members.

2. Describe the two major phases through which most small groups pass and the kinds of processes prevalent during each.

3. Explain how group rules and norms develop; be able to recognize, state, and describe their effect on the group; and adapt to them in small groups to which you belong.

4. Explain the relationship between member behaviors, the functions of those behaviors, and the development of roles in a group, and describe the three broad categories of behavioral functions.

5. Describe how a group's throughput processes help develop the group's communication network, and the effect a network has on group outputs.

6. Explain how a status hierarchy forms and the impact of status differences on group process and output.

7. Explain cohesiveness, and describe eight techniques for enhancing it in a small group.

8. Explain the theory of SYMLOG and how SYMLOG can provide insights about a small group's culture.

9. Describe how fantasy chains contribute to the formation of a small group's culture.

Key Terms

Behavior	Maintenance functions	Secondary tension
Behavioral function	Norm	Self-centered functions
Cohesiveness	Phases	Status
Communication network	Formation phase	Ascribed
Fantasy	Production phase	Earned
Fantasy chain	Primary tension	Symbolic convergence
Fantasy theme	Role	SYMLOG
Group culture	Rules	Task functions
Idiosyncrasy credit		

In previous chapters we described communication in a small group, including both the verbal and nonverbal behavior of members, as the most important throughput variable by which a group's work is accomplished. In this chapter, we begin our focus on how communication helps a group develop from a collection of individuals to a team; later chapters will extend this discussion. The system perspective serves as our framework. Small group systems create themselves through their communication behavior, producing outcomes like cohesiveness, a status hierarchy, and decisions. Likewise, they can also change themselves by revising their interaction. Note that these group characteristics can be discussed as *both* throughput and output variables because the development of functioning processes (throughput) is also one of the accomplishments (outputs) of small group interaction. Rather than focus on individual behavior *per se,* as in chapter 6, we look at the impact of member behavior on system-level variables as a whole.

Development of Group Culture

Small groups develop unique cultures just as do societies and other large groupings. **Group culture** is the pattern of values, beliefs, norms, and behaviors that are shared by group members and that shape a group's individual "personality" (sometimes called *syntality*). Many factors weave together to create a group's culture, including the content and pattern of interactions, the roles members enact and their interrelationships, the norms and rules guiding the group's interactions, and status distinctions. Each group has a unique mix of members, purposes, rules, and behaviors that cannot be duplicated exactly in other groups. For instance, some groups behave informally, with lots of joking and low power distance. Other groups display hostility, aggressive verbal behavior, and divisive conflict. Still others adhere to strict, formal interaction rules with polite, controlled communication. How do these differences come about? We now examine some of the processes most important to the development of a group's culture. We remind you that a group's culture is never static; rather, it continually evolves, adapting to meeting the changing circumstances of the group. In a sense, a group's culture is always developing, but never completed.

Tension among Members

Somehow, what starts as a collection of individuals with an interdependent purpose must become a group that functions as a unit to complete that purpose. One of the first issues a group must address is how it will manage the interpersonal tensions that are a normal part of its development. Just as individuals experience varying levels of tension, so do entire groups. In fact, a certain amount of tension is desirable. Can you imagine taking an exam when you feel so relaxed you can barely motivate yourself to read the questions? An optimum amount of tension can help us perform at peak capacity, but too much or too little impairs our ability to think and function. The same is true of groups, which must learn to manage tensions productively for the ultimate good of the group.

Primary Tension

Bormann first dichotomized tension that a group experiences into two categories, primary and secondary. **Primary tension** results from primary sources, or the interpersonal relationships among members, whereas secondary tension is directly task related. Bormann describes primary tension as being ". . . the social unease and stiffness that accompanies getting acquainted."[1] He describes the symptoms of primary tension as extreme politeness, apparent boredom, yawning and sighing, a lot of long pauses, and tentative statements uttered in soft tones. At this point, members are asking themselves, "Will they like me? Will this be a group I enjoy working with?" The politeness and apparent boredom are only a facade covering the tensions we all feel when we are with people we don't know well. However, if this primary tension is not overcome, group members will get stuck in a mode of over-politeness, formality, and hesitancy to disagree, which will hurt their ability to think critically.

A second form of primary tension, also resulting from relationships among members, can arise abruptly when there is self-centered competition for power and status within the group. Although the issue may appear to be a matter of who will perform certain jobs for the group, the real issue is the desire and struggle for personal power, which underlies much human behavior. Thus, what appears to be secondary tension is really primary tension disguised as disagreement over ideas. Power is a great motivator, as well as a potential source of friction in groups. We discuss the issue of power and leadership more fully in chapter 8. For now, it is important to realize that tension can develop among members when issues of power and leadership are not settled in a way acceptable to all members.

Several things can be done to reduce the primary tension that results in members tiptoeing around each other. For example, taking time to get acquainted is worthwhile. Members can talk about themselves, their backgrounds, interests and hobbies, experiences relevant to the group's purpose, feelings about being in the group, and so on. In fact, this movement toward intimacy via self-disclosure is a characteristic of cohesive groups.[2] It may pay to have a social hour or party, with no formal agenda. Joking, laughing together, and finding common interests can help diminish primary tensions. Even members of a group that will meet only once can profitably spend a few minutes introducing themselves so they can orient themselves to each other as parts of a group. Indeed, members who have worked together in many meetings often spend the first few moments of their meeting chitchatting and confirming their relationships before getting down to work.

Primary tensions over power are more difficult to resolve. Rules and procedures for making decisions and assigning work can help prevent or alleviate these tensions. Other times, direct confrontation may be needed. We develop these ideas in several subsequent chapters.

Secondary tension is work-related tension resulting from the differences of opinion among members as they seek to accomplish their task. It is inevitable because members perceive problems differently, disagree about goals and means for achieving them, and criteria by which to evaluate ideas. Secondary tensions are a direct result of the need to make decisions *as a group*. Sometimes these tensions become uncomfortably high.

Secondary tension looks and sounds different from primary tension. Voices become loud and strained. There may be long pauses followed by two or more members trying to talk at once. Members twist and fidget in their seats, bang fists on the table, wave their arms, interrupt each other, and may even get up and pace

Secondary Tension

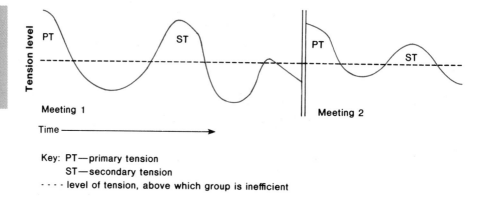

Figure 7.1
The tension cycle in a hypothetical problem-solving group.

Key: PT—primary tension
      ST—secondary tension
 - - - - level of tension, above which group is inefficient

around the room. They may try to shout each other down, call each other names, or aggressively question each other's intelligence or motives. While a couple of members verbally attack each other, the rest of the group may sit stiffly and awkwardly, not knowing what to do.

It is normal for a group to cycle between periods of high and low tension among members, and high and low productivity. Figure 7.1 represents such cycling in a hypothetical group. Above the dotted line are the periods of high tension and low production; periods of high productivity and lowered tensions, when teamwork is at a peak, are below the line.

Although it may seem easier to ignore secondary tensions because dealing with them can be uncomfortable or even painful, groups that deal with these tensions directly will experience several advantages. First, attempts to duck the tension-producing issue don't work. As Bormann says, "The problem . . . if ignored or dodged will continue to . . . impede their progress. Facing up to secondary tensions realistically is the best way to release them."[3] If secondary tension is not managed, it will continue to disrupt the group. Second, groups that find integrative ways to manage their secondary tension experience greater cohesiveness as a result of having worked through the tension. The members know they can disagree with each other yet still experience a sense of trust and commitment. Finally, the group may find that the tensions have caused the members to look more carefully at task-related issues, which usually produces a better final product.

What can group members do to manage secondary tension? Bales found that three categories of behaviors reduced tension among members: agreeing, showing solidarity, and tension release.[4] Showing agreement is socially rewarding to the person agreed with, as if to say to that person, "I value you and your opinion." The more often people are agreed with openly, the more they relax and communicate positively with each other, and the less defensive they become.

A member can show solidarity by indicating commitment to the group. Using *we* to refer to the group, speaking well of other members, offering to help, expressing confidence in the group, and talking about the importance of the group and its task are all ways to show solidarity and encourage members to move away from self-centeredness and antagonism.

Humor, too, can help release secondary tension, so long as the humor does not ridicule another member or the disagreement producing the humor is not then ignored. Enjoying a joke together makes it easier to listen better and find agreement. Humor can break uncomfortable tension and move a group through an impasse. In *Pattern for Industrial Peace,* Whyte described how a union staff representative did this repeatedly by using fishing photos whenever discussion among representatives of the steel company and union got overheated with secondary tension.[5]

Just as the occurrence of primary and secondary tension is predictable and normal in groups, other developments are relatively predictable, too. The more you know about these typical group processes, the more you will be able to identify what is usual, what is helpful, and what should be changed for the group to function more effectively. A number of researchers have studied how groups develop and change over time; they have found that groups progress through identifiable **phases.** Progression through phases is an evolutionary process that happens gradually, without clear demarcations to separate the phases.[6] The phases themselves can be identified by the types of interactions and behaviors the members exhibit.

Phases in the Development of Small Groups

Bales was one of the first researchers to investigate a group's progression through predictable phases.[7] He identified two concerns with which a group must deal. First, the group must develop the kinds of interpersonal relationships that provide stability and harmony, allowing the group to function cooperatively. These are the *socioemotional concerns.* Second, the *task concerns* involve the group's attention to its job, to completion of whatever is its task. Groups tend to cycle between these two concerns, focusing first on one, then the other. Early in the group's **formation phase,** the socioemotional dimension predominates as members attempt to work out the kinds of relationships they will have with each other. Note the connection here to primary tension. Initial reduction of primary tension, by working through interpersonal concerns, allows a group eventually to become maximally efficient in completing its task. Groups that resolve their early socioemotional issues become increasingly able to take relationships among group members for granted, and thus can shift their attention to the task. As socioemotional remarks and behaviors in a group decrease, task-related remarks and behaviors increase and eventually surpass them. In the **production phase** of a group's life cycle, when the group has reached socioemotional maturity, task behaviors will predominate. The group will achieve its peak in task efficiency. This progression can be seen over the life of an effective group, as well as over the course of a single group meeting.

It is important to recognize that groups must handle process (formation) and production (task) concerns *simultaneously.* Even at its first meeting, a group must begin the process of forming into a functioning unit by establishing the interpersonal relationships, leadership structures, and status hierarchies that enable it to work efficiently—the formation function. However, from the very beginning of its formation, the group also must deal with its task: what its charge is, how the task should be approached, who is to do what, and so forth. Thus, the group must contend with both kinds of functions throughout its life span. Although the interpersonal concerns predominate at first, task concerns are still present. If everything proceeds smoothly for the group, gradually more and more of its time can be spent directly on task concerns and less on interpersonal concerns as it moves to its production stage. However, at no point can group members disregard socioemotional concerns. Thus, we envision a group following essentially two broad developmental stages, a formation phase where process norms unfold and a production phase where group members focus on the task. These phases are not distinct. Instead, a group's attention shifts gradually, but never completely, from process to production concerns.

Development of Group Norms

When individuals begin to interact as members of a group, the full range of human behaviors is potentially available to them. Perhaps they will listen politely to each other, or maybe they will interrupt and insult one another. Somehow, the members must develop a set of rules and operating procedures to coordinate their individual behaviors into a system. Some **rules** are formalized guidelines for behavior that may be written down. For example, *Robert's Rules of Order, Newly Revised* is used by many organizations as a guide for governing face-to-face interaction.[8] Robert includes an entire section of rules that apply to any committee of an organization using his parliamentary manual.

However, most of the normal operating procedures for a group are developed gradually, with tacit rather than explicit consent of the group members. For instance, if Sam comes late to a meeting and other members make a point of chastising him, Sam will likely arrive on time for subsequent meetings and the group has "decided" on a rule that members should arrive on time. Such an informal rule, or **norm,** is seldom written down; instead, as Homans stated, it is ". . . an idea in the minds of the members of a group, an idea that can be put in the form of a statement specifying what the members . . . should do, ought to do, are expected to do, under given circumstances."[9] This section focuses on these informal rules, or norms.

Norms reflect cultural beliefs about what is appropriate or inappropriate behavior, as we discussed in chapter 5. Although the norms of an individual group may be specific to that group, chances are they will mirror general cultural norms. For instance, if physical violence is prohibited by the general culture, with disagreements handled through discussion, then a group established in the context of this larger culture will also be likely to use discussion instead of physical violence to settle disputes. As Shimanoff stated,

> When group members come together for the first time, they bring with them past experiences and expectations regarding cultural and social rules and rules for specific groups they assume may be similar to this new group. It is out of these experiences and expectations as well as its unique interaction . . . that a particular group formulates its rules.[10]

Norms are not imposed by an authority outside the group but are imposed by members on themselves and each other. They are enforced by various types of peer pressure, ranging from slight frowns to ostracism. It is important for group members, particularly new members, to be aware of these norms because to violate them may mean punishment, loss of influence, and perhaps exclusion from the group.

Norms guide and regulate the behavior of group members. They govern how and to whom members speak, how they dress, what they talk about and when, what language may be used, and so on. The whole process of communication among group members is rule-governed.[11] Rarely do norms specify absolutes; rather, they indicate ranges of acceptable and unacceptable behavior. For instance, a particular group may endorse a prompt starting time for its meetings. However, being four minutes late may be tolerated without comment, but coming fifteen minutes late would not.

During the formation stage of a new small group, norms are developed rapidly, often without members realizing what is occurring. The group's first meeting is particularly critical in establishing that group's norms. At that time, behaviors typical of primary tension in the formation phase—speaking quietly, suppressing disagreement, making tentative and ambiguous statements—can become norms if not challenged. Although members may openly discuss and state rules at their first meeting, norms usually evolve over time and seem to exist below the level of conscious awareness of most members. Often, a norm is brought to a group's awareness only after a member violates it, a new member questions it, or an observer points it out.

General norms direct the behavior of the group as a whole, whereas *role-specific norms* concern individual members with particular roles, such as the designated leader. Notice that these norms are stated as rules, even though they are not imposed on the group by an external authority or parent organization. Examples of each type of norm follow:

General norms	**Role-specific norms**
(applicable to every member)	(applicable to specific members)
Members should sit in the same position at each meeting.	The leader should prepare and distribute an agenda in advance of each meeting.
Members should address each other by first names.	The leader should summarize from time to time, but other members may do so if a summary is needed.
Other members should not disagree with the chair's ideas.	
No one may smoke during meetings.	The secretary should distribute minutes of the previous meeting at least three days before the next meeting.
Members may leave the meeting to get something to drink, but should return to their seats promptly.	Mary may play critical tester of all ideas by asking for evidence.
Members should arrive on time for meeting.	Terrell should tell a joke to relieve tension when the climate gets tense during an argument.

If norms generally exist below the level of conscious awareness, how can group members discover what their norms are? Norms can be inferred and confirmed by observation. New members, especially, should be sensitive to the group's norms so they do not inadvertently violate important ones. Fortunately, new members are not usually expected to become active participants right away, so they have time to observe and learn the rules. There are two types of behavior to watch for especially:

1. Behaviors that occur repeatedly and with regularity, by one or all members. Repetitions of a behavior are evidence that a norm exists regulating it. Thus, group members should look for answers to the following questions: "Who talks to whom?" "How do members speak?" "What kind of language do they use?" "What do they talk about and for how long?" "Where do they sit?" "When do they move about and for what reasons?" and "How is the group brought to order?"

2. Punishment of a member for infraction of a rule. The strongest evidence of a norm is a negative reaction or punishment directed at a member who violates it. Weaker support for the existence of a norm is provided when the violator corrects the sanctioned behavior, and the other members visibly approve the correction. Observers looking for norms should pay attention to behaviors that elicit negative reactions, ranging from a bit of head shaking, to surreptitious and disapproving glances passing between members, to forceful negative comments or even threats. Notice behaviors to which members react with gestures of rejection, such as frowns, head shaking, and tongue clucking. What acts do members studiously ignore, as if out of embarrassment? Listen for negative comments: "It's about time you got here," "Let's stick to issues and not go blaming each other," and "Maybe you'll have your report ready for our *next* meeting." Note, particularly, those actions that elicit negative responses from more than one person, a sure bet that a norm important to the group has been infringed.

Changing a Norm

Norms have a tremendous impact on the processes and outcomes of the group. Therefore, it is important that group members not only be aware of them but act to change them if they appear to be detrimental. For instance, a norm implying that low-status members may not disagree with high-status members interferes with the critical evaluation of ideas. Or, groups that permit members to criticize ideas as soon as they have been proposed may find that members are reluctant to make innovative suggestions and that creativity is stifled. In such cases, individuals should not "sit back and take it" but work to change the rules. However, making a frontal assault, particularly one that may be perceived as a personal attack, will not be successful but will make the person demanding the change seem like a deviant. Instead, following a few simple guidelines can help you change norms without unnecessary trauma. First, the member desiring the change must establish an identity as a loyal member of the group and speak not as an outsider but as a member committed to the group's well-being. Second, the member should carefully observe the offending behavior and keep a record of how often it occurs and what the consequences are. Armed with specific information and obvious concern for the good of the group, the member is ready for the next step, constructive confrontation.

The member should pick an appropriate time, indicate his or her concern with something that appears to be causing trouble for the group, state the specifics calmly and clearly, then ask whether other members share the concern. For instance, rather than saying, "We never get started on time and I'm sick and tired of it," the member should say instead: "For the past four meetings, we have started our work anywhere from fifteen minutes to half an hour late. We seem to have a rule that we don't have to observe our announced starting time, which makes our meetings run late. Two of us have another committee meeting directly following this one, and for each of these late meetings we have missed the conclusion of our business. This means that we need to spend additional time at the next meeting bringing everyone up to date. Does anyone else share my concern?" If the norm was subconscious, it now has been brought to the attention of the group and becomes part of the surface agenda of the group where it can be discussed openly. If the member is wrong about the norm, the group can correct the perception without disparaging the concern. However, if the individual is right, the group will appreciate the concern and likely decide to change the norm. Even if the other members agree to a new norm, they may still need gentle reminders until the new behavior becomes habituated, part of "our way of doing things."

An example will clarify how this works. A study group meeting in a small town library held weekly learning discussions to compare modern Protestant, Catholic, and Jewish theology. The intent was for members to come to an understanding of these three religious traditions. However, at times members forgot they were there to learn and attempted to convert one another. Discussion often erupted into an uproar with several people talking or shouting at once. One evening, just after the meeting had formally adjourned, a member said, "You know, I'm really bothered by our tendency to all talk at once sometimes, and not listen to each other." He turned to one of the authors who, equipped with a tape recorder, had been observing the meeting as a researcher, and said, "Jack, could some of us hear the recording you just made to see how we must sound to you?" When they heard themselves, there were groans: "Did we really sound as bad as that?" Members left the meeting in clusters of two and three, talking about what they had just realized. At the next meeting, the game of "uproar" again exploded, but this time someone said, "Remember the tape recording!" and order was resumed. There was no more interrupting for nearly an hour, and when it did occur, it lasted only several seconds before participants sheepishly shut up and offered apologies. The group had developed a new norm. Thus, although norms are developed generally without conscious intent, they are not fixed in stone and can be changed as the group's situation warrants.

Most people, when they hear the term **role,** think of parts in a play or movie. Play scripts contain interlocking roles, each of which is a different character in the cast. Just as an actor plays different roles in different scripts, like Tom Cruise as an Irish immigrant (*Far and Away*), paraplegic (*Born on the Fourth of July*), and lawyer (*The Firm*), individuals enact many diverse roles in the numerous groups to which they belong. In one group the role might be *daughter* or *son,* in another

Development of Role Structure

lead carpenter, and in yet another *church treasurer.* A given individual might be a leader in one group and play a supporting role in another. The role a person enacts in any particular group is a function of that person's personality, abilities, and communication skills, the talents of the other members, and the needs of the group as a whole.

A particular role embraces a set of behaviors that perform some function for the group. There is a difference between a *behavior* and a *behavioral function.* At the individual level, every verbal or nonverbal act by a group member is a **behavior,** but at the group level, the *function* that behavior performs in the group system is called its **behavioral function.** For example, the joke Mary tells in a group is the *behavior.* However, Mary's joke can serve a variety of *functions,* depending on how she told it, what else was happening in the group at the time, and so forth. Perhaps her joke relieved tension during an argument (a positive behavioral function), but perhaps it got the group off track or made fun of another member (negative behavioral functions). Marcus may ask a question (behavior) whose purpose (function) is to reorient the group if it seems to have lost sight of its goal. A behavioral function, then, is the impact of member behavior on the social structure (throughput) and task accomplishment (output) of the group. A member's role represents the constellation of behaviors performed by that member and the overall functions those behaviors perform for the group, just as an actor's role consists of all the lines and actions of the character in the play. Some functions are shared widely among group members (such as providing information or providing opinion), while others may become the exclusive domain of one member (such as keeping group records or joking to relieve tension).

Role Emergence

Most small groups have certain *formal* roles, usually appointed or elected positions. A *chair* has the responsibility for calling meetings, planning agendas, and coordinating the work of the other members. A *secretary* is responsible for taking notes and distributing minutes of meetings. In these cases, the duties associated with a particular role are specified in advance, sometimes in writing. However, in most small groups members create and modify their own *informal* roles as the group progresses. Informal roles, also called *behavioral roles,* reflect the personalities, behaviors, and habits of the members in a particular group; they are not specified in advance but develop through the interaction among members.

The informal role a particular individual plays in a small group is worked out in concert with the other members and is determined largely by the relative performance skills of the rest of the group members. This is accomplished primarily through trial and error. For example, Tamara may have a clear idea of how the group can accomplish its tasks; she will make attempts to structure the group's work: "I suggest we first make a list of all the things we need to do to finish our project." If no one else competes for that role, and if the other members see that structuring behavior as helpful to the group, they will reinforce and reward Tamara's statements and actions: "Okay, Tamara, that sounds like a good idea." This reinforcement, in turn, is likely to elicit more of those structuring behaviors from Tamara. On the other hand, if several members are also competent to structure the group's work, the group members collectively will reinforce the actions of the member they perceive to be the most skilled in this performance area. If Tamara is not reinforced as the group's "structurer," she will search for some other way to be valuable to, and valued by, the group. For instance, she may help to clarify the proposals of the other members ("In other words, are you saying that . . . ?") or become the group's critical evaluator ("I think there are two major flaws with that proposal."). *Every member needs a role that makes a meaningful contribution to the group.*

Because an individual's role depends on the particular mix of people in the group, that person's role will vary from group to group. Think for a moment of all the groups to which you have belonged. Your role probably changed considerably through time as you changed, as new people were added to or left a group, or as the problem facing the group changed. A major principle of small group theory is this: *the role of each group member is worked out by the interaction between the member and the rest of the group* and continues to evolve as the group evolves. Thus, a well-organized person may end up leading one group and playing a supporting role in another, depending on the characteristics and competencies of all members relative to one another.

Many group researchers have developed a number of classification schemes to describe the behavioral functions that specific remarks perform in small groups. These schemes, all oversimplified, help categorize what people say and do in a group. One common scheme classifies behaviors into the two main functions we described earlier, task and socioemotional (or maintenance). But even this oversimplifies the actual situation encountered in most groups. Assume Teresa says to Mona and Dick, "I think you guys are bypassing each other, and you should listen more carefully." That statement, even though it focuses on the ways members are relating to each other (a socioemotional concern), also has a bearing on the task accomplishment of the group, especially if Dick and Mona start paying better attention to each other. Moreover, Teresa's statement implies that she has the right to intervene with expert information about the group's process, which says something about her relationship to the group. Thus, although many researchers consider actions to be *either* task *or* relationship oriented, it is probably more accurate to say that an act may have considerable impact on *both* dimensions. Furthermore, recall that the balance of time and attention devoted to these two dimensions shifts as a collection of people develops into a small group system. Therefore, we can expect statements made earlier in the group's life to focus more on the relationship dimension than the task, and statements made later to focus more on the task. Figure 7.2 depicts these two major dimensions and illustrates how individual acts can affect each dimension to a greater or lesser degree.

Most researchers agree that both task and socioemotional needs must be met for a group to be effective. What follows is a list of behavioral functions groups need to achieve their goals. Figure 7.3 illustrates the roles three group members might enact using various combinations of the following behaviors.

Behavioral
Functions

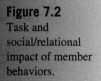

Figure 7.2
Task and
social/relational
impact of member
behaviors.

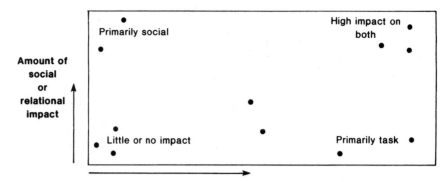

● Specific act or behavior

Task Functions

Task functions affect primarily the task output of the group. Some of the most helpful, with statements that exemplify those functions, are:

Initiating and orienting: proposing goals, plans of action, or activities; prodding the group to greater activity; defining position of group in relation to external structure or goal. ("Let's assign ourselves tasks to finish before the next meeting.")

Information giving: offering facts and information, evidence, or personal experience relevant to the group's task. ("Last year, the library spent $12,000 replacing lost materials.")

Information seeking: asking others for facts and information, evidence, or relevant personal experience. ("John, how many campus burglaries were reported last year?")

Opinion giving: stating beliefs, values, interpretations, judgments; drawing conclusions from evidence. ("I don't think theft of materials is the worst problem facing the library.")

Clarifying: making ambiguous statements more clear; interpreting issues. ("So does 'excellent' to you mean that the report should be perfect grammatically?")

Elaborating: developing an idea previously expressed by giving examples, illustrations, and explanations. ("Another thing that Toby's proposal would let us do is. . . .")

Evaluating: expressing judgments about the relative worth of information or ideas; proposing or applying criteria. ("Here are three problems I see with that idea.")

Summarizing: reviewing what has been said previously; reminding group of a number of items previously mentioned or discussed. ("So, by next week, Angie will have the research finished and Carl will have the charts done on the computer.")

Coordinating: organizing the group's work; promoting teamwork and cooperation. ("If Carol interviews the mayor by Monday, then Jim and I can prepare a response by Tuesday's meeting.")

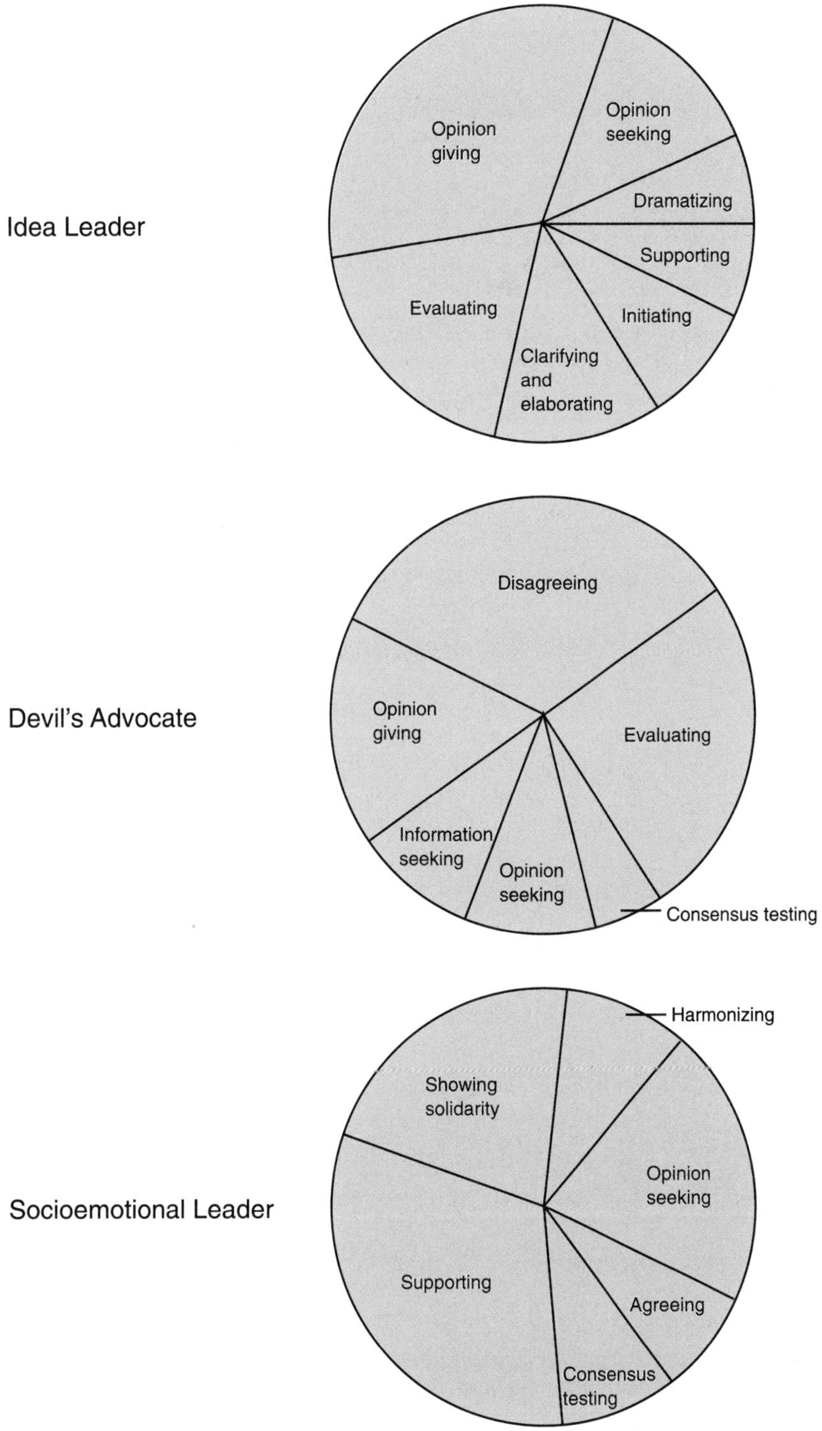

Idea Leader

Devil's Advocate

Socioemotional Leader

Figure 7.3
Roles of three members of a small group.

Consensus testing: asking if the group has reached a decision acceptable to all; suggesting that agreement may have been reached. ("We seem to be agreed that we'll accept the counteroffer.")

Recording: keeping group records, preparing reports and minutes; serving as group secretary and memory. ("I think we decided that two weeks ago. Let me look it up in the minutes to be sure.")

Suggesting procedure: suggesting an agenda of issues, or special technique; proposing some procedure or sequence to follow. ("Why don't we try brainstorming to help us come up with something new and different!")

Maintenance functions influence primarily the interpersonal relationships of members. We think the following seven functions, with sample statements, are especially vital to task groups:

Establishing norms: suggesting rules of behavior for members; challenging unproductive ways of behaving as a member; giving negative response when another violates a rule or norm. ("I think it's unproductive to call each other names. Let's stick to the issues.")

Gatekeeping: helping some member get the floor; suggesting or controlling speaking order; asking if someone has a different opinion. ("Pat, you look like you want to make a comment. Do you want to say something about the proposal?")

Supporting: agreeing or otherwise expressing support for another's belief or proposal; following the lead of another member. ("I think Tara's right; we should examine this more closely.")

Harmonizing: reducing secondary tension by reconciling disagreement; suggesting a compromise or new alternative acceptable to all; conciliating or placating an angry member. ("Jared and Sally, I think there are areas where you are in agreement, and I would like to suggest a compromise that might work for you both.")

Tension-relieving: making strangers feel at ease; reducing status differences; encouraging informality; joking and otherwise relieving tension; stressing common interests and experiences. ("We're getting tired and cranky. Let's take a ten-minute break.")

Dramatizing: evoking fantasies about people and places other than the present group and time, including storytelling and fantasizing in a vivid way; testing a tentative value or norm through fantasy or story. ("That reminds me of a story about last year's committee. . . .")

Showing solidarity: indicating positive feeling toward other group members; reinforcing a sense of group unity and cohesiveness. ("Wow, we've done a great job on this!" or "We're all in this together!")

While the preceding functions are necessary to effective small group functioning, there is another category of functions detrimental to the group. They represent an individual member's hidden agenda.

Self-centered functions refer to those member behaviors that serve the performers' unmet needs at the expense of the group. We think the following three are especially harmful:

Self-Centered Functions

Withdrawing: avoiding important differences; refusing to cope with conflicts; refusing to take a stand; covering up feelings; giving no response to the comments of others. ("Do whatever you want, I don't care," or not speaking at all.)

Blocking: preventing progress toward group goals by constantly raising objections, repeatedly bringing up the same topic or issue after the group has considered and rejected it (but it is not blocking to keep raising an idea or topic the group has not really listened to or considered). ("I know we already voted, but I want to discuss it again!")

Status and recognition seeking: stage-hogging, boasting, and calling attention to one's expertise or experience when this is not necessary to establishing credibility or relevant to the group's task; game playing to elicit sympathy; switching subject to area of personal expertise. ("I think we should do it the way I did it when I won the 'Committee Member of the Year' award.")

This list is by no means exhaustive; it could be expanded considerably with such categories as *special interest pleading, advocating, confessing,* and similar harmful functions. Self-centered functions manipulate and use other members for selfish goals that compete with what the group needs.

Networks of Communication

Concomitant with the development of somewhat specialized roles in a group is the development of a **communication network,** which refers to the pattern of message flow (who actually speaks to whom in discussions). If Terry opens a meeting, he may find the others expecting him to open all their meetings. If Andrea speaks frequently, she may find others looking (literally) to her for some comment on each new issue. Infrequent interactants will find themselves increasingly ignored. A network of who speaks to whom emerges as a function of individual competencies and commitment to the group. The network may change as new problems arise that require specific knowledge or skills, or as socioemotional concerns develop in the group. However, every small group is generally typified by one of the major network types described later.

Many types of networks have been identified. Usually a group of peers has an all-channel network in which all participants are free to comment on a one-to-one basis with all others and to the group as a whole (see figure 7.4). A wheel network, where all comments are directed toward one central person (usually the designated leader) who alone has authority to speak to the other members, should usually be avoided. A "Y," or hierarchical network, occurs when an autocratic leader speaks to lieutenants who in turn talk to subordinates. People at the ends of the Y rarely talk to the leader directly. In both the Y and wheel networks, the central person is generally satisfied with the communication and participation in the group, but the peripheral members are not. Another danger in these types of network is that the central member may suffer from information overload and become frustrated. In addition, communication in restricted networks may break down into two or more private conversations during a group meeting.

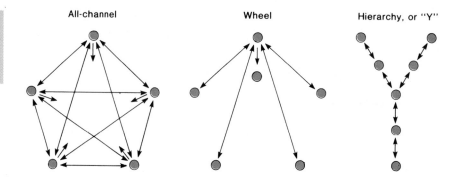

Figure 7.4
Communication networks.

All-channel   Wheel   Hierarchy, or "Y"

On the other hand, the all-channel network permits rapid communication among all members without having to get clearance from a central gatekeeping authority. Members are free to say what they want while ideas are still fresh in mind and pertinent. Communication flows freely; at least half the remarks are made to group members as a whole so all feel free to reply, and all members can hear and tune in to one-to-one or one-to-few comments. The all-channel network pays off in several ways. Morale is highest, and such groups tend to perform better on complex tasks when compared with restricted network groups. Even in all-channel groups, the flow of verbal messages may at times resemble a wheel or a hierarchy, such as during an emergency or extreme time pressure.

Status Hierarchy

Status refers to the relative importance, prestige, and power of a member in a small group. As roles emerge, each person is placed in a sort of pecking order or status ladder. Several advantages accrue to members of high status. High status is socially rewarding, so such members feel important and worthwhile. Other group members defer to them, grant them a disproportionate share of the group's attention, agree with their proposals, and seek their advice and opinions. People occupying formal, high-status roles, such as *manager,* may be given such tangible signs of status as large offices, private secretaries, and powers not granted to other members. Moreover, designated leaders are often given deference, support, and more eye contact.

Effects of status are numerous. High-status members talk more than low-status members and address each other more often than do low-status members, who address their remarks more often to high-status members than to each other.[12] Low-status members also send more positive messages to high-status members than to other low-status members, another reward of high status.[13] Low-status members are interrupted more and their comments are ignored more often than the comments of those with higher status. High-status members tend to talk more to the group as a whole, whereas low-status members express most of their comments to individuals (the classic Y network).

In addition to being granted a number of psychological or material rewards, high-status members are expected to meet certain responsibilities within the group. They are expected to work especially hard to accomplish the group's goals, and to uphold the group's norms. They may lose status by failing to fulfill the group's expectations, although they may be given additional leeway to bend the rules, called **idiosyncrasy credit,** that other members do not receive.[14] This means that, for members who have made an exceptionally valuable contribution to the group, certain rules can be bent.

Status within a small group may be *ascribed* or it may be *earned.* At first, before members know each other well and are sure what their respective contributions will be to the group, status is **ascribed** on the basis of each member's position in the society external to the small group. It is based on such things as wealth, education, occupation, personal fame, or position in the group's parent organization. For example, a committee composed of a college dean, a biology professor, an English instructor, two seniors, and two sophomores will initially have that order of ascribed status. However, status can also be **earned** or achieved based on a member's individual contributions to the group. The sophomore who conducts considerable research on behalf of the group and is a key contributor will have higher earned status than the biology professor who rarely comes to meetings and completes no assignments. In some instances, the importance of variables that contribute to ascribed status, such as sex, appears to be shifting, as we noted in chapter 5.

The most ideal group climate exists when relationships and relative status differences are somewhat flexible so that different members can become more influential as their particular knowledge and skills become pertinent to the issues or problems facing the group at any point in time. Wood found that paying undue attention to ascribed status differences negatively affected a group's ability to accomplish its task.[15] It is important to note that lower status does not mean *of little value.* Lower-status members are not necessarily unhappy in the group; cohesive groups value the contributions of each member, and each member knows it. Only when members say things like, "We could have done just as well without Morgan and Jolene on this committee," can we infer that lower status definitely means "inferior." More typically, everyone in the group might follow the lead of a normally quiet, low-status person who seems to have just the information or ability the group most needs at a given moment. That person might later slip back into a more usual low-profile position, but the contribution will have been noted and appreciated.

Cohesiveness refers to the common bonds and sentiments that hold a group together. To say a group is high in cohesiveness is to say that the relationships among members is, on the whole, attractive to them; they have a high degree of "stick to-getherness" and unity. Measuring cohesiveness is difficult and involves observing certain selected behaviors. For instance, a researcher might use members' individual assessments of how closely knit they are as a group, attendance at meetings, favorable remarks made about the group to outsiders, degree of conformity to group norms, or degree of consensus about values to judge cohesiveness.

Cohesiveness

Highly cohesive groups behave differently from less cohesive groups. They display more characteristics of primary groups than less cohesive groups.[16] They have higher rates of interaction. Members express more positive feelings for each other and report more satisfaction with the group and its products. In addition, cohesive groups exert greater control over member behaviors.[17] High cohesiveness is associated with increased ability to cope effectively with unusual problems and to work as a team in meeting emergencies. Production groups, if highly cohesive, *can* produce more than low-cohesive groups, but may not do so if members are being influenced by intragroup norms for less production. A recent meta-analysis of cohesiveness research found that, in general, highly cohesive groups are more productive, but the researchers recommend caution in generalizing these results.[18] Another study found that there is an optimum level of cohesiveness beyond which performance decreases.[19] Whether or not a cohesive group is productive also depends on the degree to which members accept their task. Greene found that cohesive groups are productive only when the members have both high acceptance of organizational goals implicit in the group's task and a strong drive (motivation and enthusiasm) to complete the task.[20] This was certainly the case with the excellent teams studied by Larson and LaFasto.[21] However, groups that are highly cohesive but socially rather than task oriented may end up accomplishing nothing.[22]

Highly successful and cohesive groups tend first to get acquainted and interested in each other as people. This type of self-disclosure increases cohesiveness, commitment to the task, and productivity.[23] Members can be heard saying, "I'm proud of our group, we really thrash out ideas until we arrive at the best, then we team up." However, high cohesiveness can also pressure members to conform to the majority or to high-status members' desires, which can result in a less-than-thorough critical evaluation of ideas. This *groupthink* phenomenon is discussed in detail in chapter 12.[24]

Although pitfalls such as groupthink are associated with high cohesiveness, there are benefits as well. A group that accomplishes its objectives, provides members with satisfaction in their participation, offers prestige in belonging, and is successful in competing with other groups is very attractive to its members. This can help produce highly committed and enthusiastic members who stay the course when problems arise.

Cohesiveness is fostered to the extent that members know and like each other as individuals, by their frequency of interaction, and by the amount of influence each exerts on the group. In addition, some evidence suggests that cohesive groups cooperate in creating a dominant sensory metaphor as a group, and that cohesiveness can be monitored through metaphor.[25] For example, when a group is first established, various members indicate their understanding by saying, "I see," "I hear you," or "I grasp that." Each of these metaphors for "I understand" concentrates on a different sense—sight, sound, or touch. In cohesive groups, members tend to converge on a particular sensory metaphor. If the visual metaphor is "chosen," for example, members will all start saying, "I see," "I've got the picture," and "I've spotted a flaw." This happens below the level of conscious awareness and indicates that the members have influenced each other in subtle but significant ways.

Interestingly, open disagreement is more frequent in highly cohesive groups, probably because a climate of trust gives each member the security needed to openly disagree on issues, facts, and ideas.[26] On the other hand, if high-status members indicate that they perceive disagreement to be a personal affront and demand compliance, then cohesiveness will be maintained at the expense of high-quality decision making.

Cohesiveness, then, is generally desirable. To enhance cohesiveness, Bormann and Bormann suggest that a group should attend to seven items, to which we add an eighth:

1. **Develop a group identity.**
   Talk about the group as *we,* not *you.* Develop nicknames for the group, insignia indicating membership, or mascots for the group.

2. **Build a group tradition.**
   Encourage traditions and rituals, which give added meaning to the group's culture. Refer to past events with pride, and encourage the group to develop a rich fantasy life, which we will discuss shortly.

3. **Stress teamwork.**
   Members, especially designated leaders or high-performance members, should avoid talking about "my accomplishments." The team performance should come before individual glory.

4. **Get the group to recognize good work.**
   Encourage members to compliment and praise one another. Low-status members, especially, need attention and recognition. Look for ways to support other members with their group work assignments, but also with non-group-related activities.

5. **Set clear, attainable group goals.**
   A long-term goal is easier to achieve if it is broken down into several short-term goals. In addition, goals should be challenging but not impossible to reach, because failure is demotivating.

6. **Give the group rewards.**
   Although many organizations reward individual performance, groups should be rewarded *as groups.* These can be tangible or intangible rewards, including recognition dinners, public praise, letters of commendation, and so forth.

7. **Treat members like people, not machines.**
   The efficient, highly oiled machine is *not* the best metaphor for the kinds of groups we have been discussing. People have human needs for warmth, affection, and esteem that should be recognized, and group work can be rewarding not just because control needs are met when a task is accomplished, but because needs for inclusion and affection are met as well.[27]

8. **Support both disagreement and agreement.**
   This means that a norm of freedom of expression and openness should be maintained. Highly cohesive groups show more disagreement, with conflict encouraged, not repressed. Often, when conflicts are resolved, group members feel closer than ever and are more cohesive.

Figure 7.5   SYMLOG diagram of a noncohesive group.

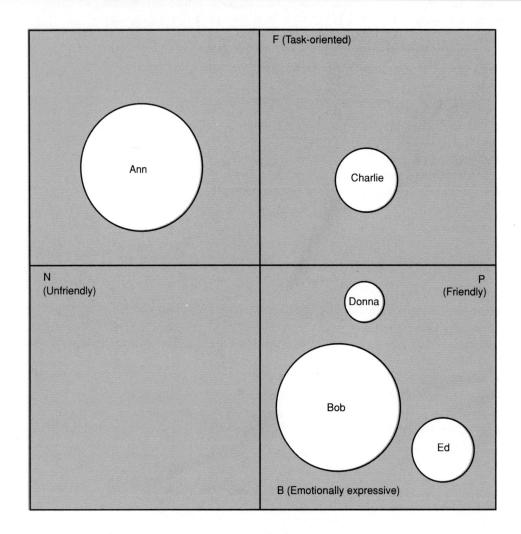

SYMLOG:
Depicting
Cohesiveness

Several of the processes we have discussed so far, in particular group cohesiveness, can be depicted using **SYMLOG,** which is an acronym for the **SY**stem for the **M**ultiple **L**evel **O**bservation of **G**roups. Developed by Bales, SYMLOG is both a theory and a methodology that permits a three-dimensional diagram to be constructed of a group.[28] Examples of such diagrams are provided in figures 7.5 and 7.6. (Instructions for producing a simplified, SYMLOG-like diagram are included in the *Instructor's Manual.*) You can see, even without detailed information about SYMLOG theory, that the first group is fragmented and polarized, but the second is unified and cohesive.

Figure 7.6   SYMLOG diagram of a unified, productive group.

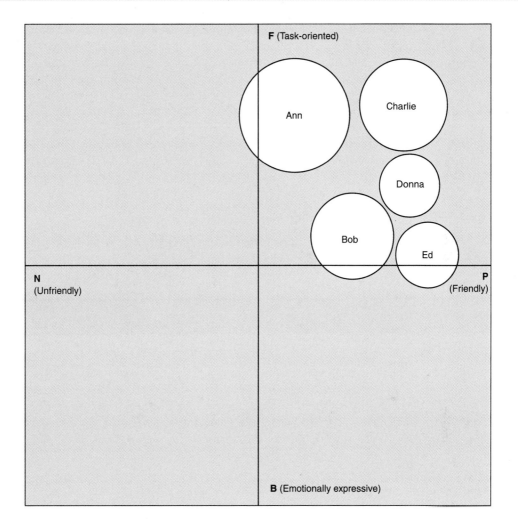

SYMLOG theory rests on the assumption that behavior of each member in a group can be classified along each of three independent dimensions: dominant versus submissive; friendly versus unfriendly; and task-oriented versus emotionally expressive.[29] SYMLOG may be used in one of two ways. With the scoring method, external observers score the verbal and nonverbal behaviors of members as they interact in real time. The rating method is easier, requiring no special training; external observers or group members themselves complete a twenty-six-question rating scale evaluating each member's behavior. The results are tallied in a particular way so each member can be placed on the SYMLOG diagram.

Each of the three dimensions is represented by a pair of letters that anchor the pole positions. For example, *P* (positive) stands for *friendly* and *N* (negative) stands for *unfriendly* behavior. On the diagram, the more friendly a member is toward the other members of the group, the farther the circle is placed to the right. The more unfriendly members are located farther to the left. (In figure 7.5, Ed is the most friendly and Ann the most unfriendly.) Task orientation is represented by *F* (forward); the more task-oriented a member is, the closer he or she is to the top of the diagram. Emotional expressiveness is represented by *B* (backward); these members are closer to the bottom of the diagram. (In figure 7.5, Ann is the most task oriented, and Ed the most emotionally expressive.) The third dimension is depicted by the size of a member's circle. *U,* for *up,* represents dominance and *D,* for *down,* represents submissiveness. (In figure 7.5, Ann and Bob are the most dominant, Donna the most submissive.)

You can readily see that the group shown in figure 7.5 is not cohesive. Ann is dominant, task-oriented, and negative toward her fellow members. She tries to dictate what happens in the group. Bob is dominant, but friendly and emotionally expressive, which gets the group off track frequently; almost certainly, Bob's behavior clashes with Ann's desire to stick to the task. Charlie, who is moderately dominant, task oriented, and friendly, is in the ideal position for a democratic, group-centered leader, but he's all by himself. Just by looking at the diagram you can tell that these people do not work well as a team. Members are dissimilar, they clash, there appears to be little cohesiveness, and there are wide variations in the degree of participation members exhibit.

The diagram in figure 7.6 tells a different story. This group seems unified, with all members in the upper right-hand quadrant (which Bales calls the *decision-making quadrant*). Members are sufficiently task-oriented to complete the group's assignment, but friendly enough toward each other that their interaction is probably harmonious. This is a picture of a productive and efficient group. As you can see, a SYMLOG analysis provides a "snapshot" of a group as a whole system whose component parts (the members) operate interdependently.

Fantasy Themes

A group's culture is produced by the interaction among group members. We discussed how roles and norms emerge as elements of a group's culture, but one of the most powerful ways in which group culture is created is through *fantasy.* Technically, **fantasy** refers to "the creative and imaginative shared interpretation of events that fulfill a group's psychological or rhetorical need to make sense of their experience and to anticipate their future."[30] Fantasy, in this sense, does not mean fictitious or unreal. It means that during certain periods of the group's interaction, rather than discussing events happening in the here-and-now of the group, the members are telling stories, relating past events, and sharing anecdotes that have a bearing *at the unconscious level* on the group's process. In other words, group members rarely set out *consciously* to establish the group's culture. Instead, they just talk. Some of that talk appears to be tangential to the group's real task, but in fact it meets psychological and rhetorical needs of the members.

When a group member says something not directly related to the present task of the group, that member has introduced a fantasy. This happens often during a discussion, with many fantasies going no further. However, sometimes group members pick up on the fantasy introduced by one group member and elaborate on it. Several members join the fantasy by adding their pieces to the story, in a kind of group storytelling. A fantasy that is picked up and elaborated by the group members is called a **fantasy chain,** first described by Bales.[31] Typically, during a fantasy chain the speed of the interaction picks up, voices become louder, and a sense of excitement can be detected. The mood is electric. The fantasy chain may last from as little as half a minute to as much as half an hour. Eventually the chain peters out, often when one member pulls the group back on task. Fantasy chaining is a rhetorical tool for creating shared images of the group and its environment. In chapter 3 we noted that communication is transactional; during fantasy chain, group members transact, without preplanned intent, to create meaning for the group. This story-telling activity plays a crucial role in determining and passing along a group's culture.[32]

Fantasy chains develop in a fairly predictable way.[33] First, some form of ambiguity or uncertainty exists in the group. One member begins the fantasy by introducing a core image that somehow relates to the uncertainty. Other members spread that core image by adding their own elements to the fantasy, creating a group, rather than just an individual, metaphor. Finally, when the fantasy chain has ended, the group members have converged on a particular picture of the group's reality.

Fantasies are *about* something; the content of the fantasy is called the **fantasy theme.** Often, there is an obvious or *manifest* theme to the fantasy chain, and a *latent,* or below-the-surface theme that, when examined, reveals the culture, values, and norms of the group. Often, fantasies have heroes and villains, plot lines, and a well-developed ethical structure that gives moral or psychological guidance to a group. To interpret the latent meaning of a fantasy, Bales suggests looking for a sudden insight rather than trying to analyze the fantasy systematically.

Fantasy is rooted in the theory of **symbolic convergence,** which was articulated and developed by Bormann. Symbolic convergence theory acknowledges that humans are storytelling creatures who create and share meaning through talk.[34] *Convergence* refers to the fact that during interaction the private symbolic worlds of individuals often overlap, or converge. When that occurs, as it *must* to some extent in a group or there would be no group, meaning is shared; the symbolic, personal communication of two or more individuals constructs a shared reality that bonds the individuals, helps them discover how they feel about certain events, reveals shared values, and can serve as a guide to action. In other words, symbolic communication theory "accounts for the creation and maintenance of a group consciousness through shared motives, common emotional activity, and consensual meanings for events."[35] We will now turn from this fairly abstract discussion to several specific examples of how fantasy helps shape a group's reality. Because fantasy chaining ties into unconscious meanings or collective needs of the participants, fantasy has a great power to motivate.

In the short and simple fantasy chain below, members of a student group are planning publicity for their annual Career Day seminar.[36] Chris asks Kevin what the previous year's group did for publicity:

Discussion	Commentary
Chris: Kevin, do you know what they did last time?	Chris asks a direct, task-relevant question.
Kevin: Yeah, somewhere I've got a list here. All they really did was put an ad in the school paper and then sent around this tacky memo to the faculty about a week ahead of time asking them to announce it in classes. It was embarrassing!	Kevin answers Chris, but introduces the fantasy about the "embarrassing" performance of last year's group.
Deirdre: I can't believe that's all they did!	Deirdre, in an animated way, picks up on Kevin's criticism of the previous group.
Lori: It was John's fault—he didn't want to do *anything,* and the group didn't do anything!	Lori adds her part.
Tony: What a bunch of lazy wimps!	Tony contributes.
Chris: We've already done more than they ever did, and we've just gotten started.	Chris contributes, and adds the idea that *this* group has already done better than the last one.
Kevin: I know! We're going to look a lot better than they did!	Kevin adds to Chris's idea.
Lori: Okay, I like trashing those guys as much as you do, but we're really getting off track.	Lori stops the fantasy by getting the group back on track.

In this segment, the group starts out addressing its task directly, but quickly gets off task as members enjoy trashing the previous year's group. Kevin introduces the fantasy, with all group members participating in the fantasy chain until Lori, the group's designated leader, stops the chain and returns the group to its task. What function has the fantasy served? The manifest theme of the fantasy is, "Last year's group did a rotten job of publicity." Remember, though, that fantasies help create a shared meanings for the *present* group. In this sequence, trashing the previous group builds up the performance of the present group by comparison, as hinted at in Chris's comment, "We've already done more than they ever did. . . ." By saying what a lousy group the previous year's group was, this group is subtly saying, "We're so much better." The group is setting standards of excellence, establishing norms of professionalism missing in the previous group that motivate the members to do better. The following is an example from the church board introduced in chapter 2. The group has been discussing routine matters when Marina initiates the fantasy:

Discussion	**Commentary**
Marina: I just noticed that spider plant in the corner. It's doing great! In fact, better than when it was in our living room!	Marina introduces the fantasy about the plant, apparently irrelevant to the group's task.
Sally: It really is healthy. Look at all the spider babies it's produced.	Sally picks up the fantasy and adds to it.
Norm: It seems to be happier here than when we had it at home. That peace lily in the corner looks pretty good, too.	Norm adds to the chain.
Sunni: You should see the plants in the sanctuary. They look so happy and healthy.	Sunni extends the fantasy to include the sanctuary plants as well.
Bill: Maybe we should bring in that half-dead shamrock in our kitchen. Do you think the environment would revive it?	Bill extends; his statement about the beneficial effects of the church environment hints at the meaning of this fantasy for this particular group.
Gary: It's all that tender, loving care!	Gary contributes.
Dick: They do look good, but we've got a lot to cover yet. Can we get back to the agenda?	Dick acknowledges, but brings the group back to its task.

The ostensible, or manifest, theme of this fantasy is the health of the plants in the church. The latent theme, which is not terribly disguised, is members' belief that they have helped create a positive, supportive atmosphere that is healthy for plants and, by extension, other living things (especially people). Thus, this particular fantasy chain reinforces the church board members' desire to do something important, life-giving, and good for the congregation. It also solidifies their commitment to the task.

Fantasies perform several functions for small groups. First, they help the members create the group's unique identity.[37] The two examples just discussed demonstrate that function. The student group helped define itself as an excellent, hard working, professional team by comparing itself favorably with the previous group. Church board members intensified their commitment to the job of establishing a new congregation and patted themselves on the back for creating a nurturing atmosphere.

Second, fantasies help a group deal with threatening or difficult information that members might feel reluctant to address directly. To illustrate, Morocco related the story of the first meeting of a research group whose student members believed their leaders were not providing them with enough direction.[38] One student recalled seeing a film about an experiment in which baby monkeys were deprived of maternal nurturing. The other members, who had seen the movie in school, began to contribute by adding details and developing a plot and dramatic image associated with the movie. The social and sexual development of the monkeys in the movie had been impaired by the lack of parental care, and this image served to symbolize the reality that group members were currently experiencing. In essence, the group was saying, "The lack of attention and help on the part of the leaders will ultimately harm us as individuals and as a group."

Third, fantasies help direct a group's actions by subtly endorsing or condemning particular courses of action. For example, Putnam and her associates describe a contract bargaining situation between two committees, one of teachers and the other of administrators.[39] The administrators constructed a fantasy chain about one of the teachers, whose constant head nodding reminded them of a woodpecker or a bird that bobs up and down on a cup. Their fantasy theme created a shared image of the teachers as well meaning but inexperienced. Later during the bargaining situation, the teachers appeared to renege on a proposal they had earlier accepted. The administrators could have made a big deal of this by escalating the conflict, but the image of the teachers as inexperienced rather than unscrupulous led them to perceive the teachers' actions as an innocent mistake. Putnam notes that this benevolent interpretation by the administrators gave the teachers latitude to err without derailing the bargaining process. The effect was to maintain good feelings all around. The fantasy, in part, inspired this outcome by molding the administrators' perceptions of the teachers' shortcomings.

Finally, fantasies can be entertaining and fun for the group. In the previous example, the administrators' committee kept itself happily entertained by imagining the teacher who nodded constantly as a woodpecker and a whirligig bird. Fantasies help groups exercise their imaginations and creativity. They are powerful shapers of a group's culture.

Summary

In this chapter, we have examined eight major process variables that need to be considered when studying how a group culture evolves from an initially loose collection of individuals: interpersonal tensions, progression of the group through identifiable phases, rules and norms, development of a role structure, communication networks, status hierarchies, cohesiveness, and shared fantasies. All groups must find ways to deal effectively with their primary and secondary tensions. Groups develop in stages, typically moving from the stage of formation to production, but always need to deal simultaneously with task and socioemotional concerns. While formal rules may exist to govern some of the group's interaction, informal rules (norms) that guide members' behaviors are developed with the tacit approval of the members themselves. From their personal behaviors and skills, group members carve out their group roles in cooperation with other group members. All groups need both task and maintenance functions to be performed, but self-oriented roles detract from the group's purpose. The ideal communication network for a small group is the all-channel network rather than the Y or the wheel. The combination of roles and placement in the communication network influences each member's status within the group. These factors affect the group's cohesiveness, which is both a product of the group's interaction and a process variable that affects the group's outcomes. The uniqueness of the group's culture is determined in part by the fantasy chaining that helps the group create its shared reality.

In the next chapter, we will consider one of the most important group processes—leadership.

1. Observe a small group during at least one discussion; take notes on what you observe and what norms these behaviors imply. Then, using the format that follows, record all the norms you infer from your observations by stating each as a rule of conduct for members. Try to identify at least fifteen or twenty norms. Briefly describe the observed behaviors on which each norm is based. Finally, indicate whether you think the norm helped the group increase its output (+), had no effect on output (0), or reduced the group's output (–).

Norm	Specific Behavior that Provides Evidence of the Norm	Impact

2. Select a small group to which you have belonged since the beginning and which has met at least several times. Describe the phases in that group's development as best you recall them. What phases did you see? How did you know when the group left one phase and entered another? Did the phases overlap? Do your fellow group members recall the phases as you do, or differently?

3. Using the list of behavioral functions as a guide, several observers should classify each remark made by each of several members of a group according to the functions. This gives you a tally of how often each person performs each function. How would you describe each member's role? Draw a role profile, similar to figure 7.3, for each person, and label the informal role each performed.

4. Rank the members you observed in the previous question according to the status of each in the group. How much relative power and influence do you think each exhibits? Why?

5. Think of at least ten groups to which you have belonged during the past year. What was your role in each? Do you have a different role depending on the group, or do you keep the same general role? Does your role change? Why or why not? What factors influence the role you perform?

6. Diagram the flow of communication in a discussion group you observe using figure 14.2, the verbal interaction diagram. Be sure to record how many times each member speaks and to whom. What is the proportion of the total statements made by each member? What sort of communication network exists in this group?

7. Think of the most and least cohesive groups to which you have belonged. List as many significant differences as you can that you believe contributed to the cohesiveness or lack of it. What do you conclude?

8. Tape record a group's interaction and listen to the tape later for the purpose of identifying fantasy themes. (Listen especially for periods when the group seems excited and the energy level appears to pick up.) What function do you think the fantasy theme is serving? What does it say about the group's shared reality?

Bibliography

Bormann, Ernest G. *Small Group Communication: Theory and Practice,* 3d ed. New York: Harper & Row, Publishers, 1990, chapters 5, 7, and 8.

Feldman, Daniel. "Development and Enforcement of Group Norms," *Academy of Management Review* 9 (1984): 47–53.

Fisher, B. Aubrey, and Donald G. Ellis. *Small Group Decision Making: Communication and the Group Process,* 3d ed. New York: McGraw-Hill, 1990, chapter 8.

Shimanoff, Susan B. "Coordinating Group Interaction Via Communication Rules." In *Small Group Communication: A Reader,* 6th ed., eds. Robert S. Cathcart and Larry A. Samovar. Dubuque, IA: Wm. C. Brown Publishers, 1992, 250–62.

Notes

1. Ernest G. Bormann, *Discussion and Group Methods: Theory and Practice,* 3d ed. (New York: Harper & Row, Publishers, 1990): 132–39.

2. David B. Barker, "The Behavioral Analysis of Interpersonal Intimacy in Group Development," *Small Group Research* 22 (February 1991): 76–91.

3. Ernest G. Bormann, *Discussion and Group Methods,* 139.

4. Robert F. Bales, *Interaction Process Analysis* (Reading, MA: Addison-Wesley, 1950).

5. William F. Whyte, *Pattern for Industrial Peace* (New York: Harper, 1951).

6. B. Aubrey Fisher and Randall K. Stutman, "An Assessment of Group Trajectories: Analyzing Developmental Breakpoints," *Communication Quarterly* 35 (Spring 1987): 105–24.

7. Robert F. Bales, *Interaction Process Analysis.*

8. Henry M. Robert, *Robert's Rules of Order, Newly Revised* (Glenview, IL: Scott, Foresman and Company, 1990): 471–521.

9. George C. Homans, *The Human Group* (New York: Harcourt Brace Jovanovich, 1950): 123.

10. Susan B. Shimanoff, "Coordinating Group Interaction Via Communication Rules," in *Small Group Communication: A Reader,* 6th ed., eds. Robert S. Cathcart and Larry A. Samovar (Dubuque, IA: Wm. C. Brown Publishers, 1992): 255.

11. Susan B. Shimanoff, "Coordinating Group Interaction."

12. J. I. Hurwitz, A. F. Zander, and B. Hymovitch, "Some Effects of Power on the Relations among Group Members," in *Group Dynamics: Research and Theory,* 3d ed., eds. D. Cartwright and A. Zander (New York: Harper & Row, Publishers, 1968): 291–97.

13. Dean C. Barnlund and C. Harland, "Propinquity and Prestige as Determinants of Communication Networks," *Sociometry* 26 (1963): 467–79.

14. E. Hollander, "Conformity, Status, and Idiosyncracy Credit," *Psychological Review* 65 (1958): 117–27.

15. Carolyn J. Wood, "Challenging the Assumptions Underlying the Use of Participatory Decision Making Strategies: A Longitudinal Case Study," *Small Group Behavior* 20 (1989): 428–48.

16. David B. Barker, "The Behavioral Analysis of Interpersonal Intimacy."

17. Harold L. Nixon II, *The Small Group* (Englewood Cliffs, NJ: Prentice-Hall, 1979): 74–76.

18. Charles R. Evans and Kenneth L. Dion, "Group Cohesion and Performance," *Small Group Behavior* 22 (May 1991): 175–86.

19. Lynne Kelly and Robert L. Duran, "Interaction and Performance in Small Groups: A Descriptive Report," *International Journal of Small Group Research* 1 (1985): 182–92.

20. Charles N. Greene, "Cohesion and Productivity in Work Groups," *Small Group Behavior* 20 (1989): 70–86.

21. Carl E. Larson and Frank M. J. LaFasto, *TeamWork: What Must Go Right/What Can Go Wrong* (Newbury Park, CA: Sage Publications, 1989).

22. Carolyn J. Wood, "Challenging the Assumptions."

23. Frederick G. Elias, Mark E. Johnson, and Jay B. Fortman, "Task-focused Self-disclosure: Effects on

Group Cohesiveness, Commitment to the Task, and Productivity," *Small Group Behavior* 20 (February 1989): 87–96.

24. Irving L. Janis, *Groupthink: Psychological Studies of Policy Decisions and Fiascoes,* 2d ed. rev. (Boston: Houghton Mifflin Company, 1983).

25. William F. Owen, "Metaphor Analysis of Cohesiveness in Small Discussion Groups," *Small Group Behavior* 16 (1985): 415–26.

26. David B. Barker, "The Behavioral Analysis of Interpersonal Intimacy."

27. Ernest G. Bormann and Nancy C. Bormann, *Effective Small Group Communication,* 4th ed. (Edina, MN: Burgess Publishing Company, 1988): 74–76.

28. Robert F. Bales and Stephen P. Cohen, *SYMLOG: A System for the Multiple Level Observation of Groups* (New York: The Free Press, 1979). Space constraints prevent including a complete description of SYMLOG theory and methodology here; we refer readers who are interested in learning to construct a complete SYMLOG diagram for their groups to a workbook, *SYMLOG Case Study Kit,* R. F. Bales (New York: The Free Press, 1980). The *Instructor's Manual* for this text includes instructions and necessary forms for completing a simplified, SYMLOG-like diagram so students can have a better idea of what SYMLOG can do.

29. Lynne Kelly and Robert L. Duran note that in some recent writings, Bales refers to the third dimension as acceptance versus nonacceptance of authority, which designation seems more appropriate when assessing group member values as opposed to behaviors; in "SYMLOG: Theory and Measurement of Small Group Interaction," in *Small Group Communication: A Reader*, 6th ed., eds., Robert S.

Cathcart and Larry A. Samovar (Dubuque, IA: Wm. C. Brown Publishers, 1992): 39–52.

30. Ernest G. Bormann, "Symbolic Convergence Theory and Communication in Group Decision Making," in *Communication and Group Decision Making,* eds. Randy Y. Hirokawa and Marshall S. Poole (Newbury Park, CA: Sage Publications, 1986): 221.

31. Robert F. Bales, *Personality and Interpersonal Behavior* (New York: Holt Rinehart and Winston, Inc. 1970): 105–8, 136–55.

32. Eric E. Peterson, "The Stories of Pregnancy: On Interpretation of Small-Group Cultures," *Communication Quarterly* 35 (1987): 39–47.

33. Catherine C. Morocco, "Development and Function of Group Metaphor," *Journal for the Theory of Social Behavior* 9 (1979): 15–27.

34. Ernest G. Bormann, "Symbolic Convergence Theory."

35. Linda L. Putnam, Shirley A. Van Hoeven, and Connie A. Bullis, "The Role of Rituals and Fantasy Themes in Teachers' Bargaining," *Western Journal of Speech Communication* (Winter, 1991): 87.

36. This fantasy chain is a slightly expanded version that occurs near the beginning of the leadership segment, part 1, of the videotape ancillary to this text, *Communicating Effectively in Small Groups.*

37. Catherine C. Morocco, "Development and Function of Group Metaphor," 15–27.

38. Catherine C. Morocco, "Development and Function of Group Metaphor."

39. Linda L. Putnam, Shirley A. Van Hoeven, and Connie A. Bullis, "The Role of Rituals and Fantasy Themes in Teachers' Bargaining."

Perspectives on Leadership in Small Groups

Central Message

Small group leadership results from communicative behaviors appropriate to group task and relational goals, other members' behaviors, the context, and other contingencies; leadership results from an *interaction* between leader and followers.

Study Objectives   As a result of your study of chapter 8 you should be able to:

1. Define the concepts of *leadership, leader, emergent leader,* and *designated leader.*

2. Explain the five sources of interpersonal influence (power) in a group and how they are involved in small group leadership.

3. Explain the three major approaches to small group leadership (trait, styles, and contingency approaches) and specific models included under each approach.

4. Name and describe seven communicative competencies important for small group leaders.

5. Describe how leaders and members are interdependent.

6. Explain *distributed leadership* and why it is an appropriate model for small, task-oriented groups.

Key Terms

Autocratic leaders
Communicative competencies
Contingency approaches
Democratic leaders
Designated leader
Distributed leadership

Emergent leader
Functions approach
Laissez-faire leaders
Leader
Leader-Member Exchange
  (LMX) model

Leadership
Power
Self-monitoring
Styles approach
Traits approach

According to Larson and LaFasto, the final ingredient for effective group performance is team leadership, with the right person serving in the leadership role.[1] However, sometimes it seems we know little more about leadership than people knew in Plato's time.[2] Contemporary writers are just as concerned about small group leadership as ancient ones were.

Because small groups are so ubiquitous, you will certainly have your turn serving as a small group leader. This can be a source of self-esteem, recognition, and appreciation; however, it can also be a nightmare.

Much of the conventional wisdom about what makes a good leader is simply wrong. Many people hold oversimplified beliefs about effective leadership that interfere with their learning to function well as small group leaders. We hope this and the next chapter will dispel those beliefs, as well as help you discover the communication competencies you must develop to perform well as a leader.

In chapter 8 we examine the concepts of *leader* and *leadership,* review historical and contemporary perspectives about leadership, describe the process of leadership emergence, examine the relationship between leaders and members, and develop an argument in favor of *distributed leadership* for most small task-oriented groups. In chapter 9 we focus on the duties commonly expected of designated small group leaders in our culture and provide specific suggestions on how to perform them.

Leadership and Leaders

The terms *leadership* and *leader* have related but separate meanings. One refers to a process, the other to a person.

Leadership

Most social scientists define **leadership** as interpersonal influence. The following definition by Hackman and Johnson reveals the importance of communication in the leadership process:

> Leadership is human (symbolic) communication which modifies the attitudes and behaviors of others in order to meet group goals and needs.[3]

This definition incorporates two important implications. First, the use of the term *modifies* suggests that influence via communication, as opposed to physical coercion or other forms of force, is the heart of the process we term *leadership.* We aren't talking about an "attitude adjustment" through force, but through interaction and persuasion, human symbolic activity. Second, this definition implies that only influence directed toward accomplishment of a *group* goal can truly be termed *small group leadership.* Thus, it excludes such behavior as one member influencing another to sabotage a group goal.

Sources of Influence (Power)

The ability to influence stems from **power** that is derived from a particular source, or base. Leaders and followers transact to create a relationship based on perceived power. Leaders can influence the conduct of others to the extent they have power that is perceived and acknowledged by followers. The bases of power identified by French and Raven include reward, punishment, legitimate, referent, and expert.[4]

Leaders can *reward* followers by giving them both tangible and intangible items such as special attention, acknowledgment, compliments, personal favors, money, and material goods. They can also *punish* by withholding these same items. For example, the frown a leader may give a latecomer is a form of punishment. *Coercion* is a special form of punishment power that uses threats or force to "influence" others. Although good leaders may effectively use punishment (especially the fear of losing something important, such as belonging to the group or the respect of the others), they do not use hardball tactics to coerce or force compliance. We do not consider coercion to be genuine leadership as we define it. As you know, coercion breeds resentment, sabotage, and rebellion, which are not desirable small group outcomes.

Legitimate power stems from a special position or role acknowledged by the followers. For instance, in a police task force, lieutenants are accepted as having the right to give orders to police sergeants, who themselves may give orders to patrol officers. In a self-managed work group or committee, the chair or coordinator has the right to perform certain actions, such as calling a meeting to order or preparing an agenda. However, legitimate power includes only influence that is accepted as appropriate by followers. Thus, a committee chair does not have the right to tell members how to dress or wear their hair, although a supervisor might have such power.

Referent power is based on attraction or identification with another person. Some referent leaders have charisma that causes others to want to associate with them and imitate their behavior. For example, one of us skipped a class in high school because the referent leader of our small group of friends suggested it. Ideally, however, discussion leaders model positive behaviors for the other members to admire and emulate, such as listening, considering all sides of an issue, and keeping remarks orderly. The more leaders are admired and respected, the more members copy their behavior, and thus the greater their power to influence the group.

Expert power is attributed by members for what another member knows or can do. For instance, if your group is responsible for producing a panel discussion for the rest of your class and you happen to be the only member who has ever participated in a panel discussion, you have expertise the others value, which gives you power in that particular group. The person with expert power is influential because he or she is perceived as having knowledge or skills vital to the group.

Usually a leader's power stems from more than one base. The more bases on which a person's power rests, the more that person has the potential to dominate a group. Conversely, the more these bases of power are distributed among members, the more likely is verbal participation to be shared, decision making to be collaborative, and satisfaction high. In other words, leadership can be provided by all members exercising their influence in service to the group goal. We expand on this idea later in the chapter.

The term **leader** refers to a person, or sometimes to a special position occupied by a person.[5] A leader in a small group is a person who influences the behavior of others through communication. We use the term *leader* to refer to three related types of individuals: a person who exerts influence toward achievement of a group's goal, a person who is perceived by the others as being a leader (influencer), and a person

Leader

Designated leaders greatly affect small groups.

Photo by James Shaffer.

who has been appointed or elected to a leadership position (e.g., chair, team leader, coordinator, or facilitator). A person elected or appointed to a leadership position is called a **designated leader.**

Having a designated leader usually helps provide stability to a group. Numerous studies have shown that small groups with stable leadership are more effective in goal achievement than small groups that fail to settle issues about who is responsible for what. A group whose energy is siphoned off in a leadership struggle produces poor outcomes, dissatisfied members, and low cohesion.[6] In contrast, groups with designated leaders *accepted by the members* have fewer interpersonal problems and often produce better outcomes than groups without designated leaders.[7] The implication is clear: even in a group where influence (and thus leadership) is widely shared, someone must coordinate the flow of communication and the work of the members.

Having the title of *designated leader* gives someone legitimate power, but that person must still *earn* the respect and support of other members. A designated leader's behavior will be evaluated and may frequently be challenged by the members. If the designated leader's power rests solely on the legitimacy of the title, someone else with more broadly based power will likely emerge as a more influential informal leader.

Even though all members of a small group bear responsibility for the success or failure of the group, the designated leader shoulders special responsibility for the work of the group. As Stech and Ratliffe say, both "group members and outsiders tend to hold the leader accountable for group beliefs, proposals, actions, and products."[8] This confers tremendous obligation on the designated leader to attend to how the group is functioning as a system and ensure that needed leadership services are provided.

As with other social scientific phenomena, the study of leadership has moved from simplicity to complexity. In this next section, we present several of the most important approaches to the study of leadership. The most useful contemporary theories are based on models of communication. We urge you not to become rigidly attached to any one theory because all of them contain useful insights; moreover, new discoveries may enable simplification of the complexity that currently exists.

A *trait* is a characteristic a person has. Some traits, such as eye color or height, are unchangeable; others, such as self-monitoring (which we discuss shortly), are subject to some control.

The earliest studies of leadership (from before the Christian epoch through the 1930s) assumed that people were collections of relatively fixed traits and that one leadership situation was much like another. Researchers who investigated leadership from this perspective looked for the trait or traits that distinguished leaders from followers. They believed that leaders were a special class of people who were born, not made. Social scientists used a number of personality measures in an effort to discover the traits of leaders. Some studies found that leaders tended to have higher IQs, and were taller, more attractive, and larger than nonleaders.[9] However, inconsistent results led scientists to reject the theory that leadership can be explained solely or even primarily on the basis of traits.

Modern trait approaches examine a variety of complex personality characteristics. Although they are labeled *traits,* they seem to represent *behaviors* that leaders perform rather than invariable, unchangeable characteristics. Researchers suggest that there is a range within which people can modify their behavior. Foreshadowing the contingency approaches to be discussed later, contemporary trait approaches hint that group situations differ; thus, the person who becomes a leader in one group may not become a leader in another. This significantly modifies the "leaders are born, not made" view.

One such contemporary **traits approach** was suggested by Bormann and his associates at the University of Minnesota, who studied the process of leadership emergence in initially leaderless groups.[10] An **emergent leader** is a group member who starts out on an equal footing with other members but eventually surfaces as leader and is acknowledged as such by the other members. Geier found that emergent leaders usually are selected by elimination during a two-stage process. At first, all members have potential to become the group's primary leader. However, during a brief first stage, members who are quiet, uninformed, or dogmatic are quickly rejected. During a longer second stage, people who try to lead in an authoritarian or

Theoretical Approaches to Leadership

Traits Approaches

Historical Trait Approaches

Contemporary Trait Approaches

manipulative manner are eliminated. Finally, the person most skilled in verbalizing ideas emerges as leader by consensus of the group. Thus, the so-called trait of "skill in verbalizing" was associated with leadership.

Several recent studies of leadership have found other traits associated with leadership emergence. One of these is **self-monitoring,** discussed briefly in chapter 6, which refers to individuals' abilities to monitor, in a given situation, both social cues and their own actions.[11] High self-monitors are sensitive to contextual cues, socially perceptive, and are able to respond flexibly according to what seems needed at any given time. Zaccaro et al. found that more than half the variance of leadership emergence was explained by self-monitoring.[12] This was confirmed by Ellis and Cronshaw, who found that male high self-monitors emerged as leaders because they were better able to adapt their behaviors to fit the needs of the group.[13] However, this was not true for women, probably because female high self-monitors sometimes pick up cues that their leadership behavior is perceived as inappropriate. They may then modify that behavior to conform to what the group deems appropriate. These authors discovered that high self-monitors do in fact monitor social cues and are able to modify their responses; they are more likely to emerge as leaders across situations. However, low self-monitors, whose actions are motivated more by internal than external cues, can also emerge as leaders in situations where they have favorable attitudes toward expressing leadership; but they will not emerge as leaders if they hold unfavorable attitudes about leadership.[14]

Verbal style, which Baker conceived as a trait-like characteristic, together with the content of communication, also is associated with leadership emergence.[15] Consistent with earlier studies, Baker found that members whose communication style was quiet, tentative, or vague were perceived as uncommitted to the group and not knowledgeable about the group's task. These members were quickly eliminated as potential leaders because others did not believe they contributed ideas or helped organize the group. Those who did emerge as leaders made more attempts to suggest procedures for the group and thus helped to get the group organized. The emergent leader's participation profiles were high in procedure giving, moderate in idea giving, and low in stating opinions. Leaders' and members' styles were consistent in what Baker describes as *mundane* style: informal, unimaginative, ordinary. High-status members who were not leaders had a dramatic style that, though unusual, was tolerated because of their perceived helpfulness to the group.

Although strict trait approaches have been discredited, it is clear that some trait-like characteristics, such as self-monitoring and communicator style, are associated with leadership. Stogdill noted that "leadership is a relation that exists between persons in a social situation, and that persons who are leaders in one situation may not necessarily be leaders in other situations."[16] We believe his conclusion that leadership is not a universal set of traits is valid; however, it seems equally clear that people with the *ability* to adapt their behaviors and who possess communication skills that help clarify the group's task and motivate other members will be influential in groups. Appropriate leader behaviors in a group are shaped by the needs of the group. A person with the ability to respond flexibly, whether that is a trait or behavior, will likely be influential in a group.

Style refers to the pattern of behaviors a leader exhibits in a group. Early style theorists attempted to discover whether there was one ideal style for small group leaders. More recent style theorists have looked at styles in relationship to member and task characteristics, which foreshadows the upcoming contingency approaches to leadership.

Styles Approaches

Considerable research has examined the behaviors of designated leaders classified as *democratic, autocratic,* and *laissez-faire.* **Democratic leaders** encourage members to participate in group decisions, including policy-making decisions ("What ideas do you have for organizing our task?"). **Laissez-faire leaders** take almost no initiative for structuring a group, but they may respond to inquiries from members ("I don't care, whatever you want to do is fine with me."). **Autocratic leaders** tightly control their groups, including making assignments, directing all verbal interaction, and giving orders ("Here's how I've structured your task. First, you will. . . ."). They ask fewer questions but answer more than democratic leaders, and make more attempts to coerce but fewer attempts to get others to participate.[17]

The autocratic and democratic styles of leadership described here correspond closely with the Theory X and Theory Y assumptions about humans described by management theorist Douglas McGregor.[18] Theory X assumes that people don't like to work and must therefore be compelled by a strong, controlling leader ("boss") who supervises their work closely. In contrast, Theory Y assumes that people work as naturally as they play, and are creative problem solvers who like to take charge of their own work. Leaders who accept the assumptions of Theory Y behave democratically by providing only as much structure as a group needs, allowing members to participate fully in decision making and other aspects of the group's work.

Research findings have been consistent about the effects of leadership style on group output.[19] Democratically led groups are generally more satisfied than autocratically led groups; most people in our culture prefer democratic groups. Autocratic groups often work harder in the presence of the leader, but they also experience more incidents of aggressiveness and apathy. Democratic groups whose leaders provide some structure and coordination are better problem solvers and their members are more satisfied than those in laissez-faire groups without structure.

Although a leadership style that provides some degree of structure appears to be the most desirable for both productivity and satisfaction, several contingent factors (including cultural values) affect how much structure and control a particular group seems to need. We next consider contingency approaches.

All **contingency approaches** assume that group situations vary, with different situations requiring different leadership styles. These approaches acknowledge that factors such as members' skills and experience, cultural values, the type of task, and the time available affect the type of leadership likely to be effective. Contingency approaches acknowledge the complexity of small group systems, with all factors such as task, members, and environment affecting each other interdependently.

Contingency Approaches

Not only do most current researchers accept contingency assumptions, but so do group members. Wood asked members of continuing small groups with task, social, and dual task-social objectives what they expected of designated leaders. Three factors emerged: task guidance, interpersonal attractiveness, and team spirit. Members of both task and dual-purpose groups rated task-oriented leadership (providing structure) as important, whereas members of social groups rated interpersonal attractiveness high and task orientation low. A moderate degree of team spirit was expected of leaders in all types of groups.[20] Griffin found that the amount of structuring and directive behavior expected from supervisors depended on the level of growth needs of subordinates. People with high growth needs (enjoy challenging jobs) most preferred participative, considerate supervisors, whereas employees with lower growth needs preferred more autocratic leadership.[21] A complex relationship was found among member needs, leadership style, and member satisfaction, giving credence to the general contingency hypothesis of leadership in small discussion groups.[22]

Downs and Pickett also examined contingencies of leader style and member needs. Groups of participants with high social needs were most productive with task-oriented procedural leaders and least productive with no designated leader. Groups of people low on interpersonal needs did equally well with designated leaders who provided task structuring only, with leaders who provided both task structuring and socioemotional leadership, and with no designated leader. Groups with some members high and some low in interpersonal needs performed somewhat better without a designated leader.

The contingency approach is also supported by Skaret and Bruning, who noted that satisfaction involves a complex interaction between leader behavior and work group attitudes.[23] The following traits of followers influence the type of leadership they preferred: degree of authoritarianism and dogmatism, need for achievement, and locus of control (whether one feels in control of one's own life or governed by fate).[24] From the research and theory surveyed, we can safely conclude that a discussion leader needs to be flexible, adapting to situational contingencies, but that in almost all situations a democratic structuring approach will be productive, or will at least *not* be counterproductive.

The Functions Approach

The **functions approach** is a subtype of contingency theories that assumes groups are most productive when specific functions are performed by leaders. The two major categories of functions are those that focus on interpersonal relationships (various writers call this *maintenance, socioemotional, social leadership,* or *initiating consideration*) and those concerned with the group's task (also called *initiating structure*). Examples of these kinds of functions were described in chapter 7.

Several researchers have attempted to identify specific task and maintenance functions needed for effective leadership. One of the earliest category systems for studying behavioral functions was the Interaction Process Analysis developed by Bales.[25] Benne and Sheats identified a variety of task and maintenance functions they claim are productive for the group, along with a set of functions that are counterproductive.[26] Several of the Benne and Sheats functions are included on the lists in chapter 7. More recently, Fisher identified four functions performed by leaders, whom he saw as providing a mediating function between group events and activities and the final outcome:

1. Leaders provide sufficient information, as well as ability to process and handle considerable information.
2. Leaders enact a *variety* of functions needed within the group.
3. Leaders help group members make sense of decisions made and actions performed within the group by doing such things as supplying good reasons for those actions.
4. Leaders focus on the here-and-now, stopping the group from jumping to unwarranted conclusions or adopting stock answers too quickly.[27]

Weick created a metaphor of *leader as medium* to explain and emphasize what he hypothesized to be the major function of leadership.[28] Task groups usually confront a variety of interpersonal and task obstacles that must be overcome. One of the most difficult is the need to reduce a vast amount of complex and often equivocal information to an understandable level. Goal achievement requires group members to devise a set of rules and procedures for narrowing the number of plausible interpretations so they can devise an appropriate course of action. Weick says the basic function of leadership is to assist the group in creating an organizing scheme of rules and procedures for problem solving.

We view the functions approach as a contingency approach because two assumptions are implicit in the model. First, at different points in the group, different functions will be needed. For instance, *initiation* is needed to get the group started; *gatekeeping* is needed to facilitate participation, and so forth. Because of the unique combination of member skills, attitudes, behaviors, and so on, each group will require a different mix of functions. Second, the model suggests that *any* member of the group can perform any of the functions, not just the designated leader. It assumes that the necessary functions must be performed by *someone* for the group to be effective, but not necessarily or automatically by the designated leader. This approach sets the stage for viewing group leadership behavior as a property of the *group*, and a function of the interaction between members and the person whose title is *leader*.

Fiedler's Contingency Model

Some contingency approaches assume that there are limits to leaders' abilities to adapt; in other words, people are relatively inflexible. Leadership behaviors are trait-like in that leaders have styles they prefer and use more effectively than other styles. Fiedler's contingency model of leadership reflects this view. He concluded that there are three factors upon which appropriate leader behaviors are contingent: leader-member relations, task structure, and leader position (or legitimate) power.[29] The central thesis of Fiedler's work is that individuals' personal needs and characteristics make them suited for leadership only in certain types of contingencies, so it is more productive to match prospective leaders to situations than to try to change the individual's style. This also implies that a group's leadership situation will

Figure 8.1
Task and relationship
needs of maturing
groups.

From P. Hersey and K.
Blanchard, *Management of
Organizational Behavior:
Utilizing Human Resources,*
4th ed. Englewood Cliffs,
NJ: Prentice Hall, 1982,
p. 152. (Reprinted by
permission).

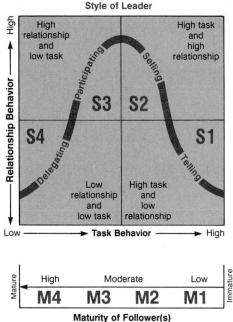

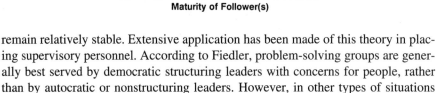

remain relatively stable. Extensive application has been made of this theory in placing supervisory personnel. According to Fiedler, problem-solving groups are generally best served by democratic structuring leaders with concerns for people, rather than by autocratic or nonstructuring leaders. However, in other types of situations (for instance, during emergencies or in leading primary groups) a more autocratic or relationship-oriented style would be more productive.

*Hersey and
Blanchard's
Situational Model*

Other contingency approaches believe that people are flexible enough to adapt their behavior to meet the needs of many groups. Representative of this approach is the model of leadership adaptability and style developed by Hersey and Blanchard.[30] These authors postulate that leadership behaviors can be located along two dimensions, relationship orientation (giving socioemotional support) and task orientation (coordination efforts, instructions, advice and so forth). A leader can be high on one, both, or neither dimension. (Figure 8.1 illustrates these dimensions.) However, whether a leader is effective depends on his or her ability to adapt to the needs of the members at all points during the life cycle, or maturity, of the group. For instance, a new group of inexperienced members needs higher task but lower relationship behaviors from the leader until members understand their charge and objectives. As members become familiar with the task, the leader should begin to increase relationship behavior. Eventually task behavior can be reduced, and, at full maturity, socioemotional support can be withdrawn, since the group's dependence on the leader is minimal. This model, which has not been widely tested empirically, implies that the leader must be able to analyze a group's situation and the maturity level of the members in order to provide the right amount of task instructions and socioemotional support. It also implies that a group's situation is not static, but changes throughout the life of the group.

Hersey and Blanchard's model places great faith in the leader's ability to adapt to the needs of the group. There is support for believing that many leaders are flexible, as the self-monitoring studies reported earlier suggested. Wood found, for example, that the discussion leaders she observed demonstrated behavioral flexibility. The comments of the designated leader varied depending on the stated purpose of the discussion and the previous success or failure of the committee. For example, leaders tended to compensate as needed, depending on what had occurred at previous meetings, by providing more or less structure. Wood noted, "The most important and obvious conclusion is that leaders of purposive discussions do engage in adaptive behavior."[31] Her results have been confirmed. Sorenson and Savage observed greater variety in the effective leaders' communicative styles than in those of ineffective leaders. In particular, leaders should attend to the degrees of dominance and supportiveness they exhibit.[32] Drecksell, too, found that leaders covered a wide range of functions, and their interaction was more complex than the interaction of other members.[33]

Chemers' *Integrative Systems/Process Model* is an example of another contingency model that assumes leaders can vary their behavior. Chemers' model reflects the complexity of a small group as a system; he assumes an interdependent relationship among all the possible input, throughput, and output variables of a small group.[34] Leadership in an open small group system involves interaction among inputs, including the leader's personal characteristics and competencies, cultural norms, situational contingencies, follower expectations and intentions, task variables, and the task itself. Process, or throughput, variables include leader/follower behaviors. Output variables include satisfaction, feedback, and group task performance. Because of its comprehensiveness, a problem with Chemers' model was pointed out by Fisher: "the number of variables that are potentially contingent on leadership and the possible combinations of those variables of situation, leader, and followers are virtually impossible to comprehend."[35] Thus, though theoretically sound, it is of limited practical value.

Chemers' Integrative Systems/Process Model

In an attempt to provide a model that acknowledges contingencies without overwhelming us with complexity, Barge and Hirokawa recently proposed a *Communication Competency Model of Group Leadership.*[36] The **communicative competencies** model is based on the assumptions that leadership involves behaviors that help a group overcome obstacles to goal achievement, that leadership occurs through the process of communication, and that communication skills (competencies) are the means used by individuals to lead small groups. This model maintains the task and relationship distinctions noted by many researchers, but provides an organizing scheme for the overwhelming array of facts and conjectures relating to group leadership. We consider it a contingency approach because it assumes that the actual context facing the leader and group is constantly shifting, so the task and relational communicative competencies needed vary from moment to moment. Group leaders must be highly flexible to draw from a personal repertoire of such competencies. We next direct your attention to the competencies we believe to be the most important to leadership and which we urge you to cultivate as personal skills.

Communicative Competencies Approach

Communicative Competencies of Effective Discussion Leaders

Knowing the behaviors and competencies that distinguish effective task group leaders can help you select a group's leader wisely and learn to be a better leader yourself. The following are specific communicative competencies exhibited by effective discussion leaders.

1. **Effective small group leaders are active communicators who encode ideas clearly and concisely.**

   Numerous studies have found emergent leaders to be high in verbal participation, although not necessarily the highest in a group.[37] Reynolds found that leaders maintained their influence by staying involved in group discussion and decision making.[38] But *amount* of talk alone is only a small part of verbal competency; Russell found that group leaders had higher levels of communicative *skills* than other members.[39]

   What are these skills? Lashbrook found that leaders were perceived as speaking more clearly and fluently than other members.[40] Facility in verbalizing problems, goals, values, ideals, and solutions characterizes effective discussion leaders. Barge and Hirokawa have theorized that the more complex the group's task, the more ambiguous the member roles, and the more negative the climate, the more important are the leader's communication skills.[41] We have already noted the importance of a leader's ability to adjust his or her communication behavior to the needs of the group.

2. **Effective group leaders communicate a good grasp of the group's task.**

   Above all else, their communication behaviors reveal extensive knowledge about the task, skills for organizing and interpreting that knowledge, and an understanding of procedures that facilitate task accomplishment.

3. **Effective group leaders are skilled in mediating information and ideas supplied by all members.**

   Such leaders are especially competent in analysis of statements and in the kinds of critical thinking that lead to thorough evaluation and integration of information. They are good at providing structure to unorganized information, at asking probing questions to bring out pertinent information, and at evaluating inferences and conclusions drawn from information. They help all members focus on activities relevant to the group's goal.[42]

4. **Effective group leaders express their opinions provisionally.**

   Most Americans prefer their leaders *not* to express ideas dogmatically. Benjamin Franklin knew this; that is why he described his leadership of the Constitutional Convention of 1776 as follows:

   [I] put on the humble inquirer and doubter . . . , never using . . . the words *certainly, undoubtedly,* or any others that give the air of positiveness to an opinion; but rather say, I conceive or apprehend a thing to be so and so; it appears to me, . . . if I am not mistaken.[43]

   Maier and Solem demonstrated that groups whose leaders suspended judgment and encouraged full consideration of minority viewpoints produced better solutions than other groups.[44] Moreover, groups whose leaders withheld their opinions about solutions until later in a discussion produced more and better alternatives to a solution than groups whose leaders expressed their opinions early.[45] Groups prefer open-minded leaders.[46]

5. **Effective group leaders express group-centered concern.**

   From interviews with ninety successful leaders in various professions, Bennis and Nanus reported that "there was no trace of self-worship or cockiness in our leaders."[47] Larson and LaFasto found that outstanding team leaders "articulate the team's goal in such a way as to inspire a desire for and eventual commitment to the accomplishment of the goal" and exhibit personal commitment to that goal in both words and deeds.[48] Furthermore, such leaders readily confront members who are more self- than group-centered.[49]

6. **Effective group leaders respect others when they speak.**

   Building on his studies of democratic leaders, Rosenfeld claimed that when ". . . people are equals with whom they work, the rewards and punishments are to be shared."[50] Such leaders are sensitive to nonverbal signals and the feelings these signify. Kenny and Zaccaro reported that leadership depends heavily on competencies in perceiving the needs and goals of members, then adjusting behaviors to these needs.[51] Effective discussion leaders are courteous.

7. **Effective group leaders share rewards and credit with the group.**

   As Fiedler and Chemers pointed out, "Leadership is an amazing ego-involving activity."[52] Leaders are often tempted to take credit for the accomplishments of the group and to consolidate their personal power. But effective leaders share as equals both within the group and when dealing with outsiders. They give credit to the group for accomplishments, and work to develop the leadership competencies of all members.[53] In short, effective leaders are skilled in communicating appreciation for efforts of members.

The Relationship Between Leaders and Members

All the contingency approaches assume an interdependent relationship between the communication behavior of the leader and the behavior, skills, preferences, and expectations of the members. In fact, although we discuss leaders and members separately, we do so only for convenience; leader/member behaviors form a unit, an interdependent system. Whether a leader's behaviors will be effective depends in large part on both the perceptions and behaviors of the other members.

Most people in our culture want their leaders to perform structuring behaviors, but to be considerate as well. Pavitt and Sackaroff found that experienced group members expected leaders to be enthusiastic and organized, and to encourage participation from all members as well as suggest procedures for the group.[54] This was confirmed by Ketrow, who found that a person who served as a procedural specialist was identified most often as a group's leader, and the task specialist was perceived as being most influential.[55] Infante and Gordon discovered that subordinates preferred a communication style they described as *affirming* (relaxed, friendly, and attentive) and low in verbal aggressiveness (attacks on others' self-concepts).[56]

One characteristic that may affect what members perceive and prefer is sex. Several studies suggest that women enact leadership differently from men, perhaps because members perceive different behavior as appropriate for men and women.

Andrews found that although men and women had equal potential as leaders, women were uncomfortable calling themselves *leader* and preferred the designations *organizer* or *coordinator,* apparently because they perceived a stigma attached to the leader label.[57] This finding is supported by Owen, who noted that women distance themselves from the label of *leader.*[58] He also observed that women became leaders by outworking men in a group, and that they used more themes of cohesion. It is likely that women's leadership behavior is constrained by expectations of members. Watson found, for instance, that women who enacted a dominant approach were less influential than women who enacted a considerate approach to leadership, especially with males.[59] However, women gave dominant female leaders higher ratings of effectiveness, but, regardless of style, women liked female bosses less than men did. Watson suggests a problem-solving approach for female leaders that takes into account the difficulties women sometimes have in dealing with perceptions of others.

Leader-Member Exchange (LMX) Model

One model that has looked systematically at the nature of the interdependent relationship of leader-member behaviors and perceptions is the **Leader-Member Exchange (LMX) model**, which suggests that supervisory leaders develop different kinds of leadership relationships with members depending on leader and member characteristics. Members differ in the amount of *negotiating latitude* they are allowed by leaders; a member with a high negotiating latitude is given a great deal of leeway to design and perform his or her job, whereas a member with low negotiating latitude is not accorded such freedom by the leader. Generally, members with higher negotiating latitude are more satisfied and more committed to the organization or group. The members' degree of negotiating latitude is transacted through a reciprocal interaction process with the leader, whose impression of the member's capabilities helps determine in large part what degree of negotiating latitude will be permitted.[60]

McClane found support for an interaction between leader and member characteristics, with the best leader-member fit determined by congruence on the need for power.[61] Leaders with high power needs gave greater negotiating latitude to members with high power needs; likewise, leaders with low power needs gave greater negotiating latitude to members with low power needs. Characteristics such as sex, locus of control, and need for achievement were not related. Clearly, leaders with high power needs take a different approach to forming groups than leaders with low power needs; both types of leaders appear to be more comfortable with members who share their assumptions about the appropriate use of power. By extension, members are more likely to be satisfied with leaders who share their assumptions by rewarding them with higher negotiating latitude.

In a different study, McClane compared groups with wide variations in the amount of negotiating latitude and groups with little variation.[62] His results suggest that high differentiation (having some members with high negotiating latitude and some with little latitude in the same group) may have an undesirable effect on a group, particularly if the members accorded high negotiating latitude are seen as an elite core group with the rest feeling like hired hands.

The foregoing discussion is designed to remind us that neither the leader nor the members operate in a vacuum; instead, their interactions are shaped by each other. Models such as the LMX remind us that, even though we isolate leadership and treat it as an individual variable for study purposes, in fact it is a *system-level* variable that is a property of the group as a whole, not of the individual called the group's leader.

We have said several times that small group leadership is the property of the *group,* not the individual who happens to hold the title of leader. We believe strongly that although a group's designated leader bears a lot of responsibility for coordinating and structuring the group's activities, all members can and should be equally responsible for the leadership of the group. **Distributed leadership** explicitly acknowledges that the leadership of a group is spread among members, with each member expected to perform the communication behaviors needed to move the group toward its goal. A group that does this is, in Hersey and Blanchard's terms, *mature;* the designated leader can largely withdraw from both task and relationship activity *because the group members themselves are able to supply these for the group.* Remember, a group may be able to function without a leader, but it cannot function without leadership. For example, Counselman reported on a group that had been active for seventeen years without a designated leader.[63] Various leadership functions had been picked up by members of the group. The most important of these were providing structure, gatekeeping, setting group norms, and adhering to the group's task. We acknowledge that this is unusual; most groups can and should use the services of a designated leader. However, this case verifies the important point we made about locus of leadership in a group: it belongs to the *group.*

Barge provided support for the distributed leadership concept when he compared two models of group leadership—one where the leader was an active, directive influence in the group, and a leaderless model, where all members engaged in the leadership process.[64] He discovered that the better predictor of group productivity was *overall* leadership activity, as opposed to the leadership activity of the designated leader alone. In contrast to what we might expect, the more productive groups were *not* more controlling or directing. Instead of demonstrating a *sender* mode, the productive groups enacted a *listener* mode, reflecting a more contemplative approach with increased sensitivity to the environment and the other members. Barge concluded that while an individual leader's behavior may not necessarily help a group achieve its goals, the overall group leadership behavior does, and group members should guard against becoming too action-oriented and insufficiently sensitive to their environments.

These findings affirm for us the concept we have of an ideal group. Most of the groups you belong to will have a designated leader, and we are not suggesting doing away with designated leaders. Instead, we invite you to consider what an ideal, responsible, mature group looks like. Even though the group has a designated leader, *all* members of ideal groups accept responsibility for their leadership. Members understand enough about the group process to know what functions are needed at what times, and they can supply those functions skillfully. Each member has,

The Case for Distributed Leadership

and acts on, a personal commitment to the group. Each member can step in to the leadership position and function effectively, with the support and contribution of the other members. Our concept of distributed leadership combines elements of several contingency approaches, particularly the functions and communicative competencies approach. It assumes members are skilled at a variety of the task and interpersonal communication competencies needed for effective leadership. It also assumes that, along with the designated leader, other members can diagnose group needs and meet them appropriately. Once again, leadership is the property of the group, and all members are responsible for effective group leadership.

Summary

Leadership was defined as using human communication skills to help the group achieve its goal. A distinction was made between *leader* and *leadership.* Leadership is group-goal-oriented influence of one member on another, whereas the leader is a person who has been appointed, elected, or has emerged to fill a *position* (or role) of group leader. The source of someone's ability to influence may be legitimate, referent, expert, reward, or punishment power. Coercion, a special form of punishment, is not considered an appropriate source of power in a group.

Several approaches to the study of leadership were examined. Early trait approaches, which assumed that leaders were born, rather than made, have been discredited. Modern trait approaches focus on complex, trait-like characteristics such as self-monitoring and verbal facility, which involve behaviors related to leadership emergence in a group. Studies of leadership emergence have shown that quiet, uninformed, and dogmatic members are quickly rejected as leaders in favor of democratic, communicatively competent members. Styles approaches examine the effect of democratic, autocratic, and laissez-faire styles on such outcomes as productivity and satisfaction. Democratically led groups are usually more satisfied; autocratic groups can be productive, especially in the presence of the leader. Current belief is that there is not one ideal style suitable for all group situations. Instead, a number of contingency factors suggest each style as being more appropriate than the others in a given situation.

The functions approach, an early contingency approach, assumes that groups need a variety of task and interpersonal functions to be performed, but not all groups need the same functions. Moreover, all members, not just the leader, can and should perform the functions. Fiedler's and Hersey and Blanchard's contingency models differ in their belief about how flexible people are. The systems approach attempts to capture the complexity of input, throughput, and output variables to be considered in determining leadership approaches, but its complexity is overwhelming. In an attempt to deal with this complexity, the communicative competencies approach focuses on the interpersonal competencies of effective leaders. A number of essential competencies were described.

Leadership is the property of the group, not just the leader. The behavior of each constrains and shapes the behavior of the other. The Leader-Member Exchange model was presented as an example of how leaders and members affect each other. Finally, a case was made for a distributed leadership model as appropriate for many small groups; this model suggests that members are as responsible for the productivity and effectiveness of the group as the leader.

1. In groups of four to six, discuss the following question for fifteen minutes; then your group's spokesperson should report your conclusions to the rest of the class:

    "In addition to the communicative competencies listed in chapter 8, what others do you think leaders of small task-oriented groups need, and why?"

2. Working alone, make a list of examples of small group leaders influencing followers through each of the five types of power. Share your examples with several classmates. Can you draw any tentative conclusions from your shared examples?

3. Discuss the notion that different types of groups need different types of leaders. What contingencies can you identify that may have a bearing? From your experience, can you give examples where a leader should have modified his or her behavior to fit the group needs? Do you think there is a *best* style of leadership to fit all situations?

4. First, list the communicative competencies you think you need to develop or improve. Second, prepare a written plan for achieving these competencies within the next year.

5. In groups of four to six, discuss the strengths and potential drawbacks of using distributed leadership in a group. Assume you are a designated leader who wants all your group members to be responsible for the group. How would you go about introducing and implementing distributed leadership?

Exercises

Bibliography

Barge, J. Kevin, and Randy Y. Hirokawa. "Toward a Communication Competence Model of Group Leadership," *Small Group Behavior* 20 (1989): 167–89.

Bennis, Warren, and B. Nanus. *Leaders: The Strategies for Taking Charge.* New York: Harper & Row, Publishers, 1985.

Cathcart, Robert S., and Larry A. Samovar. *Small Group Communication: A Reader.* 6th ed. Dubuque, IA: Wm. C. Brown Publishers, 1992, sections 7 and 8.

Hackman, Michael Z., and Craig E. Johnson. *Leadership: A Communication Perspective.* Prospect Heights, IL: Waveland Press, 1991.

Larson, Carl E., and Frank M. J. LaFasto. *TeamWork: What Must Go Right/What Can Go Wrong.* Newbury Park, CA: Sage Publications, 1989.

Notes

1. Carl E. Larson and Frank M. J. LaFasto, *TeamWork: What Must Go Right/What Can Go Wrong* (Newbury Park, CA: Sage Publications, 1989): 118.

2. B. Aubrey Fisher, "Leadership: When Does the Difference Make a Difference?" in *Communication and Group Decision-Making,* eds. Randy Y. Hirokawa and Marshall S. Poole (Beverly Hills, CA: Sage, 1986): 197.

3. Michael Z. Hackman and Craig E. Johnson, *Leadership: A Communication Perspective* (Prospect Heights, IL: Waveland Press, 1991): 11.

4. John R. P. French and Bertram Raven, "The Bases of Social Power," in *Group Dynamics: Research and Theory,* 3d ed., eds. Dorwin Cartwright and Alvin Zander (New York: McGraw-Hill, 1981): 317.

5. Marvin E. Shaw, *Group Dynamics: Research and Theory,* 3d ed. (New York: McGraw-Hill, 1981): 317.

6. Ernest G. Bormann, *Discussion and Group Methods,* 2d ed. (New York: Harper & Row, Publishers, 1975): 253–69; Nancy L. Harper and Lawrence R. Askling, "Group Communication and Quality of Task Solution in a Media Production Organization," *Communication Monographs* 47 (1980): 77–100.

7. E. P. Hollander, *Leadership Dynamics* (New York: The Free Press, 1978): 13–16.

8. Ernest Stech and Sharon A. Ratliffe, *Working in Groups* (Skokie, IL: National Textbook Company, 1976): 201.

9. Ralph M. Stogdill, *Handbook of Leadership: A Survey of Theory and Research* (New York: The Free Press, 1974): 63–82; Marvin E. Shaw, *Group Dynamics,* 2d ed. (New York: McGraw-Hill, 1976): 274–75 and chapter 6.

10. Ernest G. Bormann, *Small Group Discussion: Theory and Practice,* 3d ed., 205–14 and 291–92; John C. Geier, "A Trait Approach to the Study of Leadership in Small Groups," *Journal of Communication* 17 (1967): 316–23.

11. M. Snyder, "Self Monitoring Processes," in *Advances in Experimental Social Psychology,* 12, ed. L. Berkowitz (New York: Academic Press, 1979).

12. Stephen J. Zaccaro, Roseanne J. Foti, and David A. Kenny, "Self-Monitoring and Trait-Based Variance in Leadership: An Investigation of Leader Flexibility Across Multiple Group Situations," *Journal of Applied Psychology* 76 (1991): 308–15.

13. Robert J. Ellis and Steven F. Cronshaw, "Self-Monitoring and Leader Emergence: A Test of Moderator Effects," *Small Group Research* 23 (February 1991): 113–29.

14. Steven F. Cronshaw and Robert J. Ellis, "A Process Investigation of Self-Monitoring and Leader Emergence," *Small Group Research* 22 (November 1991): 403–20.

15. Deborah C. Baker, "A Qualitative and Quantitative Analysis of Verbal Style and the Elimination of Potential Leaders in Small Groups," *Communication Quarterly* 38 (Winter 1990): 13–26.

16. Ralph M. Stogdill, "Personal Factors Associated with Leadership: A Survey of Literature," *Journal of Psychology* 25 (1948): 64.

17. Lawrence B. Rosenfeld and Timothy B. Plax, "Personality Determinants of Autocratic and Democratic Leadership," *Speech Monographs* 42 (1975): 203–8.

18. Douglas McGregor, *The Human Side of Enterprise* (New York: McGraw-Hill, 1960).

19. Ralph K. White and Ronald Lippett, "Leader Behavior and Member Reaction in Three 'Social Climates,' " in *Group Dynamics: Research and Theory,* 2d ed., eds. Dorwin Cartwright and Alvin Zander (Evanston, IL: Row, Peterson and Company, 1960): 527–53; William E. Jurma, "Effects of Leader Structuring Style and Task-Orientation Characteristics of Group Members," *Communication Monographs* 46 (1979): 282; Malcom G. Preston and Roy K. Heintz, "Effectiveness of Participatory versus Supervisory Leadership in Group Judgment," *Journal of Abnormal and Social Psychology* 44 (1949): 344–45; George Graen, Fred Dansereau, and Takau Minami, "Dysfunctional Leadership Styles," *Organizational Behavior and Human Performance* 7 (1972): 216–36; Norman R. F. Maier and Ronald A. Maier, "An Experimental Test of the Effects of 'Developmental' vs. 'Free' Discussions on the Quality of Group Decisions," *Journal of Applied Psychology* 41 (1957): 320–23; William E. Jurma, "Leadership Structuring Style, Task Ambiguity and Group Members' Satisfaction," *Small Group Behavior* 9 (1978): 124–34.

20. Julia T. Wood, "Alternative Portraits of Leaders: A Contingency Approach to Perceptions of Leadership," *Western Journal of Speech Communication* 43 (1979): 260–70.

21. R. N. Griffin, "Relationships among Individual, Task Design, and Leader Behavior Variables," *Academy of Management Journal* 23 (1980): 665–83.

22. Cal W. Downs and Terry Pickett, "An Analysis of the Effects of Nine Leadership-Group Compatibility Contingencies upon Productivity and Member Satisfaction," *Communication Monographs* 44 (1977): 220–30.

23. David J. Skaret and Nealia S. Bruning, "Attitudes about the Work Group: An Added Moderator of the Relationship between Leader Behavior and Job Satisfaction," *Group & Organization Studies* 11 (1986): 254–79.

24. M. L. Chemers, "Leadership Theory and Research: A Systems-Process Integration," *Basic Group Processes,* ed. P. B. Paulus (New York: Springer-Verlag, 1983): 9–39.

25. R. F. Bales, *Interaction Process Analysis* (Cambridge, MA: Addison-Wesley, 1950).

26. Kenneth D. Benne and Paul Sheats, "Functional Roles of Group Members," *Journal of Social Issues* 4 (1948): 41–49.

27. B. Aubrey Fisher, "Leadership as Medium: Treating Complexity in Group Communication Research," *Small Group Behavior* 16 (1985): 167–96.

28. Karl Weick, "The Spines of Leaders," in *Leadership: Where Else Can We Go?,* eds. M. McCall and M. Lombardo (Durham, NC: Duke University Press, 1978): 37–61.

29. Fred E. Fiedler, *A Theory of Leadership Effectiveness* (New York: McGraw-Hill, 1967).

30. Paul Hersey and Kenneth Blanchard, *Management of Organizational Behavior: Utilizing Human Resources,* 2d ed. (New York: Prentice-Hall, 1972); Hersey and Blanchard, "So You Want to Know Your Leadership Style?" in *Readings in Organizational Communication,* eds. Phillip V. Lewis and John Williams (Columbus, OH: Grid Publishers, 1980): 219–34.

31. Julia T. Wood, "Leading in Purposive Discussions: A Study of Adaptive Behaviors," *Communication Monographs* 44 (1977): 152–65.

32. Ritch L. Sorenson and Grant T. Savage, "Signaling Participation Through Relational Communication: A Test of the Leader Interpersonal Influence Model," *Group & Organization Studies* 14 (September 1989): 325–54.

33. G. L. Drecksell, "Interaction Characteristics of Emergent Leadership" (Unpublished doctoral dissertation, University of Utah, 1984).

34. Martin L. Chemers, "Leadership Theory and Research: A Systems-Process Integration," in *Basic Group Processes,* ed. P. B. Paulus (New York: Springer-Verlag, 1983): 9–39.

35. Fisher, "Leadership," 203–4.

36. J. Kevin Barge and Randy Y. Hirokawa, "Toward a Communication Competency Model of Group Leadership," *Small Group Behavior* 20 (1989): 167–89.

37. Charles G. Morris and J. R. Hackman, "Behavioral Correlates of Perceived Leadership," *Journal of Personality and Social Psychology* 13 (1969): 350–61.

38. Paul D. Reynolds, "Leaders Never Quit: Talking, Silence, and Influence in Interpersonal Groups," *Small Group Behavior* 15 (1984): 411.

39. Hugh C. Russell, "Dimensions of Communicative Behavior of Discussion Leaders" (Paper presented to Central States Speech Convention, Chicago, April 1970).

40. Velma J. Lashbrook, "Gibb's Interaction Theory: The Use of Perceptions in the Discrimination of Leaders from Nonleaders" (Paper presented at the Speech Communication Association, Houston, December 1975).

41. J. Kevin Barge and Randy Y. Hirokawa, "Toward a Communication Competency Model."

42. B. Aubrey Fisher, "Leadership," 205–7.

43. "Benjamin Franklin, His Autobiography," in *The Harvard Classics, Vol. I,* ed. Charles W. Elliot (New York: P. F. Collier and Son, 1909): 18.

44. Norman R. G. Maier and A. R. Solem, "The Contributions of a Discussion Leader to the Quality of Group Thinking: The Effective Use of Minority Opinions," *Human Relations* 5 (1952): 277–88.

45. Lance E. Anderson and William K. Balzer, "The Effects of Timing of Leaders' Opinions on Problem-Solving Groups: A Field Experiment," *Group & Organization Studies* 16 (March 1991): 86–101.

46. Franklyn S. Haiman (From a paper given at the Speech Communication Association Annual Conference, Chicago, December 1984).

47. Warren Bennis and Burt Nanus, *Leaders: The Strategies for Taking Charge* (New York: Harper & Row, 1985): 57.

48. Carl E. Larson and Frank M. J. LaFasto, *TeamWork:* 121–23.

49. Carl E. Larson and Frank M. J. LaFasto, *TeamWork:* 135.

50. Lawrence B. Rosenfeld, *Now That We're All Here . . . Relations in Small Groups* (Columbus, OH: Charles E. Merrill Publishing Company, 1976): 76.

51. D. A. Kenny and S. J. Zaccaro, "An Estimate of Variance Due to Traits in Leadership," *Journal of Applied Psychology* 68 (1983): 678–85.

52. Fred E. Fiedler and Martin M. Chemers, *Leadership and Effective Management* (Glenview, IL: Scott, Foresman, 1974): 5.

53. Carl E. Larson and Frank M. J. LaFasto, *TeamWork,* 126–27.

54. Charles Pavitt and Pamela Sackaroff, "Implicit Theories of Leadership and Judgments of Leadership Among Group Members," *Small Group Research* 21 (August 1990): 374–92.

55. Sandra M. Ketrow, "Communication Role Specializations and Perceptions of Leadership," *Small Group Research* 22 (November 1991): 492–514.

56. Dominic A. Infante and William I. Gordon, "How Employees See the Boss: Test of Argumentative and Affirming Model of Supervisors' Communicative Behavior," *Western Journal of Speech Communication* 55 (Summer 1991): 294–304.

57. Patricia Hayes Andrews, "Sex and Gender Differences in Group Communication: Impact on the Facilitation Process," *Small Group Research* 23 (February 1992): 74–94.

58. William Foster Owen, "Rhetorical Themes of Emergent Female Leaders," *Small Group Behavior* 17 (November 1986): 475–86.

59. Carol Watson, "When a Woman is the Boss: Dilemmas in Taking Charge," *Group & Organization Studies* 13 (June 1988): 163–81.

60. G. B. Graen and T. A. Scandura, "Toward a Psychology of Dyadic Organizing," in *Research in Organizational Behavior* 9, eds. L. L. Cummings and B. Shaw (Greenwich, CT: JAI, 1987): 175–208.

61. William E. McClane, "The Interaction of Leader and Member Characteristics in the Leader-Member Exchange (LMX) Model of Leadership," *Small Group Research* 22 (August 1991): 283–300.

62. William E. McClane, "Implications of Member Role Differentiation: An Analysis of a Key Concept in the LMX Model of Leadership," *Group & Organization Studies* 16 (March 1991): 102–13.

63. Eleanor F. Counselman, "Leadership in a Long Term Leaderless Group," *Small Group Research* 22 (May 1991): 240–57.

64. J. Kevin Barge, "Leadership as Medium: A Leaderless Group Discussion Model," *Communication Quarterly* 37 (Fall 1989): 237–47.

Serving as Designated Leader

Central Message

A designated leader, though coequal with other members, is expected to perform a variety of administrative, structuring, and developmental activities on behalf of the group. Ideally, the designated leader encourages members to enact a variety of leadership functions while serving as a completer for functions not being supplied by other members.

Study Objectives   As a result of your study of chapter 9 you should be able to:

1. Articulate a personal philosophy of small group leadership that supports distributed leadership enacted by a group-centered, democratic designated leader.

2. Name the three major types of services expected of designated small group leaders and describe specific ways of providing them.

3. Produce written messages essential to the work of secondary small groups, including meeting notices and agendas, minutes, and reports to other groups and organizations.

4. Describe the ethical principles that guide group leaders.

Key Terms

Administrative duties
Agenda
Gatekeeper

Leader as completer
Liaison

Meeting notice
Minutes

In chapter 8 we explained that current theories of leadership focus on the leader's communication competencies, including the ability to perceive what a group needs and to adjust behavior accordingly. We supported the idea that leadership is appropriately distributed among members, who also benefit from improving their communicative competencies. However, developing these competencies can be a challenge; just because someone is designated as a group's leader does not automatically mean the group will receive the leadership services it needs. We cannot exaggerate how important it is for you to develop leadership competencies if you are to be an effective member and particularly a group leader:

> . . . the right person in a leadership role can add tremendous value to any collective effort, even to the point of sparking the outcome with an intangible kind of magic.[1]

Larson and LaFasto concluded that outstanding leaders begin by articulating a clear goal for the group in such a way that every member feels a desire for and commitment to that goal, and then developing a plan for achieving the goal that will ". . . unleash the energy and talents of contributing members." These leaders established and followed "guiding principles" that "represented day-to-day performance standards" indicative of what all group members, including the leader, should expect of each other.[2] In chapter 9 we present specific suggestions to guide your performance as a designated leader, a kind of "leader's manual." While we concentrate on typical leader responsibilities, we note again that it is appropriate for other members to perform these duties as well. We first discuss general principles guiding the leader's relationship to the group as a whole, then explain the three major types of duties leaders are expected to perform for small groups in the United States, and finally present ethical principles important for small group leaders.

Group-Centered Democratic Leadership

As we discussed in chapter 8, we believe that leadership should be tailored to fit the specific situation facing the group. In some situations, such as with members who are inexperienced or unwilling, more controlling forms of leadership are appropriate, at least initially. In other situations, with highly experienced and capable members, a designated leader may not even be necessary. However, most situations will fall between those two extremes.

Our position is that the ideal form of leadership, at least according to the standards and values of our culture, is democratic leadership that recognizes the equality of all members by encouraging member participation in all group decisions. This belief is ingrained in most Americans; it is a cornerstone of our political foundation, as is stated in the Declaration of Independence: "We hold these truths to be self-evident, that all men [sic] are created equal. . . ." We stress that this is the *ideal.* In group situations that do not seem to call for democratic leadership, then we believe the leader should exert the *least* amount of control necessary to help the group achieve its goal. Moreover, it is the leader's responsibility to work toward helping the members gain the experience, confidence, and skills they need so they *can* function effectively in a democratic group. Repeatedly, nations and corporations have shown that people coerced rather than led produce poorly and revolt when given a chance. As Donald Petersen, the CEO whose leadership during the

1980s pulled Ford Motor Company from near-bankruptcy to profitability, said: "Employee involvement requires participative management. Anyone who has a legitimate reason, who will be affected by a decision, ought to have the feeling that people want to know how he or she feels."[3] We strongly believe that the leader-follower relationship must be one of consent, with the leader as servant to the group, not the other way around. Accepting a position of designated leader means taking on special responsibilities and duties to serve the good of the group, as well as the larger organization of which it is a part. This, we believe, should be the central principle of any philosophy of small group leadership in the United States.

While it is true that certain situations call for other leadership styles, the kinds of task-oriented, problem-solving groups you will most often encounter call for democratic leadership. In a democratic relationship, attempts to coerce are perceived as unethical because they assume personal superiority and special rights on the part of the leader; they also chip away at the members' sense of self-identity. Attempts to coerce do not work because they eventually lead either to apathy or rebellion.

It may appear that we are contradicting ourselves when we say, "Be the type of leader a group needs, but be democratic." What we mean is that a leader should first recognize the group's current reality and serve the group as needed, while working toward achieving the ultimate goal of the ideal group: one where members are committed, responsible and mature; where leadership services are distributed among all members; and one where any person could serve well as the designated leader.

If group members are capable enough to serve as the group's leader, what does that leave for the designated leader to do? The metaphor we suggest is that the members are the bricks and the leader is the mortar that binds them together, as shown in figure 9.1. The bricks provide the support and substance of the group, but the mortar allows the whole group to hold its shape—completes the structure, so to speak. This concept of the **leader as completer,** as articulated by Schutz, suggests that ". . . the best a leader can do is to observe what functions are not being performed by a segment of the group and enable this part to accomplish them" or, if necessary, perform them.[4]

This concept makes several demands on both the leader and the members. Members should be competent enough both to know what the group needs at any given time and to supply that need by saying and doing the right thing. For example, if the group has digressed, a member can, and *should,* jump in with something like: "I think we've gotten off track. Can we get back to the topic?" The leader, too, should be competent enough to recognize the need and be able to jump in *if someone else in the group has not already provided the needed leadership behavior.* This means that the leader is primarily a monitor of the group's *process,* with the principle responsibility for maintaining a long-range perspective on the group's progress. This model promotes *distributed leadership,* where everyone is ultimately responsible for the group.

Leader as
Completer

Figure 9.1
The leader as "completer" of a group

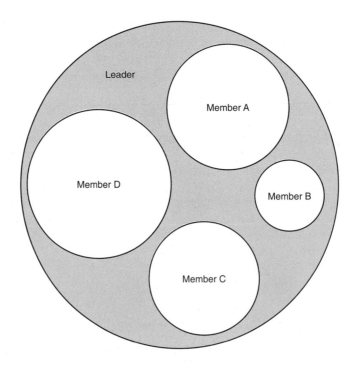

Leader

Member A

Member D

Member B

Member C

Responsibilities and Techniques of Discussion Leaders and Chairs

Although being leader of a group can be time consuming, the designated leader's duties in a continuing group need not require much more effort and time than are expected of all group members, particularly if the group has developed along the lines already suggested. In fact, in groups of peers, leaders will *not* spend more time if the other members view the job of organizing and carrying out the group's task as an activity to be shared by all members. For example, a group one of us belonged to discussed openly how leadership functions were to be distributed; one person was made responsible for calling meetings, a second for taking notes and having them distributed, and a third for soliciting items for the agenda from other members. During the discussion periods, the position of discussion leader rotated among members, as did the position of social chair. Ideally, every member can assume responsibility to supply whatever leadership services appear to be needed at any given time. This is the essence of effective discussion leadership, even though one person has been selected or has emerged as *the* leader.

In chapter 8 we presented information about contingencies that may affect the degree of control appropriately assumed by the designated leader. Contingency theory, which we support, requires leaders to be astute in their analyses of the group's situation and members' needs. Designated leaders, to function well as completers, must demonstrate tremendous flexibility to adjust their behavior to the needs of the group. Of course, leaders can rely on group members to help them by periodic, *explicit* review of the group's procedures. Considering the following situational variables can help you optimize your leadership style:

1. **Group purpose and goals.**

   Learning, personal growth, and value-sharing groups need far less structure and control than secondary groups charged with recommending solutions to complex problems. In addition, specific procedures (brainstorming, buzz group procedures, problem census, nominal group technique, etc.) require considerable procedural control.

2. **Member expectations.**

   A designated leader will initially need to conform to what members expect of the role, but this can later be changed through explicit discussion of the leader's job and through development of the members' own leadership skills.

3. **Member skills and maturity.**

   As Hersey and Blanchard reported, members who are used to working together, understand the task, and are effective communicators need less leader control than inexperienced members or newly formed groups.

4. **Member involvement in the group's task.**

   When members perceive that the task is important to them personally, they will often resist tight procedural control by a leader. Leaders should try to help members realize the importance of the task and become involved.

5. **The leader's skill and confidence.**

   Democratic leadership calls for skills in listening, organizing, summarizing and timing that take a long time to develop. Leaders should remember that the other group members can serve as a resource; a leader who believes the group needs services he or she is not able to provide should ask for the help of the other members.

6. **The time factor.**

   If a decision must be made in a hurry, a group will welcome strict control of its procedures. When time is not limited, less leader control is needed.

In problem-solving groups, the designated leader generally should focus primarily on task and procedural matters, secondarily on interpersonal relationship matters. There are three broad categories of services that designated leaders of such groups are expected to perform: administrative duties, discussion coordination, and group development. The advice we give about how to supply these services is based on research findings and the philosophy presented earlier. We suggest that each organization develop a manual of duties and responsibilities for its committees, task forces, and other small groups, including a statement of legitimate authority of the designated leaders. With such a manual, members' expectations will be much clearer and leaders will have guidelines to follow without having to guess at their duties.

Administrative
Duties

Numerous **administrative duties** must be handled; the most important ones are planning for meetings, following up on meetings, maintaining liaison with other groups, and managing the group's written communication.

Planning for Meetings

For small group meetings the famous adage holds: "To fail to plan is to plan to fail." Failure to plan results in a waste of everyone's time, ineffective problem-solving procedures, and low-quality outputs. The following checklist can guide your planning for productive meetings.

1. **Define the purpose of the meeting.**

   First, decide whether a meeting is necessary and wise. Hackman and Johnson recommend that you *not* call a meeting if other communication avenues (telephone, fax, memo) will convey the message effectively, when there isn't time for participants to prepare adequately, when one or more essential people cannot participate, and when the issues are personal and better handled privately.[5]

   Define the purpose of the meeting clearly; don't have a meeting if there's no definite purpose for it. "To talk over our coming year as a committee" is *not* adequately defined as an objective, but "To establish an agenda of problems for committee actions during the coming six months" is clear. Be sure to formulate *specific* outcomes, such as a written report, list of recommendations, and so forth, to be produced from the meeting.

2. **Establish starting and ending times for the meeting.**

   Frequently, committees and study groups meet with strict time limits imposed by other concurrent meetings, class and work schedules, and other factors over which the group has no control. Even without such external time limits, ending times should be established. Running overtime will kill member involvement and attendance and is a barrier to operating democratically.[6] Setting an ending time encourages the group to use its time well. If the work cannot be finished, plan additional meetings.

3. **If special resource people are needed for the meeting, advise and prepare them.**

   Small groups frequently need to question specialists with unique knowledge and skills or experience. For example, the church board described in chapter 2 invited church development specialists in to help board members organize activities to promote the growth of the church. Such invited resource persons need to know in advance what information to prepare and what to expect.

4. **Make all necessary physical arrangements.**

   Has the meeting room been reserved? Are handouts, notepads, chalk, charts, and possibly beverages ready? Is the room arranged for good eye contact among all members?

5. **If needed, prepare a procedure by which the group can evaluate its process.**

   Groups should periodically evaluate their throughput processes. Appropriate postmeeting reaction forms, described in chapter 14, can be prepared to help do this.

6. **Notify members of the purpose or agenda, necessary preparation, and time and place of the meeting.**

   The chair is responsible for seeing that members are notified and given ample opportunity to prepare for a meeting. In large organizations, this duty may be delegated to a staff person, such as professional secretary, but it is still the *responsibility* of the leader.

Two kinds of follow-up are needed: reminding group members of assignments to be sure they are completed and getting out necessary reports from the group to other groups or individuals. If adequate reports of minutes are kept, members can be reminded of routine assignments through these written records. Sometimes members agree to undertake special assignments. One member may agree to find bibliographic items, another to conduct a personal interview, and a third to procure copies of a relevant statute—all before the next meeting. The leader can make a brief phone call before the next meeting to ask tactfully whether the member encountered any trouble in completing the assignment; this serves as a gentle reminder and helps keep the group on track.

Following Up on Meetings

It is often necessary for a chair to prepare and send letters, memoranda, formal reports, notices of group decisions, advice prepared by the committee, and so forth to appropriate people. This includes getting copies of minutes prepared and distributed, but more especially involves writing formal resolutions, sending advisory policy statements to administrative officers, calling and conducting a press conference, or carrying out whatever decisions for action the group has made. Although the group should decide *what* to do and *who* is to do it, the *who* is often the group's designated leader.

A **liaison** serves as spokesperson from the group to other groups or the parent organization; typically, this is the designated leader's job. In most organizations, the chairs of standing committees maintain necessary coordination among the small groups that compose the organization. Many organizations have regular meetings of division managers. Whenever you act as liaison, keep in mind that you represent a *group* rather than yourself.

Liaison

Several specific occasions call for liaison. Many times two or more small groups must coordinate their work, such as when building a house or producing a play. Occasionally committee chairs will be interviewed by public media. If you anticipate this happening, you can be prepared to answer reporters' questions. The chair's statements should accurately reflect the group's work, findings, and beliefs. Any statement that is biased toward one side of an internal group controversy will cause further friction and division within the group, and the leader will lose the trust of those members who feel misrepresented.

Although discussion involves mostly oral communicating, as we've already suggested, a group needs written messages to provide continuity from meeting to meeting; to remind members of their assignments; to confirm agreements and accomplishments; to provide legal records of attendance, decisions and actions; to bring absentees up to date; and to inform the parent organization and others about

Managing Written Communication for a Group

what the group is doing. Although learning groups rarely keep records of meetings, problem-solving groups *always* should. Most committees are required to keep minutes of all meetings and to submit written reports to specified personnel. For instance, at the university where both of us work, committees of the Faculty Senate distribute reports of each meeting to all senate members and to selected administrators. Even a single-meeting conference group needs a written record. For example, one of the authors belonged to a community theatre for which the written record of an *ad hoc* personnel review committee provided evidence used in a lawsuit to support the theatre's assertion that an employee was not fired arbitrarily. Lacking this record, the theatre probably would have lost the suit.

Four categories of written messages that contribute to small group leadership are personal notes, meeting notices and agendas, meeting records, and reports and resolutions.

Personal notes.   The typical conference room is pictured with note pads and pencils at each seat because taking notes focuses group members' listening so they aren't likely to lose sight of the group goal or switch subjects. When you take notes, you shouldn't try to record a transcript of the whole discussion. Instead, focus on keeping track, maybe with just a key word or two, of the thrust of the discussion; notes should be detailed enough to prepare minutes or check the secretary's work. This helps you, as leader, summarize when needed, be sure no important concept or proposal is overlooked, and follow up between meetings to ensure that assignments are being completed. Examples of personal notes are provided in figure 9.2.

If your instructor requires you to submit a case study of your group at the end of the semester or quarter, you can use personal meeting notes, in combination with a journal, to record the development of the group. For a thorough case study, record such matters as roles members seem to be developing, leadership behaviors, communicative successes and failures, and conflict management.

Group records.   All on-going committees should maintain accurate and comprehensive **minutes** that serve as official records of the important content of meetings, especially of decisions made. Although the designated leader is responsible for seeing that minutes are recorded and distributed to members prior to the next meeting, that task may be delegated to a secretary or a volunteer from the group. Sometimes professional secretaries attend meetings for the specific purpose of writing minutes, perhaps with the help of an audio recording. Even then, the leader is responsible for ensuring that the minutes are accurate. For example, one of us, responsible for hundreds of minutes drafted by a professional secretary, found personal notes essential for editing almost every such report.

Minutes are necessary for the efficient functioning of any group. Without such a written record, members often forget important information, fail to complete assignments, or argue about what was decided. For instance, the church board mentioned in chapter 2 frequently referred to the minutes to recall what decisions

Figure 9.2 A discussion leader's personal notes.

October 4, 1991 - - - Everyone present

<u>Discussion topic</u>: what topics should we include in our class
 presentation on group polarization?

<u>Main criteria</u>:

 Judy & Bill - - - to get an "A" info must be accurate
 Bart - - - has to have practical application
 Bev - - - Dr. Brilhart wants innovative presentation
 Everybody should have a part in presenting the topic to the class.

<u>Topics</u>

 * Definition of group polarization (all agreed)
 Risky shift (Hal says can become a cautious shift w/ cautious
 members - - - this term is outdated)
 * Exercises to demonstrate when group takes risks + when it becomes
 cautious - - - Judy says there's a bunch of these in a book she has
 * Need to show how this applies in real life.

 ✗ Decisions Made
 Assignments: Me (applications); Judy & Bill (library research);
 Hal & Bev (exercises -- w/ Judy's book)

 Next meeting - - - Wed., October 11

members had made about various policies such as the rental charge for facilities, procedures for becoming a member, and so forth. The minutes prevented wasted time and unnecessary tension.

Minutes focus on the content, not the process of discussion. They are a summary record of all task-oriented information shared during the meeting, all ideas proposed as solutions, all decisions and how they were made (majority, consensus, consent), all assignments, and any plans or procedures for future action. Any special reports of procedures for future action should be attached to the minutes.

Minutes take the form of a special memorandum, though the format may vary depending on the origins and nature of the group, norms, and perhaps the history and bylaws of the parent organization. The written report of a task force or other *ad hoc* committee may take the form of a summary report, whereas standing committees (which typically consider more than one topic or problem per meeting) should number items of business in the order they were discussed. The minutes

Figure 9.3
An example of
minutes.

Report of Third Meeting of Polarization Instruction Group

Date of Meeting: Wednesday, March 9, 1994
Time and Place: 7:30–9:00 P.M. in Room 338, Craig Hall
Attendance: Bev Halliday, Inez Salinas, Terrell Washington, Bill Miklas, Judy Hartlieb

Report of Second Meeting
   Judy distributed copies of the report of the second meeting to all members. It was approved. It was decided that Judy would be responsible for recording and distributing reports of each group meeting.

Goals
   A suggested outline for problem solving presented by Terrell was followed. This led to a discussion of group polarization and to determining the actions to be taken involving the group's "problem."
   The group goals were identified as 1) understanding group polarization, 2) conducting a presentation with a class exercise on polarization for the class, and 3) each member being able to write a personal essay about the group experience.

Exercise Portion of Presentation
   After some discussion of the type of exercise to be used in the presentation, it was decided that Inez would be responsible for trying to locate a book with sample exercises that could be considered by the group at the next meeting. Bill will also have primary responsibility for this portion of the presentation and will see that copies of the test are produced and ready for the class. The other group members will individually brainstorm for exercise ideas, and further discussion of these will take place during our class meeting of Tuesday, March 15.
   Criteria for class exercises were discussed. It was concluded that the purpose of the exercise would be to demonstrate the phenomenon of group polarization at work. The exercise would be divided in such a way that each individual in the class would first take it alone and then with a small group, and see what shifts occurred.

Leader and Role
   The group determined that the leader would be responsible for developing agendas and outlines for future meetings and should serve as a overall controller and fill-in or backup person for other group members. Bev was selected by unanimous vote to fill this role as group leader.

Structure of Presentation
   A structure and time schedule of the presentation was decided on:

5 minutes—Each member of the class takes the exercise individually.
10 minutes—The class is divided into four groups, with four of our small group members serving as observers. Each group will determine how to solve the exercise problem.
5 minutes—One member of our group will present a short report on group polarization research to the class. At the same time, the four observers will be finishing their notes regarding what happened in their respective groups.
5 minutes—The four groups will each discuss what occurred in the group. The observer may start the discussion or serve as a guide/reference person, answering questions and giving insights into what happened with polarization in the group.
5 minutes—The class as a whole will have the opportunity to share what was observed and experienced within the groups. The observers may again start the discussion and open the floor to any class member's contribution.

Additional Member Roles
   Bill agreed to present the five-minute oral report on polarization to the class.
   Terrell will be responsible for arranging meeting places and will serve as a backup to any member who might be absent.

Adjournment and Next Meeting
   The meeting adjourned at approximately 9:00 P.M. Further planning will take place on Tuesday, March 15, during class time.

Board of Directors Meeting Minutes
April 14, 1992

Figure 9.4
Another example
of minutes.

Present: Bill Prior, Norm Kerris, Gary Sloane, Don Bowles, Sally Schultz (directors): Sunni Prior, Marina Kerris (invited guests); Jane Simmons, church secretary.

Call to order: Opening prayer was given by Sally. Minutes of the April 7 meeting were approved as presented.

Topic	Discussion	Actions/Recommendations
Attendance/ offering	120—Sunday, April 11 Total deposit—$1552.52 Building fund—$5858.00	
Founders Sun., May 16	Marina will attempt to get the SMSU Gospel Choir to sing for a 30-minute program. Covered dish supper to follow service. Jody (Hospitality Committee) in charge of set-up.	
Adult Sun. School	Roy Hackman will be teaching from "Spiritual Economics" starting April 25.	
Rental of facilities	Ada Cole asked cost of renting sanctuary for a workshop; Discussion centered on cost of utilities/wear and tear.	Norm moved, Don seconded, that we establish a policy of charging $30 per half day for all rentals. Passed.
Circle Suppers	Bill shared information about Circle Supper program; it has been very successful at the Columbia church. Discussion followed, and several names suggested to organize.	Sally moved, Gary seconded, that we ask Jean Ames to coordinate; that we hold them monthly on second Saturday. Passed.
Search Committee	Marina reported we have 10 applications; search committee will telephone interview and ask 3 to come for full interview.	

Meeting adjourned at 8:30 P.M. Don gave closing prayer.

Respectfully submitted,

Sally Schultz

should be signed by the writer, with a copy sent to each member as soon as possible before the next meeting. This gives members a chance to check them for accuracy and correct them at the beginning of the next meeting. Figure 9.3 is an example of minutes from a student project group that dealt with only one major topic during its entire life.

The next example of minutes, shown in figure 9.4, comes from the church board discussed earlier. Notice that the format, suggested by Sally, the secretary, allows members to see immediately what items were considered and what actions were taken without having to comb through a lot of narrative.

Figure 9.5

An example of combined meeting notice and agenda.

Date: February 21, 1994
To: Curriculum Committee (Berquist, Bourhis, Galanes, Sneegas, Stovall, Sisco)
From: Christy Drale, chair
Re: Next meeting of Curriculum Committee

The next meeting of the Curriculum Committee will be on Friday, February 25, from 1:00 to 3:00 P.M. in Craig 320.

AGENDA (by the end of the meeting we must have an answer for each of the following questions):

1. What will be the focus of our departmental assessment? (student outcomes, student perceptions, alumni perceptions, or something else?)
2. What areas of the department should be assessed?
3. Whom will we recommend as members of subcommittees to plan assessment procedures for each area decided under #2?

Meeting notices and agendas.   A notice of each meeting should be sent to all members in time to allow them to prepare for the meeting. A **meeting notice** is a memorandum that normally includes the following items:

1. Name of person to whom notice is sent.
2. Name and position of person sending notice and calling meeting.
3. When meeting will begin and end.
4. Where meeting will be held.
5. Purpose of meeting and specific outcomes to be achieved.
6. Agenda (if more than one item of business will be discussed) listing all problems or topics to be discussed.
7. Any relevant facts, reading sources, or other preparation members should make prior to meeting.
8. If this is a single-meeting group, conference, or first meeting of a new group, a list of all persons who will attend.

An **agenda** is a list of the items of business, topics, and other matters in the sequence they will be considered in the meeting. For a continuing group such as a standing committee or task force, usually the first item of business is the report of the previous meeting: should the minutes be approved as distributed or revised in some way? For a standing committee or board, the agenda might include a number of problems on which the group is working. For a task force, the agenda might be two or three questions about facts and findings on the problem to which the task force was assigned. Figure 9.5 is an example of a combined meeting notice and agenda.

When a member or subcommittee has conducted research for a group, a written copy of the major findings should be distributed to all members. If feasible, such a report can be included with the meeting notice and agenda. The report might include tables, graphs, duplicated copies of text, lists, and drawings. Likewise, prior to the meeting the report maker needs to prepare visual aids such as charts, diagrams, and graphs. Such a report can be incorporated into the minutes by mentioning it ("see attached") and stapling a copy to the official set of minutes.

Formal reports and resolutions.   Many small groups must submit written reports of their work to a parent organization or administrator. Such reports may include findings, criteria, and recommendations. You probably have read about reports to the president by special task forces on such matters as air pollution, the quality of education, and health care financing. Reports of campus task forces are regularly mentioned in student newspapers. Corporations often have teams of scientists and engineers developing new products. The end product of these hundreds of hours of work is a written report, often accompanied by a brief oral report by the group's designated leader.

Although the designated leader is responsible for submitting the report, the actual writing is usually done by one or two members. A draft of the proposed report is sent to all members, inviting their suggestions for revisions and additions. The group then meets to discuss, amend, and eventually approve the draft report. The final version is signed by all members, copied, and submitted. Usually this type of report includes sections about the problem, a summary of findings, possible solutions considered, criteria used to judge these solutions, and the group's recommendations. Any or all of these may be headings for sections of the report. You may have to do something like this as part of a project for a small group communication course.

If the final written report involves a resolution or main motion for the parent organization, the committee chair presents copies to all members of the organization and formally moves its adoption during the section of the assembly's agenda called *Reports of Committees.* The chair makes a brief persuasive speech and answers questions about the motion. Other members of the committee help in answering questions, and may make further supportive speeches. Formats for such motions can be found in any comprehensive manual of parliamentary procedure, such as *Robert's Rules of Order, Newly Revised,* or the organization may have its own special format for motions.

As you can see, management of written messages is an important part of a designated small group leader's work. Although good leaders enlist the help of members in performing these duties, they are the leader's ultimate responsibility. Clearly, good written and oral communication skills are necessary to function effectively as a leader.

Administrative duties of designated leaders precede and follow small group meetings. Now we consider what leaders are expected to do *during* actual meetings. In general, leaders should foster both creative and critical thinking about the task, while making the best possible use of members' time. The following guidelines will help you balance these broad goals.

**Leading
Discussions**

Opening remarks should set the stage for the meeting by creating a positive atmo sphere and helping focus the group on its task. They should be kept brief. Here are several guidelines:

1. **Make sure members and guests have been introduced.**
   Groups are effective only when members feel free to participate. At a first meeting, an icebreaker or brief socializing activity can help members become comfortable with each other. Name tags may be provided. If guests are present, they should be introduced and their purposes made clear to the group.

   Primary tension can hamper a group's decision making; sometimes a climate of trust or informality needs to be created or enhanced. You can suggest appropriate norms, such as to maintain confidentiality, to be respectful of each other, and to listen actively. When a new group meets for the first time, the designated leader should briefly describe his or her role and expectations of the other members. For example, both of us have explained at the first meeting of committees that we would be facilitators and coordinators, but not make decisions for the group, argue for specific proposals, try to persuade the group to espouse a particular policy, or do more than a fair share of the group work.

   Sometimes an unstructured period where members get acquainted with each other's beliefs, values, backgrounds, and attitudes regarding the problem facing the group can help. This serves primarily a socioemotional function. The designated leader who senses such a need for ventilation and encourages it may later find the job of keeping talk organized and relevant much easier. The leader must balance the need for ventilation with the need for organization and should not let it go on too long. Look for signs that the group wants order.

2. **See that any special roles are established.**
   Will the group need a recorder in addition to the designated leader? Will the group have a member acting as a special observer? The group may choose to rotate such jobs so various members receive practice performing them.

3. **Briefly review or explain the specific purpose of the meeting, the specific outcomes that should be accomplished, and the group's area of freedom.**
   Members should have been informed of these by a meeting notice, but a brief reminder helps focus members on the task. In addition, there may be questions, so addressing them early may save time and prevent misunderstandings later.

4. **Distribute any handouts.**
   Handouts may include written materials from the parent organization or administrator, copies of findings, case problems, outlines to structure the problem-solving procedure of the group, and an explanation of a special discussion technique.

5. **Suggest procedures to follow.**
   You may want the group to plan a problem-solving procedure, or you may present an outline of questions for this purpose and ask the group to adopt or modify it. For an *ad hoc* problem-solving group, we suggest that you give each member a copy of an outline of questions to guide the group's problem-solving procedure, following the general procedural model explained in chapter 10. Members should know whether decisions will be by consensus or majority

vote. If rules for committees apply, members need to know them. If a special technique, such as brainstorming or the problem census, will be used, put the procedure on a chart or handout.

6. **Ask a clear question to focus initial discussion on the first substantive issue on the agenda.**

   Your focus question may require a simple answer: "Dick, will you give us last week's sales figures?" Or it may need considerable discussion: "What do we think are the reasons for the drop-off in attendance?" In either case, the right question helps launch the group into the substantive portion of the agenda. Questions are discussed in more detail in chapter 10.

Once the group members are oriented both toward each other and the task, the leader can help the group function efficiently by helping structure the group's deliberations. The following suggestions will assist you in accomplishing this:

Structuring Discussions

1. **Keep the discussion goal oriented.**

   Be sure all members understand and accept the goal. If a digression occurs, bring the discussion back on track with statements such as: "How will this help us achieve our goal?" or "What does that have to do with what we were discussing?" Topic switching is common, so you'll need to be on constant guard against it. When an irrelevant topic crops up or someone jumps ahead in the problem-solving procedure, you can usually reroute the discussion with a comment such as: "We seem to have gotten off track. Let's finish our discussion of how serious the parking shortage is before talking about why it exists." A procedural outline in the hands of all members helps keep the discussion goal-oriented and orderly.

2. **Summarize each major step in problem solving and each major decision.**

   Before the group goes to the next issue or agenda item, be sure members have achieved closure on the current issue, with each member having the same understanding of what was decided. You can do this by summarizing, asking whether the summary is adequate, then checking to see whether the group is ready to move on: "So, we've decided that building a tunnel under National Avenue will be too costly and probably will not solve the jaywalking problem, right? [Pause to verify understanding.] Now, are we ready to go on to the next item, the overhead bridge? [Pause again to give people time to respond.]" This kind of summary helps members make the transition to the next topic. When group members start to repeat each other, suggest that agreement seems to have been reached and that the group may be ready to move on to the next question. To summarize and make transitions competently, you will need to keep complete personal notes.

3. **Help the group cover all items on its agenda.**

   To do so, you will have to watch both the time and the discussion format. First, watch the clock; nothing is more frustrating than running out of time before you have a chance to discuss an issue important to you. Members often get so involved in the discussion that they lose track of time, so it's up to the designated leader to monitor this: "We are only on our third agenda item, with fifteen minutes left. Are we ready to wrap this topic up, or would you rather deal with the remaining agenda items at a special meeting next week?"

4. Bring the discussion to a definite close.

This should be done no later than the scheduled ending time for the meeting, unless all members consent to extending the time. The conclusion can include a summary of all progress the group has made, a statement of how the reports of the meeting will be distributed to members, assignments for follow-up and implementation, commendations for a job well done, or an evaluation of the meeting to improve the group's future interactions. The designated leader may ask the recorder for help in reviewing assignments made to members and decisions agreed to by the group.

Equalizing Opportunity to Participate

While you are keeping verbal interaction organized and goal directed, you also need to ensure that everyone has an equal opportunity to speak, with no one stage-hogging or withdrawing. There are several things you can do to produce such equality:

1. Address your comments and questions to the group rather than to individuals.

Unless you want to elicit a specific item of information or respond directly to what a member has said, speak to the group as a whole. Make regular eye contact with everyone when you ask questions, especially with less talkative members.

2. Make sure all members have an equal opportunity to speak.

You may have to act as **gatekeeper,** regulating who will speak next so that everyone has a fair, equal chance. Eye contact can show you expect the less talkative members to speak. Looking at those who talk a lot encourages them to talk more and may further discourage quiet members. We suggest you make a visual survey of the entire group every minute or so. If you see a nonverbal sign that a silent member has something to say, you can help that person get the floor: "Pieta, did you want to comment on John's proposal?" or "Pieta, you seem concerned about John's proposal. Would you share your concerns with us?" That opens the gate to Pieta without putting her on the spot if she has nothing to say. Sometimes reticent members can be assigned roles that *require* their participation. For instance, someone might be asked to investigate an issue and report to the group, or be asked to serve as *devil's advocate,* which forces participation. If you know a member is well informed but has not spoken out, try encouraging participation without forcing: "Selima, I think you studied that issue. Could you give us any information about it?"

Controlling compulsive, dominating, and long-winded members is often more difficult than encouraging quiet members. Some people repeatedly interrupt and drown out the voices of others. Highly verbal people can be valuable, but verbal monopolizing must be controlled for the sake of the group. The following techniques are listed from the most subtle to the most direct:

a. When feasible, seat talkative members where you can seem to overlook them naturally, and try not to make eye contact when you ask a question of the group.

    b. When a windbag has finished one point, cut in with a tactful comment, such as, "How do the *rest* of you feel about that issue?" to suggest that someone else speak.

    c. Suggest a group rule that each person make one point, then give up the floor to others, and that no one interrupt or drown out another speaker (except when the leader does on behalf of the group).

    d. In private, tactfully ask the excessive talker to help you encourage quiet members to speak: "Your ideas have been very helpful to the group, but I'm concerned that, because you are so articulate, others feel intimidated about participating. How can you help me get Susan and Juan to contribute to the discussions more often?"

    e. Have an observer keep a count of how often or how long each member speaks, and report the findings to the group. If a serious imbalance is apparent, the group can decide what to do.

    f. As a last resort, ask the person to control talking or leave the group: "While your ideas are excellent, your constant talking prevents other members, whose ideas are equally good, from contributing. This hurts both group morale and decision making. For the sake of the group, if you will not control your talking, I think you should leave the group."

3. **Listen with real interest to what an infrequent speaker says, and encourage others to do the same.**

    Nothing discourages a speaker more than a lack of listening. Yet the evidence is clear that most people ignore comments from a member who previously has said little. Leader intervention can help an infrequent speaker get a fair hearing.

4. **Avoid commenting after each member's remark.**

    Some designated leaders fall into this pattern unaware, producing a wheel network of verbal interaction. Other leaders do this to overcontrol the group. Listen, speak when you are really needed, but don't become the constant interpreter or repeater of what others say.

5. **Bounce requests for your opinions on substantive issues back to the group.**

    Many people have a tendency to accept uncritically what a leader says (as in the phenomenon of *groupthink,* discussed in chapter 12). Under most circumstances, you will encourage both creative and critical thinking by members if you withhold your opinions until others have expressed theirs. When you *do* offer an opinion, give it as only one point of view to be considered, not as the *right* interpretation. When you are asked "What do you think we should do?" you might reply "Let's see what other members think first. What do the rest of you think about . . . ?"

6. **Remain neutral during arguments.**

    If you get heavily involved in an argument, you will lose the perspective needed to be a completer and mediator, to summarize, and to perform all the other communicative behaviors of a good leader. When you realize evaluation is needed, point that out and ask others to provide it. At most, act as a *devil's advocate* for a point of view that otherwise would not be considered. Of course, you are always free to support decisions as they emerge or point out that members have overlooked a major issue or possible negative outcome, thus encouraging critical thinking.

Stimulating Creative Thinking

Groups are potentially more creative than individuals, but often group outputs are mediocre or worse. Sometimes creativity must be stimulated deliberately. Leaders can do several things to encourage creativity:

1. **Defer evaluation and ask group members to do the same.**
   The main idea behind brainstorming, described in chapter 13, is to defer evaluation of ideas until members have no more ideas to suggest. Evaluation stifles creativity; who wants to suggest an idea that will get shot down? If you want to stimulate creativity, you (and the other members) must establish a safe climate where people feel safe to propose innovative suggestions. When a group member criticizes a suggestion, gently remind that person of the "defer evaluation" rule.

2. **Try brainstorming and other creativity-enhancing techniques.**
   This suggestion extends the first. Brainstorming not only requires deferred judgment, it also encourages members to be playful with their own and others' ideas, to use others' ideas as a springboard, and to invent wild and crazy suggestions that may turn out to be useful. In addition, there are a number of other techniques designed temporarily to disable the logical part of the mind so that the creative part of the mind can emerge.

3. **Encourage the group to search for more alternatives.**
   When no one seems to be able to think of any more ideas, you can ask an idea-spurring question: "What *else* can we think of to . . . ?" or "I wonder if we can think of five more ways to . . . ?" Often, the most creative ideas are ones that pop up after the group thinks it has exhausted its possibilities.

4. **One at a time, ask how each component of a solution or item might be improved.**
   For instance, you might ask "How could we improve the *appearance* of . . . ?" or ". . . the *strength* of . . . ?"

5. **Watch for suggestions that could open up whole new areas of thinking, then pose a general question about the new area.**
   For example, if someone suggests putting up signs in the library that show the cost of losses to the users, you might ask "How *else* could we publicize the costs of losses to the library?"

Stimulating Critical Thinking

After a group has done its creative thinking, it must then subject the various options to rigorous evaluation before it reaches a final position. All information and options should be subjected to critical evaluation, but sometimes groups develop norms of overpoliteness or conformity to the opinions of high-status members. In such cases members may be reluctant to criticize or find flaws with others' ideas. Here are ways to encourage this without evoking unmanageable secondary tension.

1. **If the group gets solution-minded quickly, suggest more analysis of the problem.**
   This is a common problem and a major source of faulty decision making. Chapter 10 presents a systematic method for helping a group focus on problem analysis.

2. **Encourage members to evaluate information.**
   For example:
   a. To check the relevance of evidence you might ask: "How does this apply to our problem?" or "How is that like the situation we are discussing?"
   b. To evaluate the source of evidence you might ask: "What is the source of that information?" "How well is Dr. So-and-so recognized in the field?" or "Is this consistent with other information on the subject?"
   c. To check on the credibility of information you might ask: "Do we have any information that is contradictory?"
   d. To encourage thorough assessment of a group member's suggestion you might ask: "How will implementing that solve our problem?" "Will that option create any problems we haven't yet foreseen?" or "How will the students (union members, secretaries, neighborhood residents, etc.) react to that suggestion?"
   e. To test a statistic you might ask how it was derived, who conducted the study, or how an average was computed.
   f. Bring in outside experts to challenge the views of the group.

3. **See that all group members understand and accept all standards, criteria, or assumptions used in making judgments.**
   For example, you might ask: "Is that criterion clear to us all?" "Does everyone agree that using our professional association's guidelines is a good idea?" or "Do we all accept that as an assumption?"

4. **See that all proposed solutions are given a thorough testing before they are accepted as final group decisions.**
   Encourage the group to apply the available facts and all criteria. Be especially careful to consider possible harmful effects of all proposed solutions. You may want to remind members of the danger of groupthink, explained in chapter 12.
   a. Ask questions such as the following to encourage thorough evaluation:
   Do we have any evidence to indicate that this solution would be satisfactory? Unsatisfactory?
   Are there any facts to support this proposal?
   How well would that idea meet our criteria?
   Would that proposal solve the basic problem?
   Is there any way we can test this idea before we decide whether or not to adopt it?
   What negative consequences might this proposal produce?
   b. Ask members to discuss tentative solutions or policies with trusted people outside the group.
   c. One or more members can be asked to take the role of critical evaluator or devil's advocate so that all ideas are challenged and everyone has a chance to air doubts.
   d. Divide the group into two subgroups under different leaders to evaluate all alternatives, then rejoin to iron out differences.
   e. Before reaching a binding solution with far-reaching consequences, hold a "second chance" meeting at which all doubts, ethical concerns, or untested assumptions can be explored.

*Fostering Meeting-to-
Meeting Improvement*

A group doesn't achieve its ultimate goal by chance. After each meeting, the designated leader should review the meeting to determine in what ways it could have been improved and especially how well the meeting's goals were accomplished. That, then, becomes the road map for improving future meetings. Here are specific suggestions:

1. **Determine how the meeting could have been improved.**

   The leader should assess whether the group's purposes were clearly communicated and whether members agreed on the goals. Was the entire agenda covered in timely fashion? Was the meeting well structured? Did members stay on the topic, for the most part? Was the thinking both creative and critical, at appropriate times? Were the members allowed to digress too often? Not enough? Did the leader take on too much of the responsibility for conducting the discussion, thereby depriving members of valuable experience? Were there any members who talked too much? Not enough? After answering these and other questions, the leader should plan strategy for the next meeting.

2. **Determine the most important changes to be made at the next meeting and adjust behavior accordingly.**

   After examining all the areas where improvements could have been made, the leader should select two or three of the most potentially harmful areas and concentrate on improving those. For example, if the agenda was half completed, the leader should keep better track of time and allow fewer digressions at the next meeting. If one or two members monopolized the floor, the leader should plan ways to curtail their participation. The leader can then share the plan with the members: "Last week, we accomplished only half the items on our agenda. This week, I'm going to pay more attention to our time, and I'll be stepping in more often to help us stick to one issue at a time. I'd appreciate your help with this, too."

Developing the Group

Developing the group involves two fundamental processes: helping the group evolve into an effective team, and helping the individual members grow to their potentials so distributed leadership can work effectively. In chapter 7 we explained how a collection of individuals develops into a group with a unique culture of communication patterns, norms, role structure, and throughput procedures. Earlier in this chapter we talked about the importance of the leader helping develop the group members' maturity level so they can increasingly assume the leadership of the group. Most members do not start out knowing how to do this; being an effective group member requires communication skills that are developed with practice. The leader can greatly facilitate the growth of the individual members.

*Helping Individuals
Grow*

An important job for the leader is to develop the members' leadership skills, including the members' abilities to assess the group's throughput processes and suggest appropriate changes. Here are several suggestions:

1. **Encourage members to assess the group's processes and suggest appropriate changes.**

   Sometimes the impetus for group growth can be supplied just by asking the group to examine itself and ask "How are we doing?" Periodic self-assessment is a characteristic of outstanding teams.[7] There are several ways for the leader to build self-assessment into the group's processes. For instance, a short period of evaluation could end each meeting, spurred by the questions: "How well do you think our meeting went today?" and "How might we make our next meeting more productive?" For example, the answer to the second question led the church board to rearrange its agenda so that "new business" now is discussed early in the meeting, before group members become tired and uncreative.

Another suggestion might be to designate someone as a process observer to share observations with the group, break into the conversation to point out something that appears to be hampering the group, suggest communicative techniques and procedures the group has overlooked, and give evaluative comments when the discussion has concluded. The job of process observer may be rotated among members, so everyone gets practice observing and assessing.

2. **Model the behavior you want others to adopt.**
   As designated leader, you can model the kind of group-centered, thoughtful, responsible behavior you think members ought to exhibit. Be sure to examine your own attitudes when a group you chair is doing poorly; your own behavior can do a lot to promote teamwork and develop the trust needed for collaboration. Encourage others to evaluate your suggestions, and react open-mindedly and nondefensively to others' criticisms.

3. **Give members practice at performing needed group duties.**
   Suggest ways in which group members can serve the needs of the group. For instance, rotate the job of recorder so several members get practice. Give members the chance to report on their areas of expertise to the group, and to perform special tasks for the group. Let members substitute for you as discussion leader or liaison to other groups. Don't jump in right away when you see that the group needs something; give the other members a chance to respond before you do.

Establishing and Maintaining Trust

True collaboration (literally, "working together") is possible only when members trust each other. Larson and LaFasto found that interviewees from outstanding teams almost always mentioned *trust* when asked about their group's climate. These authors say: "Trust is one of those mainstay virtues in the commerce of mankind. It is the bond that allows any kind of significant relationship to exist between people. Once broken, it is not easily—if ever—recovered."[8] Analysis of their data shows four components of trust: honesty (no lies, no exaggerations); openness (a combination of open-mindedness and willingness to share); consistency (predictability, dependability); and respect (treating others with fairness and dignity). The following suggestions can help you establish and retain a climate of trust:

1. **Establish norms, based on ethical principles, that build trust.**
   Among the norms that build trust are those on which three important ethical principles are based: working to understand someone, communicating to enhance another's identity and self-concept, and behaving like a responsible group member. Specific behaviors that promote these are listening actively,

encouraging others to explain themselves, helping each other with assignments or other tasks, maintaining confidentiality, getting assignments done when promised, making sure you understand someone's position before disagreeing, and feeling free to disagree without being treated as weird or politically incorrect.

2. **Confront trust violators and other problem members.**
   Two of the most common complaints are that groups tolerate members who put self over group, and that designated leaders fail "to confront and resolve issues associated with inadequate performance by team members."[9] If repeated efforts by you and the other members are unsuccessful, it is far better to remove offenders from the group than to allow trust to erode and group energy to be deflected into destructive avenues.

3. **Be a principled leader.**
   Larson and LaFasto suggest that effective team leaders exemplify the kind of group-centered leadership we have described.[10] Principled leaders put the needs of the group ahead of their individual needs and behave in ethical ways consistent with the group's norms. For instance, they do not say they want group participation, then squash members' attempts to participate. Good group leaders have a vision of the group's future, which they convey clearly; they inspire members to work toward that vision. They show personal commitment to the team's goals. Moreover, they work to unleash the talent of the other members. Leaders create leaders by giving members the experience they need to act with self-confidence.

Promoting Teamwork and Cooperation

Establishing a climate of trust will do more than anything else to develop cooperation and teamwork among members. In addition to having clear, inspiring goals and trust, there are specific things a designated leader can do to promote teamwork:

1. **Speak of "us" and "we," rather than "I" and "you."**
   The leader should convey, verbally and in every other way, that he or she is a full-fledged, committed member of the group. The designated leader also should ask what it means if another member consistently refers to the group as "you."

2. **Create symbols of group identification.**
   A sense of unity can be fostered by inside jokes, shared fantasies, logos, a name for the group (for example, a particularly effective advertising agency committee called itself the "Can Do Committee"), slogans, T-shirts, and so on.

3. **Watch for and challenge any hidden agenda item that seems to conflict with group goals.**
   If you suspect a hidden agenda item is interfering with group functioning or goal achievement, promptly bring this to the attention of the group: "Roger, you have rejected every suggestion the group has proposed without examining it fully. As a result, members are becoming frustrated and angry. Is there something going on that we should know about?" Avoidance makes such problems worse.

4. **Share all rewards with the group.**
   Designated leaders often receive praise from authority figures of a group's parent organization. Wise leaders give credit to the group. They comment about what the group has done, express pride in being a part of the group, and acknowledge the service of all members.

5. **Keep arguments focused on facts and issues, not personalities.**
   Step in at once if any member starts an attack on another's personality, ethnicity, or character. However, recognize also that members may have strong feelings about some issues, so don't squelch expressions of feeling, as long as those expressions do not denigrate others.

6. **Don't let the discussion get so serious that members cannot enjoy themselves.**
   Humor may help reduce the tensions generated when people work hard together at the job of hammering out ideas. Good task leaders may have trouble with humor. Lee observed, for instance, that many of the most efficient leaders lacked human warmth, but groups need *both* efficiency *and* satisfying interactions.[11] He suggested that task masters relax and allow digressions, which can relieve secondary tension. As leader, you *want* to let the group chain out fantasies that enrich its life and contribute to establishing shared beliefs and values. The result of such tension-relieving activity is more concerted effort by group members in the long run. If you are not skilled at tension release, enlist the help of members who are. Bring the group back to task after the joke is over or the fantasy has chained out.

7. **When a group seems to be deadlocked, look for a basis on which to compromise.**
   Perhaps you can synthesize parts of several ideas into a consensus solution or you can suggest a mediation procedure, such as the Principled Negotiation procedure described in chapter 12. However, to do so you must have been even-handed as the leader, remaining somewhat detached from the fray, while listening, observing, and maintaining perspective.

As we have suggested, the leader's behavior should serve as a model for members to follow. As Hackman and Johnson said, "Responsible leaders maintain the highest possible standards of ethics."[12] These authors suggest several principles for leaders that we believe are relevant for small groups:

Ethical Principles for Group Leaders

1. **A leader should not intentionally send deceptive or harmful messages.**
   Not only should leaders tell members the truth, they should hold *truth* to be an appropriate standard for the group's decision making. To us, this means ensuring that *all* relevant information, whether it supports the leader's position or not, is presented to the group and that the group evaluates all information in an unbiased, fair way.

2. **A leader should place concern for others above concern for personal gain.**
   This means that a leader should not take advantage of the power of the leader position for personal gain or advantage. Good leaders do not use insider information for *personal* gain. Hidden agendas, whether belonging to the

leader or members, should not be allowed to interfere with the needs of the group. Moreover, as we have mentioned previously, leaders should refrain from actions that might harm the self-esteem of members.

3. **A leader should respect the opinions and attitudes of members and allow them the freedom to consider the consequences of their actions.**
   This principle supports democratic, group-centered leadership that encourages equal opportunity for all to participate. It also supports our preference for distributed leadership and acknowledges how important it is for leaders to develop the capabilities of members.

4. **A leader should stand behind members when they carry out policies and actions approved by the leader and the group.**
   Ethical leaders support members who carry out the plans of the group and the leader. They do not save their own skins by leaving group members hanging.

5. **A leader treats members consistently, regardless of sex, ethnicity, or social background.**
   Members are valued for their contributions to the group. Ethical leaders minimize external status differences to encourage participation by all.

6. **A leader should establish clear policies that all group members are expected to follow.**
   Group procedures and rules are clearly understood, and ethical leaders follow the same rules and norms that members are expected to follow.

As with other desirable behaviors, the leader should model ethical behavior that will serve as a standard for members to follow. By doing so, the leader will help to create a climate of trust and a spirit of cohesiveness.

Summary

In chapter 9 we have presented what we believe to be the philosophical principles and communicative competencies of effective designated leaders. We believe that good leaders provide the degree of coordination and structure appropriate to the group's situation, but ideally leaders encourage group members to grow and mature so that they can assume designated leadership of the group. This allows the leader to act as a completer, providing essential group services not provided by other group members. Outstanding designated leaders articulate group goals clearly, adhere to high standards of performance, and promote equality among group members. In the United States, group leaders are expected to provide administrative services, facilitate discussions, and help the group develop. Administrative services include planning for meetings, maintaining written communication, and providing liaison for the group. Leading discussions requires communicative behaviors that initiate the discussion, keep the talk goal oriented and organized, equalize opportunities for all members to participate, stimulate both creative and critical thinking, and foster meeting-to-meeting improvement. Developing both teamwork and individual member growth requires regular evaluation of the group's processes, a climate of trust and cooperation, confronting self-oriented behaviors, and enhancing a sense of unity. Numerous specific suggestions were offered for developing such competencies. Finally, several ethical principles for designated group leaders were presented.

1. Based on your most recent experiences in group discussions, make three lists: 1) your most important strengths as a discussion leader; 2) your most important weaknesses; and 3) the steps you plan to take to remove or reduce your weaknesses.   **Exercises**

2. Think of leaders of small groups to which you have belonged and discuss the following with class members:
    a. Who was the *worst* leader? List the specific characteristics and behaviors that led to your judgment.
    b. Who was the *best* leader? List the specific characteristics and behaviors that led to your judgment.
    c. Which of the above behaviors were most important in distinguishing between the two?

3. Split the class in half. One half will serve as observers and the other as discussants; later, they will switch roles. The discussants should form groups of four or five, with approximately equal numbers of observers per group. Each group should select a designated discussion leader and a case problem or question of interest (for instance, how to improve the quality of undergraduate education at your college, how to reduce cheating, etc.). The observers should be prepared to observe the leader's behavior and answer the following questions:
    a. What functions did the leader perform? How effective was each? How appropriate?
    b. At what points during the discussion did the leader fail to supply some needed leadership service? Did someone else step in to provide it? What was the effect on the group?
    c. Overall, how effective was the leader?

4. Select a problem. Each class member should prepare and deliver a leader's opening remarks for initiating a discussion of the problem. Then, either in groups or as a whole class, evaluate each introduction.

5. After a meeting of five or six members of your class or of your project group, each member should write the minutes for the meeting. Exchange your minutes with those written by all other members of the group; compare, then see if you can agree as a group on an official report of the meeting.

6. In groups of four to six, discuss the ethical principles suggested for group leaders. Make a list of others by which you think group leaders should abide. Share your lists with the class.

Bibliography

Cathcart, Robert S., and Larry A. Samovar, eds. *Small Group Communication: A Reader,* 6th ed. Dubuque, IA: Wm. C. Brown Publishers, 1992, especially section 8.

Fisher, B. Aubrey. "Leadership: When Does the Difference Make a Difference?" In *Communication and Group Decision-Making.* Eds. Randy Y. Hirokawa and Marshall S. Poole. Beverly Hills, CA: Sage Publications, 1986, 197–215.

Hackman, Michael Z., and Craig E. Johnson. *Leadership: A Communication Perspective.* Prospect Heights, IL: Waveland Press, 1991, especially chapters 6 and 7.

Larson, Carl E., and Frank M. J. LaFasto. *TeamWork: What Must Go Right/What Can Go Wrong.* Newbury Park, CA: Sage Publications, 1989.

Notes

1. Carl E. Larson and Frank M. J. LaFasto, *TeamWork: What Must Go Right/What Can Go Wrong* (Newbury Park, CA: Sage Publications, 1989): 118.

2. Carl E. Larson and Frank M. J. LaFasto, *TeamWork,* 121–123.

3. Donald E. Petersen, cited in "Management Digest," a special advertising section of *Newsweek* (March 5, 1990): 19.

4. William C. Schutz, "The Leader as Completer," in *Small Group Communication: A Reader,* 3d ed., eds. Robert S. Cathcart and Larry A. Samovar (Dubuque, IA: Wm. C. Brown Publishers, 1979): 400.

5. Michael Z. Hackman and Craig E. Johnson, *Leadership: A Communication Perspective* (Prospect Heights, IL: Waveland Press, 1991): 129.

6. John Gastil, "Identifying Obstacles to Small Group Democracy," *Small Group Research* 24 (February 1993): 5–27.

7. Carl E. Larson and Frank M. J. LaFasto, *Teamwork,* 130–131.

8. Carl E. Larson and Frank M. J. LaFasto, *TeamWork,* 85.

9. Carl E. Larson and Frank M. J. LaFasto, *TeamWork,* 136.

10. Carl E. Larson and Frank M. J. LaFasto, *TeamWork,* 118–129.

11. Irving J. Lee, *How to Talk with People* (New York: Harper & Row, Publishers, 1952): 158–160.

12. Michael Z. Hackman and Craig E. Johnson, *Leadership: A Communication Perspective* (Prospect Heights, IL: Waveland Press, 1991): 205.

PART 4

Effective Problem Solving in the Small Group

Problem solving is the reason most secondary groups exist. Problems solved by groups affect all our lives, so it is especially important that we understand how to maximize the effectiveness of the problem-solving process in groups. This section describes the nature of problem solving, provides vital information to improve group decision-making processes, and explains how you can use conflict to enhance group problem solving and decision making.

Problem-Solving Discussion

Central Message

Problem solving is most effective when a group explores the problem thoroughly and generates a variety of possible solutions, which the group evaluates on the basis of their possible consequences. Following an appropriate adaptation of the general Procedural Model of Problem Solving helps a group do this.

Study Objectives

As a result of studying chapter 10 you should be able to:

1. Analyze the undesirable present situation, obstacles, and goal of any problem.

2. List the dimensions of a problem and explain their importance when developing a procedural outline for group problem solving.

3. Plan procedural outlines to ensure that no step crucial to the quality of the solution is overlooked.

4. List and explain six principles as guidelines for planning specific problem-solving procedures.

5. List the five components of the general Procedural Model of Problem Solving (P-MOPS), explain the importance and nature of each step, and be able to adapt the model for discussing any sort of problem.

6. Use the Single Question format to help a group engage in the vigilant interaction necessary to arrive at the best possible solution to a problem.

Key Terms

Acceptance requirements
Area of freedom
Charge
Cooperative requirements
Criteria
Decision making
Intrinsic interest
Intuitive
Obstacle

Population familiarity
Problem
Problem questions
Problem solving
Procedural Model of Problem
  Solving (P-MOPS)
Reflective thinking
Scientific method

Single Question format
Solution multiplicity
Solution questions
Structure
Systematic
Task difficulty
Technical requirements
Vigilant Interaction Theory

Although groups usually surpass individuals in solving complex problems, the adage "To fail to plan is to plan to fail" is even more true for group problem solving than for many other complex human endeavors. As Gouran and Hirokawa say,

> . . . the failure of a group to observe any overall plan for addressing the crucial issues related to the group's decision-making efforts can function to increase the probability of a faulty choice. Thus the violation of established procedures and rules for decision making is a cause for concern, and one that certainly demands the need for some counteractive influence in many cases.[1]

Rapid increases in knowledge and numbers of humans have generated increasingly complex problems for human groups, such as reducing terrorism, finding cures for "incurable" diseases like AIDS and Jacobs-Krutschfeld syndrome, controlling the federal budget, and designing safer, more energy-efficient cars. All too often, responsible authorities assume that if they assemble a group of individuals with necessary expertise, effective problem solving will result. Unfortunately, this is not the case. Not only do problem-solving group members need to have expertise about the problem, they also need to know how to proceed as a group to be sure all aspects of the problem have been examined, which Hirokawa calls **Vigilant Interaction Theory** (also referred to as *Functional Interaction Theory*).[2] For high-quality solutions, groups must attend to both information and the *process* of problem solving; indeed, without the latter they may not even be able to complete their assignments. For example, Wood reported that a group of principals and teachers she observed for more than a year were unable to complete their task. She concluded that their expertise was sufficient, but the group members lacked needed group problem-solving skills.[3]

If you ask most people what they do when they have a problem to solve, they will say something like "get the facts, weigh the alternatives, and make a decision." That's not a bad procedure, though incomplete, but extensive observation reveals that both individual and group problem solving is usually more haphazard.[4] For instance, Berg found that problem-solving groups he observed changed themes on the average every fifty-eight seconds, often without ever completing discussion of the issues or themes raised.[5] In the typical problem-solving discussion someone mentions a problem, someone else suggests a way to solve it, the group then briefly discusses the idea, and then it is adopted or something else is proposed, perhaps with brief periods of discussing the problem itself. Groups often flit from idea to idea, until time begins to run out and a decision is made quickly with no plans to implement it. As you might imagine, this haphazard procedure is unlikely to produce an adequate solution to a complicated problem, such as how to reduce the cost of health care or the level of unemployment. Vital elements of the problem will probably not be considered, innovative thinking is unlikely, and evaluation is usually less than vigilant. Some sort of systematic procedure or checklist is needed to solve complex problems effectively.

To provide a basis for you to understand the importance of both information and procedures in problem-solving discussion, chapter 10 first differentiates problem solving from decision making, analyzes the major dimensions of problems that need to be considered, presents what invariably needs to be considered when a group tackles a complicated problem, and provides two general but flexible models to ensure both the efficiency and efficacy of group problem-solving discussions.

Many writers have used the terms *problem solving* and *decision making* as synonyms, creating considerable confusion. Perhaps that is because they view making a choice among possible solutions as the most important step in problem solving. We want you to distinguish clearly between these terms, for there is a major difference between what they involve. **Decision making** refers to the act of *choosing* among options that already exist. **Problem solving** is a more comprehensive, multistep procedure through which a group develops a plan to move from an unsatisfactory state to a desired goal. Problem solving usually requires a group to make numerous decisions, but it also involves *creating* or *discovering* alternatives, not just choosing among them. Thus, decision making is one part of problem solving. An example may clarify this difference. A task force charged with solving the problem of inadequate facilities for a university performing arts department is a problem-solving group that will need to make a variety of decisions in the course of developing its proposal for correcting the inadequate facilities. In contrast, a screening committee asked to select the best site for a university performing arts center from among several approved sites is simply a decision-making group. We discuss decision making in detail in chapter 11.

Problem Solving and Decision Making

A major purpose of this chapter is to help you understand what you can do to increase the likelihood that group problem solving will be effective. In order to do so, we must first define the concept "problem" and the major variables of problems. Then we will explain the conditions that must exist for group problem solving to be effective.

Effective Problem Solving

A **problem** is a discrepancy between what actually is happening and what *should* be going on. All problems can be analyzed into three major components: an existing situation that is undesirable, a goal, and obstacles to reaching the goal, as shown in figure 10.1. Understanding the general character of these components is essential to planning problem-solving procedures.

Problem

1. **Undesirable present situation.**
   Unless someone is dissatisfied with the way things are, no problem exists; a problem, then, is in part a matter of human awareness and feelings. For example, imagine that a club to which you belong has been losing members, but no one has felt anything was wrong. At a regular meeting the secretary points out that you do not have a quorum needed to conduct business, and that attendance has been dropping gradually. Someone else says your continued existence as an organization is threatened. Now you feel concerned that the situation is unsatisfactory. Recognition of this undesirable present situation is the beginning of a problem for you.

Figure 10.1
Components of a
problem.

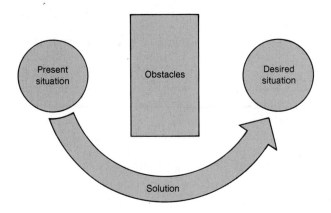

2. **Goal.**

   The perception of an unsatisfactory situation is closely associated with a goal (a desired situation), even if it's at first vague. In our example, you can already say that you want to increase your membership and attendance at meetings so your organization can survive. You might soon be able to state the goal precisely, such as, "To increase membership by 50 percent and double attendance at meetings."

3. **Obstacles.**

   An **obstacle** is anything that interferes with reaching the goal. Lack of information, inadequate funds or equipment, and a lack of needed skills would be obstacles, as would anything that must be changed, removed, or overcome. In our example, one immediately obvious obstacle is the lack of information about why membership and attendance have been dropping.

Problem solving is the procedure undertaken to arrive at a solution, including both a plan for arriving at the goal and the actual execution of the plan. Then, if the goal has not been satisfactorily achieved, further problem solving will be needed.

Problem
Characteristics

Obviously, a plan must suit the characteristics of the actual problem. In his classic synthesis of group dynamics, Shaw identified six major dimensions of the tasks in studies of small group processes, five of which are characteristics of all problems small groups tackle: *task difficulty, solution multiplicity, intrinsic interest, cooperative requirements,* and *population familiarity.*[6] Considering these and the additional characteristics of acceptance requirements, technical requirements, and the group's area of freedom will help you plan appropriate procedures for a group to tackle any problem.

   Task difficulty refers to the amount of complexity, hence the effort, knowledge, and skill needed to achieve the goal. Groups generally are asked to tackle complex problems or those for which a number of different perspectives must be considered, not simply to choose among equivalent alternatives. For instance, consider recent government task forces assigned to recommend improvements in the American health care system, reduction of the budget, and improvement of learning levels of high school graduates—problems beyond the capacity of any single person.

Solving any of these problems is much more complex than recommending an acceptable theme and effective publicity for a junior-senior prom. Only the most general steps in the problem-solving procedures for all these problems will be the same.

Solution multiplicity refers to the number of conceivable or feasible alternatives for solving the problem. To illustrate, there are usually only a few ways to get from your residence to your classroom, but there are innumerable ways to decorate your living room. Structured procedures like *brainstorming* have long been available as an aid to help us think of more possible alternatives when solution multiplicity is even moderately high.[7]

Intrinsic interest was defined by Shaw as ". . . the degree to which the task in and of itself is interesting, motivating, and attractive to the group members,"[8] reminding us of Larson and LaFasto's finding that outstanding teams had clear, elevating goals. Early research by Berkowitz found that, when group members were highly interested in their task, they preferred sharing in control of the group's procedures, but they preferred strong procedural control by a discussion leader when interest was low.[9] Our experience verifies this finding: if interest is high, members at first want to express opinions and feelings and will resist strict procedural control. After they have vented their feelings, procedural control of the problem-solving procedure is more likely to be accepted.

Ideally, groups would discuss only intrinsically interesting problems. In actuality, people are assigned to committees that deal with a variety of problems, including some of little interest to them. In such a case, this should be brought out in the open, perhaps leading to a change of attitude or a request that some other group tackle the problem.

The phrase **cooperative requirements** refers to the degree to which coordinated efforts are essential to satisfactory completion of a task. Obviously, arriving at a consensus solution for a complex problem requires a high level of cooperation in communicating, especially when members initially have different perceptions of the problem and different ideas about how to solve it. Complexity and the need for communicative competence are intertwined. Unless systematic procedures are followed for making decisions about how to solve complex problems, discussion may result in poor solutions.

The **population familiarity** dimension refers to the degree to which members have previous experience with the task and possess information essential to its successful completion. It should be no surprise to you that groups with experienced members tend to perform better than groups with inexperienced ones.[10] When population familiarity is low to start, the problem-solving procedure should concentrate on analysis of the problem. But sometimes very knowledgeable people become smug and unwilling to think of new approaches. Then procedures to increase innovation may be essential.

The **acceptance requirements** dimension refers to the extent to which a proposed solution must be acceptable to people whom it will affect. Legislation enacted to solve public problems has often backfired when acceptance requirements were overlooked. For instance, a task force recently created a planning and zoning ordinance for a county near where we work, but citizen groups, while acknowledging a need for some such law, refused to accept it. The United States has experienced epic struggles over laws controlling alcohol, marijuana, and driving. Sometimes a group must give heavy consideration to this dimension of the task, other times little or none.

The **technical requirements** dimension refers to the extent to which a solution must be technically feasible or match some standard of technical excellence. For instance, U.S. automakers have had to rethink their procedures for quality control of their products, and some have done so with great success. The Food and Drug Administration has technical standards of both safety and effectiveness that all proposed new drugs for medical problems must pass. The procedural plan for tackling any problem should encourage a group to consider both likely acceptance and technical requirements.

The group's **area of freedom** refers to the amount of authority given the group, which is either implied or stated in a *charge* to a group. A **charge** is an assignment given to a subordinate group by a parent organization or person with authority to do so. Groups not given a specific charge still need to consider the legitimate area of freedom they legally have. A charge specifies what a group is to do, including an area of freedom that defines the extent of the authority of the group. For instance, the zoning board that administered the law in the example mentioned above invited citizen groups to recommend changes in the law. Some groups, very angry that their recommendations were not made law, failed to realize that their authority was only to *recommend* and that other groups might recommend just the opposite. Here is part of the charge from a university booklet detailing what the Committee on Improvement of Instruction is supposed to do:

> This committee shall be responsible for the granting of monies to full-time . . . faculty
> for the improvement of their instructional capabilities. . . . The University committee on
> Improvement of Instruction shall make its funding recommendations to the Director of
> the Center for Improvement of Instruction and shall report its activities to the Chancellor.

This charge makes it clear that the committee's area of freedom does not include recommending that an instructor be dismissed for poor teaching, that monies be spent to improve research laboratories, or that new instructional programs be created. One of us was involved in a major conflict when an executive officer thought that he had authority to override committee recommendations for promotion, whereas the committee thought they could override the administrator. Until the area of freedom of the committee was clarified, a lot of time was wasted and bad feelings were generated. This resulted in removing the administrator and restructuring the committee. In short, be sure the problem-solving procedure includes clarification of the area of freedom given the group early on. For instance, instructors frequently assign projects to small groups in communication courses. Such an assignment is a charge. Be sure the charge and area of freedom of a classroom group is completely clear to all members.

Considering each of the problem variables described above will help you determine the appropriate procedure for solving a problem, including research inputs, discussion process, and implementation of the output. Discussing these variables should usually be done by all members very early, especially if the problem is a complex one requiring numerous meetings, so that an appropriate plan or outline can be devised to ensure that the work is at once efficient, effective, and satisfying.

Procedures and communication for group problem solving have been investigated by social scientists in many fields during the twentieth century. Basic principles for effective problem solving and decision making by small groups, as well as the efficacy of specific procedures, have been investigated by human communication scientists during the last half of this century. From their findings we present first a group of guiding principles for any discussion of complex problems by small groups, a general procedural format that can be adapted to virtually any problem, and an alternate procedure that allows a group preferring a looser structure to generate its own unique procedure without serious danger of lapses in critical thinking.

Organizing Problem-Solving Discussions

According to Hirokawa, the "quality of vigilance (or critical-thinking)" affects the quality of the solution decided upon by a problem-solving group.[11] Gouran had earlier shown how important critical thinking and communication of such thinking were to the ability of a group to reach a high-quality inference.[12] Based on considerable experimental research by Hirokawa, his students, and other researchers, Hirokawa and Rost say that vigilant interaction involves addressing four general issues before making the final decision of what to do to solve a problem. These four issues are the core of Vigilant Interaction Theory:

Vigilant Interaction Theory

1. "Is there something about the current state of affairs that requires improvement or change?"
2. "What do we want to achieve or accomplish in deciding what to do about the problem?"
3. "What are the choices available to us?"
4. "What are the positive and negative aspects of those choices?"[13]

These four subissues are also the heart of the general procedural model (P-MOPS) we present in the next section of this chapter. Productive groups usually take up these issues in a more or less organized sequence like that shown above, though the sequences may vary from discussion to discussion.[14] The single biggest error by groups that reach faulty solutions is *omission* of one or more of these steps, or failure to be thorough in discussing them. Both laboratory studies of group problem solving using college students and a field study of committees in a large utility company support vigilant interaction theory. The study of committees in the utility corporation found empirical support for the hypotheses relating all four major steps in vigilant problem-solving interaction to the quality of the groups' final recommendations for improving health of employees.[15]

   In summarizing research on the relationship between the quality of group interaction during problem-solving discussion and the quality of the final solutions reached, Hirokawa said:

   It should be clear at this point that effective group decision making usually does not happen by accident. In most cases, a group is able to make a high-quality choice because the system of reasoning that it employed in arriving at a final choice was characterized by: (1) proper understanding of the problematic situation, (2) appropriate choice-making objectives, (3) accurate evaluation of the positive and negative qualities of available choices, and (4) warranted utilization of high-quality information in arriving at a final decision.[16]

Even when groups have needed resources of valid information and member thinking skills, they may still do poorly if knowledgeable members are lacking in persuasive skills (communicative competence) or hold back on information and arguments because of personal likes and dislikes of other members—the displacement of task goals by social ones. Communicative competence and focus on the group task are essential to high-quality outcomes. Focus on the task and vigilant interaction can both be facilitated by properly structured discussion.

The Need for Structure

The **scientific method** provides a general structure for systematic group problem solving. Science as method uses disciplined observation to gain dependable knowledge about the physical world as a basis for problem solving, instead of relying on hunches, intuition, or revelation. Decisions are based on critical reasoning from reports of confirmable observations, and conclusions are held tentatively (as hypotheses and theories), always subject to change in the light of newly discovered facts. What we once believed or what we hope or wish to be true are not the criteria of science. A general description of science as a method of knowing, explaining, and predicting natural phenomena is the basis for the structural model of problem solving we espouse.

Some people tend to be **intuitive** problem solvers who size up a situation, then arrive at a solution without consciously following any perceptible procedure. The steps between feeling some difficulty and finding a solution cannot be observed—suddenly the solution is *there.* This is the so-called "Ah-ha!" or "Eureka!" experience. While we may all experience it at times, there is no way for a group to function like the brain of a human being in solving a problem.

Systematic thinkers, on the other hand, think their way through a set of logical steps, a **structure** of problem solving like the *Vigilant Interaction* issues investigated by Hirokawa. American philosopher John Dewey, in his famous book *How We Think,* described **reflective thinking.** Dewey abstracted this model from reports by students about how they had solved personal problems. Some of us use the reflective thinking model to systematize the solving of important problems. First, we are aware of a felt difficulty, then we define the difficulty, think of possible solutions for it, evaluate these potential alternatives, and finally make a decision, including, if possible, implementing and testing the decision we have chosen.[17] Although Dewey described *individual* thought processes, small group writers and researchers have adapted the steps of reflective thinking so that a group can structure its problem-solving interaction. Versions of this are sometimes presented with a title such as *Standard Agenda.*

Some of the advantages of structuring group problem-solving have been presented earlier in this chapter. There are others. For instance, Scheidel and Crowell found that uninstructed groups tended to spiral considerably from discussing problem issues to problem solutions, a sequence called "reach-testing."[18] Observers rate the quality of such discussions lower than discussions organized with the structure of Reflective Thinking or Vigilant Interaction.[19] Even low task-oriented participants rate structured discussions higher than those in which the designated leader fails to help organize the problem-solving procedure.[20] In a study by Brilhart, participants following a highly structured problem-solving procedure made a greater proportion of statements relevant to the issue of problem solving than when the leader did not clearly guide the group through such a structure.[21] Poole concluded that following a structured procedure often reminds discussants of something they forgot to do (such as analyze the problem thoroughly) in an earlier stage of problem solving and provides logical priorities.[22] So long as the logical priorities are incorporated into a sequence (e.g., problem analysis before proposing solutions), no one structure appears consistently to surpass others. In a study by Brilhart and Jochem, the quality of final decisions reached by groups following three different problem-solving structural outlines was not significantly different (though a significant proportion of the participants preferred one of these structures).[23] That no one structure produced superior final decisions was confirmed in experiments reported by Bayless and Larson, but Larson did find that using *no* structural pattern for problem solving produced definitely inferior solutions.[24]

Some theorists have argued that following a systematic linear procedure is not normal for small groups; however, the groups they observed had not been trained either in problem solving or in group procedures. Trainers in business and industry invariably have recommended teaching corporate personnel such procedures as a necessity before instituting participative management techniques such as quality circles or self-managed work teams. In a recent article, three researchers associated with a corporation in which numerous scientists conduct research and development in small teams argued forcefully for a highly systematic, structured format of problem solving by trained scientists to prevent the kinds of mistakes often attributed to "random error." These writers say that the epitome of discovery is to "methodically gather and analyze all the available data about an observable phenomenon. Contrary to what many are teaching, systematic problem solving is *not* a rigid set of specific techniques or a single prescribed discussion format . . . [but] a matter of effective group *communication* and data *handling.*"[25] The high degree of structuring helps keep the attention of the group focused by using pointed questions to which specific answers are sought, though the group may need to start discussion less rigidly.

Recent research by Hirokawa supports the importance of using systematic procedures. In one study, the groups with the highest-quality decisions used a vigilant decision-making procedure and engaged in second guessing, or retrospective questioning of previous choices.[26] In another study, Hirokawa found that it was not so much the particular procedure groups used that determined the quality, but whether certain important functions were performed.[27] That is, for effective group problem solving, groups must thoroughly and accurately understand the problem, must have a variety of acceptable alternatives, and must evaluate each alternative carefully, especially assessing the negative consequences associated with each alternative. Groups that do this, regardless of the particular decision-making technique used, perform better than those that don't. However, consistent with Larson's findings, using *any* procedure is more effective than using none because systematic procedures help ensure that the critical *functions* are attended to.

Hirokawa found that differences in decision quality are linked directly to how well groups satisfy these and other decision functions such as understanding the requirements for an acceptable choice.[28] He also found that assessment of positive and negative qualities is important at different stages of a group's deliberation. For instance, effective groups first seem to spot the serious defects when they initially screen alternatives. Once they find an alternative that appears to be free of fatal flaws, they switch strategies and begin to detail the positive aspects of the alternative. Hirokawa says, ". . . instruction needs to move away from discussion procedures and formats (e.g., 'standard agendas') and more toward the effects or consequences of those procedures and formats."[29] He views group problem solving as a complex interplay among a variety of individual-level and group-level variables that include members' cognitive and psychological characteristics, their personal motives and communication skills, decision rules under which the group operates, the relationships among the members, and the communication patterns of the group.[30]

The question remains whether individuals who rate low in critical thinking tests and low in preference for procedural order can be taught to accept and follow such systematic problem-solving procedures to advantage. The evidence indicates they can. Further, none of us appears to be purely intuitive or systematic as problem solvers; in terms of a currently popular theory, we have both left and right brain hemispheres that can function in problem solving. How much of our approach to problem solving is genetically determined and how much is learned from parents, teachers, and colleagues is open to question. But Nisbett and Ross successfully taught subjects to replace simplistic intuitive strategies (which led to many errors in problem solving) with formal structural and statistical procedures used by scientists.[31] Sternberg demonstrated that impulsive people, who did poorly in solving problems on IQ tests, could be taught to proceed more systematically and successfully.[32]

Discussion of Criteria   Systematic problem-solving procedures help groups clarify *criteria* for an effective solution. **Criteria** are the standards against which available options must be judged, and group members must agree on criteria before a solution is adopted. Theorists have long argued about *whether* and *when* a problem-solving discussion should include a step during which the group talks about, proposes, and decides on specific explicit criteria. Some textbooks have argued that reflective thinking requires deciding on criteria as part of the problem analysis, or at least before talking about solutions. Other theorists have argued that criteria should be discussed explicitly, but only after having accumulated all the possible solutions members can find or invent. Still others say little about criteria. Our experience, what little scientific evidence is available, and the psychology of problem solving individually and by groups all suggest that there is no simple single answer to the questions of whether and when to discuss criteria during group problem solving. In the first study to address this question, Brilhart and Jochem found that the quality of final decisions was not affected by *when* criteria were discussed or even whether criteria discussion was a step in the problem-solving outline followed by the group. However, significantly more of the students used as subjects preferred a sequence in which criteria were not discussed until *after* brainstorming rather than either a sequence in which criteria were decided upon before brainstorming or a sequence in which criteria were not explicitly discussed.[33]

Both Poole and Hirokawa have suggested that the actual sequence may not matter so much as the intellectual content of problem discussion (i.e., Vigilant Interaction Theory). Criteria may not need to be discussed explicitly if they are well known. In a recent study, Hirokawa et al. explored the importance of evaluation clarity in applying criteria. Evaluation clarity is high when criteria are clearly presented to the group as part of the charge or the presentation of the problem and are understood by all members. Evaluation clarity is low when standards are not presented to the group, are equivocal, or are not understood alike by all members. In their experiment, Hirokawa et al. asked students to select one of several alternative punishments for a student guilty of plagiarism. Some groups were given explicit criteria; others were not told on what basis to evaluate the possible punishments. These authors concluded that "when evaluation clarity is high, group decision performance is only weakly related to the establishment and utilization of evaluation criteria. However, when evaluation clarity is low, group decision performance is strongly correlated with a group's efforts to establish and utilize appropriate evaluation criteria."[34]

How essential for effective problem solving is it to discuss criteria explicitly? The previous studies suggest that when criteria are already well known and shared in advance of a group's problem-solving discussion, it is not necessary to discuss them. However, when there is no advance convergence among members on criteria for an effective solution (i.e., evaluation clarity is low), explicit discussion about criteria will probably improve solution quality. We think that it is a real leadership service to determine whether criteria are explicitly understood and agreed upon and, if not, to get the group to state criteria as clearly as possible before extensively evaluating alternatives. Further, if the problem is high in solution multiplicity, we recommend delaying discussion of criteria until *after* listing possible solutions. When options are few or technical demands are high, it may be wise to discuss criteria as part of the problem analysis unless they have been presented unequivocally as part of the charge or problem statement to the group.

The research reported and analyzed above suggests that systematic procedures can help groups use the critical thinking skills and knowledge of members to advantage, thus arriving at better solutions to complex problems. We are now ready to consider a structural model that uses the principles of scientific method, Vigilant Interaction Theory, and communicative competence and convergence.

P-MOPS: A General Procedural Model of Problem Solving for Structuring Problem-Solving Discussions

As we have repeatedly pointed out, the effectiveness of a specific problem-solving procedure is affected by contingencies of problem characteristics, member experiences, member traits and preferences, corporate culture, and so forth. As Pavitt recently pointed out in his summary of research concerned with formal group discussion procedures, it is highly probable that a formal procedure does improve group problem solving, but how this works is still unclear.[35] Effective problem solving requires that key issues be dealt with thoroughly. Trying to find a way to offset human tendencies to be guided by internal states more than by what others say and do in problem-solving discussions has led us to the development of a general **Procedural Model of Problem Solving (P-MOPS)**. The acronym P-MOPS has a double purpose: it helps us remember the full name of the model, and in pun-like fashion indicates that the purpose of the model is to help groups "mop up" all the details or logical necessities of high-quality problem solving. We say that this is a *general* procedural model because while it provides a systematic structure based on both scientific method and Vigilant Interaction Theory, it can be adjusted to all the contingencies faced by groups charged with or choosing to solve a problem.

The following are the major basic steps in P-MOPS:

I. Problem description and analysis: "What is the nature of the problem facing the group?"
II. Generation and elaboration of possible solutions: "What might be done to solve the problem we've described?"
III. Evaluation of possible solutions: "What are the probable benefits and possible negative consequences of each proposed solution?"
IV. Consensus decision: "What seems to be the best possible solution we can all support?"
V. Implementation of the solution chosen: "How will we put our decision into effect?"

This model assumes that the leader, perhaps with help of all members, has formulated a written outline containing specific questions about all subissues the group must consider to be sure that no important contingency will be overlooked. P-MOPS, then, is not a rigid recipe or mathematical formula, but a guide to logical implications of the vital issues involved in a complete cycle of complex problem solving. It is helpful to remind group members of these issues while they are engaged in discussion and to help keep each member focused on the *group* goal instead of diverting to personal-agenda social issues. A good way to do this is by charting: put the general outline in view of all members (visual display or handout), and chart the progress of the group on sheets of newsprint, wall boards, or a computer display. A study reported by one of your coauthors found that college students following an early version of P-MOPS much preferred to have it in front of them on a chart rather than just having the leader explain the procedure or announce each new question as the group came to it.[36] Kelly, Jaffe, and Nelson insist that the progression of a discussion must be made visual to a group as it moves through steps, perhaps on flip charts.[37] In a recent article about how computers can be used to help groups solve complex problems, Broome and Chen say two of the best uses of computer technology are for displaying ideas graphically and recording them as the group proceeds.[38] So whatever procedural outline your group follows, we suggest it be displayed to all members during the discussion, and that a visual record of the group's progress be maintained throughout.

Next we present an explanation of what is done and why at each step in P-MOPS.

I. What is the nature of the problem facing us?

Early in the discussion the group needs to focus most talk on the details of what is unsatisfactory, what led to the undesirable situation, what is ultimately desired, and what the obstacles to that goal might be. First, if the group has been given a charge, the group needs to achieve symbolic convergence on it. For instance, instructors frequently assign group projects in small group communication courses. That assignment is a charge. If you have such an assignment, make sure all members of your project group understand the charge as intended by the instructor. Sometimes student groups tackle issues beyond their area of freedom or competence, such as "What should be done to improve the U.S. Constitution?" or "How might Americans shift their goals from acquiring possessions to spiritual growth?" On questions of such breadth and abstractness, students are likely to do little more than express personal opinions in which few people would be interested. Second, be sure you are clear about the *form* your output is to take: A panel discussion presented to the class? An instructional unit? A dramatization of some theory or principle? A research paper? A video or film presentation? A written recommendation designed to solve a campus or local problem? Can you explain how you will be graded: as a group, as individuals, or by some combination of both? Will each member be required to write a case study analyzing your group? If so, what format must the paper follow? Will you need to keep a journal of group activities, or some other record?

Important principles for guiding the investigation and discussion of the nature of your problem/goal include:

A. Focus on the problem before thinking about how to solve it. What would you think if you drove your rough-running car into a garage and the service manager immediately said, "You need new valves in your engine," without so much as looking under the hood? Most of us would drive away as quickly as possible. A competent technician, after questioning you about how the car was acting, might attach an engine analysis computer before making a tentative diagnosis. As in this story, one of the most common failings in group problem solving is getting solution-centered before thoroughly analyzing the problem. Writers concerned with business groups have noted this tendency and the potential harm it can cause.[39] Time spent in this step often saves headaches later, but fudging on problem analysis leads to such outcomes as:

1. Partisanship and personalized conflict. Lacking a shared image of the details of the problem, achieving consensus is unlikely.

2. Wasted time. The back-and-forth cycling from problem to solution to more details of problem to another solution and so on is usually an inefficient use of members' time.

3. "Solutions" that don't work. If a problem is not thoroughly analyzed and all obstacles identified, the solution decided upon is not likely to overcome all the obstacles, resulting in incomplete achievement of the goal. For example, rigging a truck to burn in a crash was an easy solution to the problem of how to get footage to illustrate a design flaw, but the implicit lie of this solution cost NBC News credibility and a lawsuit, and the news director his job.

B. State the problem in the form of a single, unambiguous question, a *problem question.* Avoid beginning with a *solution question.* **Problem questions** focus on the undesired state of affairs and the goal, whereas **solution questions** suggest a solution, a means of arriving at the goal,

Solution Questions	Problem Questions
How can I transfer a man who is popular in his work group but slows down the work of other employees in the group?	How can I increase the work output of the group?
How can we increase the publicity for our club's activities so attendance will be increased?	What can we do to increase attendance at our club's activities?

and thus tend to limit the thinking of discussants to that one solution. Examples of both types of questions can be seen in figure 10.2.

C. Map the problem thoroughly. Think of the problem as an uncharted area with only vague boundaries. You must understand the terrain you will face in your campaign to arrive at the goal. To map the problem, the group must answer the following questions about the problem concerning such variables as *who, what, why, when, how long, where, how, how serious, what limitations,* and *what feelings.* Participants must *share* all they know about the situation: facts, complaints, conditions, circumstances, factors, happenings, relationships, effects, and so forth. They may discover that they need to learn a lot more before proceeding with a plan of action, so then they must answer such questions as, "How will we get the information we need?" and "Who will look up what?"

Mapping the problem should be as precise and detailed as possible. Kepner and Tregoe pointed out that one of the greatest dangers is that a group will quickly accept an apparent cause without adequate gathering of facts, analysis, and interpretation of the facts—jumping to conclusions. Instead of critically analyzing each other's arguments about causes, discussants may simply collect and present arguments in support of pet theories, and resist other possible explanations. Writing for business managers involved in problem solving, Kepner and Tregoe advised that they encourage each participant to "closely examine each hypothesis, looking for loopholes, for inconsistencies . . ." especially with regard to one's own brainchildren.[40]

Figure 10.3 illustrates the mapping of the problem, during which information is gathered, shared, and interpreted. The large circle represents all that could be known and understood about the problem. Each of the members—A, B, C, and D—come to the initial meeting with some information and opinions about it, a unique personal map represented by the four inner circles. Some information is shared by two members, some by three, and a small amount by all four. And some useful information is not yet known to *any* member. Once the members have discussed the problem freely and shared all the information they have, the group map looks like the second large circle, very close to the "real" problem.

One of the greatest obstacles to such problem-centered thinking is a member (especially if this is a designated leader) who comes to the group

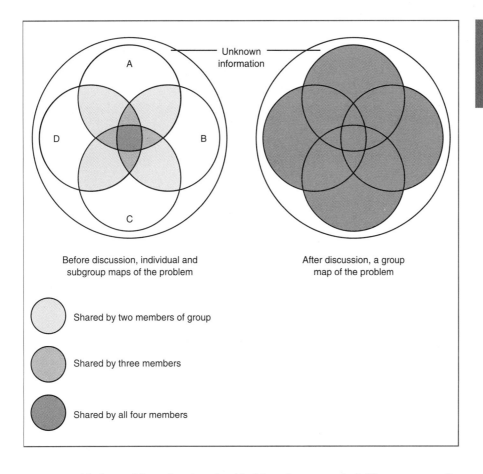

Figure 10.3
Maps of a problem before and after discussion.

Unknown information

A
D   B
C

Before discussion, individual and subgroup maps of the problem

After discussion, a group map of the problem

Shared by two members of group

Shared by three members

Shared by all four members

with the problem already solved in his or her own mind. The presenter of a problem must set preconceived solutions aside; mutual influence is a hallmark of teamwork in group problem solving.

D. Be sure the group members agree on criteria, as we discussed earlier. Unless implicit or explicit agreement exists about what criteria a solution must measure up to, consensus on a solution is unlikely. For instance, a group may decide that its solution for improving attendance at meetings must not cost money. A group of managers trying to find ways of cutting costs may decide that it will be unethical to lay off workers until *all* employees have first taken pay cuts, and it is clear the company will fail without the lay-offs.

Criteria are also expressions of values shared by members of a group. Recall Rubenstein's study of Arab and American students. When asked whether a man's wife, mother, or child should be saved from a boat wreck when only the man could swim, *all* Arabs chose the mother but *no* Americans did. The Arabs have a cultural value based on the fact that a man can have only one mother but usually can get another wife and/or child. American cultural values are different, so the choice is different

Figure 10.4
Absolute versus
relative criteria to
guide plans for a
club's annual picnic.

Absolute (*must* be met)	Relative (*should* be met)
Entertainment must not cost over $400.	Location should be convenient, that is, within thirty minutes driving time for all members.
Must be enjoyable to members and their families. (*Enjoyable* means: provide a variety of activities designed to appeal to people ranging in age from three to eighty.)	Facilities should be comfortable, for example, shelter in case of rain, electrical outlets, hot and cold running water, restroom facilities, and so on.

based on differing criteria. In short, two people having different criteria can arrive at very different solutions because they operate from different values.[41]

Criteria must be ranked or prioritized. Be sure to give highest priority to criteria that *must* be met. Ideas can then be rejected if they do not meet *absolute* criteria, and those that remain ranked on how well they meet *relative* criteria (see figure 10.4). Moreover, criteria should be stated as quantitatively as possible; criteria like "efficient" are too abstract to be measurable, but may help a group arrive at standards of "efficiency" that can be measured.

E. Be sure all members understand the group's area of freedom alike. Any policy solution must be evaluated from the standpoint of the charge. During the first step of the P-MOPS model, an outlined series of questions can guide the group's description and analysis of a complex problem. The questions in figure 10.5 are suggestive; such questions must be tailored to the specific problem and asked in the explicit language of that problem. Everyone should be encouraged to ask any and every question he or she feels needs an answer before planning a strategy to overcome all obstacles between the group and its goal.

II. **What might be done to solve the problem?**

If you try panning for gold in an Ohio stream, you probably won't make any money. You *might* succeed in finding gold in a stream in Arizona, Colorado, or California. As this analogy suggests, if there are no good ideas in the list being considered by a group, the solution recommended or adopted will fail to achieve the goal or may even make the situation worse. It is crucial in step II that a group have as many ideas as it can find and invent so it can choose the best, or, if necessary, redefine the goal and problem. You would not want to have nuggets wash out of your gold pan or lose track of a briefly mentioned idea that could turn out to be part of the best solution to a complex problem. Good technique prevents losing nuggets; *writing down each idea proposed as a solution* (preferably where everyone can see it and not forget it) will prevent losing ideas. A couple of principles can improve the group's success at finding and inventing solutions:

What does this problem question mean to us?

What is our charge and area of freedom?

What is unsatisfactory at present?

> Who (or what) is affected?
>
> When, where, and how?
>
> How serious do we judge the problem to be?
>
> How long has the problem existed?
>
> Do we need to gather any additional information to assess the nature and extent of the problem adequately?

What conditions have contributed to the problem?

> What appear to be causative conditions?
>
> What precipitated the crisis leading to our discussion?

What exactly do we hope to accomplish (the goal, desired situation)?

> What obstacles to achieving the desired goal exist?

What information do we need before we can find a satisfactory solution?

> What additional subquestions must we answer?
>
> How might we find answers to these subquestions?
>
> What are the answers to these subquestions?

How can we summarize our understanding of the problem to include the present and desired situation and causal conditions?

Figure 10.5
Questions to guide problem analysis.

1. Defer judgment during discussion while collecting and inventing proposals. This is the heart of the techniques called "brainstorming" and "Nominal Group Technique" presented in chapter 13. Judgment stifles creative thinking and increases apprehension about others' responses to ideas. Sometimes solution multiplicity is low, or thorough exploration of the problem leads to a sudden insight into a solution. In such a case, group members should still make an effort to think of other possible solutions, perhaps by asking "What else *might* we do?" If nothing else is uncovered, the solution should still be evaluated thoroughly by all available criteria, and especially for possible negative consequences. It may be refined and improved considerably through such critical thinking/discussion.

2. Often during this part of the problem-solving procedure, a participant will think of some detail of the problem that ought to be explored more fully, a sort of "Let's examine that rock again—it might have gold in it." The group will then need to cycle back to further mapping of the problem, and *should* do so instead of doggedly pursuing still further solutions at the moment just for the sake of following procedure. The group can pick up where it left off after it has backtracked to investigate and clarify the problem further, and will be better informed to make an intelligent choice among solutions. Such second-guessing is characteristic of effective problem-solving groups.[42]

III. What are the probable benefits and possible negative consequences of each proposed solution?

Once the problem has been thoroughly analyzed, with alternatives accumulated and criteria clearly understood by all members, the group is ready to evaluate the alternatives. For group problem solving to work optimally, pros and cons of each solution must be explored. Members must all have achieved communication convergence on explicit criteria if evaluation clarity is to occur. If not done previously, the first substep in this stage of group problem solving is to establish criteria. Every member must feel free to express opinions openly and honestly, without being attacked personally or attacking anyone else, for the group to achieve the best possible outcome.

Norms stressing the benefits of thorough critical examination of all issues should be developed, if necessary by discussion of them. For example:

1. Evaluation should be viewed as a cooperative venture, a team effort to prevent mistakes.
2. Feelings, ideas, opinions, and even hunches should be shared openly and evaluated without any reflection on the person who expresses them. Anonymous computer messages may be a way to support this norm in groups with residual personal struggles for power.
3. Members should insist on exploring assumptions and implications of every idea, especially the potential negative consequences. Ideally, the person who proposed an idea will *invite* such critical evaluation rather than becoming an advocate.
4. Personal attacks and *ad hominem* remarks are unacceptable as substitutes for evidence and argument. A lot of sensitivity to others' feelings and insensitivity to criticism of one's own ideas is called for. Ascribed status differences based on corporate positions, wealth, education, race, or any criterion other than relevant knowledge should play no part in evaluation discussion.
5. Members should often paraphrase what they think are the positions, feelings, and values of those with whom they disagree, always in a mood of inquiry—"Am I right?"
6. New issues should be raised or a challenge offered to an idea only when there is enough time to discuss the question thoroughly, not just before time to adjourn. If this happens, schedule another meeting to delay the final decision.
7. Trickery, bargaining, manipulation, deception, pressure to concur, and other breaches of communicative ethics are unacceptable. If noticed by any member, such unethical conduct should be pointed out at once and rebuked.

IV. What is the best possible solution we can all support?

If a decision seems to have emerged during evaluation of alternatives, the discussion leader should test for consensus. If everyone now agrees with one solution, the group is ready for the final stage of a complete problem-solving cycle. If two or more alternatives are still under consideration, the group should discuss such consensus-building questions as:

Which solution seems most likely to be accepted and supported by all persons affected by it?

Is there some compromise solution we can all accept as being likely to achieve our objectives without creating new problems?

Could we make any combination of our remaining ideas to create a solution we can all accept?

Once the group has decided what solution to recommend or adopt, the stage has been set for the final stage of this problem-solving discussion: implementation.

V. What will we do to put our solution into effect?

Unfortunately, many groups arrive at policy decisions or solutions with no plans for putting them into effect. For example, a committee charged with making a recommendation to a parent organization needs to decide who will make the report, in what form, and with what support from the entire group, and perhaps plan a campaign to prepare the general membership to accept the suggestion. A self-managing work team may actually need to make a purchase or inform a personnel office whether or not to hire a prospective new team member. A construction crew may need to acquire raw materials and schedule construction time. Competent leaders see that a group has worked out all necessary details of implementation, or that doing so has been assigned. At this point the group should decide on answers to such questions as

Who will do what, when, and how?

Do we need any follow-up evaluation of how well our solution is working? If so, how will we do that?

PERT, described in chapter 13, is a helpful procedure for planning implementation of a multistep solution.

You can see that the general Procedural Model of Problem Solving is flexible by design and can be adapted to fit almost any problem. In many cases the charge to a group will involve only some phases of the total problem-solving procedure: the group is to recommend several options, but not choose one; the group is to prepare an extensive investigation and analysis of the problem, but make no recommendations; the group is to implement a policy previously decided by another group. In such instances, only the relevant stage of P-MOPS would be used. Figure 10.8 suggests how you might adjust P-MOPS to your problem's characteristics. Examples of two leaders' outlines modifying P-MOPS are presented in figures 10.6 and 10.7. In figure 10.6, student Greg Gravenmeier dealt with all the complexities of parking on an urban campus in this outline. From the outline, you can see how major criteria were arrived at and used to evaluate proposals. Figure 10.7 is a simple leader's outline for structuring discussion of a problem for which few solutions were possible and discussion time was limited.

Figure 10.6
Leader's procedural
outline for discussion
of registration
problem.

PROBLEM QUESTION: What should be done to improve student parking at Southwest Missouri State University?

I. What is the nature of the problem students encounter with parking at SMSU?
   A. What is the scope of our concern with student parking?
      1. Do any terms in the question need to be clarified?
      2. What authority do we have?
      3. Do we need to determine the authority and duties of departments involved with campus parking?
   B. What is now unsatisfactory about student parking?
      1. What have we found to be unsatisfactory?
         a. Have any studies been done?
         b. What complaints have students been making?
      2. Does any other information exist about student parking that we need to consider?
   C. What goals does the committee hope to achieve by changes in parking that we need to consider?
   D. What obstacles may stand in the way of improving parking for students?
      1. What do we know about what is causing the problem(s) we've described?
      2. How much interest do involved persons have in this problem?
      3. What limits are there on resources that might be needed?
         a. Funds?
         b. Space?
         c. Personnel?
         d. Other?
      4. Are there any other obstacles to changing student parking?
   E. How shall we summarize the problem(s) with student parking at SMSU?
      1. Do we all perceive the problem the same?
      2. Should we subdivide the problem?
         a. If so, what are the major subproblems?
         b. In what order shall we take them up?
II. What solutions to the student parking problem(s) we've described are possible?
III. What are the relative advantages and disadvantages of each proposed solution?
   A. Do we need to further clarify our criteria?
   B. What are the advantages and disadvantages of each proposal?
      1. Might any have unacceptable negative consequences?
      2. How effective might each be?
      3. How well does each meet our other criteria?
IV. What do we agree to recommend to the proper authorities as a solution to the student parking problem?
V. How will we make our recommendations for improving student parking?
   A. To whom will our recommendations be given?
   B. In what format will we make them?
      1. Written?
      2. In person?
      3. Other, or a combination?
   C. Do we need to plan any follow-up?
   D. Who will do what, when, and how?

The Single Question Format: A Less Highly Structured Format

In the event a group chooses not to set up and be generally guided by some adaptation of P-MOPS, perhaps because members are low in Preference for Procedural Order, it is still essential for discussion to be critically vigilant to be sure of arriving at the best solution possible. As designated leader, you could ask the group to apply a procedure created by Larson, which was based on a series of studies by another researcher of how successful problem solvers reasoned.[43] When using this **Single Question format,** early in the discussion of a problem the group must decide on

I. What sort of written final exam should we have for our class?
  A. How much authority (area of freedom) do we have?
  B. What facts and feelings should we take into account as we seek an answer to this question?
II. What are our objectives (criteria) in deciding on the type of exam?
  A. Learning objectives?
  B. Grades?
  C. Type of preparation and study?
  D. Fairness to all?
III. What types of written final exam might we have?
IV. What are the advantages and disadvantages of each?
V. What will we recommend as the form of our written exam?

Figure 10.7
Leader's procedural outline for brief problem-solving discussion.

Problem Characteristic	Adaptation of Problem-Solving Procedure
1. Intrinsic interest is high.	A period of ventilation before systematic problem solving.
2. Task difficulty is high.	Detailed problem mapping; many subquestions.
3. Solution multiplicity is high.	Brainstorming.
4. Cooperative requirements are high.	A criterion step, creating and ranking explicit criteria.
5. High level of acceptance is required.	Focus on concern of people affected when evaluating options.
6. High level of technical quality is required.	Focus on evaluating ideas, critical thinking; perhaps invite outside experts to address group.
7. Population familiarity is high.	Focus on criteria and creation of multiple options.
8. Need only one or a few stages of the problem-solving process.	Shorten procedure to only steps required.

Figure 10.8
How problem characteristics affect the procedure for group problem solving.

the issues that need to be dealt with, how to answer these questions, and then proceed to do so. The list of questions provides structure to the discussion and should ensure that the major concerns of Vigilant Interaction Theory are met. Here is the format developed by Larson:

  I. What is the single question that, when answered, means the group knows how to accomplish its purpose?
 II. What subquestions must we answer before we can answer the single question we have formulated?
III. Do we have sufficient information to answer the subquestions with confidence?
    A. If "yes," what are our answers? (Then go to V.)
    B. If "no," the group continues to IV or adjourns to look for answers.
IV. What are the most reasonable answers to the subquestions?
 V. If our answers to the subquestions are adequate, what is the best solution to the problem?

Figure 10.9
An example of the
Single Question
problem-solving
procedure.

I. What is the single question. . .?
    What is the most environmentally benign, politically acceptable, and economically feasible way to dispose of solid waste from Springfield and surrounding counties?
II. Sub-questions
    In what ways could the solid waste of the Springfield area be disposed of? How much will each feasible method of waste disposal cost the citizens of Springfield and surrounding counties?
        What will facilities and start-up cost?
        What will continuing operation cost?
    Will the method generate enough revenue to pay its costs?
    What might be harmful effects of each method of disposal?
        What effects will each method have on water, air, land, and components of the environment?
        What health hazards might each method create?
    What problems might we have in getting voters to accept each method?
        What group or groups are likely to oppose each method?
        How well has this method been accepted elsewhere?
    How workable is the method?
        What personnel or training would be required?
        What has its dependability been elsewhere?
        How long will this method serve Springfield?
III. The task force engaged in extensive research efforts, including paying consultants, hiring an engineering consulting firm, and making several trips to observe facilities used by other cities.
IV. The task force recommended that a MERF (Materials Recovery Facility) with composting and limited landfill usage be recommended to voters. After an extensive information campaign involving newspapers, public forums, and broadcast media, voters approved the MERF concept. City council passed an ordinance requiring that residents not be allowed to send waste materials to private facilities to ensure generation of a sufficient amount of revenue to operate the MERF. A coordinator of the project has been hired, and a firm has been contracted with to build and operate the MERF.

You will notice that this format calls for a thorough analysis of the problem, then a search for any missing information, followed by construction of a solution based on findings and interpretations of the group. A final step, not mentioned by Larson in his original article, would be, of course:

VI. How will we put our decision into effect?

The church board to which you were introduced in chapter 2 used a version of the Single Question format to develop the church's first annual budget. Because the church was new, it had no past financial history on which to rely for budgetary information. The *single question* was, "What will be our annual budget for fiscal year 1993?" Board members knew that if they could estimate the costs of fixed expenses and the money needed by each committee, they would have a good idea of the annual budget. Thus, the subquestions asked: "What will be the individual budgets for all the subcommittees?" and "What will be our fixed expenses?" Since members did not have the information available at the initial budget meeting, they adjourned so the treasurer could meet with the committee heads to get the needed information. When all the individual subquestions were answered, the broad single question was answered as well.

An example of an initial outline that might have been created by a group following the single-question format is shown in figure 10.9. Such an outline is a product of the first part of the discussion, and it keeps being refined and added to as the group's investigations and discussions proceed toward their goal. Every member must have a copy of the questions as they are generated, answers provided, and an agenda for each meeting. Using this format calls for close teamwork and decision making by consensus.

Summary

In chapter 10 we have considered the content, interaction, and procedures of group problem-solving discussions. The concept *problem* was defined as including an unsatisfactory situation, a goal, and obstacles that must be surmounted in order to move to the goal. A review of research focusing on the structure of group problem solving led to the conclusion that some structure is needed to ensure that interaction will apply to the critical thinking faculties of members. No single sequence can be recommended, but any problem-solving discussion should deal with characteristics presented in Vigilant Interaction Theory: (1) a thorough and shared perception of the problem situation; (2) a variety of alternatives from which to choose; and (3) thorough evaluation of alternatives focusing on both the probable benefits and possible negative consequences of each. The pattern for discussion of a specific problem should be based on several important characteristics of the problem: task complexity, degree of solution multiplicity, intrinsic interest (an elevating and energizing goal), cooperative requirements, population familiarity, level of technical requirements, acceptance requirements, and the group's area of freedom.

Although no single or linear sequence can be shown to be invariably beneficial, a general sequence based on the issues raised by Vigilant Interaction Theory and the scientific method can be adapted and used. Called the Procedural Model of Problem Solving (P-MOPS), the sequence begins with description and analysis of the problem, proceeds to a search for alternative solutions, then to evaluation, deciding on a solution, and finally how to implement it. Modifications in the procedure can be made to fit any problem and group, so long as no step is overlooked. The steps need not all be taken in sequence, and considerable cycling can be expected among the steps. If a group chooses not to use the P-MOPS procedure, the Single Question procedure was suggested as an alternative in getting members to agree on the important issues to be settled and how to do so before reaching a decision on a solution.

Exercises

1. Select a problem you are concerned about, write it as a problem question, then analyze it into the three major types of components described in chapter 10.
   Use the following format:
   Problem question—
      Unsatisfactory about the current situation—
      Goal (desired situation)—
      Obstacles to achieving goal—

2. Select a problem affecting all members of the class, such as the type of final exam or some campus or community issue in which all class members have a

high level of interest. Write a paper in which you analyze this problem on each of the variables below. Give a rating number and a brief explanation of why you gave this rating for each variable.

   Task difficulty—(from high = 10 to low = 1)
   Solution multiplicity—(scale of 10 to 1)
   Intrinsic interest—
   Cooperative requirements—
   Population familiarity—
   Acceptance requirements—
   Technical requirements—
   Area of freedom—

3. As a class, select two problems for study: one should have a high level of solution multiplicity, one a low level. Each class member will write a leader's outline for structuring a group discussion of each problem, adapting P-MOPS to the characteristics of the problem. Compare outlines in small groups of four or five students each; then as a group write one outline for organizing discussion of each problem.

4. Choose a problem now faced by your school or community, then use the Single Question procedure to create a sequence of questions and subquestions for guiding a vigilant problem-solving discussion of the problem. Compare outlines or sets of questions in small groups, then combine into one outline that contains all issues group members agree should be explored before deciding on a solution.

5. Your instructor or class may decide to discuss the problems selected in exercise 3, 4, or both. If so, each group should have a designated leader whose job it is to see that the group does not overlook any issue on the outline and to post proposals and evaluations of them. As much as possible, the group should follow the sequences of issues in the outline for each problem. After the discussion or discussions, consider as a group what worked and what did not help you to achieve vigilant interaction as you discussed the problem. What should you have done differently? What have you learned from this exercise?

6. View a videotape of a problem-solving discussion (for instance, one of the groups in the previous discussion might have been recorded with a camcorder). Either as an entire class or in small groups, evaluate the vigilance, structure, omissions, and productivity of the discussion. Point out specific instances where the discussion might have been improved and where member behaviors clearly contributed to the quality of the group product.

Bibliography

Dewey, John. *How We Think.* Boston: D. C. Heath and Company, 1910.

Hirokawa, Randy Y. and Marshall S. Poole, eds. *Communication and Group Decision-Making.* Beverly Hills, CA: Sage Publications, 1986, 81–111.

Larson, Carl E. and Frank M. J. LaFasto. *Teamwork: What Must Go Right/What Can Go Wrong.* Newbury Park, CA: Sage Publications, 1989.

Pavitt, Charles. "What (Little) We Know about Formal Group Discussion Procedures: A Review of Relevant Research." *Small Group Research* 24 (1993): 217–35.

Shaw, Marvin E. *Group Dynamics,* 3d ed. New York: McGraw-Hill, 1981, chapter 10.

Worchel, Stephen, Wendy Wood, and Jeffry A. Simpson, eds. *Group Process and Productivity.* Newbury Park, CA: Sage Publications, 1992.

Notes

1. Dennis S. Gouran and Randy Y. Hirokawa, "Counteractive Functions of Communication in Effective Group Decision-Making," in *Communication and Group Decision-Making,* eds. Randy Y. Hirokawa and Marshall Scott Poole (Beverly Hills, CA: Sage Publications, 1986): 87.

2. Randy Y. Hirokawa, "Communication and Group Decision-Making Efficacy," in *Small Group Communication: A Reader,* 6th ed., eds. Robert S. Cathcart and Larry A. Samovar (Dubuque, Iowa: Wm. C. Brown Publishers, 1992): 165–77; Randy Y. Hirokawa and Kathryn M. Rost, "Effective Group Decision-Making in Organizations: Field Test of the Vigilant Interaction Theory" (Paper presented at Speech Communication Association convention, Atlanta, GA, November 1991).

3. Carolyn J. Wood, "Challenging the Assumptions Underlying the Use of Participatory Decision-Making Strategies: A Longitudinal Case Study," *Small Group Behavior* 20 (1989): 428–48.

4. Irving L. Janis and L. Mann, *Decision Making: A Psychological Analysis of Conflict, Choice and Commitment* (New York: Free Press, 1977); Irving L. Janis, *Groupthink: Psychological Studies of Foreign-Policy Decisions and Fiascoes,* 2nd ed. (Boston: Houghton Mifflin Co., 1983).

5. David M. Berg, "A Descriptive Analysis of the Distribution and Duration of Themes Discussed by Task-Oriented Small Groups," *Speech Monographs* 34 (1967): 172–75.

6. Marvin E. Shaw, *Group Dynamics,* 3rd ed. (New York: McGraw-Hill, 1981): 364.

7. See, for example, John K. Brilhart and Lurene M. Jochem, "Effects of Different Patterns on Outcomes of Problem-Solving Discussions," *Journal of Applied Psychology* 48 (1964): 175–79; Ovid L. Bayless, "An Alternative Model for Problem Solving Discussion," *Journal of Communication* 17 (1967): 188–97; and Sidney J. Parnes and Arnold Meadow, "Effects of 'Brainstorming' Instruction on Creative Problem-Solving by Trained and Untrained Subjects," *Journal of Educational Psychology* 50 (1959): 171–76.

8. Shaw, *Group Dynamics,* 364.

9. Leonard Berkowitz, "Sharing Leadership in Small Decision-Making Groups," *Journal of Abnormal and Social Psychology* 48 (1953): 231–38.

10. James H. Davis, *Group Performance* (Reading, MA: Addison-Wesley, 1969).

11. Randy Y. Hirokawa and Kathryn M. Rost, "Effective Group Decision-Making in Organizations."

12. Dennis S. Gouran, "Inferential Errors, Interaction, and Group Decision-Making," in R. Y. Hirokawa and M. S. Poole, eds. *Communication and Group Decision-Making* (Beverly Hills, CA: Sage Publications, 1986): 93–111.

13. Hirokawa and Rost, 4.

14. Randy Y. Hirokawa, "Group Communication and Problem-Solving Effectiveness II: An Investigation of Procedural Functions," *Western Journal of Speech Communication* 47 (1983): 59–74; Marshall S. Poole and Joel A. Doelger, "Developmental Processes in Group Decision-Making," in R. Y. Hirokawa and M. S. Poole, eds. *Communication and Group Decision-Making* (Newbury Park, CA: Sage Publications, 1986): 35–61.

15. Hirokawa and Rost, 20–22.

16. Randy Y. Hirokawa, "Communication and Group Decision-Making Efficacy," in Robert S. Cathcart and Larry A. Samovar, eds. *Small Group Communication: A Reader,* 6th ed. (Dubuque, IA: Wm. C. Brown Publishers, 1992): 165–77.

17. John E. Dewey, *How We Think* (Boston: D. C. Heath and Company, 1910).

18. Thomas M. Scheidel and Laura Crowell, "Developmental Sequences in Small Groups," *Quarterly Journal of Speech* 50 (1964): 140–45.

19. Dennis S. Gouran, Candace Brown, and David R. Henry, "Behavioral Correlates of Perceptions of Quality in Decision-Making Discussions," *Communication Monographs* 45 (1978): 62; William E. Jurma, "Effects of Leader Structuring Style and Task Orientation Characteristics of Group Members," *Communication Monographs* 46 (1979): 282–95.

20. William E. Jurma, "Effects of Leader Structuring Style. . . ."

21. John K. Brilhart, "An Experimental Comparison of Three Techniques for Communicating a Problem-Solving Pattern to Members of a Discussion Group," *Speech Monographs* 33 (1966): 168–77.

22. Marshall S. Poole, "Decision Development in Small Groups II: A Study of Multiple Sequences in Decision Making," *Communication Monographs* 50 (1983): 224–25; Marshall S. Poole, "Decision Development in Small Groups III: A Multiple Sequence Model of Group Decision Development," *Communication Monographs* 50 (1983): 321–41.

23. Brilhart and Jochem, "Effects of Different Patterns," 177–78.

24. Bayless, "An Alternative Model for Problem Solving Discussion," 188–97; Carl E. Larson, "Forms of Analysis and Small Group Problem Solving," *Speech Monographs* 36 (1969): 452–55.

25. Charles M. Kelly, Michael Jaffe, and Gregory V. Nelson, "Solving Problems," *Research Management* 30 (1987): 20–23.

26. Hirokawa, "Why Informed Groups Make Faulty Decisions," 557–74.

27. Randy Y. Hirokawa, "Discussion Procedures and Decision-Making Performance," *Human Communication Research* 12 (1985): 203–24.

28. Randy Y. Hirokawa, "Group Decision-Making Performance: A Continued Test of the Functional Perspective," *Human Communication Research* 14 (1988): 487–515.

29. Hirokawa, "Decision Procedures and Decision-Making Performance," 221.

30. Randy Y. Hirokawa and Dierdre D. Johnston, "Toward a General Theory of Group Decision Making: Development of an Integrated Model," *Small Group Behavior* 20 (1989): 500–23.

31. Richard Nisbett and Lee Ross, *Human Inference: Strategies and Shortcomings of Social Judgment* (Englewood Cliffs, NJ: Prentice-Hall, 1980).

32. Robert J. Sternberg, "Stalking the IQ Quark," *Psychology Today* 13 (September 1979): 42–45.

33. Brilhart and Jochem, "Effects of Different Patterns," 179.

34. Randy Y. Hirokawa, John G. Oetzel, Carlos G. Aleman, and Scott E. Elston, "The Effects of Evaluation Clarity and Bias on the Relationship between Vigilant Interaction and Group Decision-Making Efficacy" (Paper presented at the Speech Communication Association convention, Atlanta November 1991), abstract.

35. Charles Pavitt, "What (Little) We Know about Formal Group Discussion Procedures: A Review of Relevant Research," *Small Group Research* 24 (1993): 229–31.

36. Brilhart, "An Experimental Comparison of Three Techniques for Communicating a Problem-Solving Pattern. . . ."

37. Kelly, Jaffe, and Nelson, "Solving Problems," 22.

38. Benjamin J. Broome and Minder Chen, "Guidelines for Computer-Assisted Group Problem Solving: Meeting the Challenges of Complex Issues," *Small Group Research* 23: (1992): 216–36, especially 228.

39. For example, see Kelly, Jaffe, and Nelson, "Solving Problems"; Norman R. F. Maier and R. A. Maier, "An Experimental Test of the Effects of 'Developmental' vs. 'Free' Discussions on the Quality of Group Decisions," *Journal of Applied Psychology* 41 (1957): 320–23; and Randy Y. Hirokawa, "Group Communication and Problem-Solving Effectiveness: An Investigation of Group Phases," *Human Communication Research* 9 (1983): 291–305.

40. Charles H. Kepner and Benjamin B. Tregoe, *The Rational Manager* (New York: McGraw-Hill, 1965): 117–18.

41. Moshe F. Rubenstein, *Patterns of Problem Solving* (Englewood Cliffs, NJ: Prentice-Hall, 1975): 1–2.

42. Randy Y. Hirokawa, "Why Informed Groups Make Faulty Decisions," *Small Group Behavior* 18 (1987): 3–29.

43. Carl E. Larson, "Forms of Analysis and Small Group Problem-Solving," *Speech Monographs* 36 (1969): 452–55; this format has also been presented in several small group texts.

Decision Making in Small Groups

Central Message

The extent to which a group employs critical thinking has a major influence on its decision-making processes and ultimate decision quality.

Study Objectives   As a result of studying chapter 11 you should be able to:

1. Describe the relative advantages and disadvantages of group and individual decision making.

2. Understand the differences among decisions made by a leader, majority vote, and consensus including advantages and disadvantages of each procedure.

3. Explain five procedural guidelines for making group decisions by consensus and the reasons for these guidelines.

4. Describe the phases groups often experience during decision making, and explain several contingent factors that may influence these phases.

5. Describe the factors that contribute to effective group decision making.

6. Distinguish between a fact and an inference.

7. Describe five common fallacies that inhibit critical thinking, and explain how they interfere with a group's decision making.

Key Terms

Ad hominem attack	Disjunctive tasks	Group polarization
Assembly effect	Fact	Inference
Conjunctive tasks	Fallacy	Majority decision
Consensus decision	False dilemma	Overgeneralization
Critical thinking	Faulty analogy	Phasic progression

Small groups are permanent fixtures in human society. Groups, committees, and boards are being assigned increasingly important problems to solve. Throughout corporate America, workers who traditionally have been told what to do are now granted widespread decision-making authority. For example, in one recent survey of Fortune 1,000 companies, nearly *half* had self-managed work teams in place.[1] In the course of arriving at a solution, a group must make a number of decisions, both trivial and important. Every group task—from deciding whether or not a defendant is guilty and selecting the appropriate punishment, to designating which student will receive a scholarship, to choosing an employee benefits package—requires at least one and probably several decisions. As Tropman says, "Only when we begin to recognize the importance and necessity of communal decision making can we begin to prepare ourselves adequately for these roles."[2] The need to make decisions in concert with others demands that we understand how to optimize the group decision-making process. Failure to understand this process produces disasters. For example, researchers believe that the poor decision in 1986 to launch the shuttle *Challenger,* which exploded shortly after take-off, resulted from terribly flawed decision processes.[3]

We are competing with societies—Japanese, Chinese, South Korean—that are more skilled than we at collective decision making. We dare not remain complacent. As Anderson notes, it is a myth that we can work effectively in small groups without understanding their processes and dynamics.[4]

In the last chapter we focused on providing information to help you improve the comprehensive problem-solving process for those groups to which you belong. In this chapter, we narrow the focus to the decision-making process. We discuss how decisions are made by groups and how to improve group decision making.

Group versus Individual Decision Making

We previously stated that group decision making through discussion is usually superior to individual decision making. In fact, there are times when individual decision making is better. Group decision making takes more time, sometimes one or two members can dominate a discussion, and occasionally the fact that other people are present can push an otherwise well-informed discussant further in a particular direction than he or she would normally go. In trying to decide whether to have a group or an individual make a specific decision, we must balance these and other factors.

Vroom says that the decision to ask a group to make a decision should be based on analysis of three dimensions.[5] First, the quality or rationality dimension concerns whether one decision is likely to be clearly better than another. There is one best way, for example, to assemble a swing set, but many different acceptable ways to plan a party. Second, the leader must determine how important it is that the decision be accepted by group members. Some decisions, particularly those which affect members' jobs or daily lives, may appear perfectly sound but will not work if group members do not accept them. The third dimension is time. The group must have time to engage in discussion, for group decision making is considerably more time consuming than individual decision making. Therefore, a series of trade-offs is involved when an organization or authority elects to let a group make a decision.

In general, group decisions tend to be of higher quality than those made by individuals or by averaging individual decisions.[6] In fact, they usually are better even than decisions made by individual high-status members who are considered especially knowledgeable about a problem,[7] but this depends partly on the type of task. Groups have been found superior on **conjunctive tasks,** where each member possesses information needed to solve a problem but no one member has all the needed information. However, groups are not superior at **disjunctive tasks,** which require little or no coordination, often enabling the most expert member working alone to produce a correct answer.[8] Furthermore, this strongly suggests that it is the verbal interaction itself, not just summing of individual members' perceptions or opinions, that contributes to the increased quality.[9]

A number of studies support the idea that group involvement in decision making increases the acceptance of the decision.[10] Coch and French demonstrated that when workers have a voice in changing a work procedure, they are more productive and loyal than when the change is imposed on them.[11] As Block and Hoffman wrote, ". . . the effectiveness of gaining members' commitment to change through use of group decision is unquestioned. . . ."[12] The self-managed work teams in companies such as Saturn, Ford, and Johnsonville Foods epitomize this involvement.

However, group decision making is not automatically superior. Burleson, Levine, and Samter found that, although eight of ten groups that produced consensus decisions had better decisions than the individual members acting alone, two of the ten produced worse decisions.[13] Wood observed several factors that impede effective decision making, including members who do not possess needed skills and information or make conscientious efforts to acquire them from outside sources, and members whose social needs prevent them from attending to the task.[14] Poor operating procedures, especially failure to provide the kind of structure and coordination needed to accomplish the task and failure to test for consensus, hurt decision quality. Finally, adherence to ascribed status differences impaired open and honest communication, which prevented critical thinking. Miesing and Preble discovered that cohesiveness and performance norms influenced decision quality. Groups that were very cohesive and had high performance expectations performed better.[15] Hirokawa found that groups that approached decision making systematically made better decisions than groups that did not.[16] On the other hand, Gouran found that group interaction sometimes promoted collective inferential error if members accepted unusual cases as representative, passively accepted specialized knowledge, and created hypothetical stories that had no basis in fact.[17]

We can sum up the meaning of all this research comparing the quality of individual versus group decision making this way: groups are usually superior in making decisions about how to solve discussion-type problems, depending on the type of task, how high their norms are for quality (performance), whether they have sufficient cohesiveness to enforce such norms, how systematic and organized their problem-solving procedures are, and how skilled and determined the group members are at arriving at valid conclusions based on sound evidence.

As we noted earlier, group members influence each other positively as well as negatively. Such influence produces the **group polarization** tendency, sometimes called the risky or cautious shift, which refers to the finding that group members often make decisions that are more extreme (either more risky or more cautious) than the individual group members' initial preferences.[18] In other words, group members push themselves *further* in a particular direction than where they initially started. Two explanations have been proposed for this.[19]

The *social comparison theory* (SCT) suggests that as members get to know each other's values, they want to appear "correct" and may exaggerate opinions in the direction they believe the group values positively. For example, if you are mildly liberal politically and you are in a group that seems to value liberal thought, then you might be tempted to exaggerate how liberal you are. Thus, if the group or cultural norm favors risk (as with many business decisions in our culture), the group will shift toward risk; if caution is the cultural norm (as with a decision affecting a child's life), the group shifts toward caution.

The second explanation for group polarization is the *persuasive arguments theory* (PAT), which says that the number, salience, and novelty of arguments in a particular direction persuade members to move in that direction. Thus, if members favor risk (or caution), there will be more and stronger arguments presented in favor of risk (or caution); the persuasive power of these arguments shifts the group in that direction.

Studies have found some support for both SCT and PAT. Whether SCT or PAT better explains choice shift in a specific group may depend on conditions within the group. For example, Hale and Boster found that as the task became more ambiguous, SCT seemed to explain shifts better, but as task ambiguity decreased, PAT made more sense.[20] Kaplan and Miller learned that the type of task mattered; SCT explanations prevailed for tasks requiring judgment, but PAT explained the choice shifts better for intellective tasks that had correct answers.[21] Either way, decision making can be impaired or improved by the particular norms and arguments that prevail in a group. Being aware of these normal group tendencies can help group members guard against bias in decision making.

Groups frequently achieve an **assembly effect** in which the decision is qualitatively and quantitatively superior either to the best individual judgment of any member or to the average of the judgments of all the members. This is a kind of synergy that occurs in the operation of the small group as a system—the whole becomes greater than the sum of its parts. Two recent studies found evidence of the assembly effect.[22] However, Fandt discovered that synergy is achieved only when group members interact and work *interdependently* on the task; groups whose members work independently do not achieve this result.[23] For example, if group members complete individual assignments on their own and later compile their individual products into the final group product without discussing each member's individual work *as a group,* then that group will probably not achieve an assembly effect.

Groups use a number of different methods to make decisions. The three most common are by the designated leader, majority vote, and consensus.

Sometimes a designated or emergent leader will think the problem through alone and announce a decision, or will consult with the group and then announce the decision. Group members are then given instructions for executing the decision. The resulting solution may or may not be a high-quality one, but other outcomes of such control by the leader may be resentment, lowered cohesiveness, halfhearted support for the decision, and unwillingness to contribute to subsequent decisions. Members may even sabotage the decision. For example, we once observed a group of faculty members who became furious that their designated leader made an important decision without consulting them. They called a special meeting to overturn his decision. After discussing their options, they proceeded to make *exactly the same* decision he had made. Clearly their distress was not about the *content* of the decision—it was about the *process* and their belief that the leader had disenfranchised them. Indeed, many studies show that participative decision making, in which everyone affected by the decision has at least some voice in making it, reduces strife.

Making a **majority decision** through voting by a show of hands, saying *aye,* or with written ballot is probably the procedure used most often to settle a difference of opinion in democratic groups. On the plus side, everyone has an equal opportunity to influence the decision by speaking, each vote counts equally, and the decision is reached more quickly than if the group's norms require a consensus decision. Majority voting resolves conflicts by the numerical power of the majority. Of course if the vote is unanimous, consensus has been achieved. But usually the vote is split, with minority members (losers) doubting that their ideas have been understood fully and treated fairly. People in a minority may even remain silent for fear of being ridiculed for opinions that deviate from the majority opinion. Not only does the quality of the decision sometimes suffer, but the group may also experience lowered cohesiveness and commitment to the decision. When a group's by-laws *require* that a vote be taken, the group may want to discuss an issue until consensus has been reached, then vote to confirm it "legally."

A **consensus decision** is one that all members agree is the best that everyone can support. It may be, but is not necessarily, the alternative most preferred by all members. When a true consensus has been reached, the output is usually a superior-quality decision, a high level of member satisfaction, and acceptance of the result. However, unless virtual unanimity happens to exist at the beginning of a discussion of alternatives, reaching consensus may take much more time than other procedures. Furthermore, unanimity—the state of perfect consensus in which every group member believes that the decision achieved is the best that could be made—is not at all common. Sometimes a true consensus cannot be achieved, no matter

Methods of Decision Making in Groups
Decision Making by the Leader

Decision Making by Majority Vote

Decision Making by Consensus

how much time is spent in discussion. Certain personality traits, values, and other characteristics of the members affect a group's ability to achieve consensus. For example, Beatty found that groups similar in decision-rule orientation were more likely to achieve consensus.[24] Three common decision-rule orientations are attempts to minimize losses (a conservative, pessimistic approach), attempts to maximize gains (a risk-taking, optimistic approach), and the maximum expected utility approach (an attempt to derive the highest average payoffs no matter whether a pessimistic or optimistic future is envisioned). Beatty noted that the degree of comfort members felt with the decision was more important in achieving consensus than the quality of the decision itself. Groups with members whose decision-rule orientations were similar had an easier time achieving consensus. Thus, more than just the merit of the decision is involved when a group strives for consensus.

Consensus may be superficial when some members accommodate to other higher-status members, including "experts" who express their opinions with exceptional force, a designated leader, or a large majority. For example, one of us completed "Lost on the Moon," a group decision-making exercise where the group is asked to rank the utility of several items, in a group of electrical and mechanical engineers who appeared to have a great deal of expertise on technical matters. Your coauthor readily conceded to these experts. Interestingly, your coauthor's individual ranking of the items was better than the group's ranking, but compliance to the perceived expertise of the engineers deprived the group of this member's reasoning. Even though it may be uncomfortable to be the group's opinion deviate, do not suppress your opinions.

Conflict is likely in the course of arriving at consensual decisions. Expect it and welcome it, particularly the type of constructive argument that enhances critical thinking. Use your best active listening and reasoning skills. In the next chapter we present specific suggestions to help you manage conflict.

Suggestions for Achieving Consensus

The process of reaching consensus gives all members an opportunity to express how they feel and think about the alternatives, and an equitable chance to influence the outcome. Consensus depends on active listening so that all important information and points of view are understood similarly by all discussants. A consensual decision is often synergistic, with the group producing something superior to the members' individual ideas because alternatives are clarified and tested in the process of working toward consensus. Here are some discussion guidelines outlined by Hall for making consensus decisions:

1. Don't argue stubbornly for your own position. Present it clearly and logically, being sure you listen to and consider all reactions carefully.

2. Avoid looking at a stalemate as a win-lose situation. Rather, see whether you can find a next best alternative acceptable to all.

3. When agreement is reached too easily and too quickly, be on guard against groupthink (discussed in the next chapter). Don't change your position just to avoid conflict. Through discussion, be sure that everyone accepts the decision for similar or complementary reasons and really agrees that it is the best that can be reached.

4. Avoid conflict-suppressing techniques, such as majority vote, averaging, coin tossing, and so forth. Although they prevent destructive interpersonal conflicts, they also suppress constructive substantive arguments.

5. Seek out differences of opinion, which are helpful in testing alternatives and evaluation reasoning. Get every member involved in the decision-making process. The group has a better chance of selecting the best alternative if it has a wider range of information and ideas.[25]

In chapter 8 we described how groups experience phases of formation and production as they develop from a collection of individuals to a group system. Several people have observed that groups also cycle through relatively predictable phases or stages during the process of decision making and problem solving. Bales and Strodtbeck were among the first to identify this **phasic progression.**[26] During the *orientation* phase, members orient themselves to the task and to one another, if they do not already know each other. In the *evaluation* phase, they decide what they collectively think about the problem or decision. Finally, during the *control* phase, the group has reached enough socioemotional maturity for members to concentrate on completing their task. For each problem they confront, groups will tend to cycle through all three of these stages, returning to an orientation stage for a new problem once a decision has been reached about a previous problem.

> **Phasic Progression during Decision Making**

More recently, Fisher observed that experienced decision-making groups pass through four phases as they work toward deciding among a group of alternatives.[27] These phases are orientation, conflict, decision emergence, and reinforcement. They can be identified by the kinds of interactions that occur in each.

Orientation During the orientation phase, members develop a shared understanding of their task, the facts about available options, and how to interpret them. Signs of disagreement are minimal; ambiguous and favorable remarks are common. This makes sense because when group members are uncertain about the facts or concerned about how others will perceive them, they will be wary of making strong statements of disagreement that might offend another member. In this early stage, a member is more likely to say, "Well, that idea sounds like it might work, but maybe we should take time to think about it some more," than to say, "That's not going to work at all. We're going to have to try a lot harder if we are to come up with a decent solution." The first remark is ambiguous and tentative, the second is unambiguous and definite.

Conflict During the conflict phase, members offer initiatives, take stands, disagree, offer compromises, argue for and against proposals, and generally discuss ideas in a more open manner than during orientation. Ambiguous remarks fall to a low level in this phase, but disagreeing and agreeing remarks are common. For instance, Selena says, "I think we should get more information about the impact this might have before we proceed much further." Andrew replies, "Naw, we have all the information we need right now to decide." Then Tina supports Selena: "I agree with Selena. We need to know a lot more or we might really mess things up." Members argue for and against proposals, with most people taking sides. Wishy-washy behavior disappears as opinions are expressed clearly and forcefully.

Decision Emergence A group cannot stay in the conflict phase and accomplish its goal. It must move, somehow, from a position where each member argues a particular point of view to a position where members are willing to relinquish their strong stands and accept reciprocal mutual influence. This movement coincides with the reappearance of ambiguity in the group. Whereas the earlier ambiguity served as a way of managing primary tension, now it helps manage secondary tension by allowing the members to back off from staunchly held positions and save face at the same time. It would be hard on a member's self-image to switch suddenly from "I think we should accept the first proposal" to "I think we should reject the first proposal." A transition is needed; the ambiguity provides this transition, which allows the member to move from "I think we should accept the first proposal" to: "*Maybe* you are right. There might be some problems with the first proposal that I hadn't considered. Let's look at it more closely before we decide." Members move gradually toward a common group position. Near the end of this phase a consensus decision will emerge, sometimes suddenly. The members will usually know when this point is reached, and they will all indicate support for the decision. (If this does not occur, then it is appropriate for the group to resolve its disagreement by majority vote.)

Reinforcement After a group has accomplished its primary objective, it doesn't just immediately move on to a different problem or disband. Members will reinforce each other and themselves for a job well done. They will say such things as, "Wow, it took a long time but we got some really important things done," or "I really like the proposal. It's going to work beautifully," or "I'm proud of us for coming up with this. You guys are super, and this has been a rewarding experience." Members pat each other on the back and reinforce the positive feelings they have toward the decision and toward each other. This good feeling will carry over to the next meeting.

Fisher believed that unless some outside factor (like severe time pressure) interferes with the group's natural decision-making process, these phases will follow each other in a predictable way, although the proportion of time spent in each phase may vary from decision to decision. It is important to recall, however, that he studied interaction in previously developed groups that had already passed through their formation stage.

As we noted in chapter 10, Poole and his associates found that groups take a variety of paths to problem solving. Poole's investigations have called into question the idea that most groups experience a unitary linear sequence of decision-making and problem-solving phases—that is, the same phases, in the same order.[28] Group decision making is more complex than unitary sequences suggest. Poole suggests that a number of factors influence not only what phases groups experience but also in what order they occur.[29] For example, some groups experience long, drawn-out conflict phases with little socioemotional integration after the conflict. Others experience lengthy periods of idea development with no overt conflict. Poole's contingency model of group decision making describes three types of factors that affect phasic progression: objective task characteristics, group task characteristics, and group structural characteristics.[30] *Objective task characteristics* include such factors as goal clarity and potential impact of the decision. For example, if the group's goal is clear at the beginning of the process, members may be able to shorten the orientation phase. *Group task characteristics* include such factors as time and population familiarity. Members are more likely to spend extra time orienting themselves to the task and arguing the merits of various options for a novel task that is unfamiliar to them than they are for a familiar one. Finally, *group structural characteristics* refer to how members of the group work together and include such factors as cohesiveness, conflict, and history. Members who have experienced divisive conflict may either run away from potential arguments in the group or may approach group meetings with their defenses up and boxing gloves on. As you can see, group decision making is complicated, with numerous factors potentially influencing phasic progression.

It is essential to keep in mind the distinction between the phases that occur during a decision-making cycle and those that occur during the development of a group. We believe these two processes operate in conjunction with each other and can readily be synthesized. Throughout its entire life, a group must deal simultaneously with process and production concerns. In chapter 7 we described the two developmental phases, formation and production, that groups typically experience. Within each of these broad phases, a group makes a variety of decisions and may solve more than one problem. For instance, early in the formation phase of development the group may need to decide who will take notes, whether its decisions will require consensus or whether majority vote will suffice, how much information it must gather, how members will address each other, and so on. In the production phase it must investigate the problem, generate ideas, decide which of several alternatives is best, how the final report will be written and by whom, to what extent members are satisfied with the group's work and what can be done if they are not, and so forth. (Note, too, that both process and production decisions must be made in *all* stages of a group's development as a group.)

Fisher's work provides the information needed to link the group's development stages with its decision-making stages. For each new major decision a group faces, members must orient themselves to each other and to the group's new task, argue for and against the various options available, *decide* something, and achieve some sort of closure through reinforcement of the decision. Thus, from our review of the important previous work on phasic progression and from our own experience, we envision a group cycling repeatedly through phases like those Fisher described while moving gradually forward from early formation to full and efficient production at the same time solving one or more problems. This movement is captured in the spirals of figure 11.1. This back-and-forth spiral movement is typical of many continuing groups. Scheidel and Crowell observed the spiral-like progression of a group's problem-solving process and noted that a group does not move in a clear, unbroken line toward a decision.[31] This spiral-like effect has been observed by other researchers. Sabourin and Geist described the collaborative nature of group decision making as a process in which group members build on each other's proposals.[32] Fisher and Stutman also observed the messy, but ultimately progressive, nature of the spiral model.[33] It may be especially helpful for members high in preference for procedural order to know that such messy cycling between problem analysis to a decision and solution discussion is normal; they can better endure the

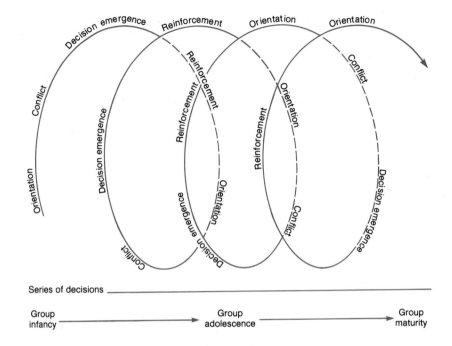

Figure 11.1
Decision making
within the
development of a
small group.

Series of decisions

Group infancy ————————→ Group adolescence ————————→ Group maturity

frustration they feel when groups do not move in an orderly linear sequence from problem analysis to solution implementation. After all, only when they are *not* engaged do troops march in steady, straight lines!

Effective Group Decision Making

There are certain steps a group can take to help ensure that it has made the best possible decision. In the following guidelines, we have synthesized the key elements of the problem-solving process that directly relate to decision-making effectiveness:

1. **Make sure members understand the problem clearly.**
   Otherwise, a group may choose a decision that attacks symptoms instead of causes or will not work as well as another option. Groups that clearly understand the choice-making situation select more wisely and avoid conflicts based on lack of similar maps of the problem.

2. **If members do not already understand the criteria for evaluating the decision, they should be discussed openly.**
   Criteria, as we explained in chapter 10, are those standards that must be met when choosing any option. For example, if the parent organization for your group has said you must stay within a prescribed budget, your eventual decision must satisfy this criterion (and *all* others as well).

3. **Evaluate all the options, using your established criteria, on the basis of both positive and negative consequences.**
   The most effective groups are able to anticipate possible negative consequences and thereby eliminate the worst options right off the bat. Think of all the things that can go wrong with each option, assessing how serious

each consequence will be, then thoroughly examine the positive aspects of each alternative. Make your final selection based on *both* evaluations.

4. **Select one option, tentatively, and "second guess" your choice.**
   The most effective groups do not simply choose to get things over with. They continue to cycle back over issues previously covered as they encounter new information or think of other things that are pertinent. Once you have made a tentative choice, go back over your choice as a group, reevaluating your information, reasoning, and assessment. In so doing you may be able to make further improvements in your chosen alternative.

The final recommendation for improving the quality of group decisions is so important that we have chosen to devote a separate section to discuss it. *Group members who want to ensure that their decisions are the best that can be made must employ critical thinking skills at each step in the decision-making process.* **Critical thinking** is the systematic examination of information and ideas on the basis of evidence and logical or probable reasoning, rather than intuition or hunch. Unfortunately, many groups do not encourage critical thinking skills. Meyers et al. found that group arguments in undergraduate groups consisted of simple assertions almost half the time and that members seldom cited rules of logic or used criteria as standards.[34] In this section we focus on how you can evaluate the evidence and reasoning that links information and ideas.

Critical Thinking and the Quality of Group Decision Making

Information—facts, ideas, opinions, data—is the raw material from which a group's decision is made. A group's final decision can be only as good as the information inputs used by the group. So you can see how important it is for a group to evaluate information it has gathered for accuracy, credibility, and relevance to the group's decisions.

Evaluating Information

It is especially important to distinguish between facts and inferences, opinions, and preferences. Failure to do so will lead a group to make poor decisions because group members often state opinions as though they are facts, thus leading other group members to accept what may be erroneous conclusions.

Distinguishing between Facts and Inferences

   A **fact** is a report that can be verified as *true* or *false*. If false, it is not a fact. Facts either exist or do not exist; they are not open to argument. A *statement of fact* is a declarative statement that describes an observation of some event. "It is raining outside" is a statement of fact. The event (the rain) is described and the statement implies how someone could verify its accuracy (e.g., by looking out the window). It is a *true* statement if it accurately describes observed events (e.g., it really *is* raining). Present events are relatively easy to verify. If the statement of fact refers to a past event, that past event must have actually been observed by somebody. However, since the past event is not *presently* available to the group for verification, only statements about it can be verified. For example, we cannot verify ourselves that George III occupied the throne of England in 1773, but we can verify that records indicate he was king. If several independent sources report the same information as fact, you can be more confident than if it comes from only one source.

An **inference** is an opinion that goes beyond what was actually observed; it makes a leap from a fact to a conclusion based on that fact. A *statement of inference* is a declarative statement that contains an opinion, preference, or conclusion. For example, "The Springfield metropolitan area is growing rapidly" is a statement of inference that goes beyond the *fact* that the area's population was 207,204 in the 1980 census and 243,300 in the 1990 census. *Rapidly* is a relative term; whether we choose to accept this inference as valid depends on what we compare the growth rate to: average growth rate for metropolitan areas in the United States, average growth rate for Missouri metropolitan areas, recent growth rate for areas of similar size, and so on. An inference *is* arguable. The following benchmarks and examples will help you recognize statements of fact from statements of inference or opinion:

Statements of Fact

Are limited to description;
Can be made only *after* observation;
Are as close to certain as humans can get;
Only a limited number of facts exist.

Statements of Inference and Opinion

Go beyond what was observed directly;
Can be made at any time without regard to observation;
Can be made by anyone, observer or not;
Entail some degree of probability, inferential risk, or uncertainty;
An unlimited number can be made about anything.

Examples:

The population of Springfield recorded in the 1990 census was 133,116.
On June 3, 1993, Jack Brilhart owned two horses.
The university library contained 2,437,532 volumes in its catalog on May 18, 1993.
After instituting lotteries, three states reduced their tax rates.
I-80 runs near both Cleveland and New York City.

Examples:

Springfield is growing rapidly.

Jack Brilhart likes horses.

The heart of a good university is its library.

We should legalize gambling to reduce the state tax.
You will get to New York from Cleveland by following I-80 (not if you have a wreck!).

Evaluating Survey and Statistical Data

Factual-type statements, including statistics or the results of surveys, need to be evaluated carefully for dependability. Surveying is a sophisticated operation and must be done correctly or the results can be misleading, especially if they are based on other than random or scientific sampling. The questions and who asks them can make a big difference in the results.

Ask the following questions when evaluating statistics: Who commissioned the study? How were the data gathered and analyzed? How were questions phrased? You may need the help of an expert to evaluate and properly interpret statistical data, especially if you are basing an important conclusion on those data.

When first introduced to the differences between facts and opinions, some students act as if statements of opinion are less valuable in a discussion. Hardly so! Facts themselves are not arguable but provide the basis for discussion and debate. Groups must deal not only with what has been verified but also determine priorities of values, ethics, goals, and procedures acceptable to all. Members make inferences about what will probably happen *if* they adopt each possible alternative. For example, facts regarding AIDS and how it is spread are fairly well known, but what a particular board of education will *do* about it depends on the values, opinions, and judgments about policies that will be acceptable to the community.

Evaluating the Sources and Implications of Opinions

Not all opinions are equal, although all people have an equal right to express their opinions. Unexamined opinions are poor guides to belief or action, and while they cannot be verified for truth, opinions *can* be evaluated for their validity and appropriate use of fact. First, consider the source of the opinion.

1. Is this person (or other source) a recognized expert on the subject? How do other experts in the field regard this person? If their opinions are different, how might this be explained?

2. Does the source have a vested interest that might have influenced the opinion? For example, a flood victim, insurance agent, politician, and taxpayer will have different opinions about whether government should reimburse victims of natural disasters for all their losses.

3. How well does the source support the opinion with documented evidence? Is the evidence well organized, with supporting statistics and tables and clear reasoning?

4. How consistent is this opinion with others expressed by the source? If not consistent, is there an acceptable explanation for the person's change?

Second, consider the implications of the opinion. To what further conclusions does it lead, and are these acceptable to the group? For example, a writer may argue that outlawing private ownership of handguns would protect us from accidents and murderers. What are the implications of this statement? That dangerous devices should not be allowed in the hands of citizens at large? That only nonessential dangerous tools that could potentially be used as murder weapons should be restricted? That eventually all potential murder weapons should be restricted? Another writer may argue that anyone with no felony record should be allowed to use a handgun after demonstrating competence in handling it safely and correctly. What are the implications of that opinion? That only convicted felons use handguns to kill another person? That most accidents would be prevented if people knew how to handle guns safely? That handguns are useful to many people? The point is that when a group decision depends on opinions, it is most important to test these opinions, especially for what they assume and imply.

Evaluating the information available to the group is only the first element of critical thinking. It is equally important to evaluate how both information sources and group members reason from this information.

Evaluating Reasoning

Critical thinking requires that conclusions (including decisions) be based both on sound evidence and clear, valid reasoning that connects information with conclusions in an appropriate and defensible way. Once you have evaluated the information (raw data), you must also look at how speakers and writers reason from that information. Are their conclusions logical and plausible, based on appropriate reasoning from information that is offered in support? Here is where *group* decision making can be clearly superior to individual decision making, because one member is usually able to spot a flaw or a reasoning error, called a **fallacy,** that another member missed. Several common fallacies observed in group discussions include overgeneralizing, making *ad hominem* attacks, suggesting inappropriate causal relationships, posing a false dilemma, and making faulty analogies.[35]

Overgeneralizing

An **overgeneralization** is a conclusion that is not supported by enough data. Because something is true about one or a few instances or persons, it is said to be true of all or most instances or persons of the same type. For example, when a person concludes that because *some* college students have defaulted on their government-guaranteed loans, *most or all* college students are irresponsible, that person has overgeneralized. Generalizations are not automatically wrong. After all, that is what statistics do—help us generalize appropriately from a relatively small sample to a large population. The problem occurs when we *over*generalize. To test generalizations, ask whether evidence other than personal testimony is being offered to support the generalization. Ask how many cases the generalization is based on, and whether the cases are typical of the phenomenon they are supposed to represent. Try to determine whether the sample offered is biased in any way.

Ad Hominem *Attacks*

An *ad hominem* **attack** is a statement that attacks a person instead of pointing out a flaw in the person's argument. The attack diverts the group's attention so members debate the merits of the person rather than the position he or she has taken on the issue. *Ad hominem* attacks may be explicit ("You can't trust foreigners to tell the truth!") or veiled ("Why do you think someone like that could help our group?"). In any case, they are a subtle form of name-calling. Determining the credibility of the person supplying information is important, but *ad hominem* attacks do not help evaluate credibility—they condemn individuals on the basis of characteristics irrelevant to the validity of opinions or accuracy of information they provide. And they do *not* help evaluate the arguments advanced by the person for or against some proposal.

Sometimes people assume that because two events are related or occurred close to each other in time, one must have caused the other. Establishing accurate causal connections is complex and difficult, even using statistical procedures. Common sense suggests that events usually have multiple and complex causes. To suggest that one single event causes another almost always oversimplifies a relationship among numerous variables. For example, we recently overheard a newscaster say that, because female graduates of women-only colleges were more likely to serve on the boards of Fortune 500 companies than graduates of coeducational schools, attendance at women's colleges probably "caused" greater career achievement. This is a preposterous statement! Numerous factors influence career achievement. Many women's colleges are both highly selective and expensive; their students are often bright, grew up in families who own or are connected to Fortune 500 companies, and can afford to attend expensive schools. Attendance at women-only colleges may indeed provide women with greater opportunities for engaging in leadership activities. More likely, native ability and family connections "cause" both attendance at women-only colleges and career achievement. Whenever group members see causal connections being posited, they should look for other reasons why the events might be linked. Only when alternative explanations have been eliminated should a causal connection be accepted as probably true, and then only tentatively.

Suggesting Inappropriate Causal Relationships

A **false dilemma** poses an either-or choice that implies, wrongly, that only two options or courses of action are possible. For example, either the university builds a new parking lot *or* students have to walk miles to get to class. Either sex education is taught by the parents *or* by the schools. Each of these statements ignores the fact that other options exist to accomplish both goals. For example, the university could provide a shuttle bus service to transport students from far-away parking lots, schedule classes early or late to alleviate parking crunches at certain times, or set up a car-pooling service to improve the parking situation. Children can be taught sex education by their parents; their teachers; their ministers, priests, or rabbis; committees composed of teachers and parents working together; teams of clergy and parents; and so forth. The either-or choices offered in both cases obscure the fact that many other options are possible—in other words, the "dilemma" is false. Just because a writer or speaker does not offer you alternatives should not blind you to their existence. Whenever you are offered an either-or choice, we encourage you to look for additional options or to think in terms of *degree* rather than *good* or *bad, effective* or *ineffective,* and so forth.

False Dilemmas

A **faulty analogy** is a comparison that asks us to stretch a similarity too far. Comparisons help us understand issues more vividly, but all comparisons have limitations. An orange house cat may look and act like a tiger, but the house cat does not eat ten pounds of meat per day and cannot hurt you much if he jumps on your lap. We have heard many students complain (we have even complained ourselves!):

Faulty Analogies

"You can't really learn how to be a public relations professional in college. It would be like trying to learn to swim from a book, but never getting in the water." At first glance, this remark hits home with those of us who know that there indeed are limitations to what you can learn in school. Examining the analogy more closely, however, reveals that many classroom activities and assignments prepare students for professional practice. For example, public relations majors practice writing for a variety of audiences, learn principles of graphic design and use them to design materials for a variety of clients, put together dynamic oral presentations, write up job specifications and budgets for proposed projects, and so on. All these are activities that public relations professionals carry out in professional practice. Whenever you hear an analogy being offered as an argument, ask yourself three things: 1) What two things are being compared? 2) How are they similar? And, more importantly, 3) How are they different? Where is the comparison inaccurate? Is some vital characteristic that might make a difference *not* compared? If the answer to either question is *yes,* the analogy has broken down and the conclusion it was used to support is possibly incorrect or incomplete. Always ask, "Is the conclusion warranted by *this* analogy?"

The fallacies we have just presented are among the most common, but by no means are they the only ones you will encounter. The important thing is for you and your fellow group members to be alert to mistakes in reasoning so you will not be led by faulty reasoning to make poor decisions.

Summary

Many decisions are made in the process of group problem solving. Just because members are capable and conscientious will not ensure that the group will make good decisions. Generally group decisions are superior to those made by individuals, but whether this is so depends on several factors, including the type of task, whether group norms support high or low production, and the decision-making procedures used. An *assembly effect* is often observed in which the group's decision is superior to the summative effect of all the individual members' decisions. Group decision making takes longer than individual decision making, and so may not always be the method of choice. Questions to consider include whether the decision must be accepted by the members, whether there is a quality component, and whether members have time to deliberate thoroughly. "Yes" answers to all three questions indicate that a group decision is warranted. Decisions in a group can be made by the designated leader (who may or may not consult the rest of the members), by majority vote, or by consensus, which is defined as the option that all members agree is the best they can all support. Suggestions for facilitating consensus include viewing the group decision as a cooperative rather than competitive process, and using disagreements to stimulate creative thinking and evaluation of alternatives.

Groups often pass through predictable phases during decision making. Bales and Strodtbeck identified three: orientation, evaluation, and control. Fisher identified four phases: orientation, in which members orient themselves to the task; conflict, in which they argue the merits of alternatives; decision emergence, during which they begin to coalesce around a single alternative; and reinforcement, when they confirm the choice and congratulate each other for a job well done. Recent researchers have questioned the notion that a single set of phases describes the decision-making pattern for most groups. Poole found, for example, that a variety of group and individual factors influences the types, length, and sequence of group decision-making phases.

Research has consistently shown that group decision making can be improved if members define the problem carefully, agree on criteria to be used, thoroughly evaluate the positive and negative characteristics of all the options, and second-guess their tentative selection. The most important thing they can do, however, is to think critically, which includes evaluating both the information available to the group and the reasoning and logic that link the information to conclusions. Members should be especially watchful for reasoning that overgeneralizes, *ad hominem* attacks, arguments based on inappropriate causal relationships, false dilemmas, and faulty analogies. Attention to these deficiencies in critical thinking will improve both the decision-making process and quality.

1. Read the following case problem, then break into groups of five or six and come to a consensus decision. Use the following questions to guide your postdecision evaluation:

   Exercises

   a. What problems in choosing did your group have?
   b. What seemed to cause these problems?
   c. Do you think you made the best choice? Why or why not?
   d. What guidelines can you write to apply what you learned?
   e. What did you learn from this exercise?

You comprise a Scholarship Awards Committee at State University. A special trust fund was established by an anonymous donor to award one full-tuition scholarship per year to a person with demonstrated need for financial assistance, a reasonable expectation of success as a student, and who is unlikely to attend college if not granted some form of aid. There are no other conditions attached to the award except that a student committee must select the winner from a list of applicants supplied by the admissions office. Admissions has given you a list of five eligible applicants and said no other information can be given to you. Who will receive the scholarship? You can award only one scholarship.

Scholarship Awards Committee

Duane, age 18, finished high school in three years. He says he rushed through because he could not have tolerated another year of the bull. His mother, a widow with two younger children to support, can only work part time in her field as a registered nurse. Duane's high school grade average was 3.0. University tests predict a 2.6 college grade point average in a science curriculum and 3.1 in nonscience. His mother is determined that Duane should be a physician. Duane says he is not sure of what job or profession he wants. He has some emotional problems; a psychiatrist he has seen recommends college because he thinks Duane needs "an intellectual challenge."

Carla, age 17, has very high recommendations from the small town high school where she earned a 3.8 grade average. In her senior year she became engaged to a driver for a feed mill, who wants her to get married at once and forget college. She is known to have spent a few nights with him on a cross-country trip to haul grain. Your university predicts she will earn 2.6 in science and 3.3 in a nonscience program. She says she wants to become a social worker "to help the poor in some big city." The minister where she attends church says she has a fine mind, but he predicts she will marry and drop out even if she starts college. Her parents are uneducated (less than high school), hard working, law abiding, and very poor.

Melissa, age 26, is a divorcee with a seven-year-old son. She had a 2.8 grade average in high school "because I goofed around," but tests predict a 2.9 in science and a 3.6 in nonscience at your university. She says she wants to become an English instructor, "in college if I get lucky, or at least in high school." She was a beauty contest winner at 18, but says she is bitter toward men and will never remarry. She gets no child support or other family assistance. Her present boss, a dress shop owner, gives her a good character reference but predicts she will marry rather than finish college.

Sam, age 19, was offered several football scholarships, but they were withdrawn when an auto accident injured his legs. He can get around well but cannot compete in athletics. His high school grade average was barely passing, but entrance test scores predict a 2.5 average in science and 3.0 in a nonscience curriculum. His father, a day laborer, says he can contribute nothing toward a college education for Sam. Sam says he is determined to become a football coach, though he has been advised that may be difficult without a college playing record.

Ray, age 27, earned a medal for bravery and lost his right hand in an Army war game. He earned a high school diploma while in the Army. The university predicts a 2.0 average in science and a 2.8 in a nonscience program. He is eligible for some veteran's assistance, but his family needs his help to support a large brood of younger children. Ray says he wants to major in business and "make enough money so my children will have better than I did."

Bibliography

Browne, M. Neil and Stuart M. Keeley. *Asking the Right Questions: A Guide to Critical Thinking,* 3d ed. Englewood Cliffs, NJ: Prentice-Hall, 1990.

Hirokawa, Randy Y. "Discussion Procedures and Decision Making Performance: A Test of a Functional Perspective." *Human Communication Research* 12 (1985): 203–24.

Isenberg, Daniel J. "Group Polarization: A Critical Review and Meta-Analysis." *Journal of Personality and Social Psychology* 50 (1986): 1141–51.

Mennecke, Brian E., Jeffrey A. Hoffer, and Bayard E. Wynne. "The Implications of Group Development and History for Group Support System Theory and Practice." *Small Group Research* 23 (1992): 524–72. Provides a thorough, current review of group development literature.

Walton, Douglas N. *Plausible Argument in Everyday Conversation.* Albany, NY: State University of New York Press, 1992.

Notes

1. Sharon Cohen, The Associated Press, "Companies Turn Workers into Bosses," in *The Springfield (MO) News-Leader,* December 2, 1990: E1–2.

2. John E. Tropman, *Effective Meetings: Improving Group Decision-Making* (Beverly Hills, CA: Sage Publications, 1980), 11.

3. Dennis S. Gouran, Randy Y. Hirokawa, and Amy E. Martz, "A Critical Analysis of Factors Related to Decision Processes Involved in the *Challenger* Disaster," *Central States Speech Journal* 37 (1986): 119–35.

4. Joseph D. Anderson, "Working with Groups: Little-Known Facts that Challenge Well-Known Myths," *Small Group Behavior* 16 (1985): 267–83.

5. Victor H. Vroom, "A New Look at Managerial Decision-Making," *Organizational Dynamics* (American Management Association, 1973), 66–80.

6. Jay Hall, "Decisions, Decisions, Decisions," *Psychology Today* 5 (November 1971): 51–54, 86–87; Jay Hall and W. H. Watson, "The Effects of a Normative Intervention on Group Decision-Making Performance," *Human Relations* 23 (1970): 299–317.

7. Irving L. Janis, *Groupthink: Psychological Studies of Policy Decisions and Fiascoes,* 2d ed. (Boston: Houghton Mifflin Company, 1983).

8. Herm W. Smith, "Group versus Individual Problem Solving and Type of Problem Solved," *Small Group Behavior* 20 (1989): 357–66.

9. Brant R. Burleson, Barbara J. Levine, and Wendy Samter, "Decision Quality," *Human Communication Research* 10 (1984): 557–74.

10. M. L. Chemers, "Leadership Theory and Research: A Systems-Process Integration," in *Basic Group Processes,* ed. P. B. Paulus (New York: Springer-Verlag, 1983), 19–20; Randy Y. Hirokawa, "Consensus Group Decision-Making, Quality of Decision and Group Satisfaction: An Attempt to Sort Fact from Fiction," *Central States Speech Journal* 33 (1982): 407–15.

11. Lester Coch and John R. P. French, Jr., "Overcoming Resistance to Change," *Human Relations* 1 (1948): 512–32.

12. Myron W. Block and L. R. Hoffman, "The Effects of Valence of Solutions and Group Cohesiveness on Members' Commitment to Group Decision," in *The Group Problem Solving Process,* ed. L. Richard Hoffman (New York: Prager, 1979), 121.

13. Burleson et al., "Decision-Making Procedure and Decision Quality," 557–74.

14. Carolyn J. Wood, "Challenging the Assumptions Underlying the Use of Participatory Decision-Making Strategies: A Longitudinal Case Study," *Small Group Behavior,* 20 (1989): 428–48.

15. Paul Miesing and John F. Preble, "Group Processes and Performance in Complex Business Simulation," *Small Group Behavior* 16 (1985): 325–38.

16. Hirokawa, "Consensus Group Decision-Making," 407–14; Randy Y. Hirokawa, "Why Informed Groups Make Faulty Decisions: An Investigation of Possible Interaction-Based Explanations," *Small Group Behavior* 18 (1987): 3–29.

17. Dennis S. Gouran, "Inferential Errors, Interaction, and Group Decision-Making," in R. Y. Hirokawa and M. S. Poole, eds., *Communication and Group Decision-Making* (Beverly Hills, CA: Sage Publications, 1986), 93–111.

18. Marvin E. Shaw, *Group Dynamics,* 2d ed. (New York: McGraw-Hill, 1976), 70–77.

19. Daniel J. Isenberg, "Group Polarization: A Critical Review and Meta-analysis," *Journal of Personality and Social Psychology* 10 (1986): 1141–51.

20. Jerold L. Hale and Franklin J. Boster, "Comparing Effects-Coded Models of Choice Shifts," *Communication Research Reports* 5 (1988): 180–86.

21. Martin F. Kaplan and Charles E. Miller, "Group Decision Making and Normative versus Informational Influence: Effects of Type of Issue and Assigned Decision Rule," *Journal of Personality and Social Psychology* 53 (1987): 306–13.

22. Burleson et al., "Decision-Making Procedure and Decision Quality," 370–73; Smith, "Group versus Individual Problem Solving."

23. Patricia M. Fandt, "The Relationship of Accountability and Interdependent Behavior to Enhancing Team Consequences," *Group & Organization Studies* 16 (1991): 300–312.

24. Michael J. Beatty, "Group Members' Decision Rule Orientations and Consensus," *Human Communication Research* 16 (1989) 279–96.

25. Hall, "Decisions, Decision, Decisions."

26. Robert F. Bales and Fred L. Strodtbeck, "Phases in Group Problem-Solving," *Journal of Abnormal and Social Psychology,* 46 (1951): 485–95.

27. For a complete summary of Fisher's work on decision-making phases, see B. Aubrey Fisher and Donald G. Ellis, *Small Group Decision Making: Communication and the Group Process,* 3d ed. (New York: McGraw-Hill Publishing Company, 1990), especially chapter 6.

28. Marshall Scott Poole, "Decision Development in Small Groups I: A Comparison of Two Models," *Communication Monographs* 48 (1981): 1–24; "Decision Development in Small Groups II: A Study of Multiple Sequences in Decision Making," *Communication Monographs* 50 (1983): 206–32; and "Decision Development in Small Groups III: A Multiple Sequence Model of Group Decision Development," *Communication Monographs* 50 (1983): 321–41; M. S. Poole and Jonelle Roth, "Decision Development in Small Groups IV: A Typology of Group Decision Paths," *Human Communication Research* 15 (1989): 322–56; and "Decision Development in Small Groups V: Test of a Contingency Model," *Human Communication Research* 15 (1989): 549–89.

29. Poole, "Decision Development II" and "Decision Development III."

30. Poole and Roth, "Decision Development V."

31. Thomas M. Scheidel and Laura Crowell, "Idea Development in Small Discussion Groups," *Quarterly Journal of Speech* 50 (1964): 140–45.

32. Teresa C. Sabourin and Patricia Geist, "Collaborative Production of Proposals in Group Decision Making," *Small Group Research* 21 (1990): 404–27.

33. B. Aubrey Fisher and Randall K. Stutman, "An Assessment of Group Trajectories: Analyzing Developmental Breakpoints," *Communication Quarterly* 35 (1987): 105–24.

34. Renee A. Meyers, David R. Siebold, and Dale Brashers, "Argument in Initial Group Decision-Making Discussions: Refinement of a Coding Scheme and a Descriptive Quantitative Analysis," *Western Journal of Speech Communication* 55 (Winter, 1991): 47–68.

35. Much of the following information is distilled from information provided in M. Neil Browne and Stuart M. Keeley, *Asking the Right Questions: A Guide to Critical Thinking,* 2d ed. (Englewood Cliffs, NJ: Prentice-Hall, 1986).

Managing Conflict in the Small Group

Central Message

If properly managed, the inevitable conflict during a small group's deliberations can improve problem solving and decision making by providing a variety of perspectives that promote critical thinking.

Study Objectives
As a result of studying chapter 12 you should be able to:

1. Define conflict and explain both the positive and negative effects it can have on a group.

2. Explain how perceptual, emotional, behavioral, and interactional dimensions operate as a system in small group conflict.

3. Describe a member who is an *innovative* or *opinion deviate* and explain how such a person can help a group improve its decision making.

4. Describe the four types of conflict that typically occur in small group interactions.

5. Define groupthink, explain the symptoms, and describe two specific techniques that can counteract groupthink.

6. Describe the ethical standards for dealing with conflict.

7. Describe the specific conflict management styles typically used to manage small group conflict.

8. Explain the principled negotiation procedure for helping a group resolve conflict.

9. Explain three alternative methods for breaking a deadlock when negotiation fails, and describe a mediation procedure a group can use if it is deadlocked.

Key Terms

Accommodation	Conflict	Inequity
Affective conflict	Deviate	Integrative approach
Avoidance	Devil's advocacy	Principled negotiation
Collaboration	Dialectical inquiry (DI)	Procedural conflict
Competition	Distributive approach	Substantive conflict
Compromise	Groupthink	

Pick up any popular general interest magazine and you will probably see an article about how to get along harmoniously at work, at home, with friends. You may even get the impression that conflict should be avoided at all costs! The truth is that whenever individuals come together in any sort of social context, disagreement and conflict are inevitable. Trying to avoid them is futile and unwise.

Americans are ambivalent about conflict. Along with values that stress agreement and "getting along," we say "stick to your guns." We have trouble reconciling the benefits of *both* harmony *and* conflict. Other cultures do not experience this tension to the same degree. For example, the same Chinese word means both *crisis* and *opportunity*. Eastern cultures, in particular, see such apparently opposing concepts as harmony and conflict as yin and yang, sides of the same coin. Americans, too, must learn to appreciate the value of each in human relationships so that both processes, managed in a balanced way, can contribute positively to a group's interaction.

In small groups, conflict is an integral part of problem solving and decision making. It is a natural byproduct of trying to come to some agreement about an issue or problem. Each member will perceive the situation in a slightly different way, have different values, priorities, and preferences. These variations in perceptions and beliefs are brought out into the open during discussion. If a group's goal is simply for members to understand each other, these differences can remain unresolved. But if a group's goal is to solve a problem or make a choice, divergent opinions must be reconciled or the group will not achieve its purpose.

Conflict is at the heart of effective decision making and problem solving. Why bother to ask a group to solve a problem if you don't think that several heads are better than one? By involving a group, you tacitly acknowledge the value of diversity, the same diversity that guarantees conflict. Conflict *should* occur during group problem solving; if it doesn't, the group members aren't doing their jobs properly by engaging in vigilant interaction to take advantage of the diversity. Failure to express disagreement and avoiding discussion of conflict-producing issues leads directly to ineffective problem solving and poor decision making.[1] For the group to receive the full benefit of the collective judgment of its members, the members must be willing to disagree, point out errors, and argue.

Although too much conflict can hurt a group or even destroy it, our experience has been that groups of students err in the direction of too little rather than too much conflict. Most of our students are afraid of disagreement and prefer groups with little or no conflict.[2] For that reason this chapter stresses the benefits of conflict. We explain how to distinguish beneficial from detrimental conflict, how to recognize the symptoms of groupthink and how to manage conflicts to produce the best possible decision or solution.

A variety of definitions exists for **conflict,** ranging from something that occurs when individuals have reached an impasse[3] to a state of genuine difference.[4] We chose Hocker and Wilmot's definition:

> *Conflict* is an expressed struggle between at least two interdependent parties who perceive incompatible goals, scarce resources, and interference from the other party in achieving their goals.[5]

A Definition of Conflict

This definition embodies several implications that are consistent with a communicative focus on conflict in small groups.

First, the notion of conflict as an *expressed struggle* indicates that conflict involves communicating. While a group member may *feel* internal (intrapersonal) distress, this distress becomes conflict *only when it is expressed,* whether clearly or in such subtle ways as not making eye contact or shifting nervously in one's chair.

Second, parties to a conflict must have an interdependent goal such that it is impossible for one person to attain the goal and not the others. Earlier we said that some groups have as their goals understanding of diverse points of view. In such groups, members do not have to coordinate their beliefs and efforts to agree on a solution. However, many secondary groups must produce something—a report, a proposal, a set of recommendations—that *all* group members must agree to. Such group members are interdependent; one cannot achieve the goal without the others. Therefore, they must find ways of reconciling diverse perspectives and beliefs affecting the decision. For example, Sam may detest Sara's views about what is appropriate treatment of laboratory animals, but that won't matter much unless both are in a group that is charged with recommending a university policy regarding treatment of laboratory animals; for the group to succeed fully, Sam and Sara must reconcile their views enough to collaborate on a policy each can support. Thus, the interdependence group members experience is accompanied by interference. Sam's disagreement with Sara interferes with Sara's having her way, and *vice versa.* This interference may take the form of Sara trying to persuade the other group members to accept her view, Sam trying to undercut Sara's credibility within the group, or Sara sabotaging Sam's car so he will miss an important meeting.

Third, this definition suggests a number of things over which people conflict, such as goals and scarce resources, to which we add values, beliefs, and ways of achieving goals. For example, we have observed numerous student groups whose members disagree on group goals. Maria's goal is to earn an A for a group presentation to the class, but Jack's goal is to do just enough to earn a C. Their divergent goals will cause a problem for the group. In contrast, assume that both Maria and Jack want to receive an A for the presentation, but Maria prefers to involve the class in an exercise followed by discussion, while Jack prefers to show and discuss a movie. In this instance, they agree on the goal but differ on the best course of action to reach the goal. Or, suppose that Sam believes that humans are superior to all other forms of life, which makes it appropriate for laboratory animals to serve human needs, but Sara values all animal life forms equally. This fundamental difference in values may make it impossible for their group to reach consensus on a policy regarding laboratory animals. You can probably tell from these examples that some conflicts, such as those over values and goals, are harder to resolve than others. In a group, the more homophilous members are with respect to basic values and beliefs, the easier it will be for the group to achieve consensus.

Fourth, parties to a conflict must *perceive* they are in conflict. This perceptual dimension is a very important one. There is nothing that automatically labels a situation as *conflict;* instead, conflict depends on how people perceive the situation. For instance, if Tyrell disagrees with a proposal you have made, you have a *choice* about how to perceive Tyrell's disagreement. You can say, "What a jerk! What makes him think he can do any better!" In this case, you have framed his disagreement as a conflict. However, you could also have said, "I wonder why Tyrell disagrees? Maybe there's something in my proposal that I forgot to consider." In this latter case, you have framed his statement of disagreement as a possible attempt on Tyrell's part to improve and strengthen your proposal. Thus, perception defines a situation as a conflict; it is a crucial element in a system that also includes emotions, behaviors, and interactions between the participants.

Perception of a situation is closely associated with emotions and behavior. To illustrate, your feelings can range from mild distress to out-of-control rage, depending on how you perceive the situation. If you think Tyrell is a jerk for disagreeing with you or believe he disagreed just to make you look bad in some way, you will feel furious. Furthermore, you may be tempted to seek revenge or escalate the intensity of the conflict. On the other hand, if you perceive Tyrell's disagreement to be motivated by a desire to strengthen your idea, then you may be only mildly hurt at his criticism, or even pleased that he cared enough to give your idea such a careful reading. In this latter case, your behavior will probably be directed toward cooperating with Tyrell and collaborating to improve the proposal, not toward escalating the conflict. Thus, no perception of conflict, no conflict.

Your perceptions, emotions, and behavior merge with the other person's perceptions, emotions, and behavior to form an interactive system. It is important to remember that you can't be in a conflict situation alone; your behaviors affect other people, as theirs affect you. Suppose you decide Tyrell is a jerk, so you rip his criticism of your proposal to shreds. That will certainly affect Tyrell, who may now conclude that *you* are a jerk who just can't take constructive criticism. Tyrell may now decide to escalate the conflict or try to destroy your credibility within the group. On the other hand, if you indicate to Tyrell that you genuinely want to know more about his criticism and the reasons for it, he may decide you are an enlightened, cooperative group member whom he can trust and on whose good judgment he can rely. This may lead him to seek your opinions, support, and ideas in the future. Thus, your perceptions, emotions, and behavior form a feedback loop with the other person's perceptions, emotions, and behavior; each element affects each other element, and none operates independently, as is shown in figure 12.1. Changing one of the elements will automatically change the others.

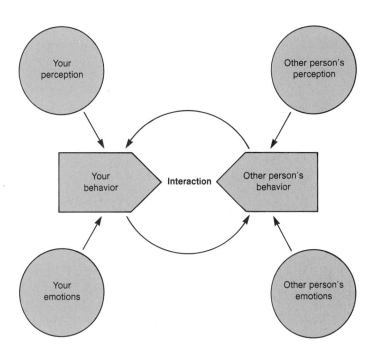

Figure 12.1
Perception, emotions, behavior, and interaction in a conflict.

Communication scholars concur that conflict has both beneficial and harmful outcomes.[6] We mentioned earlier that without the kind of conflict that comes from a critical examination of an issue, a group is unlikely to make a good decision, but we also know that conflict can be harmful. We will now examine some of these positive and negative effects.

Positive and Negative Outcomes of Conflict

Conflict positively affects the group when it produces a better decision, increases cohesiveness and teamwork, enhances member understanding, and leads to satisfaction with both the process and the product. Here are several potential benefits of conflict:

Positive Effects of Conflict

1. **Conflict can produce better understanding of both issues and people.**
   We often assume that most people see things as we do and feel as we do, and are often surprised to discover otherwise. When students discover others holding differing opinions on an issue, Smith, Johnson, and Johnson found that they become uncertain about their own positions, seek actively to get more information about the issue, are able to take the perspective of the other students, and are better able to retain information, both about their own position and those of other people.[7] They demonstrate increased understanding of both the information and the individuals.

2. **Conflict can increase member motivation.**
   People who do not care will not expend any energy disagreeing about an issue. However, when group members participate in a conflict episode they are actively involved with the issue. They are interested, excited, and pay close

attention, so they learn more about the issue. A student in one of our classes could not accept a statement by a fellow group member that nonverbal signals were more potent than words in conveying meaning. Unable to resolve the issue to his own satisfaction, he investigated the issue by using library and personal resources, and discovered the validity of the statement. His search provided some excellent examples the group was able to use in its class presentation—all because he got into an intellectual argument.

3. **Conflict can produce better decisions.**
   This outcome is the goal of good *group* problem solving. Through conflict, you discover first that others disagree, then *why* they disagree. You find flaws in reasoning, holes in arguments, factors that other members failed to consider, or implications that were ignored. Thus you help the group prevent mistakes. For example, one of us belonged to a campus staff charged with developing a plan for cutting costs at a commuter campus. The developer of the plan recommended closing the snack bar at 5:00 P.M. Another member of the staff pointed out that closing at 5:00 would leave many evening students who came to the campus directly from work without food service and might eventually lead to a drop in enrollment. After considerable debate, the committee decided to provide vending machine service, which would accomplish the goal of cutting personnel and utility costs, but not leave the evening students without food.

4. **Conflict can produce greater cohesiveness among group members.**
   When a group experiences and resolves conflict successfully, the members learn that the ties holding the group together are strong enough to withstand disagreement. Most of us who have had serious arguments with significant others can recall the closeness we feel after we have "made up." Instead of driving us apart, the conflict serves as a catalyst to strengthen the bonds between us. So it is with groups. The twin outcomes of task success and interpersonal tolerance can increase group cohesiveness. For example, in the food service story, staff members felt so good about the final outcome and so positive about each other's willingness to listen to opposing arguments that they adjourned for lunch together in a spirit of camaraderie.

Negative Effects of Conflict

Although conflict can be beneficial, we all have also seen how harmful it can be. If you have ever said to yourself after a group meeting, "I'll be glad when this project is finished, I hope I never have to work with these people again," you have experienced some of the harmful effects of conflict. These include hurt feelings, lowered cohesiveness, and even group dissolution.

1. **Conflict can cause bad feelings among group members.**
   Most of us do not like to have others disagree with us. This is particularly true when others not only disagree with an idea or proposal we give, but appear to devalue us as people. Their remarks appear caustic, even hostile. This type of perceived attack causes hard feelings. Members may be silent for fear of an attack, thereby depriving the group of valuable information and opinions.

(We discuss later how you can deal with such an attack.) Moreover, even a conflict over issues and ideas can be carried on so long that it increases tension and wears group members down to the point where they dread coming to meetings.

2. **Conflict, especially if it involves personal attacks or is carried on too long, can lower group cohesiveness.**

   If you believe that others in a group do not value your contributions, you will not be eager to spend time with that group. If you have a choice, you will spend your time with other groups that seem to value you more. Prolonged conflict and attacks on one's self-concept loosen the bonds of attraction and cohesiveness, which can cause members to reduce the effort they put forth to achieve the group's objectives.

3. **Conflict can split a group apart.**

   A member who believes a group dislikes his or her ideas, but finds support in other groups, will usually leave the group in which the conflict occurs. Conflict that goes on too long and too intensely tears members apart. One of us once observed a friendship group split up over a political issue. One side believed that busing was an appropriate way to achieve racial equality; the other side disagreed. The two sides did not simply have an intellectual disagreement; they began to impugn each other's good will, ability to reason, and commitment to democratic values. Unkind things were said, a rift occurred, and the group died.

Many people are reluctant to express opinions that differ from a group's majority opinion. (This is especially true in other cultures, such as in Oriental ones.) Expressing such disagreement will cause such a person to be seen as a deviant member by the rest of the group. A **deviate** is a member who is viewed by the other members as substantially different in some *important* way from the others. Two common types of group deviates are members who do not participate and members who express incompatible views about the issues and test opinions of the group.[8] The second type is more likely to be involved in disagreement or conflict in a group. While the deviate's role may be uncomfortable, it is a potentially valuable one for a group. Reluctant as you may be to express a deviant opinion, ethically you should do it for the good of the group. However, you do not want to appear as rebelliously blocking or withdrawing. Instead, you want to be an *innovative* or *opinion deviate,* someone who disagrees with a proposed action or decision of the group but who is strongly committed to the group and its goals.

Sometimes it is very hard for an opinion deviate to influence a group. Lindskold and Han found that it was nearly impossible for a single conciliatory member to influence a nonconciliatory group.[9] Thameling and Andrews also found that opinion deviates exerted little influence.[10] Other group members responded more emotionally to deviates than to conforming group members. A sex bias has been observed: members responded more cooperatively to male than to female deviates. Group members appeared to perceive male deviates as bright and well informed,

Expressing
Disagreement
in a Group

and showed a willingness to work with them by asking for evidence, questions, additional information, and so forth; however, they were more likely to perceive female deviates as arrogant or overly confident. These researchers suggest that an individual who wants to express a deviant opinion do so cautiously and carefully. If you first develop solid group credentials of loyalty and commitment, other members will trust your motives when you deviate from a majority opinion.

However, even with all these caveats about the difficulty of being an opinion deviate, this kind of disagreement is valuable to the group, particularly for groups in the United States and other western cultures. Valentine and Fisher found that innovative deviance accounted for one-fourth of group interaction, serving a critical thinking function.[11] Innovative deviance (in the form of contradiction, challenging statements by other members, continuing a disagreement started by others, or agreeing with an assertion someone else had attacked) was particularly helpful in the group's conflict and decision emergence phases. Furthermore, most innovative deviance occurred immediately prior to consensus, supporting the notion that conflicts can contribute to consensus. Social skill is important, too. Covey found a high correlation between social skill and the use of verbal reasoning in conflict resolution, as well as a negative correlation of social skill with verbal aggression and physical violence.[12] Thus, deviant opinions, skillfully and sensitively expressed, can help a group make better decisions.

Types of Conflict

As we have already shown, conflict in and of itself is neither helpful nor harmful to a group. What matters is what the conflict is about, how it is initiated, and how it is managed. Before we examine several types of conflict that can occur within a group and discuss the potential effects of each, we present a description of conflict in a group of students charged with selecting speakers for their university's Speaker Series.[13] Every major type of conflict occurred in this group, which is the same group of students we met in chapter 3.

The Speaker Committee—Kevin, Lori, Chris, Deidre, and Tony—had met several times, but made little progress. Kevin either missed meetings or came late; the others were angry with him. The committee couldn't agree on anything. They argued about whether they should select entertaining or educational speakers, whether they should book one major speaker or several lesser-known ones, whether they should decide by consensus or majority vote, and, most of all, what they should do about Kevin. Occasionally, one of the members would ask a question that encouraged the others to examine their decision and the criteria by which to make their decision, and occasionally a member would make a suggestion that received widespread support. In general, though, they exhibited many problems in managing their conflicts. The conflicts in this group of students illustrate the following four types of conflict:

Substantive Conflict

Substantive conflict, also called *intrinsic* conflict, is task-related conflict such as disagreement over ideas, meanings, issues, and other matters pertinent (intrinsic) to the task of the group.[14] It involves *what* the group should do. Substantive conflict is the basis for effective decision making and problem solving in a discussion group.

It is the vehicle by which ideas, proposals, evidence, and reasoning are challenged and critically examined, doubts are brought into the open, and the group works together to find the best solution. Opinion and innovative deviance described earlier are usually substantive in nature. In the example just presented, the Speaker Committee debated whether an entertaining or educational speaker would be a better choice. The ensuing argument helped members clarify the purpose of the Speaker Series and presented good reasons for considering each type of speaker. The earlier example of Maria wanting to conduct a class exercise and Jack wanting to show a movie is another instance of substantive conflict. In another example, when the university where one of us worked was ordered by the governing board to reduce programs costing about $2 million, a committee charged with recommending what programs to cut had several substantive conflicts among members. Some wanted to eliminate intercollegiate athletics, others thought various service programs could be cut, and still others wanted to do away with religious studies and masters programs in the performing arts.

Affective conflict, also called *extrinsic* conflict, is conflict that originates from interpersonal power clashes, likes and dislikes extrinsic to the group's task.[15] It represents the *who* in small group conflict and is generally detrimental to the efficient functioning of any group. For example, Speaker Series committee members Lori and Kevin did not like each other and missed no opportunity to disagree or belittle each other. When Kevin said he preferred to schedule an entertaining rather than educational speaker, Lori said, "I could have expected that from you. Let's not learn—let's party!" This statement reveals that Lori personalized the conflict with Kevin. Her dislike compounded the effects of disagreement over work procedures and ideas. She rarely failed to make sarcastic comments to Kevin throughout the meeting. Such conflict is both difficult to resolve and exceedingly harmful to the group.

Affective Conflict

Although the origin of this type of conflict is difficult to pin down, our observations of numerous groups suggest that much of it is rooted in one person's acting as if he or she is superior, and another member's refusal to accept this difference in status or power. Most of this "I am superior, more important, more knowledgeable" signaling is nonverbal, projected by subtle patterns of vocal tones, postures, and head/body angles. Much of what is called interpersonal conflict emerges from a struggle for position and power. Recent research has indicated that group members are able to differentiate between personalized (affective) and depersonalized (substantive) conflict, and that the type of conflict affects group consensus.[16] Because affective conflict can impede resolution of substantive issues, Fisher and Brown recommend disentangling relationship and substantive goals and pursuing them independently.[17] Doing so gives the parties a chance to resolve their substantive differences, even though they may never change their feelings about each other.

Procedural conflict is a type of substantive conflict over the procedures a group should follow in working toward its goals. Disagreement is about the *how* of group interaction. For instance, members of a group may disagree about whether they

Procedural Conflict

should make decisions by consensus or whether majority rule will suffice. For example, in our Speaker Series committee, Lori proposed splitting up the money available to the committee and letting each person select whatever speaker he or she wants with his/her share of the money. Tony agreed because he thought this would involve fewer arguments, but Chris accused Lori of favoring this decision-making method as a way of having fewer meetings. Deidre pointed out that if every person chose the same type of speaker, the series would be boring. The group then realized the value of consensus decision making. This disagreement over *how* the group makes its major decisions is a clear example of procedural conflict; the diversity of opinion expressed by the members helped clarify the issue to everyone's satisfaction.

Procedural conflict is sometimes used to mask affective or substantive conflict. Putnam notes that it can occur because members genuinely disagree over procedures, but it also can be used to withdraw from another substantive conflict by forcing a vote or otherwise regulating the group's work.[18] Although procedural conflict may seem to be a straightforward difference over how the group should accomplish something, it may be rooted in differing member needs for structure versus freedom. Members high in needs for procedural order are more comfortable with linear procedures than members who prefer less structured procedural order.

Conflict Over Inequity   One of the most prevalent sources of conflict in the groups we have observed is perceived **inequity** in the group: group members do not seem to have equal workloads and/or do not make equal contributions to the group. Inequity reduces satisfaction with the group and is associated with high levels of conflict.[19] In our Speaker Series committee, Kevin's work and contributions to the group were perceived as inadequate. Although Lori rode Kevin the hardest about his lack of commitment to the group, Chris, Deidre, and even Tony mentioned Kevin's lack of follow-through and failure to complete assignments for the group. When Kevin was late again, Chris said, "I'm tired of waiting for the jerk. Let's get started," and later Deidre directly confronted Kevin by listing his behaviors that indicated lack of commitment to the group ("You've missed two of the last four meetings, and were late to the ones you did come to."). Kevin's perceived inequity of effort within the group had created serious conflict between him and the other members. Kevin's continued lack of commitment to the group also contributed to Lori's strong feelings of dislike and her constant needling. She scrutinized his contributions more closely than those of the other members and criticized Kevin for statements that she accepted from other people. For example, both Tony and Kevin wanted an entertaining speaker, but Lori singled Kevin out for ridicule about wanting to party more than learn. Because of his inequity of performance, he was being required to measure up more perfectly to the group's performance norms than the others.

Although we describe these four types of conflict as though they are distinct, they are not mutually exclusive. One type can easily lead to another. Frequently two or more types blend. In our example this was most clearly seen with Lori, whose dislike of Kevin combined with Kevin's inadequate contribution to the group and his disagreement with her position (Kevin wanted an entertaining speaker, but Lori wanted an educational one). All these conflicts united to intensify Lori's dislike. Lori *looked* for things over which to be angry with Kevin. She was probably the most relieved member when Kevin eventually left the group.

We noted earlier that conflict and harmony are sides of the same coin. Just as a coin must be balanced carefully to stand on its edge, so conflict and harmony must be balanced for a group to function optimally. Too much or not enough of either one short-circuits effective decision making; both must be present. Nowhere is the imbalance seen more clearly than in the presence of *groupthink.*

Groupthink occurs when a group, often a highly cohesive one, allows the desire for harmony and consensus to suppress confrontation and substantive conflict; this causes the group to fail to examine potential solutions fully and critically. Consequently, decisions made by these groups are often seriously flawed. Just because a decision turns out badly does not *automatically* mean the processes used to formulate the decision were poor. What makes a decision faulty due to groupthink is the failure to consider all the evidence *available at the time of the decision* that could alert decision makers to potential error.

The term *groupthink* was coined by Irving Janis, who has conducted extensive analyses of a variety of major decisions by groups of policy makers.[20] Janis compared two decisions by President John F. Kennedy's National Security Council. The first was a disaster; it was the 1961 decision to invade Cuba at the Bay of Pigs shortly after Fidel Castro had established a communist government there. The second is considered a model of effective group decision making; it was the 1963 decision to blockade Cuba when missile sites were discovered and ships with nuclear warheads to arm them were photographed on their way from the Soviet Union. Janis was intrigued by the fact that essentially the same group of people made decisions of such divergent quality. He found the reason *not* in the individual decision makers but in the *throughput process* they used. Groups making effective decisions and proposing high-quality alternatives are willing to engage in open conflict over the ideas, evidence, and reasoning presented in the group. They vigilantly test all information and ideas for soundness. Janis found that Kennedy's advisors did not thoroughly test information before making the Bay of Pigs decision, which explains how such well-educated, intelligent individuals, in the face of evidence to the contrary, *as a group* allowed such a stupid decision to be made.

Groupthink, a flawed group throughput process, manifests itself in the type of communication group members exhibit. Cline compared the conversations of groupthink and non-groupthink groups and found several surprising differences.[21] Although the levels of *disagreement* were similar in both sets of groups, the groupthink groups exhibited significantly higher levels of *agreement,* and these agreements were simple, unsubstantiated ones. Group members ended up making statements and agreeing with themselves. In contrast, the agreements exhibited in non-groupthink groups were substantive in nature, with different speakers providing different evidence and lines of reasoning to support their assertions. Cline believes that in groupthink, concern for positive relationships and cohesiveness overrides critical thinking.

Groupthink

Groupthink is a common phenomenon in government, business, and educational groups. It has been implicated in a number of disastrous policy decisions, including NASA's 1986 decision to launch the space shuttle Challenger, which exploded just after take-off.[22] It has also been linked to a number of clearly unethical decisions made in American business, including Beech-Nut's decision to market phony apple juice, E. F. Hutton's decision to kite checks, and Salomon Brothers' illegal bidding in Treasury auctions.[23] In all these decisions, it appears that group members had information that should have forewarned of them impending failure, but biases affected how they processed the information, and desire for harmony and cohesiveness was allowed to prevail over critical thinking. Thus, in groupthink an absence of critical thinking sabotages the decision-making process. To help you prevent groupthink, we next discuss symptoms of groupthink and show how you can combat this common tendency.

Symptoms of Groupthink

Groupthink is more likely to occur in highly cohesive groups under pressure to achieve consensus. It is particularly likely in groups experiencing time pressures and with leaders who have a preferred solution, which they attempt to promote.[24] The symptoms identified by Janis and others fall into three main categories:

1. **The group overestimates its power and morality.**
   A group may be so optimistic that it overestimates the chances for its programs to succeed. Student groups in our classes sometimes have become so excited about creative activities they have developed for a classroom presentation that they ignore the rest of the presentation by saying, "The instructor will love it—it's more imaginative than anything else other groups have done." Unfortunately, the imaginativeness is sometimes the only part of their presentation we instructors love! In addition, the group may have such an unquestioned belief in the inherent morality of the group that the group ignores potential ethical questions that should be raised. For example, the individuals behind the burglary of the Democratic National Headquarters, which eventually led to the Watergate hearings and President Nixon's resignation in disgrace, believed that they had a morally determined duty to protect the American public by gathering intelligence to help the president. Likewise, the National Security Council under President Reagan thought the cause of the Nicaraguan contras so right that circumventing the law was justified. Similarly, President Johnson's cabinet members believed that fighting in what was essentially a civil war in Vietnam was moral because they thought it would benefit the United States and the world.

2. **The group becomes closed-minded.**
   Either a high-status leader or the group has a preferred solution, and the group closes itself off to any information contrary to this preferred course of action. A group may also stereotype outside figures who disagree so it doesn't have to pay attention to what they might have to say. NASA officials were so biased in favor of launching that they ignored or devalued information provided by engineers who opposed the Challenger launch. In the Beech-Nut case,

Figure 12.2 Groupthink in action.

company officials wanted to buy apple juice at the lowest possible cost. The
suppliers with the lowest juice prices were those most likely to be selling
phony or impure juice. Beech-Nut officials, rather than demanding that
suppliers prove their apple juice was pure, shifted the burden of proof to *their
own research and development personnel* to prove that an inexpensive
supplier's product *was not* pure before the company would switch to a
different supplier. Beech-Nut stuck to this policy even when threatened by
consumer lawsuits. Some student groups are so relieved when they arrive at
any solution to a problem that they fail to test their decision for effectiveness,
thereby producing a mediocre product.

3. **Group members experience pressures to conform.**
    Pressure to conform manifests itself in a variety of ways. First, members
    censor their own remarks, exemplified in figure 12.2. If you think everyone
    else in the group is in favor of a proposal, you will normally tend to suppress
    your own doubts and fears. Second, the group members have a shared illusion
    of unanimity, manifested by the amount of simple agreement discovered by
    Cline. Because individuals do not express doubts openly, the members think
    they all agree. Consensus is assumed rather than obtained.[25] Third, a member
    who does venture a contradictory opinion is likely to experience direct pressure
    from the rest of the group to conform: "Why are you being so negative, Jim?
    The rest of us think it's a good idea." This makes it obvious to the dissenting
    member that disagreement is perceived as disloyalty. Also, the group may
    have a number of self-appointed *mindguards* who protect the group from
    mental threats, just as bodyguards do from physical threats. For example, a

member who deliberately prevents dissonant information from reaching the group—by stopping outsiders from addressing the group, by failing to mention contrasting points of view contained in research materials, and so forth—acts as a mindguard, withholding *all* contradictory material from the group's consideration. Finally, in groups that adhere to strict status differences within the group, lower-status members are less likely to contradict higher-status members, and will avoid issues they think may produce conflict.[26]

Conformity pressures are especially dangerous when a group *must* achieve consensus. The need for consensus can lead to an "agreement norm," which curtails disagreement, ultimately causing the group to suffer.[27] Agreement reached under the duress of such a norm is only a surface consensus, not a decision deeply supported by all members as the best the entire group can back.

These symptoms of groupthink indicate that a group will probably make an incomplete survey of the information and options at its disposal, as well as a less than thorough assessment of the information and ideas. The group's search and assessment procedures are biased. We hope you can see from this discussion that group problem solving, decision making, and conflict management are linked. High-quality decision making and effective problem solving depend on members using the best critical thinking skills they can muster; in turn, critical thinking requires open and honest disagreement to reach its highest potential.

Preventing Groupthink

The designated leader of a group has a dual responsibility for building team spirit while at the same time doing everything possible to ensure full evaluation of all information and ideas presented to the group. The following suggestions for combating the tendency toward groupthink are designed to help the leader perform this difficult balancing act.

1. **Assign the role of critical evaluator to each member or establish a subgroup to serve that capacity.**
   Each member must feel responsible for helping the group achieve the best possible solution. For instance, Kroon et al. found that making members collectively accountable for the group decision counteracted two antecedents of groupthink, the group's insulation and the leader's promotion of a preferred alternative, especially for male groups.[28] However, just *saying* this to the members will not make it happen. Group leaders must make sure by their actions that critical evaluation is more important than apparent harmony or deference to the leader's position. Leaders must learn to *welcome* criticism of their own ideas and proposals, thereby modeling for the other members a willingness to be influenced by reason and evidence. For example, the president of a university where one of us worked had an advisory council established in part for this purpose. Council members were elected or appointed to represent each area of the university. At one point, the president

proposed a major reorganization of the university and invited the council to review his plan critically. The council tore the plan to shreds. The plan was eventually implemented with substantial changes, which improved it immeasurably. Had the president attempted to put the proposal into effect without first asking for and obtaining criticism, it would have failed.

Similarly, a structured group procedure called **devil's advocacy** can institutionalize the critical evaluation function within a group.[29] The procedure is as follows:

1. The group is split into two subgroups, the proposal (P) group and the devil's advocate (DA) group. Each subgroup discusses the problem separately.
2. The P group develops a set of recommendations or a solution to the problem and builds an argument for it. The group presents the recommendations, both orally and in writing, to the DA group.
3. The DA group critiques the recommendations (even if members initially agree with them). The critique is presented to the P group both orally and in writing. DA members make no recommendations of their own; they simply critique the P group's work.
4. The P group revamps the recommendations and presents them again, orally and in writing, to the DA group, which proceeds as before.
5. This process is repeated until both groups can accept the recommendations, assumptions, facts, and data. Acceptance can occur when the DA group finds nothing to object to in the recommendations, or when the P group cannot refute the criticisms.

Even if a group does not use this structured devil's advocacy procedure, members should feel free to question and challenge information presented by other members. It may be helpful to assign one or two people the specific *devil's advocate* role. If members know that Mona has been assigned this role for a particular meeting, they are more likely to view her criticisms as being part of her job and less likely to take them personally.

2. **Leaders should refrain from stating their preferences at the outset of a decision-making or problem-solving session.**

Janis found that one of the major forces leading to the Bay of Pigs decision was President Kennedy's own referent power. Kennedy's advisors admired and respected him so much that they were reluctant to criticize his ideas. Even leaders who do not have Kennedy's charisma have significant power stemming from the sources discussed in chapter 8. For example, Anderson and Balzer found that when a leader expresses an opinion early during a discussion, the group generates significantly fewer alternatives, which are less likely to be adopted by the group.[30] It is typical for members to defer to the wishes of a designated leader. However, this impairs the decision-making process, which at its most effective is based on an exhaustive search for options and vigilant appraisal of them.

3. **Leaders can establish two or more independent subgroups to work on the same problem.**

The competition of rival subcommittees may spur each of the groups to a greater effort on behalf of the full committee. Moreover, each subcommittee is likely to think of ideas, solutions, and possible consequences the other subgroup failed to consider. **Dialectical Inquiry (DI)** is another structured procedure for accomplishing such helpful competition:[31]

1. The larger group is split into two relatively equal-sized groups. Each group discusses the problem separately.
2. Group A then develops recommendations and arguments for them, including explaining the assumptions, facts, and data that underlie all the recommendations. A member of group A presents the recommendations and assumptions in writing to group B.
3. Group B then develops plausible assumptions that *negate* those presented by group A, even if group B's members initially agree with group A's proposal. Using these new assumptions, group B then develops recommendations that counter group A's.
4. The groups then meet together. First group A explains its recommendations and assumptions to the other; group B then does the same. The groups debate the merits and validity of each other's assumptions, with the goal of arriving at assumptions acceptable to all members.
5. The whole group now works with the accepted assumptions to develop the final recommendations.

The clash between competing subgroups often sparks creative and novel solutions, as well as highlighting potential flaws.

4. **Leaders should take whatever steps are needed to prevent insulation of the group.**

Sometimes a group can be so cohesive it fails to consider that others may perceive situations differently. A committee to which one of us belonged developed a sweeping proposal to alter the undergraduate curriculum. Group members had worked together for an entire year, carrying each other along on their enthusiasm and commitment. However, because they were so caught up in their own shared vision, they failed to consider some implications of their proposal for other faculty, who greeted the recommendations with dismay. The group had become insulated from external opinion.

Leaders can take several steps to offset insularity. They can encourage members to get feedback on tentative proposals from trusted associates outside the group, then report back to the group. Had the faculty committee done this, it would not have been surprised at the proposal's reception. Leaders can also arrange for outside experts to discuss their views with the group, thereby helping to ensure a broadly based foundation for making the decision.

We hope we have convinced you of the value of substantive conflict during small group problem solving. Conflict is inevitable when people meet in groups. Avoiding it *circumvents the very reason for engaging in group discussion*—that the thinking of several people is likely to be more valid and thorough than the thinking of one person acting alone. Both the attitudes of group members involved in a conflict and the procedures they use to manage the conflict affect the outcomes. Using further examples of the Speaker Series committee, we discuss both attitudes and procedures that facilitate productive conflict.

Managing Conflict

Most people have a basic attitude or approach toward managing conflict, either *distributive* or *integrative.* The **distributive approach,** also called a *win-lose* attitude, assumes that what one person gains is at another's expense. Thus, there can be only one winning side; the other or others are losers. For example, Tony and Kevin want to choose an entertaining speaker and Deidre and Lori want an educational one. The distributive orientation assumes that only one faction can win. *Either* Tony and Kevin get their entertaining speaker, *or* Lori and Deidre get their educational one. Whichever wins, the other side loses.

Basic Approaches
Toward Conflict
Management

The **integrative approach** assumes that there is some way to manage the conflict so all parties can end up winners; in other words, the main concerns of all parties can be integrated into a solution in which all involved receive what is most important to them. Someone with an integrative orientation would assume that a speaker could be found who is *both* entertaining *and* educational; thus, both factions can win. This approach has also been called a *win-win* attitude.

It may not be possible to integrate the concerns of all members into the group's final solution or decision. Perhaps members' values are so divergent they cannot be merged, or maybe resources are so scarce that needs cannot be fully met. In such cases, perhaps partial integration—*compromise*—is the best that can be achieved. However, even if a group does not develop a fully integrative solution, it *certainly* will not develop one if members begin with the premise that integration is impossible. Without an integrative orientation, members will not expend their energies to develop creative solutions but will spend time quarreling about the merits of one proposal over another in an attempt to *win* rather than find the best solution possible.

Your level of desire to cooperate determines in part how you deal with conflict. The specific style you choose is likely to be a product both of how cooperative and how assertive you are.[32] Figure 12.3 shows how these two underlying dimensions produce five common conflict management styles. (The model assumes dyadic conflict for simplicity's sake.)

Conflict
Management
Styles

While no conflict style is always best, some conflict styles are perceived as more appropriate in certain circumstances. Canary and Spitzberg found, for example, that the topic of the conflict interacted with gender of the participants to influence perceptions of both effectiveness and appropriateness.[33] We recommend a

Figure 12.3
Your conflict management style depends in part on how assertive and cooperative you are.

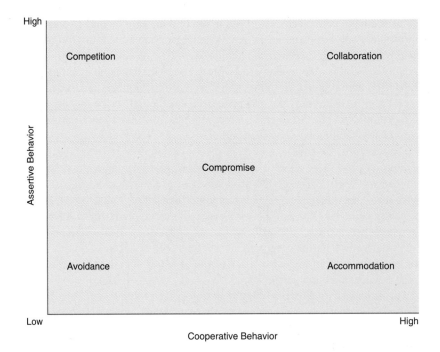

contingency view in which the most productive way for settling a conflict depends on time pressures, distribution of information and skills, group member values and needs, and other input variables. While each conflict style is appropriate under certain circumstances, the integrative approach is always acceptable in problem-solving discussions.

Avoidance

The **avoidance** style is a passive approach where a participant expends no energy discussing or exploring options. The member who disagrees but says nothing is avoiding conflict. Sometimes called *nonconfrontation,* conflict avoidance reduces satisfaction in groups.[34] Such passive behavior is appropriate only when the problem is unimportant and the risks of making a poor decision are slight. For example, a committee to which one of us belonged was asked to develop a decorating plan for a student lounge/study area. The art instructor on the committee recommended a color scheme not particularly appealing to the chemistry professor on the committee. The students liked the colors, so the chemistry professor kept his objections to himself. He reasoned that because he spent so little time in the lounge, color did not matter much to him.

Accommodation

Accommodation, also called *appeasement,* is a highly cooperative but passive approach that occurs when you give in to someone else. It may occur when the issue is not important to you, or when the relationship is more important to you than the outcome. For instance, in the Speaker Series committee, after a brief discussion about educational versus entertaining speakers, Tony said, "I can go along with an educational speaker. I just want to avoid this arguing." Tony wants to accommodate in order to end the arguments. Accommodation is appropriate only when the issue is relatively unimportant to you or the other person's needs are genuinely more important to you, but don't accommodate just to end a fight, for the resentment you carry around with you may eventually poison the relationship anyway.

Competition is a highly aggressive, uncooperative style where one person tries to win over another. Sometimes called *dominating* or *forcing,* competition is appropriate when you have strong beliefs about something *and* you perceive that other approaches will not allow your needs to be acknowledged or accommodated. However, competitive approaches can damage relationships and may end up doing more harm than good. In the Speaker Series committee, Lori and Kevin competed. Lori threatened to quit the group if only entertaining speakers were chosen, and Kevin told Tony not to accommodate so readily because he, Kevin, had plenty of good arguments left in support of entertaining speakers. Both statements imply that the speaker will do whatever is necessary to get his or her way. *Competition*

Collaboration, also called *negotiating* or *problem solving,* is a cooperative and assertive style that stems from an integrative attitude. It encourages all parties to a conflict to work together in searching for a solution that meets everyone's needs. In the Speaker Series committee, Deidre suggested that the committee look for a speaker who is both entertaining and educational. In doing this, she assumed that both important needs of the factions could be met without either faction having to give up anything, that each faction's "must have" point could be accommodated. Collaborative solutions can be ideal because all members of groups that arrive at collaborative solutions believe they have won without the others having lost. However, collaboration often takes more time than other approaches and certainly takes more energy. *Collaboration*

A **compromise,** also called a *shared* outcome, assumes that each party to the conflict will have to give up something in order to gain something more important. In the Speaker Series committee, Chris suggested a compromise when he said, "Maybe we can get two speakers, less expensive, one educational and one entertaining." Each faction would have to agree to give up the idea of bringing in one very well-known speaker. Thus, compromises entail some losses for both parties. For this reason, we recommend attempting to find a collaborative, fully integrative solution when the decision is important to all group members, where each member will be responsible for implementing the outcome, and where the group is not pressed for time. *Compromise*

However, we think compromise should *not* be considered a dirty word! When collaborative resolution is impossible or takes more time than is available, a compromise is a desirable and ethical outcome, especially if each group member feels that what he or she had to give up is fair in comparison with what others had to give up.

Expressing
Disagreements
Ethically

Ethical behaviors in conflict situations are those that promote the beneficial outcomes of conflict (e.g., greater understanding of issues, increased cohesiveness)
while minimizing the destructive outcomes (e.g., hurt feelings, personal attacks).
The following suggestions will help members behave with integrity and sensitivity
during conflicts:

1. **Do express your disagreement.**

   We have already noted that not confronting disagreements reduces satisfaction
   with the group, and failure to express honest disagreement circumvents the
   decision-making and problem-solving process in a group. By not speaking up
   when you disagree, you deprive the group of potentially valuable information.
   In a sense you deceive, because your silence suggests that you agree.

2. **Stick with the issue at hand.**

   Kreps suggests that when you disagree, you should deal directly with the issue
   under discussion. Do not bring up side issues or allow hidden agenda items to
   motivate you.[35] To do so is as unethical as to use irrelevant emotional stories to
   arouse support.

3. **Use rhetorical sensitivity in expressing your disagreement.**

   Be sensitive and perceptive enough to select words that will not connote
   negative images. Especially do not try to push others' emotional buttons. This
   means monitoring the effects of your statements on others and adjusting as
   appropriate. Use persuasion, not threats, to make your points.[36] Being
   rhetorically sensitive also means you'll follow the next ethical guideline.

4. **Disagree with the idea but do not ever criticize the person.**

   Express disagreement so that it does not devalue the person with whom you
   disagree. Individuals would rather have someone disagree honestly with them
   than disconfirm and ignore them. Members of groups with norms for
   expressing conflict cooperatively and integratively are more satisfied with the
   group's process and outcome than members of groups with norms for
   competitive and distributive expression of conflict.[37] Thus, "One flaw in your
   proposal to shut down the snack bar is that it does not consider the food service
   needs of evening students," is far superior to: "You inconsiderate bozo! What
   are the evening students supposed to do?" Above all, no name calling or
   personal attacks!

5. **Base your disagreement on evidence and reasoning.**

   Kreps notes that disagreements should be reasonable and substantive, based on
   evidence and reasoning.[38] They should not be based on rumor, innuendo,
   unsubstantiated information, or emotionalism. If you have no evidence or your
   reasoning is shown to be potentially faulty, *agree* instead of quarreling. As
   much as possible, keep the conflict issue-based.

6. **React to disagreement with a spirit of inquiry, not defensiveness.**

   Alderton and Frey believe that group members' reactions to argument are more
   important than the arguments themselves in creating group polarization.[39] If
   someone disagrees with you, do not react defensively as though you had been

attacked personally. Keep your mind open to others' ideas, evaluations, and suggestions. Listen actively to your fellow member's remarks. Be certain that the person disagreeing has understood your position correctly, then clarify any misunderstandings, and work together to search for the most effective solutions. In this way you can make conflict work *for* rather than *against* the group. This may not be easy, but it will benefit the group and you will have a clear conscience.

7. **If someone persists in attacking *you*, stay calm and speak reasonably.**
   One of the biggest challenges a group member has is to respond to a personal attack by another. The worst thing you can do is let another's attacks intimidate you into being silent! Instead, confront the attacking member calmly and reasonably, explaining how you feel and what you want the other to do: "I resent your personal attacks, and I think they are inappropriate. I am willing to listen to your objections, but I want you to stop your attacks now." If the attacker was caught up in the heat of the moment, he or she may apologize and calm down. If your initial confrontation doesn't succeed, ask for the *group's* intervention: "Do we all think personal attacks are acceptable behavior?" The other members, who probably are as uncomfortable as you, will now be encouraged to support you in confronting the attacker.

8. **Use an integrative rather than a distributive approach to solving the conflict.**
   Assume that there is a way to satisfy, at least partially, the important needs of all parties to the conflict. Use your energy to search for alternatives that integrate all parties' needs, not to destroy the other party. Act in ways that improve, not damage, the relationship. Remember that a solution satisfying all parties will be more lasting than one leaving one party feeling disgruntled or mistreated. Also, consider the ethics of a person who gains pleasure from beating another in a way that damages the *group*.

No matter how skilled at expressing disagreement and how ethical, group members can still crash on the rocks of conflict if their procedures are poor. We have selected five procedures for managing stubborn conflicts, in order of preference.

A task-oriented group experiencing a conflict must move toward resolution for the group's goals to be accomplished. There are a variety of techniques designed to help groups resolve conflict. We especially like the *principled negotiation* procedure because it is consistent with all the ethical principles we have outlined above and is an extremely effective procedure that helps a group negotiate consensus from initially divergent points of view. As described by Fisher and Ury, **principled negotiation** is an all-purpose strategy that encourages all participants in a conflict situation to collaborate by expressing their needs and searching for alternatives that meet those needs.[40] It is called "principled" because it is based on ethical principles that encourage users to remain decent individuals and not act in ways that will damage the relationship among them. It puts the integrative approach into effect.

Negotiating
Principled
Agreement

Principled negotiation is an efficient and fair way to develop a solution meeting the legitimate needs of all parties; therefore, it is likely to produce lasting solutions. Tutzauer and Roloff say the guidelines in the principled negotiation procedure are consistent with their discoveries about communication behaviors that produce integrative outcomes.[41] They found that exchanging information, asking questions instead of making demands, and foregoing rigid, inflated positions helped bargainers attain integrative outcomes. Appropriate communication techniques alone helped bargainers attain integrative outcomes regardless of their initial orientations. In addition, this type of negotiation will not harm the relationship among participants and frequently improves it. We particularly like it because it recognizes the major elements that enter into conflict—perceptions, emotions, behaviors, and interaction among individuals—and acknowledges that each must be considered. The following description of principled negotiation shows how a group can incorporate the communication principles presented throughout this book, including such concepts as rhetorical sensitivity, active listening, and integrative conflict management, into a practical, effective technique for managing conflict. The group leader, an outside consultant, or members themselves can use the procedure. Here are the four steps:

1. **Separate the people from the problem.**
   In most conflicts, the content of the disagreement becomes tangled with the relationship among the participants. Each should be dealt with directly and separately. All parties should be given the opportunity to explain, without interference, how they perceive the conflict and how they feel about it. For example, parties should share perceptions as they try to put themselves into each other's shoes. If emotions run high, allow them to be vented. Do not overreact to emotional outbursts, but listen actively and show by your actions as well as your words that you care about the needs of the other members with whom your interests conflict. The goal is not to become bosom buddies with the other party to a conflict (although that may happen), but to develop a good working relationship characterized by mutual respect.[42]

2. **Focus on interests, not positions.**
   When group members stake out certain positions ("I insist that we have an educational speaker!"), they become attached to those *positions* rather than the original *needs* the positions were designed to meet. For example, we discussed earlier the committee that debated closing the food service facility at 5:00 P.M. One side's position was that the snack bar must be closed, but the other side's position was that the snack bar must be kept open. These two positions are incompatible, and there is no way to reconcile them—in their present form, one must win and one must lose. However, when group members started to explore the *interests* behind the positions (the desire to save money and the desire to meet needs of evening students), then an avenue opened whereby both parties could have their desires met by finding a way to do *both simultaneously*—provide the students with food without raising costs. However, rigidly adhering to the initial positions precludes the discovery of this solution.

3. **Invent options for mutual gain.**

The previous example illustrates how a new option, vending service, was created that had not been apparent when the conflict started. We earlier have suggested separating the invention process from the decision process, and employing techniques like brainstorming. Negotiators should assume that the interests of all parties can be integrated into the group's final solution. For example, the same committee that debated food service options for evening students also discussed how evening students could be served by the bookstore.[43] The evening student advisor on the committee noted that the campus bookstore was open in the evenings only during the first week of the quarter. Many evening students who drove directly to campus from work could not arrive early enough for the bookstore's regular hours, and so were unable to exchange books, purchase supplies, or even browse. The advisor proposed that the bookstore hours be extended to 8:00 P.M. every evening. The campus budget officer objected strongly, noting that the proposal would result in cost increases for personnel salaries unlikely to be recovered by purchases made by evening students. Thus, the positions adopted by each person represented attempts to meet the legitimate needs of two important groups: the evening students and the budget watchdogs. However, through open discussion focused on the interests (not the positions) of each, a solution was invented that incorporated both sets of needs. The bookstore would remain open two evenings per week throughout the quarter, and would start business later in the morning the rest of the week. The total number of hours of bookstore operation was the same, so costs were not increased, but the distribution of the hours changed to meet the needs of more students.

4. **Use objective criteria.**

Negotiations will be perceived as fairer if objective criteria *agreed upon by all parties* are established as the standard for judging alternatives. Group members will profit from establishing such criteria at the beginning of any problem-solving session, but they should *insist* on it in prolonged conflicts because such criteria make negotiation less likely to be a contest of wills and more likely to be settled upon principle instead of pressure. This is an egalitarian approach in that much of the battle for dominance is removed from the negotiation process. For example, many people use the *Bluebook* to determine a fair price for used cars. You may want $5,000 for your ten-year-old Nissan Sentra, and your buyer may want to pay only $100. However, if both of you agree that the *Bluebook* is an appropriate standard and it indicates that a fair price is $800 to $1,500, depending on model and condition, this narrows the negotiating range between you and makes reaching agreement more likely.

In another example, the United Way organization of a major midwestern city nearly disintegrated as a result of arguments over which agencies should receive money. Finally, the *ad hoc* committee established a set of cost accounting procedures enabling each agency to determine how many people could be served for what amount. These procedures then served as relatively objective criteria for United Way to use in determining which agencies to fund.

Sometimes, despite a group's best intentions, even principled negotiation fails to bring about consensus, or a group is operating under a time deadline that forces members to use other methods.

When Negotiation Fails: Alternative Procedures

Settlements derived through negotiation by the group itself are preferable to solutions imposed by someone else because they tend to be more acceptable to all members. The first two alternatives involve the group in breaking a deadlock. However, sometimes a group simply is not able to break a deadlock. In that case, when a decision *must* be made, the designated leader has two remaining options.

Mediation by the Designated Leader

If a seemingly irreconcilable conflict emerges over goals or alternatives, the leader might suggest the following procedure, which is an abbreviated form of that used by professional mediators for apparently deadlocked negotiations between a union and management. The procedure represents a last-chance group attempt to arrive at an acceptable decision without resorting to third-party arbitration. If this procedure fails, other alternative procedures can be taken to resolve the conflict issue without producing consensus. Two-sided conflict is assumed for simplicity.

1. Presentation of Alternatives
   a. A proponent of side 1 presents exactly what the subgroup wants or believes and *why*. Other members supporting the position may add clarifying statements, arguments, evidence, and claims, but proponents of side 2 can say *nothing*.
   b. Side 2 can now *ask* for clarification, restatements, explanations, or supporting evidence, but may *not* disagree, argue, or propose any other alternative.
   c. A spokesperson for side 2 is now required to explain side 1's position to the complete satisfaction of all other group members, both side 1 and side 2. (Note the similarity to active listening presented in chapter 4.) Only when this person has restated side 1's proposal and supporting arguments to everyone's satisfaction is the group ready to advance to the next step.
   d. Side 2's position is now presented by a spokesperson. Exactly the same procedural rules apply as during presentation and clarification of side 1's position.
2. Charting Alternatives
   a. The designated group leader now writes both positions on a chalkboard or large poster and underneath lists *pros* (benefits, advantages) claimed by its proponents and evidence advanced in its support. Under the heading *cons* the leader should list any disadvantages, possible harmful effects, or evidence advanced against the alternative. An example of such a chart is shown in figure 12.4.
   b. When all positions have been charted, the group may want to see whether there is unanimity about any of the statements on the chart. What, if anything, do members agree upon?

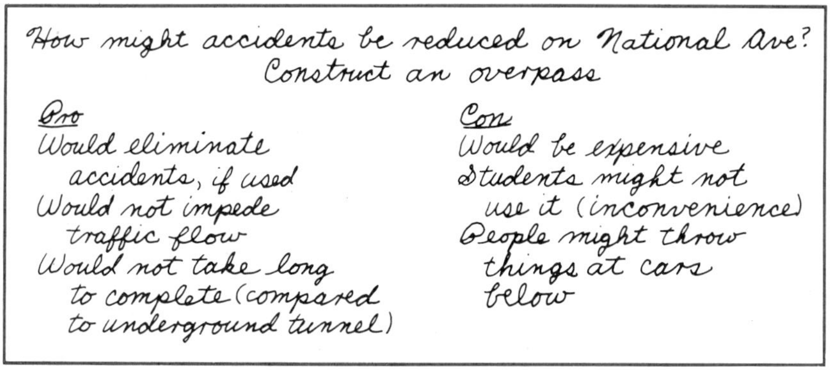

Figure 12.4
Example of a chart
of pros and cons.

3. Search for Creative Alternatives
   a. The designated leader reviews all elements of common ground shared by all group members, such as shared interest in solving the problem, shared history of the group, and so forth, then urges group members to seek a win-win resolution, an alternative all could accept. The leader may propose such a solution, or;
   b. The designated leader asks members to compromise and create an alternative that meets the minimum requirements of both sides.
4. Resolution occurs when and if a consensus or compromise alternative is adopted.

If this procedure is successful, some time should be spent by group members discussing the procedure itself, how they feel about the group and each of the other members, and how the group can manage future conflicts. Generally, when the previously described procedure is followed out of a sincere desire to resolve the conflict, the group will find at least a compromise and will develop increased cohesiveness and team spirit. Lacking a consensus or compromise, other procedures will be needed to reach a decision.

Voting is one such alternative procedure. Naturally, some members are bound to dislike the outcome, but voting may be a necessary step in overcoming an impasse. You may recall the example presented earlier where a faculty subcommittee presented a sweeping proposal to the full faculty committee, only to be met with dismay instead of enthusiasm. After repeated attempts to develop an integrative solution failed, the committee took a vote to decide the issue. One danger with voting is that the group may arrive at premature closure on an issue. Be especially careful, if this is the option you select, that the group really *is* deadlocked.

Voting

Another option is *forcing*. Here, the leader breaks the deadlock and decides on behalf of the group. For example, in the U.S. Senate the presiding officer can break a tie. As with voting, several members are likely to be disappointed, but in instances where an outside group, parent organization, or legitimate authority demands a report or where the group faces a deadline, a leader may have little choice.

Forcing

Third-Party
Arbitration

Third-party arbitration occurs when the group brings in an outside negotiator to re-solve its differences. This typically happens with joint labor-management disputes and some court-related cases. Arbitrators often have the power to resolve issues any way they please, from deciding entirely in favor of one party to splitting the differ-ence between them. Sometimes, just the threat of bringing in a third-party arbitrator is enough to force conflict participants to negotiate with each other in good faith. Usually, all parties to the conflict end up feeling dissatisfied. Thus, third-party arbi-tration should be proposed only when the leader believes the group has reached an impasse and the cost of continuing the conflict, including resentment and the possi-bility of destroying the group, will exceed the cost of arbitration. Of course, group members must agree to such a resolution procedure.

Summary

When group members use critical thinking skills, conflict is inevitable as members discuss a variety of alternatives and evaluate these alternatives from their differing perceptions, goals, values, and preferences. Conflict occurs when interdependent parties perceive incompatible goals, scarce resources, and interference in achiev-ing their goals and express this struggle outwardly. It has perceptual, emotional, behavioral, and interactional dimensions. Although conflict can cause bad feel-ings, lower cohesiveness, or group disintegration, it can also stimulate member involvement and understanding, increase cohesiveness, and produce better deci-sions. In spite of the hesitancy members may feel in expressing opinions and ideas deviant from other group members, only by being willing to risk this are the potential benefits of conflict derived for the group. Types of conflict include sub-stantive (task-oriented), affective (over personality and power differences), proce-dural (over how the group operates), and inequity (over unequal workloads or contributions by members). These types overlap, with one potentially leading to another in an actual conflict situation.

Groupthink occurs when groups suppress the conflict inherent in a thorough search for an evaluation of options and potential solutions. Symptoms of groupthink include a group's overestimation of its power and morality, closed-mindedness, and covert and overt pressures to conform. To combat these tendencies, leaders are ad-vised to assign the role of critical evaluator to each member, refrain from stating their own preferences at the outset of a group's deliberations, and take all steps nec-essary to prevent the isolation of the group from all relevant opinions. Devil's ad-vocacy and dialectical inquiry are two procedures useful for helping a group counteract groupthink.

A distributive orientation to managing conflict assumes there must be a win-ner and a loser. In contrast, an integrative (cooperative) orientation assumes that the needs of all parties can be integrated into a solution that satisfies all mem-bers. Degree of cooperation and assertiveness are variables that underlie the five common conflict management strategies of avoidance, accommodation (giving in), competition (fighting to win), collaboration (searching for an alternative that satisfies everyone), and compromise (assuming that each party will have to give up something to gain something more important). Each style is appropriate under certain circumstances.

Several ethical principles govern appropriate behavior in managing conflict. Members should express their views in a sensitive way and focus on the issues at hand, not on hidden agenda items. They should express disagreement with the idea but not attack the person or ever indulge in name-calling. Disagreements should be based on substance and fact, not innuendo and rumor. When disagreed with, members should react with a spirit of inquiry rather than defensiveness and remain open-minded to contradictory ideas. Finally, members should avoid fight-to-the-death conflict resolution strategies. *Principled negotiation* is a procedure that incorporates these ethical principles by helping parties find a satisfactory solution while not harming the relationship. Steps include separating the people from the problem, focusing on interests instead of positions, inventing options for mutual gain, and using objective criteria. If a group still cannot achieve consensus, the leader can use a mediation procedure that involves presenting the alternatives, charting the pros and cons, and searching for creative alternatives. Failing this, the group may resort to voting, forcing, or third-party arbitration to resolve a stubborn conflict.

Exercises

1. Select a group to which you now belong. Try to remember all the recent conflicts or disagreements experienced by the group. On paper, briefly describe each conflict, indicate what type it was, and explain how it was settled. Use the following format:

Description of conflict	Type of conflict	How conflict was resolved

2. Think of an extended conflict you observed or were involved in. Analyze it according to the perceptions-emotions-behavior-interaction model.
   a. How did each element of the model affect each other element?
   b. What was the relationship of the conflicting parties to each other at the *beginning* of the conflict episode and at the *end?*
   c. What do you conclude about conflict from this?
   d. Would you do anything differently if you were faced with the same situation again?

3. Your instructor should give you a problem or case study that asks you to develop a solution or proposal about an important campus or community topic that will affect a number of people. Form into groups of five or six and practice using either the devil's advocacy or dialectical inquiry procedures to develop the best possible solution to the problem.

4. Select a controversial issue for your class about which there are two or more contrasting positions. Form into discussion groups of four or five so that at least two people initially are on each side of the issue. Two classmates should

serve as observers for each group of discussants. Discuss the issue and attempt to come to some consensus. Observers should note and report on the following:

   a. What was said about the issue?

   b. How were disagreements expressed?

   c. Were there any ways that disagreement could have been expressed more appropriately? (The observers should pay particular attention to the effect on the *receiver* of the disagreeing remarks.)

5. Your class should split into dyads with one nonparticipating observer per dyad. One dyad partner should play the role of quality control manager and the other that of production manager in a manufacturing plant. Assume the production manager wants to get the quality control manager to reject fewer items so that production can be increased. Half the groups should be instructed to negotiate with a distributive orientation and half with an integrative one. Observers should note and report *exactly* what was said in attempting to settle the conflict and what appeared to be the effect. Discuss how you felt in your particular situation. Were there any consistent differences in the feelings of the participants in the two assigned orientations? What did you learn from this activity?

6. Select a controversial public issue with at least two sides. In groups or dyads, explain how you would use the principled negotiation procedure to help the competing sides resolve their differences:

   a. Imagine how people from each side feel about the situation and what their perceptions might be of themselves and people from the opposite side.

   b. First, describe, the positions of each side. Then determine what might be the needs or interests behind the positions.

   c. Determine whether there are any interests that might be compatible, and brainstorm options that bring these common interests together.

   d. Determine whether there are any objective criteria that could be used to help the parties resolve their conflict, and show how these criteria might be used.

Discuss your findings and suggestions as a whole class. What did you learn by using the principled negotiation procedure?

7. Your instructor should give you a union-management case to discuss. Select seven people from your class to act out the case—three to role-play the union team, three the management team, and one the third-party negotiator. Have this group go through the three-step mediation process under the direction of the negotiator, while the rest of the class observes and takes notes. What worked well? What worked poorly? Do you have any specific advice for the negotiator? What would you have done differently?

Bibliography

Fisher, Roger and Scott Brown. *Getting Together: Building a Relationship that Gets to Yes.* Boston: Houghton-Mifflin Company, 1988.

Fisher, Roger and William Ury. *Getting to Yes: Negotiating Agreement Without Giving In.* New York: Penguin Books, 1983.

Hocker, Joyce L. and William W. Wilmot. *Interpersonal Conflict.* 3d ed. Dubuque, IA: Wm. C. Brown Publishers, 1991.

Janis, Irving L. *Groupthink: Psychological Studies of Policy Decisions and Fiascoes.* 2d ed. Boston: Houghton-Mifflin Company, 1983.

Putnam, Linda L. "Conflict in Group Decision Making." In *Communication and Group Decision Making.* Eds. Randy Y. Hirokawa and Marshall Scott Poole. Beverly Hills, CA: Sage Publications, 1986, 175–97.

Notes

1. Carolyn J. Wood, "Challenging the Assumptions Underlying the Use of Participatory Decision-Making Strategies: A Longitudinal Case Study," *Small Group Behavior* 20 (1989): 428–48.

2. Victor D. Wall, Jr., Gloria J. Galanes, and Susan B. Love, "Small, Task-Oriented Groups: Conflict, Conflict Management, Satisfaction, and Decision Quality," *Small Group Behavior* 18 (1987): 31–55.

3. M. R. Shakun, "Formalizing Conflict Resolution in Policy-Making," *International Journal of General Systems* 7 (1981): 207–15.

4. Gordon L. Lippett, "Managing Conflict in Today's Organization, *Training and Development Journal* 36 (1982): 67–75.

5. Joyce L. Hocker and William W. Wilmot, *Interpersonal Conflict,* 3d ed. (Dubuque, IA: Wm. C. Brown Publishers, 1991): 12.

6. Morton Deutsch, "Conflicts: Productive and Destructive," *Journal of Social Issues* 25 (1969): 7–41; Kenneth W. Thomas, "Conflict and Conflict Management," in *Handbook of Industrial and Organizational Psychology,* ed. M. Dunnette (Chicago: Rand McNally, 1976): 890–934; Louis B. Pondy, "Organizational Conflict: Concepts and Models," *Administrative Science Quarterly* 12 (1976): 296–320; Brent D. Ruben, "Communication and Conflict: A System-Theoretic Perspective," *Quarterly Journal of Speech* 64 (1978): 202–12; J. Guetzkow and J. Gyr, "An Analysis of Conflict in Decision-Making Groups," *Human Relations* 7 (1954): 367–82; E. P. Torrance, "Group Decision-Making and Disagreement," *Social Forces* 35 (1957): 314–18.

7. Karl Smith, David W. Johnson, and Roger T. Johnson, "Can Conflict Be Constructive? Controversy versus Concurrence Seeking in Learning Groups," *Journal of Educational Psychology* 73 (1981): 654–63.

8. Sue D. Pendell, "Deviance and Conflict in Small Group Decision Making: An Exploratory Study," *Small Group Behavior* 21 (1990): 393–403.

9. Svenn Lindskold and Gyuseog Han, "Group Resistance to Influence by a Conciliatory Member," *Small Group Behavior* 19 (1988): 19–34.

10. Carl L. Thameling and Patricia H. Andrews, "Majority Responses to Opinion Deviates: A Communicative Analysis," *Small Group Research* 23 (1992): 475–502.

11. Kristin B. Valentine and B. Aubrey Fisher, "An Interaction Analysis of Verbal Innovative Deviance in Small Groups," *Speech Monographs* 41 (1974): 413–20.

12. Mark K. Covey, "The Relationship between Social Skill and Conflict Resolution Tactics," (Paper presented at the annual convention of the Rocky Mountain Psychological Association, Snowbird, Utah, 1983).

13. The conflict described in the following episode and used as the extended example here is segment 2 of the videotape ancillary to this text, *Communicating Effectively in Small Groups* (Dubuque, IA: Wm. C. Brown Publishers, 1991).

14. Guetzkow and Gyr, "An Analysis of Conflict," 367–82.

15. Guetzkow and Gyr, "An Analysis of Conflict," 367–82.

16. Roger C. Pace, "Personalized and Depersonalized Conflict in Small Group Discussions: An Examination of Differentiation," *Small Group Research* 21 (1990): 79–96.

17. Roger Fisher and Scott Brown, *Getting Together: Building a Relationship That Gets to Yes* (Boston: Houghton-Mifflin, 1988): 16–23.

18. Linda L. Putnam, "Conflict in Group Decision Making," in *Communication and Group Decision-Making,* eds. Randy Y. Hirokawa and Marshall Scott Poole (Beverly Hills, CA: Sage Publications, 1986): 175–96.

19. Victor D. Wall, Jr., and Linda L. Nolan, "Small Group Conflict: A Look at Equity, Satisfaction, and Styles of Conflict Management," *Small Group Behavior* 18 (1987): 188–211.

20. Irving L. Janis, *Groupthink: Psychological Studies of Policy Decisions and Fiascoes,* 2d ed. (Boston: Houghton-Mifflin Company, 1983).

21. Rebecca J. Welsh Cline, "Detecting Groupthink: Methods for Observing the Illusion of Unanimity," *Communication Quarterly* 38 (1990): 112–26.

22. Dennis S. Gouran, Randy Y. Hirokawa, and Amy E. Martz, "A Critical Analysis of Factors Related to Decisional Processes Involved in the *Challenger* Disaster, *Central States Speech Journal* 37 (1986): 119–35.

23. Ronald R. Sims, "Linking Groupthink to Unethical Behavior in Organizations," *Journal of Business Ethics* 11 (1992): 651–62.

24. Gregory Moorhead, Richard Ference, and Chris P. Neck, "Group Decision Fiascoes Continue: Space Shuttle Challenger and a Revised Groupthink Framework," *Human Relations* 44 (1991): 539–50.

25. Carolyn J. Wood, "Challenging the Assumptions Underlying the Use of Participatory Decision-Making Strategies."

26. Ibid.

27. Anne Gero, "Conflict Avoidance in Consensual Decision Processes," *Small Group Behavior* 16 (1985): 487–99.

28. Marceline B. R. Kroon, David van Kreveld, and Jacob M. Rabbie, "Group versus Individual Decision Making: Effects of Accountability and Gender on Groupthink," *Small Group Research* 23 (1992): 427–58.

29. Richard L. Priem and Kenneth H. Price, "Process and Outcome Expectations for the Dialectical Inquiry, Devil's Advocacy, and Consensus Techniques of Strategic Decision Making," *Group & Organization Studies* 16 (1991): 206–25.

30. Lance E. Anderson and William K. Balzer, "The Effects of Timing of Leaders' Opinions on Problem-Solving Groups," *Group & Organization Studies* 16 (1991): 86–101.

31. Ibid.

32. R. H. Kilmann and K. Thomas, "Developing a Forced-Choice Measure of Conflict-Handling Behavior: The MODE Instrument," *Educational and Psychological Measurement* 37 (1977): 309–25.

33. Daniel J. Canary and Brian H. Spitzberg, "Appropriateness and Effectiveness Perceptions of Conflict Strategies," *Human Communication Research* 14 (1987): 93–118.

34. Hal Witteman, "Group Member Satisfaction: A Conflict-Related Account," *Small Group Behavior* 22 (1991): 24–58.

35. Gary L. Kreps, *Organizational Communication,* 2d ed. (New York: Longman, 1990): 193.

36. Fisher and Brown, *Getting Together.*

37. Gloria J. Galanes, "The Effect of Conflict Expression Styles on Quality of Outcome and Satisfaction in Small, Task-Oriented Groups," (Unpublished doctoral dissertation, Ohio State University, 1985).

38. Gary L. Kreps, *Organizational Communication,* 2d ed.

39. Steven M. Alderton and Lawrence R. Frey, "Argumentation in Small Group Decision-Making," in *Communication and Group Decision-Making,* eds. Randy Y. Hirokawa and Marshall Scott Poole (Beverly Hills, CA: Sage Publications, 1986): 157–73.

40. Roger Fisher and William Ury, *Getting to Yes: Negotiating Agreement Without Giving In* (Boston: Houghton-Mifflin Company, 1981; Penguin Books, 1983).

41. Frank Tutzauer and Michael E. Roloff, "Communicative Processes Leading to Integrative Agreements," *Communication Research* 15 (1988): 360–80.

42. Fisher and Brown, *Getting to Yes.*

43. A version of the discussion about this issue is depicted on the ancillary videotape, *Communicating Effectively in Small Groups* (Dubuque, IA: Wm. C. Brown Publishers, 1991). Segment 3 depicts an ineffective discussion, and segment 4 shows an effective discussion where this major issue of bookstore hours is resolved.

PART 5

Group Discussion and Observation Techniques

Individuals skilled in a variety of group problem-solving techniques are valued and sought-after members of any organization. So are people who can observe a group discussion, analyze the process, spot problems, and provide appropriate recommendations for improvement. These final two chapters provide information and techniques to help you put your understanding of small group communication to work for the benefit of any group or organization to which you belong.

Special Discussion Techniques and Methods

Central Message

Special techniques can be used to improve the regulation of discussion, enhance the effectiveness of several aspects of problem solving, and improve overall problem solving in organizations. For any of these techniques to be effective, all members must understand the procedure and follow it closely.

Study Objectives

As a result of studying chapter 13 you should be able to:

1. Explain how to keep discussions orderly by using the guidelines for committees in *Robert's Rules of Order, Newly Revised.*

2. Explain how the problem census and RISK techniques can be used to uncover problems, and describe the procedures for each technique.

3. Explain how buzz groups and focus groups can generate information for a variety of uses, and describe the procedures for each technique.

4. Plan and lead brainstorming and synectics sessions to enhance group members' creativity.

5. Explain the purpose and central principle of the Program Evaluation and Review Technique (PERT).

6. Describe the purpose and procedure for conducting the Nominal Group Technique.

7. Explain the purposes and basic procedures of both quality circles and self-managed work groups, and the organizational climate and training necessary for either method to be productive.

8. Describe advantages and disadvantages of teleconferences in comparison to face-to-face meetings, and explain how these types of meetings can best supplement each other.

Key Terms

Brainstorming
Brainwriting
Buzz group session
Focus groups
Nominal Group Technique

Problem census
Program Evaluation and Review
  Technique (PERT)
Quality circle

RISK technique
Self-managed work groups
Synectics
Teleconference

Up to now we have emphasized small group communication theories and processes. Chapter 13 shifts the focus to specific group formats and techniques. We have included a variety of techniques that were developed for small groups that are components of larger organizations. These techniques can be modified or combined to serve specific group or organizational purposes.

Regulating Group Discussions

Appropriate group regulation gives each participant an equal opportunity to speak and ensures that decisions are made democratically. The larger a group, the more important it is to have formal procedures to regulate interaction so order can be maintained. Many organizations and large assemblies have adopted *Robert's Rules of Order, Newly Revised* as their parliamentary code.[1] Robert also includes a code of rules for board and committee meetings of organizations. When an organization adopts *Robert's Rules of Order,* the committees of that organization are bound to use Robert's rules for committees, which are much less formal and detailed than the parliamentary rules that govern large meetings. These rules make it unnecessary (and undesirable) for members to keep uttering "question," "point of order," or "I move to table the motion."

The bylaws of a parent organization may have special rules governing committees; if at any point these contradict what Robert says, the bylaws rule. Chairs of committees need to know the organization's bylaws and, if the organization has adopted a parliamentary manual, what that manual says about committee procedures.

We have summarized Robert's rules for committees below for three reasons: first, because Robert is the parliamentary authority adopted by most American organizations; second, so you can know how to act in committees covered by *Robert's Rules;* and third, so you can use these rules properly if you are in the formal role of chair.

Administrative matters

1. The chair of a committee may be selected in one of three ways: appointed by the parent organization, selected by the committee members, or the first person named to the committee is automatically the chair.

2. A committee meets on call of its chair or any two members.

3. A quorum (minimum number of members needed for the committee to take any legal action) is a simple majority of committee members, unless specified otherwise by the parent organization.

4. Formal reports of committees should contain only what was agreed to by a majority of those present at a regular and properly called (notice given to each member) meeting at which a quorum was present. Usually the chair makes formal reports from a committee in writing, but reports of less formal action or works in progress may be given orally to a parent organization.

5. If a committee has been unable to reach consensus and a minority of its membership wants to make a report or recommendation to the parent organization different from that of the majority, it is usually permitted to do so as soon as the "majority" committee report has been made. This is not a *right* of a committee minority, but during debate under parliamentary rules the

members who did not agree with the majority may speak their opposition. However, no one has the right to allude to what happened during the committee's private discussions unless the entire committee has agreed that this is to be permitted.

Responsibilities of the chair

6. The chair is responsible for records of the committee but may delegate the work, or a separate secretary position may be created. The chair is still responsible for supervising this process.

7. Unlike *presiding* officers, committee chairs can take stands on issues without leaving the chair position. They can also make motions and vote on all questions, as can all other members of the committee. (In some large committees, it may be decided that the chair will act as if in a large assembly; if so, the chair should do so *at all times,* not participating in the substance of a discussion and voting only to create or break a tie.)

Discussing, making motions, and voting

8. Members do not need the formal recognition of the chair to speak, but may speak whenever they want *so long as they do not interrupt others.*

9. Many of the motions required in an assembly are irrelevant. A member can discuss virtually anything informally in committee sessions, so there is no need for points of order, motions to table, or matters of personal privilege. In short, the bulk of what is called *parliamentary law* is obstructive to committee meetings.

10. Motions do not need a second. A motion is a proposal for the group to take some action.

11. There is no limit to how many times a member can speak on an issue, and motions to limit or close discussion are *not* permitted.

12. Informal discussion is permitted with no motion pending. In a parliamentary discussion, members cannot discuss an issue without a motion, but in a committee meeting no motion is needed until *after* the discussion has indicated that consensus or majority decision has been achieved.

13. A majority of those actually voting is required before any decision can be made. Usually a vote is taken to confirm a decision already sensed by the group. "Straw" (nonbinding) votes can be taken at any time to determine whether a majority or consensus exists before a binding vote is taken. The leader might say, "I think we have consensus on this. Would all who favor the proposal please raise your right hand?"

14. No motion is needed to record a vote. When a proposal is clear to all members, a vote can be taken and the outcome recorded as a decision.

15. The chair can ask if all members consent or agree with an idea or proposal. If no one objects, the decision is made and reported in the minutes. For example: "It was decided by consent that Jean and Bob should draft a resolution to present at the next meeting of the club."

16. A motion to reconsider a previous vote can be made at any time, with no limit to how many times a question can be reconsidered. Unlike in a parliamentary body, even a person who voted with the losing side can move to reconsider. Thus, a person who was absent or did not vote can ask for reconsideration of a previous decision if the action has not yet been carried out.

17. Motions can be amended in committee, but this is best done informally. If time is available, it is preferable to decide changes by consensus rather than by voting.

In summary, only a minimum of rules of order and precedence is required in committees of organizations that have adopted *Robert's Rules of Order*. Voting is done to show that a legal majority supported all reported findings, recommendations, and actions. Voting is *not* done to shut off discussion. Any issue within the freedom of the committee can be presented for discussion at any time, and discussion can be quite informal and as lengthy as needed.

Group Techniques for Increasing Problem-Solving Effectiveness

We live in an increasingly competitive world. Survival and success depend on an organization's or group's ability to tap the potential of *all* members in working toward its goals. Group members must cooperate and coordinate efforts to be of most help to the groups, organizations, and societies to which they belong.

In this chapter we present a selection of small group techniques for improving organizational effectiveness. Knowing when and how to apply these techniques will enhance your value to your group or organization. When you believe that one of them can help your group or organization, consult this book or some other manual. All the techniques we have selected may be tailored for specific contexts or purposes by modifying them or combining them with other techniques. If you decide to use any of them, make sure you or the group coordinator explains the procedures carefully before the group tries them. Providing participants with a handout or chart is worthwhile.

We have classified these techniques by their major function, though many can serve more than one type of function: identifying problems, generating information, enhancing creativity, and improving problem solving within organizations.

Identifying Problems

People closest to a problem (such as cooks and waiters in a restaurant, teachers in a school, or production workers in a factory) are often more aware of difficulties and problems than managers are. The following two techniques help bring to overall awareness the individual perceptions of *all* individuals in an organization. Making such perceptions widely available can help prevent costly or life-threatening events later on.

The Problem Census

The **problem census** is a "posting" technique used to identify important issues or problems. It is particularly useful for building an agenda for future problem-solving meetings, program planning by an organization, or discovering problems encountered by organization members but not generally known. For instance, a university department where one of us worked periodically conducted a problem census that developed into an agenda for a series of future meetings. The census first identified the list of problems, then different faculty members assigned themselves to researching and presenting an outline of each of the problems on the list to the committee for eventual problem solving. The following are the steps for conducting a problem census:

1. Seat the group in a semicircle facing a chart or board.

2. Explain the purpose of the technique, which is to bring out all problems, concerns, questions, or difficulties any member of the group would like to have discussed.

3. The leader then asks each participant, in round-robin fashion, to present one problem or question. This continues until all problems have been presented.

4. The leader posts each problem as it is presented by writing it clearly on the chart or board. The leader must accept totally whatever is presented, never challenging or disagreeing, but asking for clarification or elaboration as needed. Often, the leader can distill a long problem statement into a concise phrase, but should always ask the speaker if the distillation is accurate before posting it. Each filled page of the chart is fastened to the wall for all to see. (A computer display for doing this is available in some organizations.)

5. The group now establishes a priority order for the entire list, usually by having members vote for their top three or four choices. *All* the problems are retained on the agenda; voting just prioritizes the list.

6. The group may now find that some of the questions can be answered or solved at once by other members to the satisfaction of the presenter. Such questions are removed from the list.

7. Each remaining problem is dealt with in turn, based on the number of votes it received, at this or subsequent meetings. Some issues may call for a factual presentation by a consultant, some may be handled by a brief lecture, and some by distributing printed material. Other problems will require extensive analysis and discussion by the entire group or an *ad hoc* subcommittee.

Once a group has decided on a solution, that solution has to be evaluated carefully. Recall that earlier we talked about second-chance meetings where members can raise last-minute doubts, and we reported Hirokawa's research showing that one crucial function a group should perform is evaluation of negative consequences.[2] The **RISK technique** is designed specifically to allow an organization to assess how a proposed change or policy might negatively affect the individuals and groups involved.[3]

The RISK Technique

A special task force or selected committee of affected employees can use the RISK procedure to benefit not only themselves but the entire organization. Generally this procedure works best in groups of fifteen or fewer people who already know each other. For instance, suppose the CEO of an organization has tentatively decided to restructure a particular department. The CEO could then ask members of that department to participate in a RISK session to identify possible problems

(RISKS) that the proposed restructuring might cause. Minor concerns can then be dealt with immediately, and possible major problems can be identified and perhaps resolved before they occur. More important, if the proposed plan has a *fatal* flaw, the CEO may decide not to implement it. There are six basic steps in the RISK technique:

1. The leader presents the proposed solution or change in detail, and asks members to think of any risks, fears, or problems with the proposal.

2. Members may either brainstorm as a group to generate problems or may first work individually, using the brainwriting procedure described later.

3. The problems are posted in round-robin fashion on a chart or board. Once this has been done, members should study the list and add to it any additional concerns that occur to them. It is *absolutely imperative* that the leader be nonjudgmental. If members feel threatened they will not reveal their real concerns. Often the risks felt to be most serious by some members will be voiced after a considerable lull, so the leader should not try to rush this process.

4. After this initial meeting, all risks are compiled into a master list and circulated to all participants, who are asked to add anything else that occurs to them.

5. At a second meeting, additional risks felt by any member are added to the master list. Then members discuss each risk one by one. They decide whether each is serious or one that can readily be resolved and removed from the list. Members should be encouraged to share their feelings—fears, doubts, concerns—during this interaction.

6. The remaining risks are processed into an agenda and handled the same way as items from the problem census. If the risks cannot be resolved, the proposed plan should be seriously reconsidered and either modified or discarded.

Generating Information and Ideas

Organizations and groups need information for a variety of purposes. The following two procedures are all-purpose techniques that enable group and organization members to provide information about a number of matters that can later be used in numerous ways.

Focus Groups

Long used in advertising and marketing research, **focus groups** enable an organization to identify problems, interests, concerns of employees and the general public, potential markets, and possible directions for innovation. Focus groups engage in unstructured or loosely structured discussion about a topic presented to them by a facilitator, who simply announces the topic and lets group members respond freely in whatever way they choose. This free-association discussion is usually tape recorded for later content analysis. Focus groups are often used to discover what customers look for in a product or how they may react to possible name or design changes. However, they also have provided information about employee morale, patients' feelings about how they were treated in a medical center, neighborhood reaction to proposed public facilities, and so on.

The uses of focus groups can be quite versatile. For example, the church board introduced in chapter 2 used focus groups of congregation members to assess how things were going and what kinds of activities the congregation would like the board to undertake. Every three or four months, the board would schedule focus group interviews after church services for all interested congregation members, with one or two board members serving as facilitators for each group of five or six people. The focus groups would discuss one or more open-ended questions such as "What do you like best (or least) about attending church here?" and "What kinds of activities or events would you like to see happening at church?" The information provided in these discussions helped identify strengths of the new church on which the board could capitalize, and also led directly to the establishment of a Friday evening workshop series on a potpourri of topics, ranging from enhancing self-esteem to managing conflicts to interpreting dreams. Congregation members were highly supportive of the focus groups and reported that they appreciated being asked their opinions. Recently, one of us participated in a focus group commissioned by a television station to help select a new anchor for the evening news. The group members watched a series of audition tapes, then discussed the strengths and weaknesses of each applicant.

A **buzz group session** is used to organize a large meeting into many small groups that work concurrently on the same question. Purposes may be to generate questions for a speaker or panel, to identify problems or issues, to compile a list of ideas or possible solutions, and generally to stimulate personal involvement and thinking by members of a large assembly. For example, one of us participated with five hundred educational leaders in Kentucky who met to work out techniques for promoting a Minimum Foundation Program for public education in that state. Organizers sought a favorable vote of taxpayers in a special election to support a state tax for local schools based on need. This meant higher taxes and a flow of money from wealthier to poorer districts. Several times the buzz group technique helped identify specific local problems, inexpensive advertising and promotional techniques, arguments for the program, and so forth. Although the conference was large, every attendee participated actively in discussion, and enthusiasm and involvement was remarkable. The procedure is as follows:

Buzz Groups

1. The chair presents a target question—as concise, limited, and specific as possible—to the entire assembly, which may be seated in rows in an auditorium or at small tables. The question should be displayed on a larger poster or blackboard for all to see. The following are examples of such questions:

   What techniques could be used to publicize the Minimum Foundation Program to citizens of each county or city?

   What new projects might local unions undertake to help members with social problems?

   What are the arguments for (or against) a Materials Recovery Facility (MERF) for Springfield?

Figure 13.1
Buzz group seating
in an auditorium.

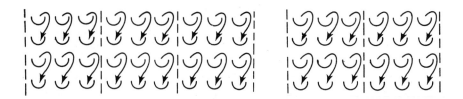

2. Divide the large group into work groups of six by seating them at small tables or, if in a large auditorium, by counting off by three in each row. Then have alternate rows turn to face each other as shown in figure 13.1. Each group should be given a copy of the target question on an index card.

3. Appoint a recorder-spokesperson for each group based on seating: "The person sitting in the forward left-hand seat will be its recorder. The recorder should write down on the card *all* ideas presented, then have the group rank-order them." Assistants should then pass out blank cards.

4. Next, ask each group to record as many answers to the target question as it can think of in five minutes. Spend one minute evaluating the list to decide whether any items should be eliminated and in what order to present them. Thus, discussion occurs in groups of six members for six minutes. This procedure is sometimes called Phillips' 66 because it was developed and popularized by J. Donald Phillips, former president of Hillsdale College in Michigan, who served as consultant for the Kentucky Conference.

5. When the five minutes are up, warn the groups and allow an extra minute if all seem involved. Then, ask each group to evaluate and rank order its list.

6. At this point you may do any of several things, depending on group size and overall meeting plan:
   a. The cards are collected and edited to eliminate duplications. A tally is made of the number of times each item was listed. The total list is duplicated and distributed to the entire group at a subsequent meeting or is presented to some special group for processing.
   b. The chair asks each recorder to report orally from his or her seat, in round-robin fashion, one *new* item from the card as a secretary records all items on a chart or board in front of the room. The list is processed as above or according to the problem census technique described earlier.
   c. Each recorder presents the complete list to the speaker or panel.

This versatile technique has many variations. For example, groups may have more than six minutes and may even follow a brief outline provided by the leader.

Enhancing Group
Creativity

Sometimes, innovation is a group's or organization's main goal. In order for groups to maximize their creativity, they must be allowed to function in an environment where judgment is eliminated and where linear thinking is replaced by holistic, intuitive thinking. Later, at a more appropriate time, critical thinking is reintroduced to evaluate the creative ideas generated by the group. The following techniques help a group enhance its creativity.

The **brainstorming** technique was developed by an advertising executive who recognized the need for imagination and a spirit of playfulness for successful advertising campaigns.[4] In order for the group's creativity to be released, members must feel safe in a nonthreatening environment that is free of judgment.[5] Because critical evaluation kills creativity, the main principle behind brainstorming is "no evaluation," at least during the brainstorming process. Evaluation of the ideas takes place *after* the group has listed as many ideas as possible, either by the same or a different group. Brainstorming is widely used wherever solution multiplicity is needed. It has been used to solve thousands of problems in such diverse industries as banking, engineering and design, marketing, medicine, decorating, programming, education, government, and food science (to name a few). Brainstorming is often used as the second step in the general Procedural Model of Problem Solving, and can be used in conjunction with other techniques. The basic procedure has four steps and involves four major rules:

Brainstorming

1. **The group is given a problem to solve.**
   The problem can vary from quite specific (What shall we name our new soft drink?) to highly abstract (How can we improve living conditions in the residence halls?).

   Problems for brainstorming should have high solution multiplicity, and group members may engage in some preparation prior to brainstorming. In one recent case with which the authors are familiar, a team brainstorming names for a new pudding to be test marketed in the United States first ate some of the pudding, then talked about its taste and what it reminded them of in a freewheeling, unstructured discussion. Then they brainstormed more than five hundred possible names!

2. **Members of the group are encouraged to generate as many solutions as possible.**
   Four general guidelines are followed during this period of brainstorming:
   a. *No evaluation is permitted.* This means that no criticism, laughing at, or other negative reactions are permitted to any idea presented. Trying to think imaginatively while being critical is like trying to accelerate with one foot on the gas pedal and one on the brake.
   b. *Quantity is sought.* The more ideas listed, the better. If there is a lull in ideas, the facilitator should encourage more by asking the group to think of ways to modify previously listed ideas, add a few more, or consider other characteristics of the problem.
   c. *Innovation is encouraged.* Members are asked to provide unusual ideas, even those that seem wild and crazy at first mention. Remember, every new idea was unique at its inception.
   d. *Hitchhiking is encouraged.* Members are asked to build on or modify ideas presented by other members of the group. A member with a hitchhiked idea snaps his or her fingers for immediate attention and to get the idea charted at once.

Brainstorming produces many possible solutions to a problem.

3. **All ideas are charted so the entire group can see them.**

   The facilitator writes the ideas on large sheets of plain paper, then posts the sheets along the walls so everyone can see the ideas. (Computer displays are now available for this.) Looking at the posted ideas often triggers new ideas. The sheets can later be used to write the report of the meeting.

4. **All ideas are evaluated at a different session.**

   After the brainstorming technique has been used to generate a long list of possible solutions, critical thinking is used to evaluate each idea, possibly to modify or improve on some of them, or to select for the solution or policy only those ideas that meet essential criteria such as feasibility, effectiveness, and acceptability. Sometimes a different group evaluates them. If the same group does the evaluating, it should take a break, even if only a short one.

   Brainstorming variations. There are several variations to brainstorming that adhere to the same "no evaluation" theme but are designed to overcome obstacles that sometimes impede creativity. These obstacles can include inhibition of participants, one or two dominant speakers, or fixating on a few ideas.[6] One such variation is **brainwriting.** Brainwriting capitalizes on the fact that group members are sometimes more productive when working alone but in the presence of others. During brainwriting, members are given a specified time limit—ten or fifteen minutes—and asked to write down as many ideas as they can generate during that time. They are encouraged to write as fast as they can without stopping and, as with brainstorming, to hitchhike on their own ideas. When the time period has elapsed, members share their ideas, in round-robin fashion, and proceed just as with regular brainstorming.

Another variation, *electronic brainstorming,* capitalizes on the fact that anonymity can remove inhibitions. Members sit at computer terminals and type in their ideas. No member knows who contributed the ideas, which are displayed on a large screen visible to all. Gallupe et al. found that electronic brainstorming groups generated more ideas, and more high-quality ideas, than oral brainstorming groups, particularly in larger groups.[7] Members were less fearful of being evaluated, and were more satisfied with electronic brainstorming than oral brainstorming.

Finally, there are a number of computer software programs that have recently been developed to help individuals define problems and enhance their creativity. Each program has different strengths and weaknesses, which Pastrick has evaluated.[8] These programs can easily be used by group members for the benefit of the group.

Metaphoric and Analogic Thinking

Metaphoric and analogic techniques encourage group members to focus on similarities between dissimilar things, thereby hoping to gain fresh perspective on the problem or issue to be solved. For example, we have heard the story about the man who developed Velcro after noticing, when he returned from a hike in the woods, how burrs stuck to his socks and pants. This illustrates how an idea in one domain may help solve a problem or suggest an innovation in another domain.

An example of a technique that encourages metaphoric thinking is **synectics,** developed by William Gordon.[9] It encourages linking apparently unrelated elements so as to gain an unexpected insight into a problem. It starts by having the individual or group identify the essence of the problem, then identifying a metaphor or analogy that captures that essence. Group members are encouraged to search for metaphors that seem unrelated to the problem and to use a different sensory perception. For example, if the problem is visual, group members are encouraged to develop a hearing or touch metaphor. The point is to make the usual seem unusual, thereby opening mental doors for new insights to occur. The final step of the procedure is to force-fit the analogy to the problem under consideration so the way to a solution may be opened.

Harriman provides an example of how this generation of "distant analogies" works.[10] A food science manager had a problem with organic debris floating in flavored syrup, which detracted from consumer appeal. The only method he knew to remove the debris also wasted large amounts of the syrup. Needing a fresh perspective, he prevailed on a nonexpert colleague for help. Together they created several images (analogies or metaphors) of "debris" in nature: raking piles of leaves, roadside litter, logs floating down a stream, a canoe floating toward a dam, and so forth. The canoe image reminded the manager that tidal currents change the characteristics of water's surface tension, which in turn reminded him that he had once helped clean up a harbor by using this principle. These images and recollections suggested that he could change the surface characteristics of the syrup (i.e., make it less "sticky") to make the debris easier to remove without wasting syrup.

Discussing the following questions, adapted from ones suggested by Miller, can help groups or individuals use analogy and metaphor to arrive at innovative solutions:

1. **Look for a personal analogy.**
   Identify with the object and view the problem from the perspective of the object. For example, if you want to create a safer car, imagine that you are the car and ask, "How could I operate more safely?"

2. **Look for a direct analogy.**
   Look for a direct comparison of events from diverse fields. For example, the Velcro illustration shared earlier compares something from nature with something man-made.

3. **Look for a symbolic analogy.**
   Imagine different ways of identifying the function or purpose of a solution by filling in the following: "How can we invent [something] that [performs a function] like an [analogy]?" For example, you might ask: "How can we invent [a safer car] that [stays on track] like a [train]?"

4. **Look for a fantasy analogy.**
   Use your imagination to ignore objective reality and discover what new ideas you can find. For instance, imagine that you can shrink yourself to take a trip through your veins and arteries to look for new ways of getting rid of cholesterol deposits.[11]

Metaphoric and analogic techniques may sound odd, but they work by forcing individuals out of their habitual thinking ruts so they can perceive a problem from a different perspective. They may feel uncomfortable to group members because they make what seems like a clear-cut problem ambiguous, uncertain, and strange. But that is precisely the point! If habitual ways of thinking could solve the problem, then innovation would not be needed. Analogy-based creativity techniques provide a potentially rich source of solutions.

Implementing Ideas with PERT

The **Program Evaluation and Review Technique (PERT)** is helpful during the final stage of problem solving, implementation. Sometimes a solution is highly complicated, involving a variety of materials, people whose work must be coordinated, and steps that must be completed in a specific sequence. For example, think of what is involved in constructing a large building on campus or making something like the space shuttle. PERT was developed to expedite such detailed operations so they can be done efficiently and so people can keep track of each step of a complex project. The procedure can be simplified to help even a student project group keep track of who will do what by when. Siebold summarized the main points of PERT:

1. Describe the final step (how the solution should appear when fully operational).
2. Enumerate any events that must occur before the final goal is realized.
3. Order these steps chronologically.
4. If necessary, develop a flow diagram of the process and all the steps in it.
5. Generate a list of all the activities, resources, and materials needed to accomplish each step.
6. Estimate the time needed to accomplish each step, then add all the estimates to get a total time for implementing the plan.
7. Compare the total time estimate with deadlines or expectations and correct as necessary (by assigning more people or less time to a given step).
8. Determine which members will be responsible for each step.[12]

The preceding techniques are for improving group work during specific steps in problem solving. Those that follow use groups to improve the overall performance of organizations in general.

Everything we presented in the chapters devoted to problem solving and decision making can be applied to any group in an organization to improve its effectiveness. However, there are a number of specific small group procedures that can be used to tap the personal resources of members for organizational objectives. We have selected the Nominal Group Technique, quality circle, self-managed work group, and teleconferencing as the procedures you are most likely to use.

Improving Organizational Problem Solving

As we said with brainwriting, often people working individually in the presence of others can generate more ideas for solving problems than the same number of people interacting. Delbecq and Van de Ven developed the **Nominal Group Technique** as an alternative that capitalizes on this while minimizing weaknesses that groups sometimes exhibit. *Nominal* means "in name only"; a nominal group alternates between verbal interaction and individual work in the presence of others.[13] It works better for major problems and long-range planning than for routine meetings.[14] The Nominal Group Technique helps reduce secondary tension, prevents aggressive conflict, and eliminates the chance for some members to make speeches. In an organization, it allows members to express their concerns without fear of reprisals.[15] In one recent demonstration of its effectiveness, the Nominal Group Technique was used, in combination with a decision analysis technique, to help a complex organization with many independent divisions select a common integrated computer system.[16] Consensus was achieved and participants were satisfied with the process. On the other hand, the Nominal Group Technique is not

The Nominal Group Technique

by itself a complete problem-solving process, it may reduce cohesiveness, and it can produce less member satisfaction than fully interactive formats.[17] One of us used a modification of this technique to help a manufacturer identify and generate possible solutions for problems consumers were having with package directions for a product.

Essentially, the Nominal Group members (six to nine) work individually in each other's presence by writing their ideas, recording these ideas on a chart as a group and clarifying them, then evaluating them by a ranking procedure until a decision has been reached. The procedure may vary, but it always involves a cycle of individual work followed by discussion. Following are the steps for the designated leader as outlined by Delbecq:

1. State the known problem elements or characteristics of a situation that differ from what is desired. At this point there should be *no* mention of solutions and no interaction. Members are seated at a table facing a chart or board. A large group can be divided into several small working groups, each with a leader.

2. Ask participants to generate a list of the emotional, personal, and organizational features of the problem. Then give a clear definition of the problem. (Steps 1 and 2 can be combined, with the leader presenting the problem and moving the group at once into step 3.)

3. Allow the group five to fifteen minutes to brainwrite. Each person is asked to write all ideas for solving the problem that he or she can think of. (The leader also generates a list of ideas.)

4. In a round-robin session that includes the leader, list the ideas on a chart for all members to see. If two members have the same idea, put a tally by the idea, but don't record it twice.

5. Take the group through the list item by item, for clarification and elaboration, but *not* evaluation. Anyone may ask another person for clarification of an idea on the list. Questions such as "What does number 6 mean?" or "Do you understand item 4?" are now in order for discussion, but no lobbying, criticism, or argument are allowed yet.

6. Give each person the same number of note cards (five or so) on which to write the items he or she most prefers. The person arranges the cards and ranks them according to preference, writing 5 on the top card to 1 on the bottom.

7. All cards are collected. The ratings are added for each item, and divided by the total number of people in the group. Most items will have a fractional rating. Items no one rated are removed from the list.

8. Engage in an evaluative discussion of the several items with the highest ranks. This should be a full and free discussion with critical thinking, disagreement, and analysis encouraged.

9. If a decision is reached, fine. If not, re-vote on the remaining items and discuss further. This process can be repeated several times as needed until a clear synthesis of a few ideas or support for one idea has emerged. The result is acted on or submitted to the appropriate group for action.

The name **quality circle** has been given to small groups of employees who meet at regular intervals on company time to discuss work-related matters. The ultimate purpose of the quality circle is to increase productivity, improve the quality of what is produced, and enhance employee involvement.[18] Quality circle members share their opinions with management in an attempt to solve all sorts of job-related problems. Quality circle techniques were originally developed jointly by American and Japanese management experts working to help postwar Japan prepare to compete for world markets. The participative nature of quality circles meshed well with Japanese culture, although the concept had been rejected by U.S. managers, who saw quality circles as encroaching on their authority.

Quality Circles

Many American companies have instituted quality circles, sometimes called *work effectiveness teams,* to help them compete more successfully. Corporations using quality circles or some variation of them include Ford Motor Company, General Motors, Hewlett-Packard, Burlington Industries, Ethyl Corporation, Anchor Hocking, Control Data, Galion, Sheller-Globe, 3M, Dresser Industries, Firestone, W. R. Grace, Sony, Honda, Weyerhauser, Northrup, SmithKline Beecham, American Airlines, Dow Chemical, Procter & Gamble, Xerox, and Kraft Foods.[19] Nonprofit organizations like the Red Cross, Boy Scouts, and a number of school systems also have quality circles. Workers participating in these groups perceive improvements in their communication with superiors, subordinates, and peers, as well as positive effects on their power and influence.[20]

Employees in a quality circle meet with a team leader (in the United States, usually a supervisor; in Japan, an elected worker) on company time to discuss production problems, or to react to problems presented to them by management. Usually they meet for an hour a week, but time varies from company to company. Quality circles may work on any problem, from how a restaurant can serve customers more quickly to how a country can develop its exports. All ideas agreed upon are submitted to management, which must react to every suggestion by adopting it; modifying, and then adopting it; investigating it further; or rejecting it with an explanation why. Many companies combine the quality circle with employee bonus systems, which reward either individuals or groups for profit-making or money-saving ideas. Often, the quality circles are one part of a *Total Quality Management* program instituted throughout a company. You will note that any of the techniques discussed thus far—standard decision-making and problem-solving methods, the RISK technique, brainstorming, the Nominal Group Technique, etc.— can be used as needed by the quality circle to enhance its effectiveness.

Although quality circles can be quite effective, merely instituting them in a company will not guarantee success. Sometimes unions see them as a ploy to increase production without improving benefits (perhaps a valid criticism in some cases), and occasionally managers implement quality circle programs without having enough foresight into how the programs will work within that company's culture. Potential problems identified by Lawler and Mohrman include middle managers who feel threatened and resist the ideas presented, failure to implement ideas, groups becoming discouraged by management's failure to respond, and management's failure to reward groups financially for their contributions.[21] For quality circles to work, management must be strongly committed to the quality circle program, the program must be part of a long-range plan for organizational development, and participants must be adequately trained in small group dynamics and participative problem solving.[22] Employees must know that their ideas for increasing efficiency will not ultimately cost them jobs or earnings. They must know that their ideas will be respected and dealt with and that they will share in the tangible benefits, such as cost savings, their ideas bring. The employees must have a commitment to the company, but must also be assured of the company's commitment to them. If they are used as a trick to squeeze every ounce of work possible out of employees without rewarding them, quality circles won't work.

Self-Managed Work Groups	**Self-managed work groups,** also called *autonomous work groups,* are teams of peers who determine their own work schedules and procedures within prescribed limits. Sometimes the groups have considerable freedom, even up to the point of hiring and firing team members. Self-managed work groups eliminate many traditional supervisory positions and reduce the number of middle managers. The team performs such management functions as deciding which member will perform which job, what supplies to order, and what the work schedule will be. Members are cross-trained so that each member can perform several or all of the jobs needed by the team. For example, the custom-order team for one office furniture manufacturer originally included a salesperson skilled at pricing, a furniture designer, a craftsperson who could create specialized parts, and three skilled assemblers. Members cross-trained each other so now the whole team goes to a prospective client's office to listen and offer suggestions. This team's success has contributed significantly to the company's profits.[23] The fact that members of a self-managed work group are cross-trained provides the team tremendous flexibility to deal with absent workers. Members are less likely to become bored or frustrated, and they are more likely to help each other out than in traditional assembly line organizations. Self-managed work teams are used in such companies as Volvo, Saturn, Sherwin-Williams, and Procter & Gamble. As you may surmise, before a self-managed work program can be installed, workers and managers must undergo extensive training in group attitudes, techniques, and procedures.

A self-managed work group elects its own leader, who is *not* a supervisor, but a coordinator with legitimate authority from the group. The company's management establishes the work group's area of freedom and assigns what must be produced, but the work group has considerable latitude to decide everything else. Some self-managed work groups even establish their own annual budgets, prepare reports, develop specifications for jobs, and solve technical problems that arise in the course of completing jobs. They may even bid for new company business.

Many of the same concerns about quality circles hold for self-managed work teams. Middle managers and unions often feel threatened by them. However, companies using this technique report a 20 to 40 percent increase in production over traditional work organizations.[24] The self-managed teams require less supervision time, produce higher-quality products, have less absenteeism, and generally have higher morale and job satisfaction than employees under traditional line supervision.

The teleconference is another group technique that expedites the work of many organizations. Face-to-face meetings are expensive, but representatives of departments in large corporations, administrators and faculty of multicampus universities, and individuals involved in cooperative ventures among different organizations and nations need ways to share ideas and information quickly. One solution is the electronically mediated meeting, the **teleconference.** These meetings can take the form of video conferences, where participants can both see and hear each other; audio conferences, where participants can hear but not see each other; and computer conferences, where participants send messages displayed on computer monitors.

Teleconferencing

Videoconferences are prohibitively expensive for most companies at present, but audioconferences, including telephone conference calls, are routine. Computer conferences are becoming increasingly sophisticated and accessible. With the advent of "electronic highways" in the future, we expect the frequency of teleconferencing to increase exponentially. Recent studies have shown that decisions made by computerized conference groups were just as good as ones made by face to face groups, but computer groups were less likely to reach agreement.[25] The *type* of computerized technique appears to make a difference. Murrell found that using the window method, where each participant could see the responses of all other participants at once, produced higher decision quality than a message system, where participants had to complete a message before they could interact.[26] Some studies have found that computer conferences can provide some advantages over face-to-face meetings. Dubrovsky et al. discovered that inequalities due to status and expertise were minimized with electronic mail conferences.[27] Hiltz et al. suggest that computer programs permitting anonymity may help create greater and more equal participation.[28] On the other hand, computer-mediated group decision making leads to more delays, more outspoken advocacy, and more extreme or risky decisions, along with more equal participation, than face-to-face meetings.[29]

From the more than one hundred studies of teleconferencing, we can develop practical guidelines for making electronic meetings productive.[30] For audioconferencing, speaker phone equipment is readily available, relatively inexpensive, and requires no special studios. It can be set up in any office. However, audio conferences lack "social presence."[31] The sense of sharing, belonging, and recognition of each other as individuals can be low. Many key nonverbal cues are absent, and electronic equipment can fail at the most inopportune times. On the other hand, the potential for *greater* equality of opportunity to participate exists in the control equipment used by conference leaders.

For teleconferencing to work best, Johansen, Vallee, and Spangler recommend that the participants hold an extended face-to-face conference beforehand to form a sense of "groupness."[32] A post-teleconference meeting can be useful as well. It seems that for complex tasks, face-to-face meetings are still preferable, with teleconferences well suited to routine meetings.

Several factors can improve routine teleconferences. A trained moderator is essential, all participants should be aware of the rules and guidelines for speaking, and all speakers should abide by specified time limits.[33] Electronic meetings are not qualitatively different from face-to-face ones, but additional coordination efforts are required because less information (e.g., nonverbal cues) is exchanged.

At present, teleconferences are recommended for routine meetings, but as travel costs skyrocket and technological limitations decrease, the need for teleconferences to replace both routine and significant meetings will increase. Several up-and-coming computer-related innovations promise to increase the utility and effectiveness of mediated meetings. For instance, recent and continuing advances in Group Decision Support Systems and electronic highways, specially designed information systems technology tailored to help groups maximize a variety of group outcomes, may one day reverse this recommendation.[34]

Summary

Leaders of committees created by organizations governed by *Robert's Rules of Order* should know and follow Robert's rules for committees. Quite different from Robert's rules for assemblies, the less formal committee rules provide for equality among members and guide the leader's behavior.

A variety of group techniques to help promote group and organizational effectiveness were presented in chapter 13. The first group of techniques is directed at improving specific stages of the problem-solving process. Two of these techniques help members identify problems. The problem census uses a polling-posting method to help a group build an agenda for future problem solving, and the RISK technique spots unforeseen negative reactions to a proposed change of policy or procedure so they can be dealt with before it is too late. Two additional techniques help groups generate information for a variety of purposes. Focus groups are unstructured group meetings that can be recorded and content-analyzed to provide a wealth of information for numerous applications, and buzz groups allow every member of a large group to participate regarding the purpose of the group. Two more techniques help a group enhance creativity. Brainstorming, including its written and electronic variants, uses the principle of deferred judgment to encourage members to discover playful, inventive ideas, and synectics encourages members to use unusual or distant analogies to generate a sudden insight into a problem. Finally, PERT is a special technique for working out the implementation of a complex solution. The solution is broken down into steps and organized so that the timing and coordination of people and materials is efficient and effective.

The second group of techniques presented in chapter 13 is designed to improve problem solving at the organizational level through the efforts of designated small groups. The Nominal Group Technique helps groups reach solutions to long-range problems with a minimum of secondary tension. Quality circle members meet to improve the quality and quantity of products and the work climate. Self-managed work groups of cross-trained members allow production personnel to manage the scheduling and details of their work.

The final method presented, teleconferencing, allows members of small groups to meet, even when they are dispersed geographically. Electronic media are employed so that audio, video, or computer conferencing can occur. Such meetings supplement, but do not replace, face-to-face meetings. Although electronic meetings are currently recommended for routine business, advances in information technology, such as Group Decision Support Systems, may make computer-mediated problem-solving meetings more useful and widespread in the future.

All the techniques and methods described in this chapter were designed to be used in a variety of organizational contexts. As you recommend or use them, feel free to adapt them to your specific circumstances.

Exercises

1. Conduct a problem census focusing on the question "What topics should our class select for discussion that would be intrinsically interesting and involve the whole class?" Use the rank-ordered topics in future exercises.

2. Select a topic from your problem census and use the Nominal Group Technique to discuss the problem. Your instructor will coordinate and time the exercise, but students should lead each of the groups.

3. Your instructor will assign small groups of students to prepare and demonstrate as many of the techniques described in the chapter as time permits.

4. Prepare and follow a PERT plan for a major group project. Each member must sign acceptance of the PERT plan.

5. As a whole class or in subgroups of six to twelve each, participate in a formal brainstorming session considering questions such as, "What use might Goodwill Industries make of the thousands of used belts donated in collection boxes?"

6. With the instructor's blessing, form a quality circle of volunteers to meet every two weeks, discuss problems in the class and what might be done to solve them, and other ways the class could be made more interesting. The circle should give consensus recommendations to the instructor. The instructor should make some reaction to each suggestion at the next class meeting by either incorporating it or explaining why the suggestion was declined.

Bibliography

Baird, John E., Jr. *Quality Circles: Leader's Manual.* Prospect Heights, IL: Waveland Press, 1982.

Krueger, Richard A. *Focus Groups: A Practical Guide for Applied Research.* Newbury Park, CA: Sage Publications, 1988.

Kuhn, Robert L., ed. *Handbook for Creative and Innovative Managers.* New York: McGraw-Hill Book Company, 1988, especially chapters 10, 13, and 14.

Moore, Carl M. *Group Techniques for Idea Building.* Newbury Park, CA: Sage Publications, 1987.

Robert, Henry M. *Robert's Rules of Order, Newly Revised.* Glenview, IL: Scott, Foresman and Company, 1990.

Siebold, David R. "Making Meetings More Successful: Plans, Formats, and Procedures for Group Problem Solving." In *Small Group Communication: A Reader.* 6th ed., eds. Robert S. Cathcart and Larry A. Samovar. Dubuque, IA: Wm. C. Brown Publishers, 1992, 178–91.

Notes

1. Henry M. Robert, *Robert's Rules of Order, Newly Revised* (Glenview, IL: Scott, Foresman and Company, 1990): 471–521.

2. Randy Y. Hirokawa, "Discussion Procedures and Decision-Making Performance: A Test of a Functional Perspective," *Human Communication Research* 12 (1985): 203–24.

3. Norman R. F. Maier, *Problem-Solving Discussions and Conferences: Leadership Methods and Skills* (New York: McGraw-Hill, 1963): 171–77.

4. Alex Osborn, *Applied Imagination,* rev. ed. (New York: Charles Scribner's Sons, 1975).

5. Paul Kirvan, "Brainstorming: It Is More Than You Think," *Communication News* 28 (1991): 39–40.

6. Graham Hitchings and Sara Cox, "Generating Ideas Using Randomized Search Methods: A Method of Managed Convergence," *Management Decision* 30 (1992): 58.

7. R. Brent Gallupe, Alan R. Dennis, William H. Cooper, Joseph S. Valacich, Lane M. Bastianutti, and Jay F. Nunamaker, Jr., "Electronic Brainstorming and Group Size," *Academy of Management Journal* 35 (June 1992): 350–70.

8. Greg Pastrick, "Brainstorming Software: A Free Flow of Ideas," *PC Magazine* 10 (April 30, 1991): 329–36.

9. Russell L. Ackoff and Elsa Vergara, "Creativity in Problem Solving and Planning," in *Handbook for Creative and Innovative Managers,* ed. Robert L. Kuhn (New York: McGraw-Hill Book Company, 1988): 77–90.

10. Richard A. Harriman, "Techniques for Fostering Innovation," in *Handbook for Creative and Innovative Managers,* ed. Robert L. Kuhn (New York: McGraw-Hill Book Company, 1988): 136–37.

11. William C. Miller, "Techniques for Stimulating New Ideas: A Matter of Fluency," in *Handbook for Creative and Innovative Managers,* ed. Robert L. Kuhn (New York: McGraw-Hill Book Company, 1988): 124.

12. David R. Siebold, "Making Meetings More Successful: Plans, Formats, and Procedures for Group Problem Solving," in *Small Group Communication: A Reader,* 6th ed., eds. Robert S. Cathcart and Larry A. Samovar (Dubuque, IA: Wm. C. Brown Publishers, 1992): 187.

13. Andre L. Delbecq, Andrew H. Van de Ven, and David H. Gustafson, *Group Techniques for Program Planning: A Guide to Nominal Group and Delphi Processes* (Glenview, IL: Scott, Foresman and Company, 1975): 7–16.

14. Ibid., 3–4.

15. Alan Honeycutt and Bill Richards, "Nominal Group Process in Organizational Development Work," *Leadership & Organization Development Journal* 12 (October 1991): 24–28.

16. James B. Thomas, Reuben R. McDaniel, Jr., and Michael J. Dooris, "Strategic Issue Analysis: NGT + Decision Analysis for Resolving Strategic Issues," *Journal of Applied Behavioral Science* 25 (May 1989): 189–201.

17. Andre L. Delbecq, "Techniques for Achieving Innovative Changes in Programming," (Presentation at the Midwest Regional Conference of the Family Service Association of America; Omaha, NE: April 20, 1971).

18. June P. Elvins, "Communication in Quality Circles: Members' Perceptions of Their Participation and Its Effects on Related Organizational Communication Variables," *Group & Organization Studies* 10 (1985): 479–507.

19. William V. Ruch, *Corporate Communications* (Westport, CN: Quorum Books, 1984): 205–19.

20. Elvins, "Communication in Quality Circles," 479–507.

21. E. Lawler and S. Mohrman, "Quality Circles after the Fad," *Harvard Business Review* (1985): 65–71.

22. Gerald M. Goldhaber, *Organizational Communication,* 4th ed., (Dubuque, IA: Wm. C. Brown Publishers, 1986): 283.

23. Thomas Owen, "Self-Managing Work Team," *Small Business Reports* (February 1991): 53–65.

24. Henry P. Sims, Jr. and James W. Dean, Jr., "Beyond Quality Circles: Self-Managing Teams," *Personnel Journal* (1985): 25–32.

25. Starr Roxanne Hiltz, Kenneth Johnson, and Murray Turoff, "Experiments in Group Decision Making: Communication Process and Outcome in Face-to-Face versus Computerized Conferences," *Human Communication Research* 13 (1986): 225–52.

26. Sharon L. Murrell, "The Impact of Communicating Through Computers," (Unpublished doctoral dissertation, State University of New York at Stony Brook, 1983).

27. Vitaly J. Dubrovsky, Sara Kiesler, and Beheruz N. Sethna, "The Equalization Phenomenon: Status Effects in Computer-Mediated and Face-to-Face Decision-Making Groups," *Human Computer Interaction* 6 (1991): 119–46.

28. Starr Roxanne Hiltz, Murray Turoff, and Kenneth Johnson, "Experiments in Group Decision Making, 3: Disinhibition, Deindividuation, and Group Process in Pen Name and Real Name Computer Conferences," *Decision Support Systems* 5 (June 1989): 217–32.

29. Sara Keisler and Lee Sproull, "Group Decision Making and Communication Technology," *Organizational Behavior and Human Decision Processes* 52 (June 1992): 96–123.

30. Robert Johansen, J. Vallee, and K. Spangler, *Electronic Meetings: Technical Alternatives and Social Choices* (Reading, MA: Addison-Wesley, 1979): 2.

31. John A. Short, E. Williams, and B. Christie, *The Social Psychology of Telecommunications* (London: John Wiley and Sons, 1976).

32. Johansen, Vallee, and Spangler, *Electronic Meetings,* 113–15.

33. Larry L. Barker, Kathy J. Wahlers, Kittie W. Watson, and Robert J. Kibler, *Groups in Process: An Introduction to Small Group Communication,* 3d ed. (Englewood Cliffs, NJ: Prentice-Hall, 1987): 208.

34. Marshall S. Poole, Michael Holmes, and Gerardine DeSanctis, "Conflict Management in a Computer-Supported Meeting Environment," *Management Science* 37 (August 1991): 926–53; Leonard M. Jessup, Terry Connolly, and David A. Tansik, "Toward a Theory of Automated Group Work: The Deindividuation Effects of Anonymity," *Small Group Research* 21 (August 1990): 333–48; Hiltz, Turoff, and Johnson, "Experiments in Group Decision Making."

Observing Group Discussions

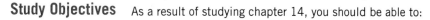

Central Message

By using appropriate methods and instruments, observers can study group communication processes and provide vital information groups can use to evaluate and improve their procedures and outputs.

Study Objectives   As a result of studying chapter 14, you should be able to:

1. Explain the potential benefits of nonparticipant observation of small group interaction for both the observer and observed.

2. Prepare an observation guide appropriate for observing a small group.

3. Report observations to groups in ways that are helpful to the group members.

4. Devise instruments for charting the flow and frequency of verbal participation, obtaining postmeeting reactions of members to a variety of characteristics of their discussion and outputs, and for evaluating both individual members and groups.

Key Terms

Consultant	Nonparticipant observer	Rating scales
Content analysis	Postmeeting reaction forms	Reminder
Critique	(PMRs)	Verbal interaction analysis

We have repeatedly stressed the importance of observing the group communication process while also participating in it. However, you cannot both observe and participate during the same instant. Rather, the participant-observer shifts attention back and forth between observing and participating. Sometimes you have seen clearly what your group needed, and then have been able to supply it (the completer function), but sometimes you have not been able to determine what was missing, what was wrong, and what was needed—or even that there was anything wrong with the meeting at all. The most skillful among us has become so engrossed in discussing an issue about which we care deeply that we lose the observer perspective. In the excitement of a moment of argument we lose sight of the group as a whole and the entirety of problem solving.

A **nonparticipant observer** can be of real assistance in helping a group perceive what is going on and make corrections in its process and direction. Feedback from a nonparticipant observer and/or postmeeting reaction questionnaires can benefit an *entire* group, including the discussion leader. Evaluation of its processes can be beneficial to both small groups and the organizations that created them.[1] We have two main purposes in this chapter: first, we explain the functions nonparticipant observers perform and how to perform them; second, we present examples of several types of instruments that both participants and observers can use to gather information and sometimes feed it back into the group for improvement of future discussion. Included among these instruments are interaction analysis diagrams, member and observer rating scales, postmeeting reaction questionnaires, and content analysis schemes. Seeing some variable(s) of the group's interaction represented in a diagram or table may produce the insight and incentive members need to change their participation.

Roles of Nonparticipant Observers

Every student of discussion and group communication needs to spend considerable time observing interaction of discussion groups. As many of our students have remarked, "It looks different when you are sitting outside the circle." We have witnessed the "Ah-ha!" reactions of student observers as they finally *saw* a phenomenon occurring that previously had been only an abstract idea. These observations frequently lead to voluntary change, so we encourage you to observe as much small group interaction as you can.

As a nonparticipant observer, you can do four things with your observations: learn from the examples of others, remind a group of techniques or principles of discussion it has overlooked, provide critical evaluations of the discussion, and suggest new techniques and information to improve the group's communication. We next examine these functions in detail.

Learning

A principle function of a nonparticipant observer is to learn more about group dynamics from observing and analyzing interaction. We often give our small group students an assignment to observe a group and to report the findings to the class. The first assignment is frequently to observe a recorded discussion. Such observers do not usually make a report of their observations to those observed, although sometimes a group being observed live will request a report. Small group

The fishbowl is an excellent arrangement for training observers.

researchers, many of whose studies have been cited and discussed in this book, frequently gather data by observing small groups in their natural settings or in a social laboratory. They seek to establish valid generalizations about small group communication from analysis of their observations. To accomplish that, they must control personal biases by focusing attention on specific measurable communicative behaviors and outcomes.

As a student-observer, you can observe any small group meeting legally declared open to the public, such as most meetings of boards, councils, and committees of governments where a "sunshine" law exists. You can obtain permission to observe many other small groups by describing your purpose as a learner and promising to maintain the confidentiality of details that are the private business of the group. Our students have observed meetings of groups such as church study-discussion classes, college classes, student activity committees, executive committees of sororities and fraternities, teaching teams, department managers, management staffs, task forces, school boards, boards of regents, quality circles, and self-help groups such as Adult Children of Alcoholics.

A team of observers usually produces more insight into a group's processes than an individual observer; team members learn a lot from sharing and discussing insights. An observation team may be able to arrange a fishbowl set-up, with observers sitting in a circle outside the discussion group. All observers can focus on the same aspects of group dynamics, such as leadership sharing, or each can watch for and report on different phenomena (e.g., leadership, roles, use of information, nonverbal signals, etc.). Observers may be assigned to watch the behavior of specific participants on a one-on-one basis, then later share their observations with their assigned *alter egos,* as well as with the rest of the observation team.

Reminding

Often group members need just to be reminded of principles and techniques they already know but have temporarily overlooked in the excitement of a lively argument. When the observer notices some difficulty with the communication process or problem-solving procedure, he or she may remind the group of the principles or techniques that have temporarily been overlooked. Facilitators of quality circles are primarily there to remind (advise) the groups. You can see that the **reminder** role is somewhat analogous to that of a parliamentarian in a large assembly or a coach during pauses in a game. For example, facilitators in quality circle programs are reminder-observers to the circles, often serving as advisors but not as participants during problem-solving discussion. It is useful for continuing classroom discussion groups to rotate this reminder role among the members so each has the chance to develop skills without any one person being left out of the discussion for too long. When you have become a skilled participant-observer you may even be able to act as an unappointed reminder to non-classroom groups to which you belong. Here are a few guidelines to help you remind in a sensitive and helpful way:

1. Focus on communication process and procedures, not on issues and content of the discussion.

2. Keep in mind that the group is responsible for its own changes—you are in no position to give orders or tell the members what to do, but only to remind and suggest. To do this, phrase most of your remarks in the form of descriptions of what you have observed, questions, and suggestions. For example: "I wonder if the group realizes that we have discussed _____ , _____ , and _____ in the space of only four minutes?" "Are we ready to list possible solutions, or do we need to explore the problem more fully before proceeding into the next stage of problem solving?" "I wonder if Jake and Maria understand each other's proposals?" or "Some members do not appear to have much chance to be heard. Does the group want to do more gatekeeping to ensure that such members' contributions are not missed?" Comments phrased in these ways remind the group of principles of effective discussion without criticizing specific members and possibly arousing defensiveness.

3. As a rule, focus on trends and tendencies rather than singling out individual members for comment.

4. Give the group a chance to correct itself before you intervene. Interrupt discussion only when you think the group will not become aware of a problem until it has wasted a lot of time or created harmful quarrels out of what could be productive argument. Allow a little frustration to motivate change, but not enough to lower morale or produce severe secondary tension.

Consulting

Sometimes a nonparticipant observer can be a helpful **consultant** to a group by providing new resources for the members to use, such as procedures and techniques designed to solve specific group difficulties. With the advent of quality circles and self-managed work teams, workers who select coordinator-leaders from their own ranks need access to specialized information or procedures not readily available to most workers. Managers remaining after such corporate changes often need help in reviewing their roles and working well with the new participative management program. Helping in such ways is also part of the facilitator role. Committees and task forces of all kinds may need consultants to help them resolve communication, relational, and procedural difficulties. You can see that *any organizational communication specialist needs to be prepared to serve as a consultant to small groups in the organization of which he or she is a part.*

To serve as a small group consultant, you will need a thorough grasp of small group dynamics, techniques, and communicative competencies. You will need to know and use a variety of observational, feedback, and evaluation instruments. Examples are presented in the next part of this chapter, and there are others available in literature with which you should become familiar if you serve as a consultant. Here are some guidelines for making your remarks as a consultant more acceptable and effective with the people you observe and advise:

1. Begin post-observation remarks by *stressing the positive,* pointing out what a leader and group are doing well.

2. Emphasize what you think matters most or most needs improvement. Avoid overwhelming a group with more advice and suggestions than it can handle at one time.

3. Avoid arguing. Present your observations, opinions and advice; be sure they are understood as you intend; then leave group members free to decide whether or how your evaluations and advice will be used. You are not an umpire with authority to stop the game or throw players out. The people you advise have the authority to decide what to change; you have only the power of expertise.

4. If during a discussion you decide to advise the designated leader, do so *without interrupting the meeting.* If possible, whisper or write suggestions to the leader.

5. When someone asks for your advice, give it as precisely, clearly, and briefly as possible. If the group asks for an explanation or demonstration of some technique or competency, prepare it carefully.

6. Critical comments to a leader (or any member) should usually be made *in private,* where the person will not appear to be under attack or lose face with other members.

7. If a group asks for information or procedures with which you are not familiar, you may need to augment your knowledge by consulting print resources or expert individuals who can help you. Ethically, you cannot bluff.

A primary responsibility of many consultants, teachers, and trainers is to provide a **critique,** a descriptive analysis of the group's functioning accompanied by an evaluation that focuses on both the strengths and weaknesses of the group interaction. Your instructor may often do this. Corporate communication specialists in training and development staffs are often called on to provide evaluations of both groups and individual members to managers. Fandt demonstrated that such accountability led to higher levels of performance, higher satisfaction with both

Critiquing

process and product, and higher cohesiveness in groups evaluated than in groups not being evaluated to superiors. All research subjects were managerial personnel.[2] Greenbaum and associates claim that failure to evaluate adequately the procedures and output of the circles is often a major factor in the demise of quality circle programs.[3]

If you become a facilitator for quality circles, self-help groups, or self-managing teams, you will need competencies of a constructive critic when providing direct feedback and advice. You can begin to develop these competencies as a critic-observer for groups of classmates.

In general, a critic's postmeeting judgments should cover at least four aspects of a group's discussion processes and culture: (1) inputs to and content of the problem-solving discussion; (2) the group process, including patterns of verbal interaction, member roles (including any ego-centered behavior and ethical lapses), communication process, decision making, and problem solving as a whole; (3) the group product, including how well it has been evaluated by the group, how appropriate it is to the goals or problem described by the group, and how committed members seem to be to making it work; and (4) leadership, especially the role of the designated leader and the sharing of leadership functions.[4] As a critic, you should use criteria appropriate for the type of group you observe, whether it is a public or private learning discussion or a problem-solving, advisory, or action group.

Ethical Guidelines for Nonparticipant Observers

Immediately after observing a discussion, the critic usually makes a detailed feedback statement to the group, describing selected aspects of the discussion and expressing opinions about strong and weak points. While doing so, it is *essential* to respect both the individual members and the group as an entity. Critic observers should behave so that the group will welcome nonparticipant observers in the future. The ethical standards that apply to critic observers are analogous to those that universities use when faculty and students conduct research involving human subjects. Within the past twenty years, most universities have instituted Human Subjects Review committees to ensure compliance with these guidelines. Unfortunately, such committees were necessitated by inappropriate and unethical treatment of some human subjects. The relationship of group members to nonparticipant observers is similar to that of subjects to researchers, so we propose that, as observer, you adhere to the following standards of personal conduct:

1. People observed must not be harmed either physically or psychologically by the observation and feedback. It is thus unethical knowingly to do anything that will cause embarrassment, emotional upset, physical danger, and so forth. For example, it would be unethical for a critic-observer to make fun of a group member in front of the rest of the group, but it would not be unethical to speak with that member privately to describe the effect of the offending behavior on the group.

2. Observers must never lie to people they observe. For example, it would not be ethical to say an evaluation of the group or members will *not* be given to a superior manager in a corporation or military unit, then later to provide such evaluations to the superior. We also think it is unethical to tell a group that you think its decision-making procedures were vigilant when you think they are sloppy and uncritical.

3. All criticism should be *constructive.* When you point out a problem, you should also suggest what to do to correct it. You are there to *help,* not to judge. You will be more helpful if you present positive evaluations before talking about what needs to be changed: "I like . . . , but. . . ."

4. The privacy and confidentiality of group members must be respected at all times. It is not ethical to share with outsiders what you have observed in a specific group unless: (1) you told the group you were going to do so *before* observing and the group granted you permission to do so; or (2) you so thoroughly disguise the identity of the group and its members (as in a statistical summary) that no one can possibly identify the group and members in your report. It is not ethical to receive confidential information from one member and share it with another without permission to do so. Unless a group meeting has been legally declared open to the public, it is a reprehensible violation of confidentiality to report the details or substance of group business to outsiders.

When the purpose for which you are observing includes reporting findings (for instance, reporting observations as the product of a class observation project), you will need to get permission to do so from the group members *before* you do your observing. The persons to be observed may be more willing to let you report if you offer to use pseudonyms instead of real names. In general, treat observed persons just as you would want to be treated if your roles were reversed.

Planning for Observing

While observing a group you may feel overwhelmed by all that is going on. Planning your observation in advance will help you focus on variables most important to your purposes and functions as an observer. One way to cope with information overload is to record the group's discussion on audio or video tape (but only after obtaining permission from the group) for more detailed analysis at a later time. That way, you will worry less about missing something important and can make notes about parts of the discussion to review later. Before trying to observe systematically or with some sort of content analysis scheme, we suggest you practice observing numerous discussions for which you do not need to make any reports. Practice using the sorts of observational instruments and techniques you intend to use to gather data for research, consulting, and reminding. Only after you have become familiar with the tools and confident and consistent in their use are you ready to serve as a consultant, not just a learner. This is a lot like any skill—most of us need a lot of practice on a musical instrument before we are ready to give a concert.

Here is a list of questions you can use as a general guide from which to select a more limited list of questions for a specific observation. If you have been asked to observe interaction as a group member or outside consultant or reminder, this list can help you decide what processes are going well and then focus on characteristics that group members may want to change.

Group Purpose/Goals

Is there a clear and accepted group goal?

Has the committee achieved a clear understanding of its charge?

Do members seem to know and accept limits on their area of freedom?

Can members describe what sort of output is needed?

Setting

How adequate are meeting facilities, such as seating arrangement, privacy, and comfort?

How adequate are facilities for recording and displaying group progress (information, ideas, evaluations, decisions, and so on)?

Communication Skills and Network

How competently do members encode verbally and nonverbally?

How carefully are members listening to understand each other?

How equally is participation spread among the members?

Is the network of verbal interaction all-channel or unduly restricted?

Group Culture, Norms, and Communication Climate

To what degree is the group climate characterized by openness, trust, and teamwork?

What attitudes toward each other and the content of information and ideas are members manifesting?

Are any self-centered hidden agenda items interfering with progress toward the goal?

Are any norms interfering with cohesiveness and progress?

Are arguments being expressed sensitively and managed to test ideas and achieve consensus, or to win?

Role Structure

Is there a designated leader?

If so, how well is this person performing the role? With what style? Are others encouraged to share in leader functions?

If not, how is leadership distributed? Are any needed services missing?

Are all necessary functional roles being provided?

Are there any ego-centered behavioral roles?

Problem-Solving and Decision-Making Procedures

How vigilant are the group's problem-solving procedures?

Do members seem to be adequately informed or are they planning how to get needed information before reaching decisions?

Are information and ideas being evaluated thoroughly for effectiveness and possible negative consequences, or accepted without question?

Are criteria shared by all group members, or explicitly discussed and agreed upon?

Are there any tendencies toward groupthink?

Has some procedure or agenda for the discussion been accepted by the group? If so, how adequate is it and how well is it being used?

Are information, interpretations, proposals, and decisions being recorded?

Are these provided in some record visible to the entire group?

How creative is the group in finding alternatives?

How frequently are summaries being made and used to focus and move discussion toward the goal?

How are decisions being made?

If needed, is the group making adequate plans to implement its decisions? To evaluate the adequacy of its actual solution(s), and possibly make changes later?

Might procedural changes or special techniques such as brainstorming, committee procedural rules, Nominal Group Technique, or computer charting be beneficial to the group?

Obviously, you cannot consider all these questions at the same time. You should first concentrate on one or two factors that seem most important to understanding a group, or in which a group most needs awareness and assistance. After increased experience you will probably discover that you can pay attention to more factors, or rapidly scan what is happening and then decide where to focus your attention.

Just as athletic teams, music groups, and actors need *regular* evaluations and advice to perform optimally, so do task forces, standing committees, boards, quality circles, and self-managed work teams. Any group can benefit from periodic evaluation. Regular reviews should be scheduled, whether or not aided by a consultant critic. For instance, Hill's *Learning Thru Discussion* procedure includes an evaluation of the discussion as part of each meeting of a learning group.[5] If "How are we doing?" sessions are not scheduled, too often no group evaluations occur, or evaluation takes the form of gripe sessions among a few members with little benefit to the entire membership as a system. In addition to scheduled evaluations, taking a break for an unplanned evaluation may correct a dangerous pattern of behavior before a crisis occurs.

Instruments for Observing and Evaluating Discussions

Figure 14.1
Verbal interaction
diagram.

Group _____

Time _____

Begin _____

End _____

Place _____

Observer _____

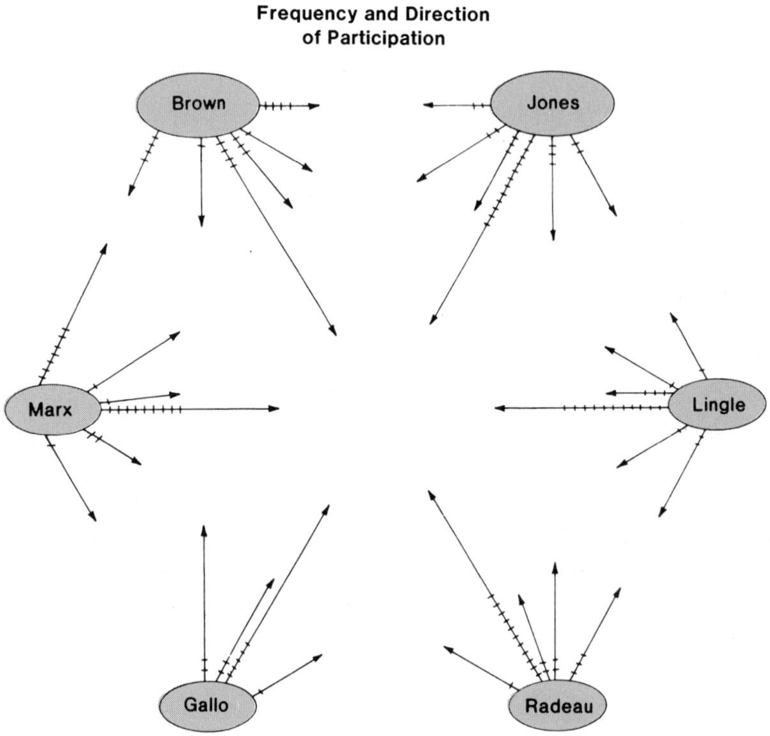

**Frequency and Direction
of Participation**

This final section of chapter 14 is devoted to instruments and techniques for observing and evaluating groups and their members. Many of the forms were developed for classes in small group communication, discussion, and leadership. They can be used as presented or adapted to suit particular situations and needs.

Verbal Interaction
Analysis

A diagram of a **verbal interaction analysis** made by an observer reveals much about relationships among members of a group. The diagram in figure 14.1 shows who talks to whom, how often each member participates orally, and whether the group has members who do not speak up or who dominate the discussion. Notice

Figure 14.2
Displaying data
from a verbal
interaction
diagram.

Group _____ *G.E. "Tigers" 2.C.* _____ Place _____ *Conf. Rm. 14* _____
Observer _____ *Snow* _____ Date _____ *10-9-93* _____
Beginning time _____ *1:03* _____ Ending Time _____ *1:54 pm* _____

TO:

FROM:	Brown	Jones	Lingle	Radeau	Gallo	Marx	Group	Total Percent
Brown	—	5	2	4	2	5	5	23 / 16.1
Jones	3	—	3	4	4	3	13	30 / 21
Lingle	2	2	—	3	2	4	12	25 / 17.5
Radeau	3	3	4	—	0	2	12	24 / 16.8
Gallo	3	3	2	0	—	0	6	14 / 9.8
Marx	8	2	2	3	2	—	10	27 / 18.9
Total number / percent	19 / 13.3	15 / 10.5	13 / 9.1	14 / 9.8	10 / 7	14 / 9.8	58 / 40.6	143 / 100

the information at the top of the figure that identifies group, time, and persons involved. The names of the participants are located around a circle according to seating during the discussion. Each time a member speaks, an arrow is drawn from the person's position toward the person to whom the remark was addressed, or a longer arrow is drawn toward the center of the circle when a member speaks to the entire group. Subsequent remarks in the same direction are indicated by short cross marks on the shaft of the arrow.

For ease in interpreting a verbal interaction diagram, numbers and percentages can be displayed in a chart like the one in figure 14.2. Judging from the numbers shown in this example, who do you think was discussion leader of the GE Tigers? Are there any other reasoned inferences you can make about this group from the data? You could modify this procedure and instrument to capture the frequency of some nonverbal behaviors such as eye contact and body angles.

Content analysis procedures examine the actual content of remarks (topics, types of remarks, fantasy theme structure, etc.) made during a discussion. One type of content analysis focuses on who performs what behavioral functions and how often. From such a descriptive analysis, members' roles can be described. The example in figure 14.3 classifies the behaviors of members according to the functions they enact during the observed discussion. Specific behavioral functions are listed along the left side of the chart, and the participants' names in the cells at the head of each column. Each time a member speaks, the observer judges the functional meaning of that statement to the group and places a tally mark in the appropriate cell of the chart. After the discussion the tally marks are converted to numbers and percentages, as shown in figure 14.4. From this analysis, can you tell who was probably task leader of this group? Who is the social or maintenance leader? Do any individuals seem to be interfering with the group's progress toward its goal?

Content Analysis

Figure 14.3
Content analysis of behavioral functions of members.

Group _____ Place _____ Observer _____

Date _____ Beginning time _____ Ending time _____

Participants' Names

Behavioral Functions						
1. Initiating and orienting						
2. Information giving						
3. Information seeking						
4. Opinion giving						
5. Opinion seeking						
6. Clarifying and elaborating						
7. Evaluating						
8. Summarizing						
9. Coordinating						
10. Consensus testing						
11. Recording						
12. Suggesting procedure						
13. Gatekeeping						
14. Supporting						
15. Harmonizing						
16. Tension relieving						
17. Dramatizing						
18. Norming						
19. Withdrawing						
20. Blocking						
21. Status and recognition seeking						

A content analysis form could be developed for virtually any set of categories into which observable member behaviors could be classified, such as types of statements, functional stage in problem solving, kinds of questions, ways of expressing inferences, and so on. You might use verbal interaction analysis to trace development of fantasy chains, the progression of an idea from initial introduction through its final form and disposal by the group, types of conflicts, or how information is

Group __EXECUTIVE COMMITTEE__   Place __CU LOBBY__
Observer __ANDY__   Date __8-28-91__
Beginning time __4:30 P.M.__   Ending time __6:30 P.M.__

Figure 14.4
Displaying data from analysis of behavioral functions of members.

Participants' Names

Behavioral Functions	Mary	John	Edna	Dave	Jodi	Total number / percent
1. Initiating and orienting	5	3				8 / 5.7
2. Information giving	6	5		2	3	16 / 11.4
3. Information seeking			3			3 / 2.1
4. Opinion giving	8	8	4	2	1	23 / 16.4
5. Opinion seeking			2			2 / 1.4
6. Clarifying and elaborating			3			3 / 2.1
7. Evaluating	2	4			1	7 / 5
8. Summarizing	2					2 / 1.4
9. Coordinating	8					8 / 5.7
10. Consensus testing				3		3 / 2.1
11. Recording			5			5 / 3.6
12. Suggesting procedure	3		6			9 / 6.4
13. Gatekeeping			1	5		6 / 4.3
14. Supporting	2		2	6		10 / 7.1
15. Harmonizing				3	2	5 / 3.6
16. Tension relieving					6	6 / 4.3
17. Dramatizing		5			3	8 / 5.7
18. Norming				4		4 / 2.9
19. Withdrawing		1				1 / .7
20. Blocking	2	5				7 / 5
21. Status and recognition seeking		4				4 / 2.9
Total number / percent	38 / 27.1	35 / 25	26 / 18.6	25 / 17.9	16 / 11.4	140 / 100

used by a group. One thing that matters is that the observer is able to classify the remarks consistently, identifying approximately the same behaviors and classifying them about the same way as another independent observer, or with oneself at two different times (using a recording of the discussion).

Many different types of questionnaires and observer forms have been prepared for studying and improving small group interaction. Some of these use open-ended or multiple-response questions; some use rating scales. **Rating scales** are items or composites of several items that ask a respondent to render a numerical evaluation

Questionnaires and Rating Scales

Postmeeting reaction (PMR) sheets can help diagnose problems in a group.

of some factor observed. You are probably familiar with the 10–0 scale used by judges of some Olympic competitions and the scales by which consumer products are rated in magazines. In chapter 7 we introduced you to SYMLOG, a rating technique in which behaviors of group members are rated on three major dimensions; these ratings are then entered in a three-dimensional chart to describe group-level characteristics and problems. The scales and other forms that follow are provided for your use and to give you ideas about creating others for specific purposes.

Postmeeting reaction forms (PMRs) are questionnaires given to participants at the end of a meeting to get objective feedback for improving future discussions by the group. Because they are anonymous, participants are likely to be candid and honest in their comments and ratings. A PMR form may be planned by an entire group, a leader, an instructor, a consultant, organizers of a large conference, or by a student of small group communication. The questionnaires are distributed, completed, and collected after a discussion. Responses should be tallied and reported back to the group as soon as possible on a duplicated summary sheet or wall chart. The chart provides the basis for an evaluation discussion and planning changes in group procedures.

Questions and scales should be tailored to fit the purposes and needs of the person(s) preparing the questionnaire. Questions can be about any aspect of group discussion: the substance of the discussion, interpersonal relations, procedures, and

Figure 14.5
Postmeeting
reaction (PMR)
form.

Instructions: Check the point on each scale that best represents your honest judgment. Add any comments you wish to make that are not covered by the questionnaire. Do *not* sign your name.

1. How clear were the *goals* of the discussion to you?

   very clear   somewhat vague   muddled

2. The *atmosphere* was

   cooperative and cohesive   apathetic   competitive

3. How well *organized and vigilant* was the discussion?

   disorderly   just right   too rigid

4. How effective was the *leadership* supplied by the chairperson?

   too autocratic   democratic   weak

5. *Preparation for this meeting* was

   thorough   adequate   poor

6. Did you find yourself *wanting to speak* when you didn't get a chance?

   almost never   occasionally   often

7. How satisfied are you with the *results* of the discussion?

   very satisfied   moderately satisfied   very dissatisfied

8. How do you feel about *working again* with this same group?

   eager   I will   reluctant

   Comments:

techniques. Several types of questions may be mixed on a questionnaire, depending on what the preparer of the questionnaire wants to learn. Three examples of PMR forms are shown in figures 14.5, 14.6 and 14.7. Figure 14.7 was developed to provide feedback to leaders of learning discussions.

Rating scales can be put into feedback questionnaires or used by critic-observers to report judgments about any aspect of the group and its discussion, including group climate, norms, structure, interpersonal relationships, speaking,

Figure 14.6
Postmeeting reaction
(PMR) form.

1. How do you feel about today's discussion?

   excellent _____ good _____ all right _____ so-so _____ bad _____

2. What were the strong points of the discussion?

3. What were the weaknesses?

4. What changes would you suggest for future meetings?

(You need not sign your name.)

Figure 14.7
Postmeeting reaction
(PMR) form for
leading discussion.

Leader's Name _____

Instruction: Circle number on each scale that best indicates your reaction.

1. *Preparation* for leading the discussion seemed
   thorough and appropriate   very inadequate

   | 7 | 6 | 5 | 4 | 3 | 2 | 1 |

2. *Organizing and guiding* the discussion were
   clear and orderly   rigid or haphazard

   | 7 | 6 | 5 | 4 | 3 | 2 | 1 |

3. *Spreading of participation* was
   just right   completely neglected

   | 7 | 6 | 5 | 4 | 3 | 2 | 1 |

4. The *style* or philosophy of the leader was
   group centered stimulator   autocratic ("expert")

   | 7 | 6 | 5 | 4 | 3 | 2 | 1 |

5. *Participating* in the discussion was
   satisfying and enjoyable   boring or frustrating

   | 7 | 6 | 5 | 4 | 3 | 2 | 1 |

Comments:

Group Characteristic	5 Excellent	4 Good	3 Average	2 Fair	1 Poor
Goal clarity and interest					
Organization of discussion					
Vigilance; evaluation					
Communication: speaking					
Communication: listening					
Cooperation, teamwork					

Date _____   Group _____
Time _____   Observer _____

Figure 14.8
Problem-solving discussion rating scale.

listening, content of remarks, and so on. The set of scales in figure 14.8 can be used to evaluate any small group discussion. The composite scale in figure 14.9, based on a similar one developed by Patton and Giffin, may be used to identify deficiencies in problem-solving procedures.[6]

Almost any characteristic of individual behavior can be evaluated with an appropriate scale. Figure 14.10 shows a simple rating form that can be completed by a critic-observer and given to each participant; participants can even complete these scales anonymously about each other, and then distribute them to the persons rated. Versions of this form (originally devised by a group of students for their own use) have been used extensively by one of the authors. It is easy to understand, can be completed quickly, and focuses on some of the most important variables of a participant's behavior; figure 14.11 is similar in purpose but more comprehensive. Figure 14.12 is useful for rating the level of assertiveness of participants, while indicating whether nonassertive participation was evaluated as passive or aggressive.

The previous forms can be used as presented or modified to rate designated leaders, but figures 14.13 and 14.14 were devised specifically for that purpose. Exceptionally comprehensive, figure 14.13 has been modified substantially over the years from one originally devised for rating Air Force personnel as discussion leaders. Figure 14.14 is designed to help a leader engage in introspective evaluation after a discussion, identifying specific successes and failings, and then providing an overall rating.

Figure 14.9
Problem-solving
procedure scale.

Instructions: Based on behaviors and interaction you observed, rate the degree to which the group measured up to each criterion.

Poor 1			Fair 2		Average 3	Good 4	Excellent 5

1	2	3	4	5	1. Concerns of all members were established regarding the problem.
1	2	3	4	5	2. Components of the undesirable situation and obstacles to change were clearly described.
1	2	3	4	5	3. The goal was clearly defined and agreed upon by all members.
1	2	3	4	5	4. Possible solutions were listed and clarified before extensive evaluation of them.
1	2	3	4	5	5. Criteria for evaluation were previously understood and accepted, or discussed and agreed upon by all members.
1	2	3	4	5	6. Based on facts and reasoning, predictions were made regarding the probable effectiveness and possible negative consequences of each proposed solution.
1	2	3	4	5	7. Consensus was achieved on the most desirable/acceptable solution.
1	2	3	4	5	8. A realistic plan was developed for implementing the solution and, if appropriate, for evaluating its effectiveness.
1	2	3	4	5	9. Overall, the problem-solving process was thorough, vigilant, and systematic.

Date _____

_____   Observer _____
(Name of participant)

1. Contributions to the *content of the discussion.* (relevant information, issue-centered arguments, adequate reasoning, etc.)

5	4	3	2	1
Outstanding in quality and quantity		Fair share		Few or none

2. Contributions to *efficient group procedures.* (agenda planning, responding to prior comments, summaries)

5	4	3	2	1
Always relevant, aided organization		Relevant, no aid in order		Sidetracked, confused group

3. Degree of *group orientation and cooperation.* (listening to understand, responsible, agreeable, group centered, open-minded)

5	4	3	2	1
Very responsible and constructive				Self-centered

4. *Speaking competency.* (clear, to group, one point at a time, concise)

5	4	3	2	1
Brief, clear, to group				Vague, indirect, wordy

5. *Overall value* to the group.

5	4	3	2	1
Most valuable				Least valuable

Suggestions:

Figure 14.10
Participant rating scale.

Figure 14.11
Discussion
participant
evaluation scale.

Participant's name _____

Instruction: Circle the number that best reflects your evaluation of the discussant's participation on each scale

Superior   Poor
1 2 3 4 5   1. Was prepared and informed.
1 2 3 4 5   2. Contributions were brief and clear.
1 2 3 4 5   3. Comments relevant and well timed.
1 2 3 4 5   4. Spoke distinctly and audibly to all.
1 2 3 4 5   5. Willingness to communicate.
1 2 3 4 5   6. Frequency of participation [if poor, too low ( ) or high ( )].
1 2 3 4 5   7. Nonverbal responses were clear and constant.
1 2 3 4 5   8. Listened to understand and follow discussion.
1 2 3 4 5   9. Openmindedness.
1 2 3 4 5   10. Cooperative, team orientation.
1 2 3 4 5   11. Helped keep discussion organized, following outline.
1 2 3 4 5   12. Contributed to evaluation of information and ideas.
1 2 3 4 5   13. Respectful and tactful with others.
1 2 3 4 5   14. Encouraged others to participate.
1 2 3 4 5   15. Overall rating as participant.

Comments: Evaluator _____

Discussant _____ Date _____

Observer _____ Time _____

Figure 14.12
Assertiveness
rating scale.

   The check mark on each scale indicates my best judgment of your degree of assertiveness as a participant in the discussion.

Behavior	Nonassertive	Assertive	Aggressive
Getting the floor			
	yielded easily	usually refused to let others take over or dominate	interrupted and cut others off
Expressing opinions			
	never expressed personal opinion	stated opinions, but open to others' opinions	insisted others should agree
Expressing personal desires (for meeting times, procedures, etc.)			
	never, or did so in a pleading way	stated openly, but willing to compromise	insisted on having own way
Sharing information			
	none, or only if asked to do so	whenever information was relevant, concisely	whether relevant or not; long-winded, rambling

Manner			
Voice			
	weak, unduly soft	strong and clear	loud, strident
Posture and movements			
	withdrawn, restricted	animated, often leaning forward	unduly forceful, "table pounding"
Eye contact			
	rare, even when speaking	direct but not staring or glaring	stared others down
Overall manner			
	nonassertive	assertive	aggressive

Figure 14.13
Comprehensive
leader rating scale.

Date _____   Leader _____
Time _____   Observer _____

Instructions: Draw a line through any item not applicable to the discussion you have just observed. Use the following scale to evaluate the designated leader's performance as discussion leader.

5—superior   4—above average   3—average   2—below average   1—poor

Personal Style and Communicative Competencies

To what degree did the leader:
_____ Show poise and confidence in speaking?
_____ Show enthusiasm and interest in the problem?
_____ Listen well to understand *all* participants?
_____ Manifest personal warmth and a sense of humor?
_____ Show an open mind toward all new information and ideas?
_____ Create an atmosphere of teamwork?
_____ Share functional leadership with other members?
_____ Behave democratically?
_____ Maintain perspective on problem and group process?

Preparation

To what degree:
_____ Were all needed physical arrangements cared for?
_____ Were members notified and given guidance in preparing to meet?
_____ Was the leader prepared on the problem or subject?
_____ Was a procedural sequence of questions prepared to guide discussion?

Leadership Techniques

To what degree did the leader:
_____ Put members at ease with each other?
_____ Equalize opportunity to speak?
_____ Introduce and explain the charge or problem so it was clear to all?
_____ Control aggressive or dominant members with tact?
_____ Present an agenda and/or procedural outline for group problem solving?
_____ Encourage members to modify the procedural outline?
_____ State questions clearly to the group?
_____ Guide the group through a thorough analysis of problem before discussing solutions?
_____ Stimulate imaginative and creative thinking about solutions?
_____ Encourage the group to evaluate all ideas and proposals thoroughly before accepting or rejecting them?
_____ See that plans were made to implement and follow up on all decisions?
_____ Keep discussion on one point at a time?
_____ Rebound questions asking for a personal opinion or solution to the group?
_____ Provide summaries needed to clarify, remind, and move group forward to next issue or agenda item?
_____ Test for consensus before moving to a new phase of problem solving?
_____ Keep complete and accurate notes, including visual chart of proposals, evaluations, and decisions?
_____ If needed, suggest compromise or integrative solutions to resolve conflict?
_____ (Other—please specify _____)

Instructions: Rate yourself on each item by putting a check mark in the "Yes" or "No" column. Your score is five times the number of items marked "Yes." Rating: *excellent*, 90 or higher; *good*, 80–85; *fair*, 70–75; *inadequate*, 65 or lower.

	Yes	No
1. I prepared all needed facilities.	___	___
2. I started the meeting promptly and ended on time.	___	___
3. I established an atmosphere of supportiveness and informality by being open and responsive to all ideas.	___	___
4. I clearly oriented the group to its goal and area of freedom.	___	___
5. I encouraged all members to participate and maintained equal opportunity for all to speak.	___	___
6. I listened actively, and (if needed) encouraged all members to do so.	___	___
7. My questions were clear and brief.	___	___
8. I saw to it that unclear statements were paraphrased or otherwise clarified.	___	___
9. I used a plan for leading the group in an organized consideration of all major phases of problem solving and all components of vigilant interaction.	___	___
10. I saw to it that the problem was discussed thoroughly before solutions were considered.	___	___
11. I actively encouraged creative thinking.	___	___
12. I encouraged thorough evaluation of all proposed solutions, both for effectiveness and negative consequences.	___	___
13. I integrated related ideas or suggestions and urged the group to arrive at consensus on a solution.	___	___
14. I prompted open discussion of substantive conflicts.	___	___
15. I maintained order and organization, promptly pointing out tangents, making transitions, and keeping track of the passage of time.	___	___
16. I saw to it that the meeting produced definite assignments or plans for action, and that any subsequent meeting was arranged.	___	___
17. All important information, ideas, and decisions were promptly and accurately recorded.	___	___
18. I was able to remain neutral during constructive arguments, and otherwise encourage teamwork.	___	___
19. I suggested or urged establishment of needed ethical standards and procedural norms.	___	___
20. I encouraged members to discuss how they felt about group process and procedures.	___	___

Figure 14.14
Discussion leader self-rating scale.

Summary

In chapter 14 we have examined the functions of nonparticipant observers as learners, reminders, consultants, and critics. Students can develop insights into small group dynamics and improve their competencies by observing numerous discussions. They may also be called upon to assist groups in such roles as reminder or consultant. Communication consultants in organizations should be prepared to do so. Because no one can keep track of all variables at once, it is important that observers focus on certain variables at a time, usually by planning carefully to collect data to answer relatively specific questions. Prepared observation forms and questionnaires can help observers do this. Special questionnaires, called postmeeting reaction forms, can be used to provide feedback to groups as the basis for improvement of future discussions.

A number of forms were included in the chapter as models from which you can prepare specific tools for observing verbal interaction, doing content analyses of behaviors and discussion content, and providing evaluations to group members. We urge you to practice with such forms to develop your personal competencies as a nonparticipant observer so that you can function competently as a consistent scholar, reminder, consultant, and critic.

Exercises

1. Divide your class into groups of five or six. Select an area of small group discussion to evaluate, and, individually, develop a form to assess that phenomenon. Then share your individual forms, and use them as input to preparing as a group the best form you can to accomplish the same purpose.

2. Divide your class into project groups of five or six members. Each group should select an existing small group to observe and evaluate. You may want to check your student activities or similar office for lists of on-campus organizations or groups whose meetings you might observe. Class members may have special access to groups in local business or government organizations.

   This project will last for the entire term. Although you may be given some time in class for meetings, expect that you will have to schedule numerous meetings outside of class time.

   You will need to decide what group to observe, on what aspects of the group to focus (e.g., leadership, roles, decision-making procedures and effectiveness, conflict management, problem-solving procedures, collection and use of information, etc.), and what observation techniques and/or forms to use. Then you will carry out your observations and prepare a report of your findings to the rest of the class, using appropriate visual and other aids. You may also be required to submit a written report to your instructor and perhaps one to the group observed.

3. Because you will be a *member* of a group that forms the observation team for exercise 2 or of some other project team (such as an advisory task force), you should assume the role of participant-observer in your own project group. Pay particular attention to how your group develops from a collection of individuals, the norms that develop, communication among members, power relations, how leadership emerges, the vigilance of problem-solving interaction, how decisions are made, the overall culture of the group, and the

quality of its outputs. Then write an essay describing the group and evaluating it, using an outline of a set of questions such as those that follow. These are only suggested headings or sections for your paper; your group will be unique, so concentrate on the factors that are most important to understanding and evaluating it. You will almost certainly need to keep a journal in which you keep records of what you observe as soon as possible after each meeting, and of communication or other activity involving members *as members* between group meetings.

1. What was the *goal* of the group? How did the group develop this objective? How stimulating was this goal to members? How well does it represent interests of members? Did any hidden agendas detract from this goal?

   Questions for
Evaluating a
Project Group

2. How did a group structure and culture emerge? Were there any noticeable phases in this emergence? How could you tell if the group was emerging from one phase to another?
   a. What *norms* governing behavior emerged? How? What effects did they have on teamwork, productivity, and morale? If there were any counterproductive norms, what efforts were made to change them?
   b. What sort of relationships developed among members? Did you have any passive or aggressive behavior to contend with? How were primary and secondary tensions handled?

3. What do you perceive to be the *role* that each member developed? How did these roles evolve? Were any behavioral functions needed by the group missing? Why do you think no one served as "completer" for these functions?

4. Did the group have a designated *leader?* If so, who? How did this person become leader? What services did the leader provide? How adequately? What leadership services did other members provide? If no leader emerged or was named, were necessary leadership services provided, and if so, how?

5. How adequate was *communication* in the group? What communication network existed among members? How well did members encode verbally? Listen to each other? Were there any specific problems with language, attitudes, or nonverbal signals? How adequately were records (especially minutes) maintained and used? Charting of group progress in problem solving?

6. How well were discussions structured? How systematic were problem-solving discussions? How well were the prime qualities of Vigilant Interaction Theory achieved?

7. How were decisions made? What techniques were used for major issues facing the group? How good were the results of these decisions? If prolonged conflicts emerged, how were they managed and with what effects?

8. Overall, how do you evaluate your project group? Your personal contributions to it? Those of each other member? If you could, what changes would you make in the group, and why? What might have been done to bring about such changes?

Notes

1. Patricia M. Fandt, "The Relationship of Accountability and Interdependent Behavior to Enhancing Team Consequences," *Group & Organization Studies* 16 (1991): 300–312; Harold H. Greenbaum, Ira T. Kaplan, and William Metlay, "Evaluation of Problem-Solving Groups," *Group & Organization Studies* 13 (1988): 133–47.

2. Fandt, 305–7.

3. Greenbaum, Kaplan and Metlay.

4. Greenbaum, Kaplan and Metlay, 137–39, 145.

5. W. Fawcett Hill, *Learning Thru Discussion* (Beverly Hills, CA: Sage Publications, 1977): 30–31.

6. Bobby R. Patton and Kim Giffin, *Problem-Solving Group Interaction* (New York: Harper & Row, 1973): 213–14.

Making Public Presentations of the Group's Output

Often groups must make public presentations of their output, which may take the form of a report, a set of findings or recommendations, and so forth. The group's leader or selected representatives may present a report from the group to the parent organization, a political body, an open meeting of interested community representatives, or another type of public gathering. The members of the audience at such public gatherings may themselves become participants who will discuss the report of the group. The following information presents formats for a variety of public discussion sessions in which group members may find themselves participating. Of course, these formats are also used for events other than public presentation of group reports; we present them here because they are so useful for groups.

A **panel discussion** is a public presentation in which a small group of people representing varying perspectives informally discusses issues relevant to an important question in front of a listening audience. For example, a panel might discuss abortion laws, solutions to congested parking on campus, what might be done to solve a community's solid waste problem, or the responsibility of society to the victims of crimes. A panel format is sometimes used with a group of aspirants for political office.

Panel Discussions

Groups may participate in panel discussions in a variety of ways. A group may be asked to plan and conduct an entire panel discussion, in which case the entire group must research and present fairly all relevant points of view about the issue. More typically, a group known to support a particular point of view will be asked to supply a representative to serve as a panelist with other panelists who represent different viewpoints. The **moderator** of a panel coordinates the discussion so it does not ramble and so all viewpoints are represented. Participants need to be both knowledgeable about the question under discussion and articulate in expressing their, or the group's, opinions. Panelists generally have an outline of questions to follow, but their speaking is relatively impromptu. Panelists need not agree on anything except which issues to discuss; the lively argument that often ensues can make for an intellectually stimulating program. The panel format is excellent for presenting an overview of different points of view on an issue of public concern. CNN and C-SPAN often include such a discussion in their programming.

A panel of political journalists from the Washington Post and Knight-Ridder speaking to a college group.

Preparing for Panel Discussions

Panel and other public discussions call for special physical arrangements and other preparations. First, all discussants should be able to see each other and the audience at all times to facilitate direct interaction. Seat panelists in a semicircle in front of the audience with the moderator either at one end or in the center; thus, panelists have eye contact with each other and the audience. Second, panelists should be seated behind a table, preferably with some sort of cover on the front. Two small tables in an open V make an excellent arrangement. Third, a large name card should be placed in front of each panelist. Fourth, microphones, if needed, should be plentiful enough and unobtrusive. In a large assembly, if a floor mike is required for questions from the audience, it should be placed strategically and audience members instructed in its use. Finally, visual displays of the topic or question under consideration help keep the discussion organized. A chalkboard or easel can be used for this purpose.

The discussion outline for a panel discussion could follow a problem-solving pattern or one of the learning discussion formats suggested in Appendix C. The moderator should ask panelists in advance to suggest questions and subquestions for the discussion. After these are compiled into a rough outline the moderator intends to use, panelists should receive a copy in advance so they have a chance to investigate and think of possible responses to each question.

The moderator prepares a special outline and uses it during the panel discussion. The outline has an introduction, sequence of questions to be raised, and a planned conclusion format. The moderator acts as a conversational traffic officer directing the flow of the discussion. Moderators ask questions of the group of panelists, see that each panelist has an equal opportunity to speak, and clarify ambiguous remarks or ask panelists to do so. They do not participate directly in the arguments. They summarize each major topic or have the panelists do so and keep the discussion moving along the major points of the outline. A moderator's outline might look like this:

Introduction

"What should be the law governing abortions in the United States?"

I. Ladies and gentlemen, the question of what the law should be governing abortions in the United States has been a subject of heated argument, physical confrontation, intensive lobbying, court cases, sermons, and pamphlets—and far too little calm, thoughtful discussion.

II. Today we are fortunate to have a panel of thoughtful experts who represent all major points of view on this subject.

    A. Father Jon McClarety has made an intensive study of the Catholic theology and arguments underlying the church's stand against legalized abortions. He is a member of the Department of Philosophy and Theology of Holy Name Academy.

    B. Robert Byron is an attorney for the Legal Aid Society who has served his society in appeals to the Supreme Court that led to the current legal status of abortions.

    C. Ms. Martine Giles, founder and director of the Adoption Alternatives Agency, has helped arrange more than 300 private adoptions nationally.

    D. Ms. Dorothy Mankewicz, a social worker and volunteer lecturer for Zero Population Growth, has assisted many women who wanted abortions.

    E. Professor Maha Kasakrim is historian of ethical and social values at Western State University and author of two books dealing with the abortion law controversy.

III. Our panelists have agreed to discuss four specific issues that are part of the question you see on the poster before you. "What should be the law governing abortions in the United States?"

    A. When does a human life begin?

    B. Who has the right to decide whether or not a woman should be allowed to have an abortion?

    C. What would be the effects of greater restriction on the right of choice to have an abortion?

    D. Under what conditions, if any, should abortions be legal?

IV. Each panelist will give a brief statement of his or her position on each issue and the reasoning behind it, then the panelists will question and debate their positions informally. After fifty minutes, the floor will be opened for questions from you, our listening audience. While discussion is proceeding, you may want to jot down questions as they occur to you so you can remember them for the forum period (described later).

Body of the Discussion

I. "When does a human life begin?"
   A. Father McClarety: _____
   B. Ms. Mankewicz: _____
   C. Professor Kasakrim: _____
      and so on.
   (All four issues are discussed, with the moderator summarizing; seeing that
   each panelist gets an opportunity to present a position on each issue, and
   question, support, or argue with the others; and moving the group to the next
   major question at a prearranged time.)

Conclusion

I. Let's see if we can summarize what we have learned about each other's
   positions. I'd like each of you to summarize in a minute or less your position
   and arguments. (Often the moderator does the summing up, with panelists
   being free to correct or supplement.)
II. I believe all of us in this room are now better prepared to cope with this vital
   issue. We now understand each other's positions as well as possible, and the
   values and beliefs supporting them.
III. Now I wonder what questions our listeners have for the panel? Please raise
   your hand if you want to ask a question, and wait for me to recognize you by
   pointing. I will give each person a chance to ask one question before allowing
   anyone to ask a second question. Your questions can be directed to a particular
   panel member to answer or to the entire group. If you want a particular panel
   member to answer, state that person's name. Okay, what's our first question?
   The lady to my right wearing the maroon blazer—please state your question
   loudly enough for all present to hear. (Suggestions for conducting a successful
   forum discussion are provided later in this appendix.)

Public Interviews

The leader or selected members of a group may be asked to participate in public
interviews about the group's work. A **public interview** may be conducted by
one or more interviewers of one or more interviewees at a time. *Meet the Press* and
This Week With David Brinkley are examples of this format, as are press conferences and some political candidate debates. Interviewers and interviewees may
agree in advance on a list of major questions or topics to be discussed and on the
range of topics for discussion, or the program may be entirely spontaneous. The
interviewer's responsibility is to represent the audience by asking questions the
audience most wants or needs to have answered, and to help the interviewees clarify their responses. The interviewee's responsibility is to present fairly and clearly
the point of view of the group represented.

Forum Discussions

Sometimes when a group presents a report to a large gathering, members of the
audience are permitted to ask questions or express opinions about the group's work.
Forum discussion refers to this period of verbal interaction during which audience
members interact in an organized way with the presenters. The term *forum* also
refers to a discussion held by a large gathering of people, such as a university
faculty meeting or a town meeting. Frequently a forum follows a panel or interview

A forum discussion often follows a panel discussion.

presentation. Audience members should be told in advance that a forum will follow the public presentation so they can think of questions or comments. Microphones often are set up at strategic places for audience members to use. Sometimes, audience members are asked to supply their questions or comments in written form to a moderator, who reads them aloud for the entire gathering, followed by responses from panelists or interviewees.

Strict procedural control is needed for a successful forum. The moderator should control the forum so the discussion is interesting and fair to all participants. The following are guidelines to ensure fairness without letting the discussion bog down on one issue:

1. During the introduction to the panel or other program, announce that there will be a forum or question and answer period. This allows listeners to be thinking of questions and remarks.

2. State whether only questions or both questions and comments will be permitted.

3. Just before the audience participation segment, announce definite rules to assure equal opportunity for all to speak, such as:
   A. Raise your hand and wait to be recognized before speaking.
   B. No one may speak a second time until each person who wants the floor has had it once.
   C. Comments or questions should be addressed either to a specific panelist by name or to the entire panel.
   D. Remarks must be limited to not more than _____ seconds.
   E. Speak loudly enough to be heard by everyone or go to the floor microphone.

4. Tell the audience whether there will be a definite length of time for the forum and stick to the time.

5. If the audience is large, recognize people from various parts of the room in a systematic pattern.

6. Encourage different points of view by asking for them: "Does anyone want to present a *different* point of view from that we have just heard?"

7. If a question cannot be heard by all, restate it.

8. If a question is unclear or long, paraphrase it to the originator's satisfaction.

9. When the allotted time is nearly up, state that there is just enough time for one or two more questions or comments.

10. If no one seeks the floor, wait a few seconds, then thank the panel and audience for their participation and either dismiss the meeting or go on to the next item on the agenda.

Informational Resources for the Group

A group's output can be only as good as its input and throughput allow. No matter how committed members are to the group and how skilled they are at the process of discussion, critical thinking will be impaired if members don't have accurate, relevant, valid, and complete information with which to work. Groups that attempt to gather as much relevant information as possible *before* they begin their problem-solving or decision-making procedures will produce better outputs—decisions, solutions, reports, recommendations—than groups whose inputs are inadequate.

Appendix B is designed to help group members improve their input resources by assessing the information they have, deciding what additional information they need, and then obtaining it, evaluating it, and organizing it for easy referencing by the group. The four steps, in order, are 1) review and organize your present stock of information and ideas, 2) gather needed additional information, 3) evaluate all the information and ideas you have collected, and 4) organize the information and ideas into a tentative outline. This comprehensive information-gathering procedure is especially useful for important problems and decisions where making a mistake would be costly or worse. In such cases, the search for information should be exhaustive and evaluation thorough. For problems with little danger of making a costly mistake, the group can adapt the procedure or focus on just those steps that are most relevant.

Group members probably already have some information about the subject or they would not be discussing it. Taking a systematic inventory of the information you currently have saves time and makes it easier for you to recall what you have when you need it. You probably noticed that this is the third step in the Single Question problem-solving procedure described in chapter 10.

Review and Organize Your Present Stock of Information and Ideas

1. **Place the problem or subject in perspective.**
   To what is it related? What will it affect, and what affects it? For example, when the church board mentioned in chapter 2 decided on a new location for the church, it had to consider the financial condition of the church, long-range plans, the availability of public transportation and parking facilities, types of activities planned for the church, and so forth.

2. **Make an inventory of information you have about the subject.**
   Each member should contribute what he or she knows, similar to the mapping procedure described in chapter 10. This should be a fairly unstructured, freewheeling process. All this information should be written down.

3. **Organize the information into a rough draft of a problem-solving outline.**
   Look over the information for main issues, topics or questions about the problem. You may want to use the guidelines suggested in chapter 10.

4. **Look for deficiencies.**
   The rough draft will reveal where the group has gaps in its information and suggest specific information to gather and opinions or ideas that need to be supported.

Gather Needed Information

The group is now ready to plan how it will correct the deficiencies in its knowledge and thinking. *Planning* is important; otherwise, haphazard information gathering produces "garbage in" that results in "garbage out" conclusions.

Groups cannot expect to deal with all this information in a single meeting. Even if members are familiar with the topic in advance, they need time to think about the information and spot gaps. This usually takes two meetings, often more. The following two-step procedure helps assure that the group overlooks nothing important:

1. **The group should identify and list all the major issues or topics, along with subtopics, that it needs to explore further.**
   These issues were suggested by the rough outline produced during step 1 above. Additional topics or deficiencies should be added as they occur to members. A list should be produced of all additional information needed.

2. **The group should assign research responsibilities to individual members.**
   Items from the list produced in step 1 should be distributed equitably to the members and deadlines established for completion of the research. This increases individual responsibility and involvement. Ideally, members are allowed to choose voluntarily the topics of most interest to them. A group secretary or chair should keep track of who has agreed to undertake what research.

As a general rule, all members should do some common background study, with two or more members examining each major source on the topic. This helps offset individual perceptual biases and helps prevent the group from relying on one "specialist" for each topic.

Ways of gathering information are suggested below. Since this information has likely been covered in previous communication and composition classes, we review it only briefly.

Note Taking

Information and ideas slip from memory or become distorted unless we make accurate and complete notes. Saying that a key piece of information appeared "in a book by some DNA researcher" is useless because fellow members cannot evaluate the credibility of the information or the source. The best system of

<table>
<tr><td>

SELF-MONITORING   Why related to leadership emergence

Robert J. Ellis and Steven F. Cronshaw, "Self-Monitoring and Leader Emergence: A Test of Moderator Effects," in *Small Group Research*, Vol. 23, No. 1, February, 1992: 113–129.

"It is possible that low and high self-monitors are equally effective at identifying the needs of a group, but only high self-monitors are proficient at modifying their behavior to respond to such needs." p. 124

</td></tr>
</table>

Figure B.1
A note card listing a topic heading, a specific subject, and exact details of the source.

note taking is to record each bit of information or data on a separate index card, along with the topic heading and the full bibliographic reference, as shown in figure B.1.

Note cards provide both accuracy and flexibility. They can be arranged in groups to help synthesize and interpret the evidence collected. They can be consulted with ease during a discussion without having to leaf through a disorganized notebook. For those of you with a computer and a data management program, the information from your note cards can be entered into your computer and sorted in a variety of ways with ease.

Three important sources for gathering information useful to problem-solving discussions are direct observation, reading, and interviews.

Direct Observation

Many times, needed information can come only from firsthand observation by group members, and often only direct observation can breathe life into a table of statistics or survey results. For example, a group of students trying to improve conditions in a self-service coffee shop of a student union spent time observing and recording how many customers did and did not bus their waste materials, the kinds of litter on the floor and tables, and placement and condition of waste containers and signs encouraging users to keep the room clean.

Reading

For many topics and problems, the major source of information will be books, journals, newspapers, government documents, and other printed pages. First, it is important to narrow down the print sources likely to yield relevant information. To do that, you need to compile a **bibliography,** which is a list of published sources on a particular topic or issue. Although ideally you would like to locate and evaluate all recent printed information on your topic before making any final decision, that is not always possible. Be sure, however, that you do not limit yourself to only one or two sources or to sources that support only one point of view. This will produce a bias in your information with no way to cross-check validity.

To compile your bibliography as efficiently as possible, first prepare a list of key terms—descriptors—on the topic. For instance, a group investigating, "What type of lottery should our state conduct?" might use the following descriptors: *lottery, sweepstakes, gambling, crime, revenue,* and *betting.* Once you start your search, you may encounter additional terms, such as *victimless* or *wagering.* A reference librarian's help is indispensable in using printed sources of all kinds, including *Sociological Abstracts, Psychological Abstracts, ERIC, Facts on File,* and others. The abstract sources are significant time savers because they provide brief summaries of articles or books so you can determine whether you should read the entire publication for details.

In addition, most major bibliographies, indexes, and abstract compilations are now accessible by computer. Computerized data bases such as *InfoTrac, Sociofile, Atlas,* and *PsychLit* can be invaluable in locating information about a topic. Although some of these data bases may entail a fee, they make it extremely easy for you to locate relevant items quickly, so they are usually worth the money. The list of descriptors your group generates provides a starting point for a computer file search.

A good library manual, available at virtually every college or university library, helps in building a bibliography and locating print materials. Also helpful are bibliographies of bibliographies, such as *A World Bibliography of Bibliographies and Bibliographic Sources* and *Bibliographic Sources.* Bibliographies are also found at the end of most books, doctoral dissertations, and research articles. Do not overlook indexes to periodicals, such as *The Readers Guide to Periodical Literature, The New York Times Index,* and *Education Index.* Federal and state government publications, in special sections of many libraries, also contain vast amounts of information. The *Monthly Catalog of U.S. Government Publications* and the *Monthly Checklist of State Publications* will help you locate relevant information in these publications. Other useful sources include the *Congressional Quarterly Weekly Report* and the *Congressional Digest.*

Even while you start to compile a bibliography, you can begin reading. A good strategy is for all members of the group to read some of the same things to provide a common background, then divide up the rest of the bibliography. When you evaluate a book for usefulness, read the index and table of contents for clues. Skim rapidly until you find something pertinent to your group, then read carefully. Take notes of the most important ideas and facts, and make copies of particularly valuable information for the rest of the group.

For controversial problems or topics, read as many contrasting interpretations and viewpoints as possible. For example, before developing a campus policy regarding use of laboratory animals for research, study the writings of those who favor and oppose using animals. Although it is easier to remember opinions that support your own, making an effort to understand other points of view is essential for effective group discussion and problem solving. Doing that will also help you increase your level of cognitive complexity.

Interviews

Sometimes you need first-hand information or explanations by a knowledgeable individual; interviews can help you obtain information you cannot get in other ways. For example, members of the group that observed the operation of the campus coffee shop also interviewed a number of customers to determine how they felt about its condition and ask their reasons for not busing their wastepaper and leftovers. They also interviewed the manager to determine why materials that contributed to litter were being used. The church board interviewed ministers at other churches for suggestions about running a church until a full-time minister could be hired. Most people are flattered to be asked for their information and opinions, but remember that your interviewees are busy and would prefer that you read first, then interview them for clarification.

Interview questions may be open-ended ("Why do you eat in the snack shop?") or closed-ended ("If trash containers were more conveniently located, would you use them? Yes _____ No _____"). In-depth interviews using open-ended questions often yield unexpected information and provide richer data. However, answers to open-ended questions are more difficult and time-consuming to tally. In contrast, closed-ended questions can be asked of many people quickly and are easily tabulated if formulated properly. You may want to use both.

It is invalid to generalize findings from a casual or haphazard sample to a larger population. For example, interviews about location of a new sanitary landfill with fifty people who happen to enter a particular door of City Hall will not provide an accurate picture of the beliefs of residents of that city, or even of people who go to City Hall. A scientifically designed sample (a *representative* sample) must be taken if results of interviews are to be generalized to members of a larger population. Unless some member of your group has been trained as a survey researcher or you can get such a person to help you, *student groups should generally not undertake a sample survey.*

Useful information may crop up anywhere, anytime. You may hear something relevant to your topic or problem while listening to the radio or watching television. Some televised material, such as the program content of C-SPAN, is cataloged and available for purchase or rent. Lectures or public speeches are another source of information. An idea may occur to you when you are not consciously thinking about the group's problem—for example, while riding to school, jogging, or talking with friends. Most of us find it helpful to keep a small notepad or a few notecards with us so we can jot down ideas when they occur, lest we forget or distort them. The important thing is to be alert for unexpected information and record it promptly.

Other Information Sources

3. **Evaluate the Information and Ideas You Have Collected.**
   The information and ideas you have gathered must be evaluated for accuracy and credibility. Many of your ideas may collapse in the presence of contradictory information, or some of your information may be spurious, from suspect sources, in direct contradiction to other evidence, or irrelevant. Now is the time for the group to cull the misleading, unsubstantiated, or wrong information so your decision or solution will not be faulty.

   In chapter 11 we discussed ways you can evaluate information and reasoning. In particular, examine the following questions:
   1. **Are the sources believable?**
      Is the person a recognized expert? Is there anything—vested interest, known bias—that could have biased his or her opinion? For instance, ideas about medical care in the United States from representative physicians, insurance agents, and pharmaceutical salespeople are likely to be biased in different ways.

2. **Is there a clear distinction made between facts and inferences?**
   Are opinions stated as though they are facts? Can the facts be verified by independent credible sources?
3. **Are statistical data validly gathered, analyzed, and explained?**
   Was the sample representative? Were appropriate statistical procedures used to analyze the data? Are the results appropriately generalized, or overgeneralized?
4. **Are conclusions (inferences) supported by good reasoning?**
   Are there any fallacies that call the conclusions into question? Can you draw different but equally valid conclusions from the same set of evidence?

4. **Organize Your Information and Ideas.**
   The most efficient way to organize the group's information is to write a tentative outline based on a P-MOPS or Single Question sequence for problem solving (see chapter 10). Ask yourself, "What are the questions that must be answered by our group to arrive at a full understanding of the problem or subject?" Your answers can serve as tentative main points in your outline.

   Once you have decided on some tentative major issues or topic areas, you can arrange your notes into piles, one per issue or outline item. Some of the piles can be further divided into subheadings. For example, information concerning the nature of the problem might be arranged under such subheadings as "who is affected," "seriousness of the problem," "contributing causes," "previous attempts to solve the problem," and so forth. Organizing your information like this makes it easier for you to locate pertinent information when a topic arises during group discussion, helps you prepare questions the group needs to consider, and generally helps you and the group conduct an orderly and comprehensive discussion of a complex topic.

   When you prepare for a problem-solving discussion, your outline likely contains some possible solutions you have found or thought of. You may have evidence or reasoning that shows how similar solutions were tried on a similar problem or even some suggestions about how to implement a plan. However, such thinking and planning should be *tentative*. It is easy to become dogmatic about an issue after you have spent hours preparing to discuss it, but it is absolutely essential that your mind be open. It is inappropriate and harmful to the group for members to come to a discussion prepared to defend their solutions against all comers. Remember that experts at the cutting edge of their fields are usually less dogmatic and sure of themselves than people who know much less. Instead, the ideal group member has the attitude of being prepared to contribute some reliable information and perhaps some ideas for testing by other members, to listen with understanding, and to ask probing questions, thereby shaping but not forcing the solution.

   We emphasize again that the information-gathering strategies we have suggested here can be modified to suit the particular needs of the group. For consequential decisions that will affect many people, something like this full procedure should be used. However, for relatively minor problems with few risks of making a mistake, the group can focus on the parts of this procedure most relevant to the group's problem.

Planning for and Leading Learning Discussions

Learning discussions are held primarily for the enlightenment of either the discussants themselves or a listening audience. No matter whether the learning discussion is private or public, learning is more than the acquisition of facts. It assumes change comes about in a person due to experience, with *education* meaning the structuring of situations to facilitate change. *Cognitive* or intellectual learning ranges from the ability to recognize and recall specific information to the ability to combine and create, *affective* learning involves changes in feelings and values, and *psychomotor* learning pertains to physical skills. The group approach to learning is well documented as frequently superior to lecture, video, or an individualized instruction format.[1] Cooperative group interaction is an effective way to learn for students of all ages.[2] From years of observing and leading various kinds of learning groups; conducting training programs for teachers, students, and study-discussion leaders; and serving as consultants, we have attempted to develop some principles and techniques for planning and conducting learning discussions. There are a number of settings in which learning discussions occur. They range from impromptu situations to occasions organized specifically for the purpose of engaging in learning discussions, including study groups of all kinds. Much of our learning outside the traditional collegiate structure occurs in discussion groups sponsored by continuing education divisions of universities, churches, libraries, and other civic and educational institutions. Because of the prevalence of such learning activities, we will describe both private and public discussion formats.

Private learning discussions exist not for the purpose of reaching decisions but for the *personal growth and enlightenment of their members.* There is no need to reach agreement; rather, what is sought is appreciation for and understanding of other points of view. Examples include classroom groups, study groups, library discussion groups, training programs, and encounter and other experiential growth groups. Private learning discussions are suitable for such diverse purposes as sharing perceptions of a book, film, or other work of art; exploring the merits of competing policies; analyzing case problems; or generating ideas for improving one's life.

Private Learning Discussions

Organizing
Learning
Discussions

Although not all private learning discussions, such as affective groups or encounter sessions, need to be organized, discussions for classes and study-discussion groups generally benefit from some structure. Many of the same logical patterns used to organize essays and informative public speeches can be applied. Usually, the designated leader will provide the organizing framework or ask the group to create one.

1. **Organizing learning discussions by topic or major issue.**
   In this common pattern, the group discusses a set of topics or issues, each of which is phrased as a question. These should be basic issues that must be understood for members to gain an overall view of the subject and to share their differing reactions to it. The designated leader should prepare a set of questions and subquestions to guide exploration of these major issues, but the group should ultimately decide what will be discussed, modifying the leader's guide as desired. The following outline is an example of general questions used by a group to discuss the films they saw:
   I. What were our reactions to the theme of the picture?
   II. How good was the acting?
   III. How well was the picture staged and costumed?
   IV. How effective were lighting and photography?
   V. Would we recommend this picture to our friends?

2. **Organizing learning discussions by comparison sequence.**
   A **comparative outline** might be used to compare two or more policies, objectives, or organizations. The group might begin by discussing criteria and goals, or with the first of the topics to be compared. For example, a classroom group comparing the merits of various ways of generating electricity used the following outline:
   I. What are the advantages and disadvantages of generating electricity from fossil fuels?
   II. What are the advantages and disadvantages of generating electricity from nuclear fuel?
   III. What are the advantages and disadvantages of generating electricity with solar radiation?

3. **Organizing learning discussions by other sequences.**
   Other logical sequences can be employed to structure the discussion. For instance, a chronological sequence fits a discussion of a historical trend, such as the changing role of women in the United States from revolutionary times to the present. A causal sequence is appropriate for discussing possible effects of new technologies. In short, the subject matter should determine the sequence.

Discussions of
Works of Art

Many learning groups, both in and out of the classroom, have found enlightenment and pleasure in discussing such works of art as poetry, paintings, short stories, sculpture, and architecture. A **fine arts discussion format** has proven helpful in countless discussions: (1) the group examines the work of art together; (2) group members discuss what they perceive in the work of art and what it means to them; and (3) the group again examines the work of art. This format allows relatively little time to be spent discussing the artist, the artist's motives, or the artist's life. If artistic techniques are considered, they are left until near the end of the discussion.

The following set of questions can be used to guide discussion of a poem. With ap-   *Literature*
propriate modifications, a similar sequence of questions could be used to organize
discussion of any other art form. With any specific work of art, some questions may
be fruitless or meaningless, and others may be needed to open up other avenues of
perception and interpretation. Beliefs of members about how one *ought* to react to a
poem or other work should not be allowed to block discussion.

Introduction: Someone reads the poem aloud.

I. What situation seems to be occurring in the poem?
   A. What seems to be taking place?
   B. What other actions are described by the persons in the poem?
II. What seems to be the speaker's feelings about the situation?
   A. How does the speaker feel in the beginning of the poem?
   B. In the middle?
   C. At the end?
III. What kind of person does the speaker appear to be?
   A. What kind of person might feel like this?
   B. What kind of person might change this way (or remain unchanged)?
IV. What generalizations does the poem suggest?
   A. What ideas does the poet assume to be true?
   B. Does the poet arrive at any insights, answers, or solutions?
   C. How do we feel about these ideas?

Conclusion: A group member reads the poem aloud.

Some of the questions in the previous general outline may not fit a particular
poem. You must plan questions for the specific poem, depending on what it is about,
how it is written, and the reactions it evokes in you. This adaptation is illustrated in
the following poem and outline for a discussion by a group of college students.

Invictus
William Ernest Henley

Out of the night that covers me,
    Black as the Pit from pole to pole.
I thank whatever gods may be
    For my unconquerable soul.

In the fell clutch of circumstance
    I have not winced nor cried aloud.
Under the bludgeonings of chance
    My head is bloody, but unbowed.

Beyond this place of wrath and tears
    Looms but the Horror of the shade,
And yet the menace of the years
    Finds, and shall find, me unafraid.

It matters not how strait the gate,
    How charged with punishments the scroll,
I am the master of my fate;
    I am the captain of my soul.

  I. What do you think the speaker in *Invictus* is talking about?
    A. In the first stanza, what might "night," "Pit," "gods," and "unconquerable soul" refer to?
    B. What might the second stanza be about?
    C. The third stanza?
    D. The fourth stanza?
 II. What sort of person does the speaker appear to be?
    A. What do you think is the speaker's attitude toward dying?
    B. What do you think is the speaker's attitude about an afterlife?
    C. What else does the poem suggest about the speaker?
III. What beliefs and assumptions underlie the poem?
    A. What does the poem assume to be true?
    B. What do we think about these beliefs?
 IV. Do you like the poem? Why, or why not?

Visual Objects

An outline of questions for discussing a visual object, such as a painting, sculpture, clothing, building, or photograph should focus on various characteristics or features of the object, not the whole. The discussants are led to shift the visual focus in this way and to describe what they see from each new perspective such as shape, color, line, texture, and area. As part of her work in one of our classes, a student prepared the following outline to lead discussion of an abstract painting.

Introduction: A painting is hung in front of the group seated in a semicircle, and the group is asked to examine it silently.

  I. What different elements do you see?
    A. What do you notice about the texture?
    B. What colors do you notice?
    C. What do you notice about the shapes?
    D. Do you observe anything in the lines?
 II. Overall, what do you perceive?
    A. Does it seem to portray any specific object, idea, or event?
    B. Do your personal experiences or ideas affect your perceptions in any way?
III. What feelings do you experience from looking at the picture?
    A. What emotions does it arouse?
    B. Does it move you to want to take any action?
    C. What seems to be evoking your reaction or arousal?
 IV. What does the painting seem to say to you?
    A. Does it have any specific message or theme for you?
    B. What might be the purpose of this painting? Is it strictly aesthetic?
  V. How do you evaluate the painting?
    A. Do you think the artist said what he wanted to say?
    B. Do you feel it was worth saying?
    C. How did the artist achieve this, or what prevented him from achieving it?
    D. Has the painting or our discussion of it revealed anything new or important to you?
    E. Does it have any universality or significance?

A learning group may want to explore possible ways to cope with some type of problem that members encounter as individuals. There is no need for them to come to any decision about a solution as a group. The desired output is for each individual to understand better what is involved and have more options when encountering a problem of the sort discussed. If the members are quite heterogeneous in backgrounds and values, more learning is likely than if they perceive and handle the problem in about the same way.

Often a learning discussion is desultory when addressing a vague, general problem such as "What should you do if someone threatens your life with a weapon?" Rather than beginning with such a general question, the discussion leader can usually evoke more enthusiasm and involvement by using a real or hypothetical case for the group to discuss. A copy of the case is given to each member, and discussed as if the group members were actually trying to solve it. The discussion can be organized using the general Procedural Model of Problem Solving. Then members are asked to generalize from the specific case to similar past or future situations. The following are examples of case problems written to stimulate learning discussions. You can write similar cases from your observations.

The Grade Inflation Case

In recent years, a pervasive problem has arisen on many American college and university campuses—grade inflation. Cumulative final averages have never been so high. This problem has hit home at Robert Burns University. Recently, employers who interview graduates have complained to the chancellor, voicing strong objections to grading policies. They claim that it is now impossible to use a student applicant's grades as a basis for comparison with other applicants and for predicting what sort of employee a student might make. Corporate representatives say that almost all students have above average grades, and 60 percent have at least a 3.1 average.

A preliminary check of records revealed some eye-opening statistics. In 1962, the average SAT score of freshmen was 1,148 and the average final cumulative grade point was 2.3 for those students when they graduated. In 1985, the average SAT score of freshmen was 997, but the average final grade point average was 3.2 when those students graduated. Prior to 1967, the SAT served as a dependable predictor of a student's academic accomplishments, but it no longer does.

A survey of teaching practices at Robert Burns University revealed that most professors curve grades on at least half of their assignments in order to raise the class average. Professors say they are reluctant to give below a C grade because low grades are damaging to students' self-concepts and to their chances for employment in desirable jobs as well as admission to graduate schools. Many said they are reluctant to grade below a B.

College textbook publishers report that they are editing for a tenth-grade reading level, because the higher levels at which they used to edit are too difficult for the majority of today's beginning college students. Some publishers say they must edit freshman texts at even lower reading-difficulty levels, or the books are not adopted.

The provost of Robert Burns University has charged you, as a committee of concerned students from the student senate, to consider whether grade inflation is a serious problem at the university. If you find that it is, he has asked you to recommend a new grading policy to combat the problem and to suggest how to implement the policy and make it effective in restoring grades to their former usefulness and credibility.

The Teacher's Dilemma

An English teacher in a consolidated, rural high school has had extensive dramatic experience and as a result was chosen by the principal to direct the first play in the new school. Its success may determine whether or not there will be future plays produced at the school; if well done it can bring prestige to both the teacher and the school. As a result, the teacher (a friend of mine) is exhausting every means available to her to make the play an artistic success. She has chosen the cast except for the leading female part. The principal's daughter wants the part, and the principal told the teacher he wants his daughter to have it. But she is a poor actress and would jeopardize the success of the show. Tentatively, the teacher has chosen someone who should do an excellent job in the role, but the principal has implied that if his daughter is not selected, he will appoint another director in the future.

What should I tell my English teacher friend to do?

Guidelines for Leading Private Learning Discussions

Based on educational research and philosophy, we suggest the following specific guidelines for leading cooperative learning discussions:

1. **Always establish a cooperative group goal.**
   Remember the concept of promotive interdependence? The group's outcome should be presented as *sharing* individual knowledge to help all members understand each other, listen, and consider each other partners, not competitors.

2. **Give rewards to the group, not to individual members.**
   Praise for good work is directed to the group. Such comments as "That was a really fine discussion" or "I got a lot from all of you" are group oriented and stress the cooperative relationship.

3. **Keep the focus on common experience.**
   Similar to mapping the problem, participants should be reading the same articles or books, looking at the same painting or movie, or studying the same problem. Meaningful discussions evolve from members sharing differing perceptions of the same phenomena. Members are more satisfied when discussion is kept relevant than when it rambles to peripheral topics.[3]

4. **Limit the number of issues or topics.**
   Greater learning and more satisfaction are found in groups where the number of distinguishable topics per session is limited.[4] Plan three to five basic issues per hour, including several subquestions under each broad issue.

5. **Plan a variety of open-ended questions.**

   Open-ended questions encourage a variety of answers from different points of view. For example, "Which political party do you think has done the most to help the poor?" is a relatively closed question, but "What kinds of activities and policies help poor people?" is more open-ended. While closed-ended questions are appropriate, especially for helping establish facts, open-ended questions elicit greater discussion.

6. **Be guided by the nature of the subject.**

   The pattern for a learning discussion, as explained earlier, is usually inherent in the subject. Let the topic and the information guide the logical sequence for discussion.

7. **Focus on how the subject relates to interests of the members as a group.**

   Recall the information about intrinsic interest from the previous chapter 10. Groups perform best when members are interested in the discussion. One method of ensuring this is to poll the group, orally or in writing, for questions members would like to explore. However the leader elects to do this, the discussion will be more productive if it relates to the personal concerns and experiences of the members. For example, compare the following two sets of questions for guiding a discussion of Arthur Miller's *Death of a Salesman.* Which would *you* rather use?

   1. What method of character introduction is used?
   2. Which point of view does the author use?
   3. What are some figures of speech used by Miller?

   versus

   1. Does anything seem unhealthy about Willy's inability to face reality?
   2. Do we think it was wrong for Biff to quit trying after he surprised Willy in the hotel in Boston? Why or why not?
   3. What should we do when someone else fails us, like a teacher or parent?

8. **Don't pass off pseudodiscussion as a cooperative learning discussion.**

   In a pseudodiscussion, the leader has already arrived at an interpretation, value, or solution. Unfortunately, many so-called learning discussion leaders employ the *form* of discussion to disguise a lecture or a persuasion attempt. The purpose of a learning discussion is not to discover the *correct* interpretation but to explore people's opinions, perceptions, and interpretations. If you want to promote one interpretation or position, say so; do not hide behind a pseudodiscussion.

Many groups exist to provide support and psychological learning for their members. Two techniques are presented here that can apply to a wide range of such situations and types of groups.

Affective discussion, a term coined by Epstein, was originally developed to help school children ventilate their feelings. However, the technique can be adapted for any learning group where fears, suspicions, prejudices, and other negative feelings interfere with productive thinking, communicating, and relating to others.[5] The purpose of an affective discussion is to help persons express and explore strong

Special Techniques for Learning Groups Concerned with Feelings and Interpersonal Relations

feelings. The group usually consists of six to ten people seated in a tight circle. In a traditional classroom, a teacher can seat part of the class in front or back of the room, while other students work at their seats, or can divide the class into several smaller groups that have been instructed in the procedure. The technique has been used most successfully by one of us to help groups of graduate students cope with their fear of statistics or thesis writing. It also is excellent for dealing with issues like racial prejudice.

An affective discussion begins with the assumption that all persons have feelings and that any feeling is "okay" to have. We need to express our feelings without apology and have them accepted in a supportive atmosphere, without criticism, in order for adequate intra- and interpersonal communication to occur. In an affective discussion, the designated leader plays little part other than to facilitate expression and empathic listening. Judgment and other defensive responses likely to elicit defensive reactions must be avoided, otherwise, the free and honest sharing of feelings is inhibited. Comments to avoid include:

That's right.

That's wrong.

Don't you mean . . . ?

That's not a nice thing to say.

Gasp.

How can you say something like that?

That's a (liberal, conservative, socialist) idea.

Helpful comments that facilitate candid expression might be:

What do *you* think?

How do you feel about that?

Let him finish his thought.

It's all right to say what you feel.

I don't know.

It's not a matter of right or wrong but what you feel.

The key, again, is nonevaluation. The leader must be totally accepting. Present the opening question, then *listen,* perhaps making an occasional facilitative comment showing understanding and acceptance. The leader of an affective discussion needs to be laissez-faire much of the time.

Encounter discussion can be a means to personal growth and improving interpersonal relations for the participants. *Encounter* means that members of the learning group explore their reactions to each other, describing openly and honestly what they feel. If done in an accepting and caring way, such descriptions by other members of a group regarding how they are responding to you can be a means for gaining self-insight and self-acceptance. A high degree of interpersonal trust is essential if encounter discussion is to be productive because members can feel threatened when others let them know how their behavior is perceived and responded to.

The value of receiving such information is that the person will have more energy available for constructive work rather than protecting an image. As we express some of our inner feelings, others can better understand us, accept us, and identify with our feelings, fears, and needs. For example, an encounter group to which one of us belonged had a member perceived by others as aloof, withdrawn, and cold. After encounter discussion, this individual revealed her fear of interacting with others and her shyness. Others began to respond to her differently once they understood her better, and she began to see how her refusal to talk was misinterpreted by others.

The vehicle by which such growth can be facilitated is interpersonal feedback, which is defined as information one person gives to another about how the first has perceived and been affected by the behavior of the second. A mirror provides an analogy—the member giving the feedback holds a mirror up to the person receiving the feedback, describing and reflecting the behavior but *not judging it.* Since self-images are based on what we *think* others think of us, such feedback can modify our self-concepts by providing a "reality check" with what other members really *do* see in our behavior.

In feedback sessions, comments should be limited to what happens among members of the group while it is in session. Talking about other situations members have been in, topical issues, theorizing, or conducting amateur psychoanalysis sessions should be avoided. Participants should state their remarks as their personal reactions and feelings, describing how they feel and what they were reacting to. Members must avoid name-calling, accusing, or telling each other how they *should* behave.

Feedback sessions should be conducted in the presence of your instructor or some experienced group trainer. If no experienced trainer is available, you can still benefit from limited interpersonal feedback. The important thing is for each member to be free to invite or not to invite the reactions of others. The following guidelines may be helpful:

1. **Describe rather than pass judgment.**
   No one should feel condemned as a person. A description of one's own reactions leaves the receiver of feedback free to react as he or she sees fit. For example, "You were nasty" is evaluative and may elicit defensiveness, but "I felt myself growing angry when you . . ." gives the person valuable information free of judgment.

2. **Be as specific as possible.**
   To be told, "You are domineering" may do more harm than good. In contrast, "When we were talking about how to proceed, I thought you refused to consider anyone else's ideas, so I felt forced to accept your suggestions, face an attack from you, or leave the group," gives the receiver concrete, helpful information.

3. **Consider the needs of the receiver.**
   What can the receiver hear, accept, and handle at this time? A lambasting to relieve your own tension will be counterproductive. Strive for balance between negative and positive feedback.

4. **Deal only with behavior the receiver can change.**
   For example, you would not tell a stutterer that such hesitations drive you nuts. However, you might let someone know that withdrawal from conversation looks like sulking and you don't like it.

5. **Don't force feedback on another.**
   Let the recipient invite comments (unless you respond immediately after something is said or done). If someone indicates he or she wants to hear no more, stop. What you say won't be accepted or understood in any case.

6. **Check to see whether your feedback is understood.**
   Did the receiver understand what you mean? Watch for reactions, perhaps asking the person to restate your point.

7. **See whether the other members agree with you.**
   You may find that other participants do not respond as you did to a particular person. Ask, "How do the rest of you feel about that?" often. Lack of agreement can provide you with important feedback about your *own* perceptions, reactions, and behavior.

8. **Expect slow moments.**
   At times there will be a lot of hesitation and fumbling. Group members typically are hesitant to express feelings openly until interpersonal trust has been established and they feel safe. Expect the exchange of frank feedback to take a long time to develop.

Notes

1. D. W. Johnson and R. T. Johnson, *Learning Together and Alone* (Englewood Cliffs, NJ: Prentice-Hall, 1975), 191–92; W. J. McKeachie, "Recitation and Discussion," in *Achieving Learner Objectives,* 3d ed., ed. O. E. Lancaster (University Park, PA: The Pennsylvania State University, 1963), section F.

2. P. H. Witte, "The Effects of Group Reward Structures on Interracial Acceptance, Peer Tutoring and Academic Performance," (Unpublished doctoral dissertation, Washington University, 1972); Johnson and Johnson, *Learning Together and Alone,* 193–96; Elizabeth Hunter, *Encounter in the Classroom* (New York: Holt, Rinehart and Winston, 1972), 1–15.

3. John K. Brilhart, "An Exploratory Study of Relationships between Evaluating Process and Associated Behaviors of Participants in Six Study-Discussion Groups," (Ph.D. dissertation, Pennsylvania State University, 1962), 283–93.

4. Brilhart, "An Exploratory Study," 275–82.

5. Charlotte Epstein, *Affective Subjects in the Classroom: Exploring Race, Sex and Drugs* (Scranton, PA: Intext Educational Publishers, 1972), 12–13.

A

Abstract   general, nonspecific, or vague.

Acceptance requirements   the degree to which the solution for a given problem must be accepted by the people it will affect.

Accommodation   the conflict management style, high in cooperativeness and low in assertiveness, where one person appeases or gives in to the other.

Active listening   listening with the intent of understanding a speaker the way the speaker wishes to be understood and paraphrasing your understanding so the speaker can confirm or correct the paraphrase.

Activity group   a group formed primarily for members to participate in an activity, such as bridge, bowling, hunting, etc.

Activity orientation   the extent to which a culture emphasizes *doing* or *being,* taking charge or going with the flow.

Ad hominem attack   an attack on a person rather than his or her argument, often involving namecalling; distracts a group from careful examination of an issue or argument.

Administrative duties   one of the major categories of responsibility of a designated leader; includes planning, sending meeting notices, keeping written records, and other administrative functions.

Affective conflict   conflict resulting from personality clashes, likes, dislikes, and competition for power.

Affective discussion   a discussion whose purpose is to let group members express and explore feelings, especially fears, in relation to some topic or concept.

Agenda   a list of items to be discussed at a group meeting.

Aggressiveness   behavior designed to win or dominate that fails to respect the rights or beliefs of others.

Ambiguous   a characteristic of any word or statement that can reasonably be understood in more than one way.

Area of freedom   the scope of authority and responsibility of a group, including limits on the group's authority.

Assembly effect   a type of group synergy or nonsummativity whereby the decision of group members collectively is superior to adding together (summing) the wisdom, knowledge, experience, and skills of the members individually.

Assertiveness   behavior that manifests respect both for your own and other's rights as opposed to aggressiveness and nonassertiveness.

Attitude   a network of beliefs and values, not directly measurable, that a person holds toward an object, person, or concept; produces a tendency to react in specific ways toward the object, person, or concept.

Authoritarianism   tendency to accept uncritically the information, ideas, and proposals of authority figures such as a high-status group member or leader; produces preference for strong leaders and subservience as a follower.

Autocratic leader   a leader who tries to dominate and control a group.

Avoidance   the passive conflict management style that ignores a conflict.

B

Backchannel   nonverbal vocalizations such as *mm-hmm* and *uh-huh* that are uttered while another is speaking; partly determined by one's culture, can indicate interest and active listening.

Behavior   any observable action by a group member.

Behavioral function   the effect or function a member's behavior has on the group as a whole.

Bibliography   a list of sources of information about a topic; usually includes books, journal or magazine articles, newspaper stories, interviews, and so forth.

Boundary spanner   a group member who monitors the group's environment to import and export information relevant to the group's success.

Brainstorming   a small group technique for stimulating creative thinking by temporarily suspending evaluation.

Brainwriting   individual brainstorming producing a written list.

Buzz group session method whereby attendees at a large group meeting can participate actively; the large meeting is divided into groups of about six persons each who discuss a target question for a specified time, then report their answers to the entire large assembly.

Bypassing a misunderstanding that results from two people not realizing they are referring to different things by the same words, or have the same referent for different words.

C

Charge the assignment or goal given to a group, usually by a parent organization or administrator of the parent organization.

Cliche a trite, stereotyped phrase or saying used to explain some event.

Closed system a system, such as a small group, with relatively impermeable boundaries, resulting in little interchange between the system and its environment.

Code a set of specific symbols used in a language, such as sounds, syllables, and words.

Cognitive complexity the personal trait that refers to the level of development of a group member's construct system for interpreting signals; cognitively complex individuals are able to synthesize more information and think in more abstract and organized terms than are cognitively simple individuals.

Cohesiveness the degree of attraction members feel for the group; unity.

Collaboration the assertive, cooperative conflict management style that assumes a solution can be found that fully meets the needs of all parties to a conflict; a problem-solving conflict management style.

Collectivist culture a culture in which the needs and wishes of the group predominate over the needs of any one individual; the idea of an individual following a path separate from the group is inconceivable.

Committee a small group of people given an assigned task or responsibility by a larger group (parent organization) or person with authority.

    Ad hoc or special committee a group that goes out of existence after its specific task has been completed.

    Standing committee a group given an area of responsibility that includes many tasks and continues indefinitely.

Communication a process in which signals produced by people are received, interpreted, and responded to by other people.

Communication apprehension (CA) anxiety or fear of speaking in a variety of social situations; reticence; shyness.

Communication network the interpersonal channels open for interaction; collectively, who talks to whom.

Communicative competencies the communication-related skills and abilities of members that help groups achieve their goals.

Competition the uncooperative, aggressive conflict management style where one person attempts to dominate or force the outcome to his or her advantage.

Complete communication transaction interchange during which the person who sends a signal is responded to by the receiver, and in turn acknowledges the response.

Compromise the conflict management style that assumes each party must give up something to get something; a shared solution to a conflict situation.

Concrete words low-level abstractions referring to specific objects, experiences, and relationships.

Conference group a group composed of representatives from two or more groups; typically conferences try to find ways to coordinate efforts, reduce conflict, etc.

Conflict the expressed struggle that occurs when interdependent parties (including group members) perceive incompatible goals or scarce resources and interference in achieving their goals.

Conjunctive task a type of group task where each member possesses information relevant to the decision, but no one member alone has all the needed information, thus requiring a high level of coordination among members.

Consensus decision a choice that all group members agree is the best one that they all can accept.

Consultant a nonparticipant observer who works with a group to determine what it needs, then attempts to help by providing inputs, such as special techniques, procedures, and information.

Content analysis an analysis of the content (topics, behaviors, specific words or ideas, fantasy themes, etc.) of a group's discussion.

Contingency approaches the study of leadership that assumes the appropriate leadership style in a given situation depends on factors such as members' skills and knowledge, time available, the type of task, and so forth.

Cooperative requirements the degree to which members' efforts need to be coordinated for a group to complete its task successfully (see also "conjunctive task").

Criteria standards for judging among alternatives; may be *absolute* (must) or *relative*.

Critical thinking the systematic examination of information and ideas on the basis of evidence and logic rather than intuition, hunch, or prejudgment.

Critique analysis and criticism of something, such as identification of strengths and weaknesses in a small group's process and interaction.

Crosscultural communication examination of a particular dimension or variable as it occurs in two or more cultures.

Cultural identity the identification with and acceptance of a particular group's shared symbols, meanings, norms, and rules for conduct.

Culture the patterns of values, beliefs, symbols, norms, procedures, and behaviors that have been historically transmitted to and are shared by a given group of persons.

D

Decision making choosing from among a set of alternatives.

Defensive listening thinking of how to defend some aspect of one's self-image while appearing to listen to what another is saying.

Democratic leader an egalitarian leader who coordinates and facilitates discussion in a small group, encouraging participation of all members.

Designated leader a person appointed or elected to a position as leader of a small group.

Deviate a group member who differs in some important way, such as degree of participation, values, or opinions, from the rest of the group members; *opinion* or *innovative* deviates help groups examine alternatives more thoroughly by expressing opinions different from those held by the majority, thus forcing the group to take a closer look.

Devil's Advocacy (DA) a structured group procedure designed to prevent groupthink wherein a subgroup challenges the tentative solution proposed by a group.

Devil's Advocate a group member who argues against a proposal to test its validity.

Dialect a regional variation in the pronunciation, vocabulary, and/or grammar of a language.

Dialectical Inquiry (DI) a structured group procedure designed to prevent groupthink wherein two subgroups develop deliberately opposing solutions to a problem and challenge each other's assumptions and solutions as a way to ensure that the ultimate solution is the best possible.

Discussion (small group discussion) a small group of people communicating with each other to achieve some interdependent goal, such as increased understanding, coordination of activity, or solution to a shared problem.

Disjunctive task a type of group task in which members work on parts of the group problem independently, with little or no coordination of effort through discussion needed.

Distributed leadership the concept that group leadership is the responsibility of the group as a whole, not just the designated leader; assumes all members can and should provide needed leadership services to the group.

Dogmatism a tendency to hold rigidly to personal beliefs; close-mindedness to evidence and reasoning contrary to one's beliefs.

E

Egalitarianism belief in the equality of all people, resulting in the preference for participation in problem solving by all group members rather than by just a few high status members.

Emergent leader member of an initially leaderless group who, by virtue of information and communication competencies, rises from within a group to enact leadership functions and is viewed as the leader by all or most members.

Emotive words words that evoke specific emotions, connote more than they denote, and serve as triggers for recalling pleasant or unpleasant experiences.

Encounter discussion a discussion for the purpose of personal growth of the members and improving interpersonal relations, using honest feedback among members.

Environment the context or setting in which a small group system exists; the larger systems of which a small group is a component.

Ethics the rules or standards that a person or group uses to determine whether conduct or behavior is right and appropriate.

Ethnocentrism the belief that one's own culture is inherently superior to all others; tendency to view other cultures through the viewpoint of one's own culture.

F

Fact a verifiable observed event; a descriptive statement that is true.

Fallacy a reasoning error.

False dilemma either-or thinking that assumes, incorrectly, that only two choices or courses of action are possible.

Fantasy a statement not pertaining to the *here-and-now* of the group that offers a creative and meaningful interpretation of events meeting a group's psychological or rhetorical need.

Fantasy chain a series of statements by several or all group members in which a story is dramatized to help create a group's view of reality.

Fantasy theme what the content of the dramatization of a fantasy or fantasy chain is about; the *manifest* theme is the overt, surface content, and the *latent* theme is the hidden, underlying meaning.

Faulty analogy an incomplete comparison that stretches a similarity too far; assuming that because two things are similar in some respects, they are alike in others.

Feedback some part of the output of a system that is returned to the system as input to influence or control future operations of the system; information given to a group to help it take corrective action when necessary; information about a member's communicative behavior to help that member understand how his or her actions are responded to by others.

Focus group a special group procedure that encourages freewheeling discussion focusing on a specific topic or issue, often used to analyze people's interests and values for market research.

Focused listening focusing attention on major ideas and issues rather than details of another's message so as to be able to review and recall those issues readily.

Forum discussion a large audience interacting orally, usually following some public presentation.

Functions approach the study of functions performed by leaders; the theory that leadership is defined by the functions a group needs and that can be supplied by *any* member.

G

Gatekeeper any member of a small group controlling who speaks during a discussion; any controller of the flow of messages among members.

Gender learned and culturally transmitted sex-role behavior of an individual.

Group three or more people with an interdependent goal who interact and influence each other.

Group culture the pattern of values, beliefs, and norms shared by group members, developed through interaction and incorporating members' shared experiences in the group, patterns of interaction, and status relationships.

Group dynamics a broad field of inquiry concerned with the nature of groups, including how groups develop and interact, and their relationship with individuals, other groups, and institutions.

Group polarization the tendency for group members to make decisions that are more extreme (more risky or cautious) than they would make individually.

Grouphate the feeling of antipathy and hostility many people have against working in a group, fostered by the many ineffective, time-wasting groups that exist.

Groupthink the tendency of some cohesive groups to fail to subject information, reasoning, and proposals to thorough critical analysis leading to faulty decisions.

H

High-context communication communication wherein the primary meaning of a message is conveyed by features of the situation or context instead of the verbal, explicit part of the message.

High-level abstraction a word, phrase, or statement commonly used to refer to a broad category of objects, relationships, or concepts; typically refers to intangibles such as *love, democracy,* etc.

I

Idiosyncracy credit additional leeway in adhering to group norms, given to a member for valuable contributions to the group.

Individualistic culture a culture in which the needs and wishes of the individual predominate over the needs of the group.

Individual-level variables characteristics of the individual members of a group that affect the group's interaction, such as traits, attitudes, values, beliefs, and skills.

Inequity conflict conflict about perceived unequal workloads or contributions to the group effort.

Inference a statement that includes more than a description of some event, thus going beyond fact; an inference involves some degree of uncertainty or probability and cannot be checked for accuracy by direct observation.

Input the energy, information, and raw material used by an open system, which is transformed into output by throughput processes.

Interaction mutual influence by two or more people through the communication process.

Intercultural communication interaction between and among individuals from different cultures or subcultures.

Interdependence the property of a system such that all parts are interrelated and affect each other as well as the whole system.

Interdependent goal an objective shared by members of a small group in such a way that one member cannot achieve the goal without the other members also achieving it.

International communication interaction between and among individuals from different countries (may be more intra- than intercultural).

Interpersonal communication transactional process in which one person's verbal and nonverbal behavior evokes meaning in another.

Intracultural communication interaction between and among individuals from the same culture or subculture.

Intrapersonal communication "interaction" within a single individual; signals are generated, transmitted, and interpreted entirely within the nervous system of one person.

Intrinsic interest extent to which the task itself is attractive and interesting to the participants.

Intuitive problem solving problem solving that is impulsive, not systematic or characterized by any step-by-step procedure.

K

Kinesics study of communication through movements.

L

Laissez-faire leader a do-nothing designated leader who provides minimal services to the group.

Leader a person who uses communication to influence others to meet group goals and needs; any person identified by members of a group as leader; a person designated as leader by election or appointment.

Leader as completer a leader who determines what functions or behaviors are most needed for a group to perform optimally, then supplies them or encourages others to do so.

Leader-Member Exchange model the leadership model based on the finding that supervisors develop different kinds of leadership relationships with their subordinates, depending on characteristics of both the leader and members.

Leadership influence exerted through communication that helps a group achieve goals; performance of a leadership function by any member.

Learning discussion a discussion designed to enhance the knowledge, perceptions, and interactions of the members, but where group consensus is not necessary.

Learning group (study group) a group conducting a learning discussion.

Least-sized group the principle that the ideal group contains as few members as possible so long as all necessary perspectives and skills are represented.

Liaison communication between or among groups; interfacing; a person who performs the liaison function.

Listening receiving and interpreting oral and other signals from another person or source.

Low-context communication communication wherein the primary meaning of a message is carried by the verbal or explicit part of the message.

M

Maintenance functions relationship-oriented member behaviors that reduce tensions, increase solidarity, and facilitate teamwork.

Majority decision decision made by vote, with the winning alternative receiving more than half the members' votes.

Meeting notice a written message providing the time, place, purpose, and other information relevant to an upcoming meeting.

Message either a set of signals from one person to others or interpretation/response of a listener to a set of signals.

Mind raping insisting that what a speaker meant is what the *listener* would have meant by the same words, even after the speaker protests.

Minutes a written record of every relevant item dealt with during a group meeting, including a record of all decisions.

Moderator a person who controls the flow of communication during a public presentation such as a panel or forum discussion.

Multiple causation the principle that each change in a system is caused by numerous factors.

N

Nominal Group Technique a special procedure in which group members brainwrite to generate ideas, then interact to pool, clarify, and evaluate these ideas until a solution has been accepted by weighted voting.

Nonparticipant observer an individual who is not a member of a group but who observes the group's interaction for the purpose of studying small groups or providing appropriate feedback to the members.

Nonsummativity the property of a system that the whole is not the sum of its parts, but may be greater or lesser than the sum.

Nonverbal signals messages other than words to which listeners react.

Norm an unstated informal rule, enforced by peer pressure, that governs the behavior of members of a small group.

O

Obstacle something that interferes or stands in the way of solving a problem, such as lack of information or resources, or attitudes of people who must support the solution.

Open system a system with relatively permeable boundaries, producing a high degree of interchange between the system and its environment.

Output anything that is produced by the throughput processes of a system, such as a tangible product or a change in components of the system; in a small group, outputs are such things as reports, resolutions, changes in cohesiveness, and attitude changes in members.

Overgeneralizing assuming that because something is true about one or a few items, it is true of all or most items of the same type.

P

Panel discussion a small group whose members interact informally and impromptu for the benefit of a listening audience.

Paralanguage nonverbal characteristics of voice and utterance, such as pitch, rate, tone of voice, fluency, pauses, and dialectical variations.

Paraphrase restatement in one's own words of what one understood a speaker to mean.

Participant-observer an active participant in a small group who is at the same time observing and evaluating its processes and procedures.

Passiveness nonassertive behavior that allows one's own rights and beliefs to be ignored or dominated, often to avoid conflict, even at the expense of good decision making.

Personal growth group a group of people who come together to develop personal insights, overcome personality problems, and grow personally through feedback and support of others.

Phase a stage in the development of a small group or in the process of making a decision.

   Formation phase the stage in the development of a group during which relationship issues predominate as members work out their relationships with each other.

   Production phase the stage in the development of a group during which task concerns predominate after a group has reached some socioemotional maturity.

Phasic progression   the movement of a group through fairly predictable phases or stages, each of which is characterized by specific kinds of statements.

Population familiarity   the degree to which members of a group are familiar with the nature of a problem and experienced in solving similar problems or performing similar tasks.

Postmeeting reaction form (PMR)   a form, completed after a discussion, on which group members evaluate the discussion, the group, and/or the leader; PMR responses are usually tabulated and reported back to the group.

Power   the potential to influence behavior of others, derived from such bases as the ability to reward and punish, expertise, legitimate title or position, and personal attraction or charisma.

Power distance   the degree to which a culture emphasizes status and power differences among members of the culture; in low power-distance cultures, status differences are minimized, but in high power-distance cultures, they are highly emphasized.

Preference for procedural order   a trait characterized by need or desire to follow a clear, linear structure during problem solving and decision making.

Prejudice   a preconceived opinion about something based on partial information or limited experience, accompanied by the tendency to reject contradictory information.

Primary group   a group whose main purpose is to meet members' needs for inclusion and affection.

Primary tension   tension and discomfort in members that stems from interpersonal (i.e., primary) sources, including the social unease that occurs when members of a new group first meet or during competition for power among members.

Principled negotiation   a general strategy that enables parties in a conflict to express their needs openly and search for alternatives that will meet the needs of all parties without damaging the relationship among parties.

Problem   the difference between what actually happens and what *should* be happening; components include an existing but undesired state of affairs, a goal, and obstacles to achieving the goal.

Problem census   a technique in which members of a small group are polled for topics and problems that are then posted, ranked by voting, and used to create agendas for future meetings.

Problem question   a question calling the attention of a group to a problem without suggesting any particular type of solution in the question.

Problem solving   a multistage procedure for moving from some unsatisfactory state to a more satisfactory one, or developing a plan for doing so.

Problem-solving group   a group that discusses to devise a course of action to solve a problem.

Procedural conflict   conflict resulting from disagreement about *how* to do something.

Procedural Model of Problem Solving (P-MOPS)   a five-step general procedure, based on the scientific method, for structuring problem-solving discussions; P-MOPS is adaptable to any type of problem.

Process variable   (see Throughput variable)

Program Evaluation and Review Technique (PERT)   a procedure for planning the details to implement a complex solution that involves many people and resources.

Proxemics   the study of uses of space and territory between and among people.

Pseudolistening   responding overtly as if listening attentively, but thinking about something other than what the speaker is saying.

Public interview   one or more interviewers asking questions of one or more respondents for the benefit of a listening audience.

Q

Quality circle (quality control circle)   a group of employees meeting on company time to investigate work-related problems and to make recommendations for solving these problems.

R

Rating scale   a pencil-and-paper instrument to measure quantitatively some factor involved in a discussion.

Referent   whatever is denoted by a symbol or statement.

Reflective thinking   a generic term for systematic thinking during problem solving; also, a systematic procedure for organizing a problem-solving discussion that emphasizes criteria and quality, as opposed to quantity and innovation, in creating alternatives.

Regulator   nonverbal signal used to control who speaks during a discussion.

Reminder   a nonparticipant observer who helps a group by reminding members of principles or techniques they may have forgotten or overlooked during discussion.

Rhetorical sensitivity   speaking and phrasing statements in such a way that the feelings and beliefs of the listener are considered; phrasing statements so as not to offend others or trigger emotional overreactions.

RISK technique   a small group procedure for communicating and dealing with all risks, fears, doubts, and worries that members have about a new policy or plan before it is implemented.

Role   a pattern of behavior displayed by and expected of a member of a small group; a composite of a group member's frequently performed behavioral functions.

Rule   a statement prescribing how members of a small group may, should, or must behave, which may be stated formally in writing, or informally as in the case of norms.

S

Scientific method the procedure by which systematic observation is used to gain knowledge about the physical world; used as the basis for effective problem solving.

Secondary group a group whose major purpose is to complete a task, such as making a decision, solving a problem, writing a report, or providing recommendations to a parent organization.

Secondary tension tension and discomfort experienced by group members that stem from task-related (i.e., secondary) sources, including conflicts over values, points of view, or alternative solutions.

Self-centered functions actions of a small group member, motivated by personal needs, that serve the individual at the expense of the group.

Self-managed work group a small group of peers who determine within prescribed limits their own work schedules and procedures.

Self-monitoring the extent to which someone pays attention to and controls his or her self-presentation in social situations; high self-monitors are able to assess how others perceive them and adapt their behavior to elicit a desired response.

Sex biologically determined female-ness or male-ness.

Sign a signal that has an *inherent* relationship with what it represents, such as a blush or scar.

Signal any stimulus a person can receive and interpret, including both signs and symbols.

Single Question format a special procedure for structuring problem-solving discussions that facilitates critical thinking and systematic problem solving, but is more suitable for members low in preference for procedural order than more highly structured linear procedures.

Small group a group of at least three but few enough members for each to perceive all others as individuals, who meet face-to-face, share some identity or common purpose, and share standards for governing their activities as members.

Small group communication the scholarly study of communication among members of a small group, among two or more groups, and between groups and larger organizations; the body of communication theory produced by such study.

Social loafer a person who makes a minimal contribution to the group and assumes the other members will take up the slack.

Sociofugal furniture and environmental arrangements that discourage group interaction.

Sociopetal furniture and environmental arrangements that facilitate group interaction.

Solution multiplicity extent to which there are many different possible alternatives for solving a particular problem.

Solution question a question directed to a group in which the solution to a problem is suggested or implied.

Status the position of a member in the hierarchy of power, influence, and prestige within a small group.

Ascribed status status due to characteristics external to the group, such as wealth, level of education, position, physical attractiveness, and so forth; status given on the basis of a member's input characteristics.

Earned status status earned by a member's valued contributions to the group, such as working hard for the group, providing needed expertise, being especially communicatively competent, and so forth; status that comes from performance during a group's throughput processes.

Structuration the concept that a group creates and continuously re-creates itself through members' communicative behaviors; the group's communication both establishes and limits how the group develops.

Structure organization; arrangement of parts of a system; steps in a procedure.

Styles approach the leadership approach that studies the interrelationship between leader style and member behaviors.

Subculture a grouping that sees itself as distinct, but is part of a larger culture.

Substantive conflict conflict resulting from disagreements over ideas, information, reasoning, or evidence.

Symbol an arbitrary, human-created signal used to represent something with which it has no inherent relationship; all words are symbols.

Symbolic convergence the theory that humans create and share meaning through talk and storytelling, producing an overlapping (convergence) of private symbolic worlds of individuals during interaction.

SYMLOG *SY*stem for the *M*ultiple-*L*evel *O*bservation of *G*roups, both a theory about member characteristics and effects on group interaction, and a methodology that produces a three-dimensional "snapshot" of a group at a given point in time.

Synectics a special group technique that encourages members to use unusual analogies and metaphors to create innovative solutions to problems.

Syntactic rules rules governing the appropriate usage and arrangements among code units of a language, such as the rules for constructing phrases and sentences.

System an entity made up of components patterned in interdependent relationship to each other, requiring constant adaptation among its parts to maintain organic wholeness and balance.

Systematic problem solving organized problem solving that follows a definite series of steps or sequence, such as those provided by P-MOPS.

System-level variables features or characteristics of the group as a whole, such as cohesiveness, interaction patterns, norms, roles, and so forth, that affect the group's interaction.

T

Task difficulty   degree of problem complexity and effort required.

Task functions   task-oriented member behaviors that contribute primarily to accomplishing the goals of a group.

Technical requirements   the degree to which the solution for a given problem is technically feasible or must meet standards of technical excellence.

Teleconference   a meeting of participants who communicate via mediated channels such as television, telephone, or computer rather than face-to-face.

Throughput   also called **process,** the actual *functioning* of a system, or how the system transforms inputs into outputs.

Trait   a relatively enduring, consistent pattern of behavior or other observable characteristic.

Traits approach   the approach to leadership that assumes leaders have certain traits that distinguish them from followers or members of a group.

U

Uncertainty avoidance   the degree to which members of a culture avoid or embrace uncertainty and ambiguity; cultures high in uncertainty avoidance prefer clear rules for interaction, whereas cultures low in uncertainty avoidance are comfortable without guidelines.

V

Variable   an observable characteristic that can change in magnitude or quality from time to time.

Verbal interaction analysis   an analysis of who talks to whom and how often during a discussion.

Vigilant Interaction Theory   the theory that suggests that group members not only must have expertise about a problem, but must also be knowledgeable about the *process* of problem solving, especially to ensure that all aspects of the problem have been examined and that the pros and cons of all the alternatives have been thoroughly assessed.

W

Worldview   one's beliefs about the nature of life, the purpose of life, and one's relation to the cosmos.

NAME INDEX